Hardware Acceleration for Machine Learning

Hardware Acceleration for Machine Learning

Guest Editors

Sergio Spanò
Gian Carlo Cardarilli
Luca Di Nunzio

MDPI Basel • Beijing • Wuhan • Barcelona • Belgrade • Novi Sad • Cluj • Manchester

Guest Editors
Sergio Spanò
Department of
Electronic Engineering
Tor Vergata University
of Rome
Rome
Italy

Gian Carlo Cardarilli
Department of
Electronic Engineering
Tor Vergata University
of Rome
Rome
Italy

Luca Di Nunzio
Department of
Electronic Engineering
Tor Vergata University
of Rome
Rome
Italy

Editorial Office
MDPI AG
Grosspeteranlage 5
4052 Basel, Switzerland

This is a reprint of the Special Issue, published open access by the journal *Electronics* (ISSN 2079-9292), freely accessible at: https://www.mdpi.com/journal/electronics/special_issues/A6WWZQYK09.

For citation purposes, cite each article independently as indicated on the article page online and as indicated below:

Lastname, A.A.; Lastname, B.B. Article Title. *Journal Name* **Year**, *Volume Number*, Page Range.

ISBN 978-3-7258-7855-0 (Hbk)
ISBN 978-3-7258-7856-7 (PDF)
https://doi.org/10.3390/books978-3-7258-7856-7

Contents

About the Editors

Sergio Spanò

Sergio Spanò received his bachelor's degree (2015), master's degree (2018), and Ph.D. with honors (2022) in Electronic Engineering from the University of Rome "Tor Vergata." Since 2022, he has been an Adjunct Professor and Research Fellow at the same institution, where he conducts teaching and research activities in the field of electronics. He is also an Adjunct Professor at the "Guglielmo Marconi" University and, since 2025, at the "San Raffaele" University of Rome. He possesses industrial experience in the space and telecommunications sectors, collaborating on research and development projects for high-performance and low-power systems.

Gian Carlo Cardarilli

Gian Carlo Cardarilli was born in Rome, Italy. He received the Laurea degree (summa cum laude) from Sapienza Università di Roma, in 1981. Since 1984, he has worked at the Tor Vergata University of Rome, where he is currently a Full Professor of digital electronics and electronics for communication systems. From 1992 to 1994, he was employed at the University of L'Aquila. From 1987 to 1988, he worked with the Circuits and Systems Team, EPFL, Lausanne, Switzerland. He works in the field of computer arithmetic and its application to the design of fast signal digital processors. He also regularly cooperates with companies, such as Alcatel Alenia Space, Italy; STM, Agrate Brianza, Italy; Micron, Italy; and Selex S.I., Italy. His research interests include VLSI architectures for signal processing and IC design and the design of special architectures for signal processing. In this field, he has published more than 160 papers in international journals and conferences.

Luca Di Nunzio

Luca Di Nunzio received a master's degree (summa cum laude) in electronics engineering and a Ph.D. in systems and technologies for space from the Tor Vergata University of Rome, in 2006 and 2010, respectively. He is currently an Adjunct Professor at the Digital Electronics Laboratory, Tor Vergata University of Rome, and an Adjunct Professor of digital electronics at Guglielmo Marconi University. He has experience with several companies in the fields of electronics and communications. His research interests include reconfigurable computing, communication circuits, digital signal processing, and machine learning.

Preface

The rapid transition of machine learning from cloud-based environments to embedded and edge-centric platforms has created an urgent demand for hardware acceleration solutions that can reconcile complex computational requirements with stringent power and latency constraints. This Reprint, titled "Hardware Acceleration for Machine Learning", captures this critical intersection of research and engineering by curating a diverse set of studies that explore the next generation of intelligent systems. Our primary aim in assembling this collection was to provide a comprehensive and technically rigorous perspective on how diverse hardware paradigms—ranging from FPGAs and SoC architectures to optimized software–hardware co-design and neuromorphic computing—can collectively drive the future of sustainable AI deployment.

This collection is intended for researchers, system designers, and practitioners working at the forefront of embedded AI, electronics, and digital system design. By highlighting advancements in fields as varied as cybersecurity telemetry analysis, industrial smart grid monitoring, and efficient training optimization, this Reprint offers a roadmap for those seeking to overcome the limitations of general-purpose processors in resource-constrained environments. We hope that this synthesis of methodologies, benchmarking techniques, and novel architectural designs serves as an invaluable reference, fostering innovation and guiding the development of truly scalable, high-performance, and energy-efficient hardware platforms for the next decade of intelligent edge applications.

Sergio Spanò, Gian Carlo Cardarilli, and Luca Di Nunzio
Guest Editors

electronics

MDPI

Editorial

Hardware Acceleration for Machine Learning

Sergio Spanò *, Gian Carlo Cardarilli and Luca Di Nunzio

Department of Electronic Engineering, Tor Vergata University of Rome, 00133 Rome, Italy;
g.cardarilli@uniroma2.it (G.C.C.); di.nunzio@ing.uniroma2.it (L.D.N.)
* Correspondence: spano@ing.uniroma2.it

1. Introduction

In recent years, hardware acceleration for machine learning has made significant strides, evolving from general-purpose solutions to increasingly specialized heterogeneous platforms designed to integrate artificial intelligence directly into embedded systems and edge architectures. This evolution is driven by the need to maintain or even increase computational performance while simultaneously reducing power consumption, latency, and memory footprint, objectives that software advances alone can no longer achieve [1–3].

Recent literature documents how embedded machine learning accelerators are converging toward "versatile" solutions capable of supporting a variety of models and workloads while remaining constrained by tight power budgets. Garreau et al. [1] provide a comprehensive overview of this landscape, analyzing architectures and hardware–software co-design strategies for integrated ML systems. In parallel, several proposals systematically address low-power VLSI architectures for the edge, with dedicated processors capable of executing AI inference on IoT nodes under extreme energy constraints, as shown in works on low-power edge AI processors [4,5].

Beyond the purely circuit-level dimension, comprehensive architectures have emerged for the efficient processing of complex neural networks in embedded and real-time contexts. In the FPGA domain, Dehnavi et al. [6] propose a CNN accelerator based on a novel "Convolutional Processing Element" capable of reducing idle states and external memory accesses, thereby simultaneously improving throughput and energy efficiency. Complementarily, the Pflow framework introduces an end-to-end heterogeneous chain for CNN inference on FPGAs, decoupling model description from hardware details and achieving significant speedups and efficiency gains [7]. At the system level, this trend toward heterogeneous platforms is further exemplified by solutions like TaPaSCo-AIE, which leverages AMD AI Engines with Vitis 2022.2 and streaming infrastructure for highly energy-efficient acceleration in large-scale neural scenarios [8].

Energy and performance optimization of inference architectures is also addressed along methodological lines, with proposals combining quantization, approximation, and dataflow-driven acceleration techniques to drastically reduce consumption while maintaining accuracy. An example is the VLSI architecture for edge AI described in Progress in Electronics and Communication Engineering, which integrates strategies such as approximate computing, clock gating, and quantization to achieve power savings exceeding 40% compared to baseline solutions [9]. Parallelly, comprehensive surveys relate model compression, accelerator specialization, and new forms of algorithm–hardware co-design, highlighting how efficiency increasingly depends not only on peak throughput but also on data movement optimization and memory hierarchy [2].

It is noteworthy that hardware acceleration for AI now has a cross-cutting impact on diverse application domains beyond classical signal or image processing. In the materials field, for instance, Zhang et al. [10] analyze how advanced deep learning techniques paired with hardware acceleration solutions enable new modes of materials design and information extraction from large scientific databases. These results reinforce the idea that architectural choices, from general-purpose processors to accelerator-centric systems, neuromorphic solutions, and heterogeneous frameworks, are now an integral part of the innovation process across multiple sectors.

In this context, the Special Issue "Hardware Acceleration for Machine Learning" in *Electronics* aims to provide an updated and coherent snapshot of this rapidly evolving ecosystem. The selected contributions cover the full spectrum from low-power IoT applications to embedded FPGA and SoC implementations, ASIC edge solutions, and efficient data-processing algorithms, continuing the path traced by previous Special Issues of the journal on advanced devices and circuits for extreme operational scenarios. This collection thus serves as a reference for researchers and designers interested in combining machine learning's potential with truly implementable, scalable, and energy-sustainable hardware platforms, while opening new research perspectives for next-generation intelligent systems.

2. Overview of Contributions

The eight articles comprising the "Hardware Acceleration for Machine Learning" Special Issue synthesize cutting-edge developments in hardware acceleration strategies for machine learning, showcasing the latest research advances across key embedded platforms and optimization techniques. These contributions encompass comparative framework analyses for deep learning inference, low-power RTL designs for CNN accelerators, unified FPGA/CGRA pipelines for edge AI, adaptive optimizers for training efficiency, performance analyses of preprocessing techniques, general-purpose hyperdimensional computing accelerators, breaking DSP walls in edge AI, and integer-state dynamics in quantized SNNs, as detailed in Contributions 1–8.

Ratul et al. (Contribution 1) present an exhaustive, multi-dimensional benchmarking study evaluating five leading deep learning inference frameworks, including PyTorch version 2.3.0, ONNX Runtime version 1.17.1, TensorRT version 8.6.2.3, Apache TVM version 0.21.0, and JAX version 0.4.28. All frameworks undergo rigorous testing on the NVIDIA Jetson AGX Orin edge AI platform, a high-performance embedded solution with Ampere GPU architecture. The evaluation encompasses both traditional convolutional neural networks, such as ResNet-152 with 60.2 million parameters, MobileNetV2 optimized for mobile deployment, ultra-compact SqueezeNet, balanced EfficientNet-B0, and classic VGG16, as well as modern transformer architectures, including Swin Transformer and real-time YOLOv5s object detector. Testing utilizes the complete ImageNet ILSVRC2012 validation dataset comprising 50,000 high-resolution images across 1000 classes and measures critical performance dimensions, including inference latency, throughput expressed as images per second, peak system memory utilization, instantaneous power consumption, and classification accuracy through both Top-1 and Top-5 metrics across batch sizes ranging from 2 to 128. Key findings reveal TensorRT achieves superior performance in larger batch configurations through sophisticated layer and tensor fusion, kernel-level autotuning for Jetson hardware, and dynamic tensor memory allocation that minimizes fragmentation. ONNX Runtime demonstrates superior cross-platform portability, leveraging execution providers and graph optimizations like constant folding and operator fusion, while PyTorch establishes a flexible research baseline with cuDNN acceleration. Apache TVM excels through AutoTVM empirical cost-model tuning, generating hardware-specific kernel sched-

https://doi.org/10.3390/electronics15091857

ules, and JAX shows promising just-in-time compilation via XLA, though it is constrained by memory limitations at scale. The study maintains near-identical prediction accuracy across all frameworks after FP16 mixed-precision optimization, providing developers with actionable guidance on framework selection, balancing deployment complexity against runtime efficiency and hardware utilization characteristics.

Gundrapally et al. (Contribution 2) present a comprehensively power-optimized implementation of the Tiny YOLOv4 object detection network specifically targeting the AMD Xilinx ZCU104 FPGA-SoC (Advanced Micro Devices, Inc. (AMD), Santa Clara, CA 95054, USA) evaluation platform. Starting from a Tensil toolchain-generated register-transfer-level RTL baseline for COCO dataset-trained fixed-point quantized inference, the authors introduce three novel RTL-level low-power design methodologies meticulously applied to computational critical paths. Local Explicit Clock Enable (LECE) provides fine-grained control over flip-flop and pipeline register updates by gating clock signals only during valid computation cycles, operand isolation strategically decouples inactive input datapaths from downstream functional units using conditional logic guards to suppress unnecessary signal transitions within multipliers and adders, and Enhanced Clock Gating (ECG) employs XOR-based multi-stage gating logic across wide datapaths and deep pipelines to minimize switching activity with lower power than conventional AND/OR schemes. Vivado 2022.2 post-place-and-route synthesis and implementation analysis reports significant power improvements, including a 29.4 percent total on-chip power reduction from 5.044 watts (baseline) to 3.561 watts (optimized configuration), alongside 33.9 percent dynamic power savings from 4.338 watts to 2.866 watts. Resource utilization is also substantially reduced to 9.0 percent CLB LUTs versus 20.9 percent (baseline), 1.4 percent CLB registers versus 10.8 percent, and 1.3 percent DSP slices versus 41.9 percent, while maintaining 32.2 percent Block RAM tile occupancy equivalent to 3.77 megabytes for feature map buffering. Real-time validation through the PYNQ Jupyter Notebook interface demonstrates 9.87 frames per second live object detection processing from USB camera input, achieving 43.9 GOPs per watt efficiency, representing a 1.37 times improvement over comparable FPGA implementations. These results validate RTL power optimization efficacy for battery-constrained applications, including drones, surveillance systems, and autonomous vehicles, without compromising COCO-trained detection accuracy.

Bagui et al. (Contribution 3) conduct a methodologically rigorous comparative analysis quantifying the impact of three distinct data preprocessing pipelines on support vector machine classifier performance for MITRE ATT&CK framework tactic-level cybersecurity threat detection. The study leverages two unprecedented, large-scale Zeek network connection log datasets generated through University of West Florida Cyber Range facilities: UWF-ZeekData22, containing 9.28 million attack records matched against 9.28 million benign samples dominated by Reconnaissance (9.28 M instances) and Discovery (2086 instances) tactics, and UWF-ZeekDataFall22, with 350 K attack and 350 K benign records spanning Resource Development (275 K), Reconnaissance (51 K), Discovery (17 K), Defense Evasion (3 K), and Privilege Escalation (3 K) tactics. Processing occurs within the Hadoop distributed file system, utilizing Apache Spark version 3.5.0 with explicit MapReduce-style parallelization across GPU-enabled clusters. Preprocessing pipelines systematically compare minimal processing through mean imputation, StringIndexer conversion, and uid/label dropping against dimensionality reduction via normalized Principal Component Analysis and supervised Linear Discriminant Analysis. Binary classification targets individual tactics versus benign traffic, while a multinomial One-vs-Rest SVM is used for multi-tactic discrimination. Comprehensive evaluation metrics encompass accuracy, precision, recall, F1 score, and AUROC, alongside preprocessing and classifier

 https://doi.org/10.3390/electronics15091857

execution times across CPU, GPU, and MapReduce-GPU execution environments. Binomial LDA consistently performs best across all statistical measures and demonstrates the fastest execution times, particularly under GPU and MapReduce-GPU acceleration, outperforming both PCA and minimal preprocessing baselines. This represents a pioneering tactic-level Zeek log classification approach, advancing production cybersecurity machine learning pipelines through dimensionality reduction optimized for massive-scale network telemetry analysis.

Mylonas et al. (Contribution 4) construct a fully open-source unified hardware-aware artificial intelligence acceleration pipeline that seamlessly bridges the Brevitas version 0.12.0 quantization-aware training and post-training quantization frontend with two distinct acceleration backends. The FINN version 0.10.1 flow generates high-throughput customized FPGA dataflow architectures emphasizing streaming processing elements and parallel pipelines, while the CGRA4ML framework targets low-power coarse-grained reconfigurable array mappings through temporal processing element reuse and dynamic runtime reconfiguration. A novel model intermediate representation translation layer from QONNX version 0.4.0 to QKeras version 0.9.0 handles Conv/ConvTranspose nodes alongside standard activation functions, including ReLU, facilitating Brevitas model portability across flows. The pipeline demonstrates practical effectiveness through the comprehensive deployment of an autoencoder neural network for anomaly detection targeting wind turbine fleet monitoring within realistic smart grid cyber-physical systems testbed environments. Quantization-aware trained and post-training quantized models deploy equivalently across both acceleration paths on the AMD ZCU104 evaluation platform, achieving up to a 10 times inference speedup per individual flow relative to the software baseline, alongside a 37 times aggregate throughput improvement and over an 11 times higher energy efficiency through detailed power-performance-area analysis. Reconstruction mean-squared error accuracy remains preserved across hardware-accelerated implementations compared to the reference execution, with FINN excelling in ultralow latency requirements and CGRA4ML demonstrating advantages in sustained low-power operation for continuous, time-critical edge monitoring applications within industrial energy infrastructure.

Martino et al. (Contribution 5) construct a comprehensively host-agnostic, AMBA AXI4-compliant, plug-and-play Binary Spatter Code hyperdimensional computing accelerator intellectual property core targeting Xilinx Zynq XC7Z020 system-on-chip platforms hosted on Digilent Zybo Z7-20 evaluation boards. The design advances beyond prior instruction-set-coupled approaches through fully standalone, modular implementation featuring synthesis-time scalable SIMD parallel datapaths, runtime configurable hypervector dimensionality via dedicated control-status registers, multi-bank scratchpad memory hierarchy with configurable bank count and depth, and optimized functional units that eliminate the area-intensive permutation shifter through block-cyclic memory address reordering while preserving bijectivity and decorrelation properties essential for BSC algebra. Clipping unit redesign employs packed comparator arrays with shift-append reconstruction, reducing dynamic multiplexers to 16 LUTs and 34 flip-flops versus hundreds in the baseline. AXI4-Lite memory-mapped control plane handles configuration alongside high-bandwidth AXI4-Stream DMA-driven data paths couple to external DDR through Xilinx DMA engine with asynchronous FIFO clock domain crossing isolation. Complete Linux userspace multi-layer C software stack, released via GitHub repository commit 3ae3b46, provides a unified dual-mode API supporting both pure software emulation for verification and hardware dispatch, abstracting low-level register programming, DMA buffer management via pre-allocated contiguous physical memory regions, and composite pipeline orchestration for encoding, training, and inference workflows. Compared with

 https://doi.org/10.3390/electronics15091857

an embedded dual-core ARM Cortex-A9 software baseline, primitive-level speedups reach 431 times across binding (XOR), bundling (saturating counters), permutation, similarity (Hamming distance accumulation), clipping (majority vote), and associative search operations, yielding average 68.45 times training and 93.34 times inference acceleration across end-to-end classification benchmarks. Full RTL code, testbenches, and software artifacts enable reproducible research and accelerate broader adoption of hyperdimensional computing for robust, noise-tolerant edge intelligence applications.

Aboulsaad and Shaout (Contribution 6) introduce AdamN, a sophisticated drop-in compatible replacement optimizer for the widely adopted AdamW algorithm that fundamentally enhances first-order stochastic optimization through principled nested momentum accumulation and exact bias-correction mechanisms. The core methodological advance replaces AdamW's conventional single exponential moving average numerator with a compounded EMA-of-EMA structure applied to raw gradients, producing triangular-with-exponential-tail temporal kernels that extend effective gradient-history memory while preserving instantaneous responsiveness to fresh gradient information. An analytically derived exact double-EMA debiasing factor simultaneously eliminates both inner and outer cold-start initialization biases without requiring ad hoc warmup schedules, enabling stable convergence from iteration zero at identical first-order computational complexity. Extensive empirical validation across diverse architectures and tasks confirms transformative practical benefits. On ResNet-18 trained for CIFAR-100 classification, AdamN matches AdamW's final test accuracy while reaching critical 80 percent and 90 percent training accuracy milestones 127 s and 165 s faster in wall-clock time, respectively. Fine-tuning the Llama 3.1-8B language model on small-domain datasets demonstrates halving the required optimization steps or 2.25 times faster time-to-target perplexity. Vision Transformer transfer learning from ViT-Base/16 pretraining to CIFAR-100 with batch size 256 achieves 88.8 percent test accuracy versus AdamW's 84.2 percent, reaching 40/80 percent validation milestones by epoch three compared to AdamW's epoch 59 for the 80 percent threshold. Language modeling on token-frequency imbalanced Wikitext-2-style datasets with training-only token corruption reduces rare-token perplexity without warmup dependency while matching head- and mid-frequency performance. Controlled ablation studies isolate nested momentum and exact debiasing contributions, confirming their synergistic role in reducing total training epochs, energy consumption, and deployment costs across vision and natural language processing workloads.

Liu and Heiyan (Contribution 7) introduce AEMAC, a breakthrough software–hardware co-designed edge artificial intelligence accelerator that fundamentally circumvents the critical "DSP wall" limitation constraining convolutional neural network scalability on entry-level Xilinx Zynq-7020 FPGAs, which possess only 220 DSP48E1 slices that are rapidly exhausted by competing SoC workloads. The architecture elegantly decouples arithmetic computation from DSP resource availability through a synergistic two-level strategy: a software-side dynamic integer scaling mechanism maps narrow-range floating-point activations (typically clustering near zero post-ReLU) into optimal integer domains via 99.9th percentile alignment, preventing outlier-induced saturation, complemented by a hardware-side strictly zero-DSP tri-mode computing engine leveraging abundant slice LUT fabric with a 2-bit Tiny mode for extreme sparsity regions ($|x| < 3$), a 4-bit Approx mode for moderate values ($|x| < 12$), and an 8-bit Precise mode for large magnitudes. A statistical bias compensation mechanism derived from quantization-noise analysis counteracts systematic -0.5 N negative bias inherent to logic-efficient floor truncation through conditional +1 injection via the accumulator CARRYIN port during low-precision modes, achieving global error cancellation via mode hybridization, where Tiny/Approx positive

https://doi.org/10.3390/electronics15091857

bias offsets Precise-mode negative bias, yielding near-zero expected error $E \approx 0$ across sparsity-dominated neural distributions ($\beta \approx 0.5$–0.8). The Vivado 2020.2-validated single-core implementation consumes 56 LUTs and 33 registers with a shallow four-stage critical path ensuring 100 MHz operation. A 64-core cluster sustains 26.1 GOPs/W at 0.490 W under worst-case random workloads. Micro-level arithmetic fidelity analysis confirms a 16.7 percent reduction in mean absolute error reduction versus naive truncation. On a CIFAR-10 custom lightweight CNN, end-to-end Top-1 accuracy is recovered to 64.74 ± 0.12 percent, matching the FP32 baseline of 64.64 percent compared with 64.19 ± 0.15 percent for uncompensated quantization. The approach scales to an industry-standard ResNet-20 (92.02 percent) and MobileNetV2 (91.30 percent via depthwise-to-group convolution adaptation satisfying the $N \geq 36$ statistical boundary for Law of Large Numbers-based error cancellation). ImageNet ResNet-18 bit-accurate simulation recovers accuracy within 0.71 percent versus an 8.34 percent drop under naive quantization. Trace-driven hardware verification confirms bit-true equivalence against the software golden model even under a worst-case $N = 4608$ accumulation depth.

Zhang (Contribution 8) systematically formalizes quantized spiking neural networks as deterministic discrete-time dynamical systems modeled through bounded integer-state update maps incorporating hardware-relevant implementation semantics, including shift-based leakage approximation, unsigned saturation clipping rather than wraparound overflow, and no-reset post-spike dynamics. The integer-state neuron evolution follows a canonical form $V_{t+1} = (V_t \gg k) + \sum_j w_{ij} S_{jt}$ with $S_{t+1} = [V_{t+1} \geq \theta_i]$, generating spikes via threshold comparison, where the right shift implements an exponential decay factor $1/2^k$, avoiding costly multipliers. Theoretical analysis establishes the network as a discrete map $F : \mathbb{Z}^N \rightarrow \mathbb{Z}^N$ on a bounded integer lattice of cardinality $\left(2^b\right)^N$, guaranteeing a finite number of reachable states and eventual periodicity, since deterministic updates from any initial condition must eventually revisit prior states, forming cycles. Extensive simulation sweeps characterize quantization-sensitive temporal regimes across network sizes $N = 30$–130 neurons, connection densities 0.1–0.9, bitwidths $b = 1$–16, over $T = 1000$ steps. One-to-two-bit configurations collapse to quiescence due to insufficient state resolution for sustained suprathreshold dynamics; 3-bit systems mark a critical transition exhibiting intermittent spiking; 4–16 bitwidths sustain rich recurrent activity patterns. For $N = 64$ and sparsity = 0.5, the median empirical recurrence lengths are 8.0 and 10.5 steps for 4-bit and higher precisions, respectively. Observed attractor structures, including fixed points (silence/saturation), short periodic orbits (rhythmic synchronization), and long bounded transients, underscore precision as an active dynamical design parameter rather than a mere approximation error source. The findings position bitwidth selection as a strategic lever controlling spike timing stability, activity persistence, and computational repertoire in hardware spiking systems, motivating precision-aware training, FPGA/ASIC co-design frameworks, and attractor-based analysis beyond continuous-time approximations.

In conclusion, driven by escalating requirements for resource-efficient machine learning deployment across the edge computing continuum, from battery-constrained IoT sensors to industrial cyber-physical infrastructure, these contributions establish comprehensive advances across the acceleration spectrum. Framework benchmarking guides practical inference-engine selection; RTL power methodologies enable sustainable CNN deployment; unified quantization pipelines democratize FPGA/CGRA accessibility; nested optimizers accelerate development-to-production timelines; preprocessing advances cybersecurity telemetry analysis; hyperdimensional accelerators unlock noise-robust paradigms; DSP-free architectures shatter resource bottlenecks; and integer-state SNN theory reframes quantization as dynamical control. Collectively, these works illuminate pathways toward

https://doi.org/10.3390/electronics15091857

next-generation heterogeneous SoC integration, advanced quantization-aware training regimes, neuromorphic–digital hybrid systems, and beyond-CMOS computational substrates capable of sustaining exponential AI scaling within planetary energy constraints.

Author Contributions: Conceptualization, S.S., L.D.N. and G.C.C.; methodology, S.S.; validation, S.S. and L.D.N.; formal analysis, S.S. and G.C.C.; investigation, S.S. and L.D.N.; resources, S.S. and G.C.C.; data curation, S.S. and L.D.N.; writing—original draft preparation, S.S.; writing—review and editing, S.S., L.D.N. and G.C.C.; visualization, S.S. and L.D.N.; supervision, G.C.C. All authors have read and agreed to the published version of the manuscript.

Funding: This research received no external funding.

Conflicts of Interest: The authors declare no conflicts of interest.

List of Contributions

1. Ratul, I.J.; Zhou, Y.; Yang, K. Accelerating deep learning inference: A comparative analysis of modern acceleration frameworks. *Electronics* **2025**, *14*, 2977.
2. Gundrapally, A.; Shah, Y.A.; Vemuri, S.M.; Choi, K. Hardware Accelerator Design by Using RT-Level Power Optimization Techniques on FPGA for Future AI Mobile Applications. *Electronics* **2025**, *14*, 3317.
3. Bagui, S.S.; Eller, C.; Armour, R.; Singh, S.; Bagui, S.C.; Mink, D. Analyzing Performance of Data Preprocessing Techniques on CPUs vs. GPUs with and Without the MapReduce Environment. *Electronics* **2025**, *14*, 3597.
4. Mylonas, E.; Filippou, C.; Kontraros, S.; Birbas, M.; Birbas, A. A Unified FPGA/CGRA Acceleration Pipeline for Time-Critical Edge AI: Case Study on Autoencoder-Based Anomaly Detection in Smart Grids. *Electronics* **2026**, *15*, 414.
5. Martino, R.; Pisani, M.; Angioli, M.; Barbirotta, M.; Mastrandrea, A.; Rosato, A.; Olivieri, M. A General-Purpose AXI Plug-and-Play Hyperdimensional Computing Accelerator. *Electronics* **2026**, *15*, 489.
6. Aboulsaad, M.; Shaout, A. AdamN: Accelerating Deep Learning Training via Nested Momentum and Exact Bias Handling. *Electronics* **2026**, *15*, 670.
7. Liu, C.; Heiyan, J. Breaking the DSP Wall: A Software–Hardware Co-Designed, Adaptive Error-Compensated MAC Architecture for Efficient Edge AI. *Electronics* **2026**, *15*, 1586.
8. Zhang, L. Integer-State Dynamics in Quantized Spiking Neural Networks: Implications for Hardware-Oriented Design. *Electronics* **2026**, *15*, 1756.

References

1. Garreau, P.; Cotret, P.; Francq, J.; Cexus, J.-C.; Lagadec, L. A survey on versatile embedded Machine Learning hardware acceleration. *J. Syst. Archit.* **2025**, *167*, 103501. [CrossRef]
2. Xu, B.; Banerjee, A.; Gupta, S. Hardware Acceleration for Neural Networks: A Comprehensive Survey. *arXiv* **2025**, arXiv:2512.23914. [CrossRef]
3. Cardarilli, G.C.; Di Nunzio, L.; Fazzolari, R.; Giardino, D.; Matta, M.; Re, M.; Silvestri, F.; Spanò, S. Efficient ensemble machine learning implementation on FPGA using partial reconfiguration. In *International Conference on Applications in Electronics Pervading Industry, Environment and Society*; Springer International Publishing: Cham, Switzerland, 2018; pp. 253–259.
4. Bhaggiaraj, S.; Antony, S.M.; Sankar, B.U. Design and optimization of low-power VLSI circuits of IoT edge devices. *ICTAT J. Microelectron.* **2024**, *10*, 1727–1731.
5. Bennet, M. Low-Power VLSI Architectures for Edge Computing: Advancing Energy-Efficient AI Inference at the Device Level. *Int. J. Emerg. Trends Comput. Sci. Inf. Technol.* **2023**, *4*, 1–9.
6. Dehnavi, M.; Ghasemi, A.; Alizadeh, B. FPGA-based CNN accelerator using Convolutional Processing Element to reduce idle states. *J. Syst. Archit.* **2025**, *167*, 103468. [CrossRef]
7. Wan, Y.; Xie, X.; Yi, L.; Jiang, B.; Chen, J.; Jiang, Y. Pflow: An end-to-end heterogeneous acceleration framework for CNN inference on FPGAs. *J. Syst. Archit.* **2024**, *150*, 103113. [CrossRef]

 https://doi.org/10.3390/electronics15091857

8. Heinz, C.; Kalkhof, T.; Lavan, Y.; Koch, A. TaPaSCo-AIE: An Open-Source Framework for Streaming-Based Heterogeneous Acceleration Using AMD AI Engines. In *2024 IEEE International Parallel and Distributed Processing Symposium Workshops (IPDPSW)*; IEEE: New York, NY, USA, 2024; pp. 155–161.
9. Vaduganathan, D.; Brinda, B.M. Design and Optimization of Energy-Efficient VLSI Architectures for Edge AI in Internet of Things (IoT) Applications. *Prog. Electron. Commun. Eng.* **2026**, *3*, 24–28.
10. Zhang, J.; Yu, J.; Qiu, N.; Liu, Y.; Song, Y.; Zhang, L.; Du, S. Advanced artificial intelligence algorithms and hardware acceleration techniques applied to material structure design. *AI Mater.* **2026**, *2*, 3. [CrossRef]

https://doi.org/10.3390/electronics15091857

electronics

MDPI

Article

Integer-State Dynamics in Quantized Spiking Neural Networks: Implications for Hardware-Oriented Design

Lei Zhang

Faculty of Engineering and Applied Science, University of Regina, Regina, SK S4S 0A2, Canada;
lei.zhang@uregina.ca

Abstract

Spiking neural networks (SNNs) support energy-efficient machine intelligence because event-driven computation and sparse activity map naturally to low-power digital hardware. In practical implementations, however, membrane states, synaptic weights, and thresholds are represented with finite-precision integer arithmetic. Quantization, clipping, and overflow can therefore alter network dynamics rather than merely approximate a higher-precision model. This paper adopts an integer-state dynamical perspective, modeling a quantized SNN with a hardware-relevant update rule as a deterministic map on a bounded integer lattice. Rather than claiming recurrence itself as a new property, we focus on how finite-precision representation and implementation semantics shape observed recurrent regimes and activity patterns. We introduce a shift-based update rule with integer-valued states and investigate its behaviour through simulation-based analysis with network sizes $N = 30$–130, connection densities 0.1–0.9, and bit widths 1 to 16 over T = 1000 steps. The results show bounded and recurrent temporal structure with strong quantization sensitivity. The observed regimes depend heavily on the semantics of representation and the scaling choices. These findings suggest that numerical precision can act as a dynamical design variable and provide useful implications for hardware-oriented SNN design, while motivating future work on attractor analysis and FPGA/ASIC validation.

Keywords: integer-state SNN; finite-state dynamics; periodic attractors; hardware-aware quantization; overflow/clipping semantics; FPGA/ASIC co-design

1. Introduction

The rapid growth of computation- and data-intensive learning systems has created a strong demand for specialized hardware platforms capable of delivering high performance under strict energy and latency constraints [1–3]. Spiking neural networks (SNNs) provide a promising direction because discrete spike events enable sparse, event-driven computation with intrinsic temporal structure [4,5]. This paradigm links modern machine intelligence with established spiking-neuron models from computational neuroscience, offering both computational efficiency and biophysical interpretability [6,7]. Recent progress in training algorithms and open-source tooling has significantly lowered the barrier to building and evaluating deep SNNs, supporting broader experimentation, reproducibility, and deployment-oriented analysis [8–10].

At the hardware level, spike-based computation has been validated across multiple neuromorphic and digital platforms. Large systems such as TrueNorth and SpiNNaker established key architectural foundations for massive parallelism and asynchronous communication [11,12], while Loihi introduced programmable neuron and synapse models with on-chip learning for practical workloads [13,14]. In parallel, FPGA- and ASIC-based SNN accelerators exploit integer arithmetic, sparse spike events, and localized synaptic memory to improve efficiency and throughput, forming a broad hardware design space for SNN acceleration [15–19].

Despite this progress, the dynamical effects of finite-precision numerical representations in digital SNNs remain insufficiently studied. In digital implementations, membrane states, synaptic weights, thresholds, and accumulators are represented using bounded integers or fixed-point numbers [15,16]. Meanwhile, recent research on fast and hardware-friendly SNNs increasingly couples latency and efficiency to quantization and low-bit representations, including ANN-to-SNN conversion calibrated or trained under quantization [20–25]. Importantly, low precision in SNNs is no longer limited to synaptic weights: several works explicitly quantize membrane potentials and thresholds, or pursue end-to-end integer-only formulations, to reduce memory and frequent read/write overhead while preserving task performance [26–30]. These developments motivate a closer look at how bit width, clipping, saturation, and overflow semantics reshape the dynamics of the recurrent system, not merely its numerical approximation error [31–35].

In finite-precision SNN implementations, these effects may appear not only as amplitude distortion but also as changes in spike timing, saturation behaviour, and activity stability over time. This makes finite precision relevant not only to numerical approximation, but also to the qualitative temporal behaviour of the implemented recurrent system. In this work, we adopt an integer-state perspective, modeling a digital SNN as a deterministic update map on a bounded integer lattice. Under this view, trajectories are inherently bounded and eventually recurrent, and thresholding and saturation introduce implementation-dependent temporal patterns [15,16,36]. This perspective reframes precision from a source of approximation error to an implementation-level design variable that influences attractor structure, spike timing, and activity persistence [1,34]. It also provides a clearer lens for interpreting learning in constrained state spaces, including surrogate-gradient-based training under discrete or quantized dynamics [8,37,38].

Unlike prior quantized-SNN studies that primarily optimize task accuracy, latency, or compression through quantized training, ANN-to-SNN conversion, or integer-only inference [20–23,26–30], the present work does not propose a new training algorithm or hardware accelerator. Instead, it isolates the state-update semantics and studies how bit width, clipping, and leakage change the observed finite-horizon temporal patterns of the implemented recurrent system. Under the tested unsigned no-reset semantics, 1-bit and 2-bit settings are effectively quiescent, 3-bit settings mark a transition, and 4–16 bit settings sustain activity; in the focused $N = 64$, sparsity $= 0.5$ configuration, the median empirical recurrence length is 8.0–10.5 steps for 4-, 8-, and 16-bit settings.

This paper makes three main contributions. First, we formalize an integer-state SNN update rule based on bounded arithmetic and shift-based leakage, enabling the network to be analyzed as a finite discrete-time system under explicit finite-precision assumptions [35,36]. Second, rather than claiming recurrence itself as a new property, we characterize how quantization, clipping, overflow, and related implementation semantics change observed temporal categories such as quiescent activity, sustained spiking, and short recurrent cycles [15,16,23,26]. Third, we provide simulation-based evidence showing precision-dependent transitions in these temporal patterns and discuss their implications for hardware-oriented SNN design, while leaving full FPGA and ASIC validation to future work [17,18,34].

https://doi.org/10.3390/electronics15081756

The remainder of the paper is organized as follows: Section 2 introduces the integer-state formulation and update rule. Section 3 develops the discrete dynamical interpretation. Section 4 discusses hardware implications. Section 5 presents experimental results and analysis.

2. Integer-State SNN Formulation

2.1. Discrete-Time Neuron Model

SNNs are often modelled using discrete-time approximations of continuous-time neuron dynamics, particularly for digital hardware or event-driven simulations. Integrate-and-fire (LIF) models remain attractive because they capture accumulation, leakage, thresholding, and spike generation while remaining computationally lightweight [4–7].

Equations (1)–(3) define a minimal discrete-time integrate-and-fire neuron model suitable for digital implementation. In a generic discrete-time setting, the membrane potential of neuron i evolves according to Equation (1):

$$V_i(t+1) = \alpha V_i(t) + \sum_j w_{ij} S_j(t) \tag{1}$$

where $V_i(t)$ denotes the membrane potential at time step t, w_{ij} represents the synaptic weight from presynaptic neuron j to neuron i, and $S_j(t) \in \{0,1\}$ denotes the spike output of neuron j. The parameter α models the leakage or decay of the membrane potential over time. A spike is generated whenever the updated membrane potential crosses a threshold θ_i according to Equation (2):

$$S_i(t+1) = \begin{cases} 1, & V_i(t+1) \geq \theta_i, \\ 0, & \text{otherwise.} \end{cases} \tag{2}$$

Following spike emission, the membrane potential may be reset or reduced according to a threshold-subtraction rule in Equation (3):

$$V_i(t+1) \leftarrow V_i(t+1) - \theta_i \tag{3}$$

This formulation is intentionally minimal. The purpose of the present paper is not to propose a new biological neuron model but rather to provide a hardware-oriented state-space abstraction in which the effects of finite precision, bounded arithmetic, and deterministic update semantics can be discussed more directly.

In the present paper, Equations (1)–(3) are introduced as a generic discrete-time reference form. The exploratory simulations reported in Section 5 do not use the threshold-subtraction reset in Equation (3); instead, they are conducted under an unsigned no-reset setting together with the integer-state shift-based update rule introduced later in Equation (6). Accordingly, Equation (3) is included here to indicate a common discrete-time spiking formulation, whereas the actual simulation results in this study are generated using bounded integer-state updates without post-spike reset.

2.2. Integer-State Representation

In many software-oriented SNN studies, neuron states and synaptic parameters are represented using floating-point values. In contrast, digital neuromorphic processors, FPGA-based accelerators, and fixed-point SNN pipelines often rely on limited-precision arithmetic in order to reduce memory footprint, simplify arithmetic units, and improve energy efficiency [13,15,16,31]. Motivated by this implementation reality, we consider an

 https://doi.org/10.3390/electronics15081756

integer-state formulation in which membrane potentials, synaptic weights, and thresholds are represented on a bounded integer lattice in Equation (4):

$$V_i(t) \in \mathbb{Z}., \quad w_{ij} \in \mathbb{Z}., \quad \theta_i \in \mathbb{Z}. \tag{4}$$

Under this assumption, the network update remains structurally similar to the standard discrete-time integrate-and-fire form in Equation (1), but the state evolution now takes place entirely within a finite or effectively bounded integer state space determined by the bit width and clipping semantics of the implementation. This shift in viewpoint is important: once the neuron states are represented in bounded integer form, the resulting network is no longer merely a floating-point model with quantization noise, but a discrete dynamical system whose reachable trajectories and long-term behaviour are shaped by the representation itself. The integer-state constraint in Equation (4) therefore makes the role of bit width explicit and directly links hardware resource limits to state-space size and dynamical behaviour.

Such an integer-state representation offers several conceptual and practical advantages. First, it aligns naturally with the arithmetic primitives available in digital hardware, where additions, comparisons, shifts, and bounded accumulations are cheaper than floating-point operations. Second, it makes the role of bit width explicit, thereby connecting hardware resource constraints with state-space size and dynamical behaviour. Third, it provides a more suitable abstraction for discussing recurrence, clipping, boundedness, and finite-state effects in hardware-oriented SNNs [16,31–33].

2.3. Hardware Interpretation

The integer-state viewpoint is particularly useful when SNNs are mapped to digital hardware. In practice, many neuromorphic and FPGA-based implementations employ fixed-point or integer-valued state variables together with lightweight update operations. A common example is the replacement of a real-valued leakage coefficient by a shift-based approximation in Equation (5):

$$\alpha = 1 - 2^{-k} \tag{5}$$

which yields the hardware-friendly update rule in Equation (6):

$$V_i(t+1) = V_i(t) - (V_i(t) \gg k) + \sum_j w_{ij} S_j(t) \tag{6}$$

where $\gg k$ denotes a right-shift by k bits. This form is attractive because it avoids multiplication and can be implemented using only integer subtraction, addition, comparison, and bit-shift operations. In the remainder of this paper, Equation (6) serves as the canonical integer-state update rule used in our simulations.

From a hardware-design perspective, such an update rule reflects the constraints that naturally arise in digital neuromorphic systems: bounded state variables, quantized weights, finite accumulator widths, and programmable decay rules. Architectures such as Loihi, SpiNNaker, and a variety of FPGA-based SNN accelerators demonstrate that low-precision spike-based computation is not merely an approximation of a higher-precision model, but a practical implementation regime in its own right [12,13,15,16].

Therefore, in this paper, the integer-state SNN formulation should be understood as a hardware-relevant abstraction: a simplified but meaningful representation that captures the essential interaction among quantization, bounded arithmetic, and spike-based recur-

 https://doi.org/10.3390/electronics15081756

rence. This abstraction provides the foundation for the discrete dynamical interpretation developed in the next section.

2.4. Implementation Semantics Used in This Study

To avoid ambiguity between the generic neuron model in Section 2.1 and the exploratory setting used in Section 5, we explicitly summarize the implementation semantics adopted in this study. The simulations reported in this paper use an unsigned integer-state formulation without post-spike reset. At each time step, spikes are generated according to $S_i(t) = 1[V_i(t) \geq \theta_i]$, and the membrane state is then updated by the shift-based rule in Equation (6). Bounded arithmetic is implemented by saturation clipping: Whenever the pre-clipped update falls below 0 or exceeds $2^b - 1$, it is clipped to the nearest boundary of the representable range rather than wrapped around. Therefore, the reported dynamics should be interpreted as properties of this specific finite-precision update semantics rather than of a generic reset-based or wrap-around-overflow model.

3. Discrete Dynamical Perspective

3.1. Integer-State Network as a Discrete Map

When membrane states, thresholds, and synaptic interactions are represented using bounded integers, a hardware-oriented SNN can be interpreted as a discrete-time state-transition system. Define the vector of neuron states for a network of N neurons at time step t as

$$\mathbf{X}(t) = [V_1(t), V_2(t), \ldots, V_N(t)]^\top \tag{7}$$

Under the integer-state formulation introduced in Section 2, the network evolves according to the discrete map denoted as

$$\mathbf{X}(t+1) = F(\mathbf{X}(t)) \tag{8}$$

Here, F is the deterministic update map for implementing leakage, synaptic input accumulation, thresholding, and any reset or clipping operations. Equations (7) and (8) clarify that F is not merely a numerical approximation of a continuous dynamical system; rather, it defines the actual evolution rule of the finite-precision network [4,6,13,16].

This perspective is useful because it shifts the analysis from floating-point neuron trajectories to state-space structure. Rather than evaluating how closely a digital implementation approximates a continuous SNN, we instead study how the finite-state update rule organizes trajectories, recurrence, and long-term dynamical behaviours. Thus, the network can be viewed as a quantized dynamical map whose properties depend explicitly on bit width, state bounds, threshold rules, and clipping behaviour.

3.2. Properties of Integer-State Dynamics

Several important properties follow immediately once the network is treated as a deterministic map on a bounded integer state space. First, if each neuron state is represented with a finite bit width and the update rules enforce bounded arithmetic, then the total number of reachable network states is finite. Second, because the update map F is deterministic, each state has a unique successor. These two properties together imply that every trajectory must eventually revisit a previously visited state. After a state is revisited, the trajectory necessarily enters a periodic cycle. Therefore, with a bounded finite-state and deterministic update, the network must eventually enter either a fixed point or a finite repeating cycle.

https://doi.org/10.3390/electronics15081756

However, this statement requires careful interpretation. It is not intended as a complete attractor classification theorem for all quantized SNNs, nor does it claim that all practical networks exhibit short or easily interpretable cycles. Rather, it provides a structural boundary condition: finite-precision SNNs are constrained to evolve within a finite-state graph, and their long-term behaviour must be recurrent in a finite-state sense. The key challenges are to characterize how long the transient can be, understand how the recurrence depends on the representation choices, and determine whether the resulting cycles are functionally useful or merely an implementation artifact [16,31,34,35].

3.3. Possible Attractor Types

From this discrete dynamical perspective, the system may exhibit several qualitatively distinct long-term behaviours.

Fixed points: A fixed point is any state $\mathbf{X}^\star$ satisfying $\mathbf{X}^\star = F(\mathbf{X}^\star)$. In the context of spiking networks, a fixed point may represent complete silence, a clipped steady pattern, or a stable balance among state variables.

Periodic orbits: A periodic orbit of period T satisfies $\mathbf{X}(t+T) = \mathbf{X}(t)$ for some positive integer T. In hardware SNNs, such periodic behaviour may appear as rhythmic spike patterns, recurrent synchronization, or finite-state cycles created by quantization and deterministic updates.

Long transient dynamics: Although a bounded finite-state system must eventually repeat, the transient before recurrence can still be long and complex, especially in higher-dimensional networks with heterogeneous thresholds, sparse connections, and mixed excitatory/inhibitory interactions. From the perspective of practical observation, such transient trajectories may appear irregular or chaos-like over finite windows, even though they remain fundamentally finite-state and ultimately recurrent. The goal here is not to claim formal chaos, but to emphasize that quantized SNNs can still exhibit complex transient dynamics before settling into a repeated orbit.

This taxonomy is useful because it distinguishes three interpretation levels: fixed-point collapse, periodic recurrence, and long bounded transients that may still be computationally relevant. In hardware systems, all three regimes matter because they lead to different functional and implementation consequences, such as quiescence, oscillation, or sensitivity to scaling and clipping.

3.4. Conceptual Implications

Viewing quantized SNNs as finite-state discrete maps has several implications for both theory and hardware design. First, it clarifies that deterministic low-precision implementations are not simply noisy approximations of continuous models, but dynamical systems in their own right. Second, it indicates that precision, clipping, and update rules should be treated as dynamical parameters, not only as engineering constraints. Third, it provides a vocabulary for analyzing recurrence, boundedness, and temporal structure in a way directly relevant to digital implementation.

In this paper, the discrete dynamical perspective serves a conceptual purpose rather than supplying a complete theoretical framework. It provides a principled way to interpret hardware-oriented SNNs as bounded finite-state systems, and motivates the experimental question in Section 5: whether simple quantized networks exhibit bounded, recurrent, and quantization-sensitive temporal behaviours under lightweight simulation settings.

 https://doi.org/10.3390/electronics15081756

4. Implications for Hardware Design

4.1. Integer-State Neurons on Digital Hardware

The integer-state formulation introduced in Section 2 naturally aligns with digital neuromorphic and hardware-accelerated SNN implementations. If membrane states, thresholds, and synaptic weights are represented using bounded integers or fixed-point values, neuron updates reduce to a small set of primitive hardware operations: integer addition, subtraction, comparison, clipping, and bit-shift. Compared with floating-point implementations, this representation avoids expensive arithmetic units and aligns with FPGA logic, ASIC datapaths, and low-power neuromorphic cores [12,13,15,16].

A representative example is the shift-based leakage rule discussed in Section 2, where the decay parameter is approximated as $\alpha = 1 - 2^{-k}$ in Equation (5). Then, the neuron update follows the integer-state rule in Equation (6), which can be implemented efficiently using bounded accumulators, right shifts, and threshold comparisons. This computation style is especially attractive for digital spike-processing pipelines because it clarifies the link between representation, arithmetic cost, and temporal behaviour. Instead of treating finite precision as an afterthought, the integer-state formulation incorporates it into the computational definition of the model.

4.2. Benefits of Integer Representation

The hardware significance of integer-state SNNs goes beyond ease of implementation, as emphasized in surveys on neuromorphic hardware and efficient deep-learning accelerators [1,15,35]. First, bounded integer states reduce area and energy costs by replacing floating-point units with simpler datapath operations, consistent with findings in energy-efficient DNN accelerator designs and low-precision computation studies [1,3,31]. Second, integer bit width explicitly defines the storage memory cost and controls the size of the reachable state space, affecting the system's tendency to saturate, become quiescent, or enter bounded recurrence, as discussed in analyses of neuromorphic circuit behaviour and memory constraints [16,39]. Third, integer-state implementations improve timing predictability, aiding pipelined FPGA designs, event schedulers, and real-time neuromorphic execution—a feature highlighted in hardware neuromorphic platforms such as TrueNorth and Loihi [11,13]. Finally, bounded arithmetic makes clipping and overflow observable and analyzable, allowing these effects to be treated as design variables rather than hidden numerical artifacts, aligning with studies on quantized neural networks, low-precision arithmetic, and neuromorphic information processing constraints [1,16,31,34].

These benefits are crucial for hardware-aware SNN design because quantization changes both resource usage and temporal dynamics. A narrow state range may save memory and logic but increase clipping risk and potential collapse into quiescent or highly constrained trajectories; a wider state range reduces clipping but may alter recurrence structure and effective scaling. In other words, precision is not solely an engineering trade-off between cost and accuracy. In finite-state SNNs, precision also shapes the temporal pattern class of the implemented system.

4.3. FPGA and ASIC Implementations

The neuromorphic literature already shows that spike-based computation can be implemented efficiently using finite-precision digital hardware. Examples include TrueNorth [11], SpiNNaker [12], and Loihi [13,14]. Despite their different architectural philosophies, these systems rely on integer or fixed-point neuron states, programmable decay dynamics, event-driven communication, and bounded local computation to support scalable spike processing. FPGA-based SNN implementations also use bit-serial arithmetic,

https://doi.org/10.3390/electronics15081756

parallel neuron pipelines, event routing, and sparsity-aware scheduling [15,16], all of which naturally support integer-state representations.

Although the paper does not yet provide a full FPGA or ASIC realization of the proposed integer-state framework, the conceptual mapping developed here is intended to support such follow-up hardware implementations.

4.4. Conceptual Takeaways

From the perspective of this paper, the key hardware lesson is that quantization should be treated as a dynamical design variable. A hardware-oriented SNN is not merely a continuous spiking model implemented approximately with fewer bits. Once bounded integer arithmetic is enforced, the system becomes a finite-state computational object whose reachable trajectories, recurrence structure, and clipping behaviour depend directly on representation rules. This observation links the abstract analysis in Section 3 with the exploratory simulations in Section 5. Both suggest that finite-state effects play a central role in the behaviour of digital SNNs.

The integer-state perspective, therefore, supports a co-design view of spike-based hardware. The network model influences hardware architecture through bit width, clipping, thresholding, and decay implementation, while hardware constraints feed back into the effective network dynamics. For this paper, the significance of this point is conceptual but important. If finite precision changes the temporal behaviour of the network, hardware-aware SNN design should not be viewed merely as a cost-minimization problem. It should also address how implementation choices shape the discrete dynamics of the network.

5. Preliminary Experiments

To illustrate the qualitative phenomena discussed in Sections 2–4, we performed lightweight exploratory simulations using a finite-state unsigned SNN model without reset—neurons do not reset their membrane state after spiking. The goal of this section is not a complete theoretical validation, but to demonstrate that bounded finite-state SNNs can exhibit recurrent and quantization-sensitive temporal behaviour under practically relevant parameters. The experiments, therefore, serve as phenomenon demonstrations supporting the conceptual claims of this work.

Metric Definitions: For clarity, we define the empirical summary metrics used throughout this section as follows. The firing rate is computed as the total number of emitted spikes divided by NT, where N is the number of neurons, and T is the simulation horizon. The active neuron fraction denotes the proportion of neurons that emit at least one spike within the tail observation window used for recurrent-pattern analysis. The pseudo-rank is defined as the matrix rank of the final tail segment of the membrane-state trajectory and is used here as an empirical surrogate for the richness of the tail dynamics rather than as a formal dynamical invariant. The empirical cycle length is estimated from the joint tail sequence of membrane states and spike outputs by searching for the smallest candidate period for which three consecutive tail blocks are identical; it is therefore reported as an empirical indicator of repeated finite-state behaviour rather than as a mathematically exact orbit classification. Unless otherwise noted, these quantities are computed from the simulated trajectories under the finite observation horizon described below, and repeated-experiment summaries are obtained by aggregating results across runs with the same parameter setting.

The global sweep covered network sizes $N = 30, 32, \ldots, 130$ and connection densities ranging from 0.1 to 0.9 with a step size of 0.1. The bit-width settings were evaluated from 1 to 16 bits in increments of 1 bit. The lower range (1–4 bits) represents extreme quantization,

 https://doi.org/10.3390/electronics15081756

8-bit corresponds to typical neuromorphic precision, and 16-bit provides a high-resolution regime approaching near-continuous dynamics. In all experiments, the simulation length was fixed at $T = 1000$. Thresholds were sampled from the interval $[4, 8]$, and the shift-based leakage parameter was set to $k = 1$, corresponding to a decay factor $\alpha = 1 - 2^{-k} = 0.5$. In addition to the full sweep, a focused repeated experiment was conducted at $N = 64$ and sparsity 0.5, as this operating region consistently produced bounded recurrent dynamics in exploratory trials. For each bit width from 1 to 16, the same network topology was simulated across 5 predefined random initial conditions to ensure reproducibility.

Figures 1–4 provide a focused dynamical view of a representative 8-bit network instance at $N = 64$ and sparsity $= 0.5$, including the connectivity matrix, membrane-state trajectories, spike raster, and a delay-embedded state visualization. Figures 5 and 6 summarize the effect of bit width on firing activity under two parameter settings, while Figure 7 reports the corresponding median empirical cycle length across the global sweep. Tables 1–3 provide numerical summaries supporting the interpretation of these figures.

5.1. Focused Dynamical Views

Figure 1 shows the random sparse integer connectivity matrix for a representative 8-bit network instance in the focused configuration. Although the weights are sampled from a simple bounded integer range, the resulting interaction structure can still generate nontrivial temporal behaviour under repeated iteration. In this paper, the connectivity matrix is not presented as a learned structure, but as an illustrative finite-state interaction pattern from which the observed dynamics arise.

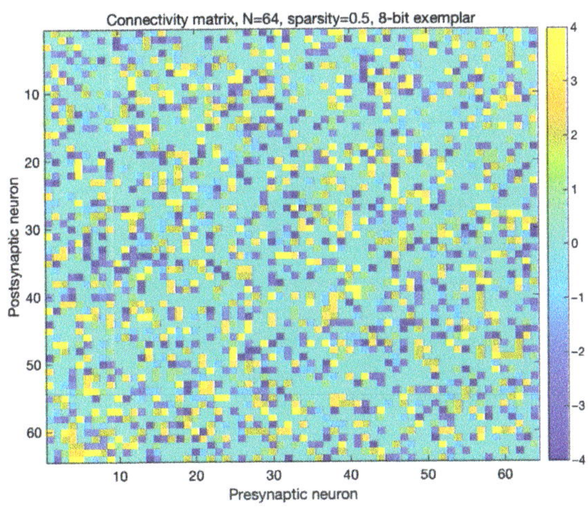

Figure 1. Representative sparse integer connectivity matrix for the focused exploratory configuration ($N = 64$, sparsity $= 0.5$, 8-bit exemplar). The bounded weight structure provides the interaction topology from which the observed finite-state dynamics emerge.

Figure 2 shows membrane-state trajectories for representative neurons under the same focused configuration. The state variables remain bounded and exhibit repeated but nontrivial temporal structure, rather than diverging or collapsing. This behaviour is consistent with the discrete-state viewpoint developed earlier: finite precision constrains the trajectories while still permitting recurrent temporal patterns over finite windows.

https://doi.org/10.3390/electronics15081756

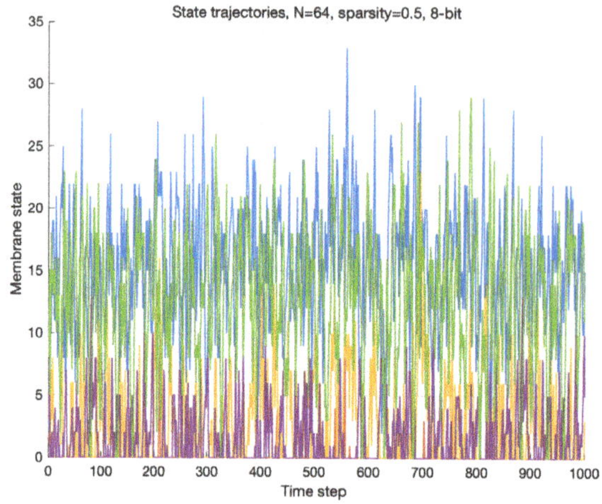

Figure 2. Representative membrane-state trajectories for the focused exploratory configuration ($N = 64$, sparsity $= 0.5$, 8-bit). Different colors denote different representative neurons. The trajectories remain bounded and show short-to-moderate recurrent temporal structure.

Figure 3 shows the corresponding spike raster. The network exhibits sustained, structured spike activity throughout the simulation horizon, indicating that the focused regime is neither quiescent nor saturated. Instead, recurrent spike patterns emerge in a bounded state space, representing the qualitative phenomenon targeted by the integer-state interpretation proposed in this work.

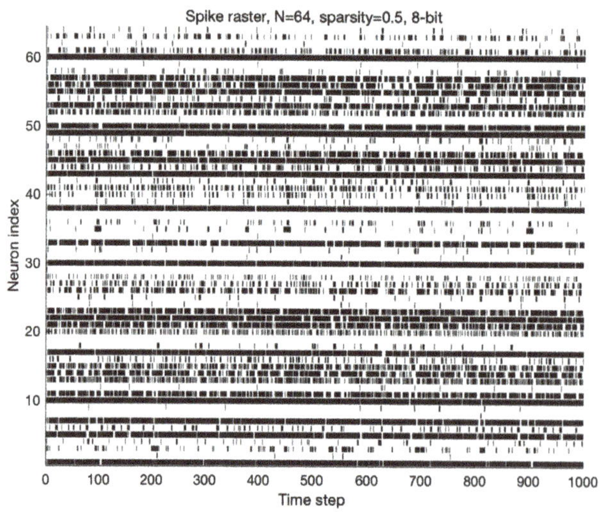

Figure 3. Spike raster for the focused exploratory configuration ($N = 64$, sparsity $= 0.5$, 8-bit). The spike trains exhibit sustained yet structured activity rather than immediate silence or saturation.

Figure 4 shows a delay-embedded visualization of the state evolution for a representative neuron. This figure provides an exploratory geometric view of bounded recurrence rather than a rigorous attractor proof. For this work, this figure serves an interpretive role by making the finite-state temporal structure visually explicit without overstating the theoretical completeness of the analysis.

 https://doi.org/10.3390/electronics15081756

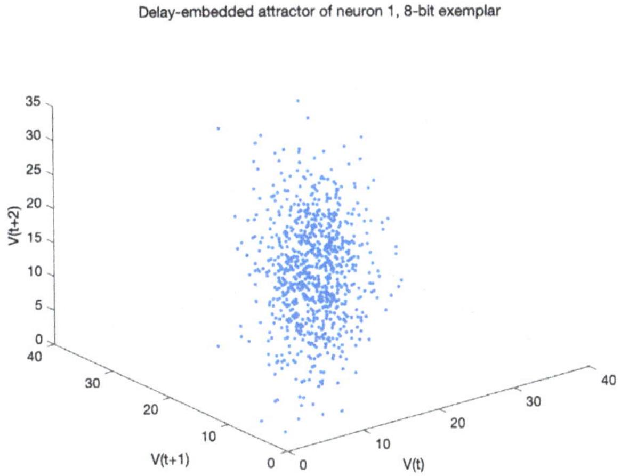

Figure 4. Delay-embedded state visualization for a representative neuron in the focused 8-bit configuration. The figure provides an exploratory geometric view of bounded recurrent structure rather than a formal attractor classification.

5.2. Global Bit-Width Effects

While Figures 1–4 focus on a representative network instance, Figures 5 and 6 summarize the behaviour of the global sweep as the bit width changes.

Figure 5 shows the average firing rate as a function of bit width across the full parameter grid ($k = 1$, sparsity= 0.5). For 1-bit and 2-bit settings, the mean firing rate is effectively zero, indicating a quiescent regime. At 3 bits, activity begins to emerge but remains below the levels observed at higher precision, suggesting a transition near a minimal precision threshold. For bit widths of 4 bits and above, the mean firing rate stabilizes within a narrow range, indicating that sustained activity becomes robust beyond this threshold under the unsigned no-reset formulation. This behaviour suggests the existence of a minimal precision threshold separating quiescent and active dynamical regimes in integer-state SNNs.

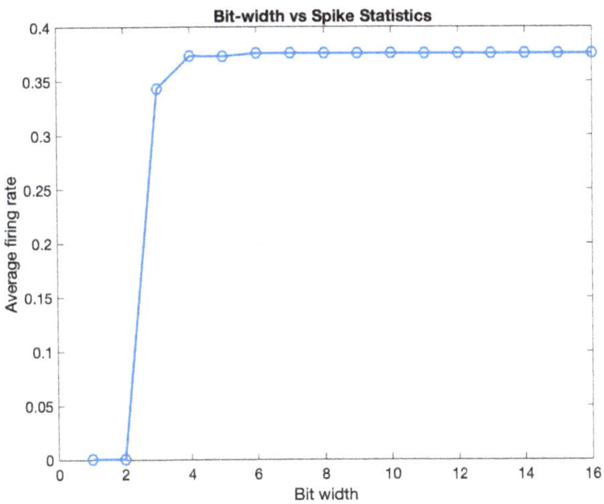

Figure 5. Average firing rate as a function of bit width across the global parameter sweep. ($k = 1$, sparsity $= 0.5$). Blue circle markers denote the per-bit averages, and the solid blue line connects them for visual guidance.

 https://doi.org/10.3390/electronics15081756

Figure 6 shows the corresponding relationship for a different parameter setting ($k = 8$, sparsity$= 0.2$). While both settings exhibit a similar transition from quiescent to active regimes around 3–4 bits, the structure of the active regime differs between them. For $k = 1$ and sparsity 0.5, the firing rate quickly converges to a stable plateau, indicating a precision-insensitive regime. In contrast, for $k = 8$ and sparsity 0.2, the plateau exhibits measurable variation across bit widths, suggesting that longer memory and reduced connectivity increase sensitivity to quantization.

These results indicate that precision acts as a dynamical control variable whose effect depends on the interaction between leakage and network sparsity.

Figure 7 shows the median empirical cycle length across the global sweep. The results indicate that bounded recurrence is not restricted to one precision setting. Instead, short repeating temporal patterns appear across multiple bit-width choices, supporting the view that integer-state SNNs should be studied as discrete finite-state systems in their own right.

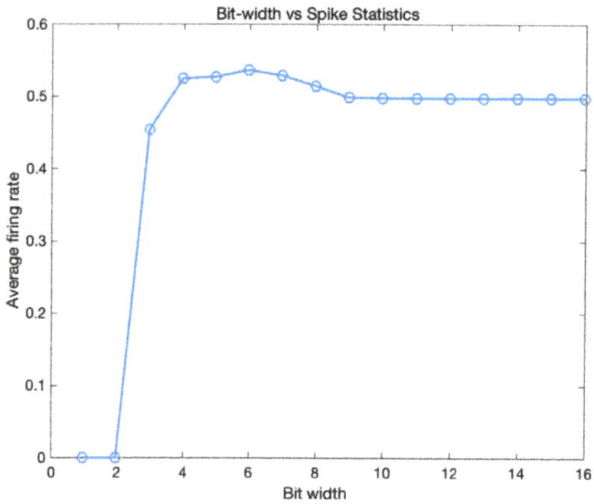

Figure 6. Average firing rate as a function of bit width across the global parameter sweep. ($k = 8$, sparsity $= 0.2$). Blue circle markers denote the per-bit averages, and the solid blue line connects them for visual guidance.

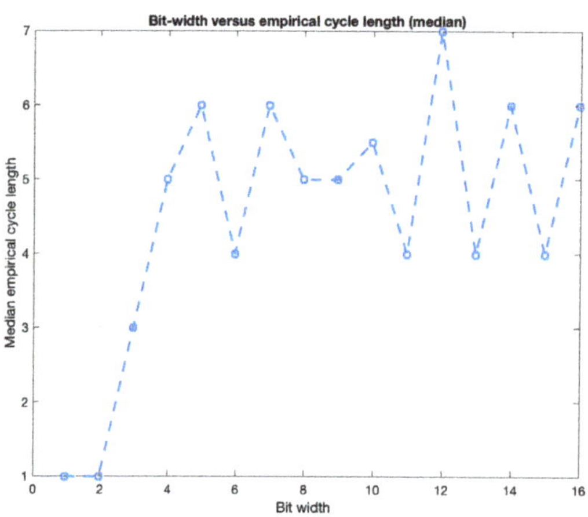

Figure 7. Median empirical cycle length as a function of bit width across the global parameter sweep. Blue square markers denote the per-bit medians, and the dashed blue line connects them for visual guidance. Bounded recurrence appears across multiple precision regimes rather than being confined to a single bit-width setting.

 https://doi.org/10.3390/electronics15081756

5.3. Quantitative Summary

The numerical summaries reinforce the qualitative patterns shown in Figures 1–7. Table 1 reports the global sweep summary by bit width. The mean firing rate remains close to 0.36 across 4-, 8-, and 16-bit settings, while the mean pseudo-rank surrogate and the median empirical cycle length remain nontrivial. These results indicate that the exploratory model frequently supports bounded recurrent temporal structure over the explored parameter space.

Table 1. Global sweep summary by bit width. The results indicate that bounded recurrent and quantization-sensitive dynamics are observed across all three tested precision levels.

Bits	Mean Firing Rate	Active Neuron Fraction (Mean)	Pseudo-Rank (Mean)	Empirical Cycle (Median)
4	0.3646	0.5883	44.1634	4.5
8	0.3629	0.5597	41.6057	5.5
16	0.3626	0.5715	43.5708	5.0

Table 2 focuses on the repeated experiment at $N = 64$ and sparsity $= 0.5$. In this region, the mean firing rates remain around 0.40, and the median empirical recurrence period lies in the range of approximately 8–10.5 time steps. This confirms that the focused operating region repeatedly produces visually rich bounded recurrence under the exploratory update semantics.

Table 2. Focused repeated results for the exploratory configuration $N = 64$ and sparsity $= 0.5$. This region repeatedly produced visually rich bounded recurrent behaviour.

Bits	Mean Firing Rate	Std Firing Rate	Pseudo-Rank (Mean)	Empirical Cycle (Median)
4	0.4068	0.0678	27.4667	10.5
8	0.4179	0.0759	25.1333	10.0
16	0.4045	0.0672	27.9000	8.0

Table 3 lists representative top recurrent cases from the global sweep according to the pseudo-rank surrogate. These examples suggest that larger networks with moderate connection density can produce especially rich tail dynamics under the exploratory unsigned integer-state update rule.

Table 3. Representative top recurrent cases from the global sweep, ranked by the pseudo-rank surrogate. These examples suggest that moderately connected, larger networks often exhibit richer bounded-tail dynamics in the exploratory regime.

N	Sparsity	Bits	Pseudo-Rank	Firing Rate
130	0.2	8	126	0.3588
128	0.2	4	126	0.3206
130	0.3	4	124	0.3877
130	0.2	16	124	0.3635

5.4. Interpretation

Taken together, Figures 1–7 and Tables 1–3 support three practical conclusions. First, finite-state integer SNNs can exhibit bounded and recurrent temporal behaviour over broad

 https://doi.org/10.3390/electronics15081756

regions of parameter space, even without learning or external drive. Second, bit width should not be interpreted only as a storage or arithmetic parameter, since it also interacts with clipping, effective dynamic range, and recurrence structure. Third, the particular region around $N = 64$ and sparsity $= 0.5$ appears to provide a useful operating point for visually exposing bounded recurrent behaviour in the exploratory regime. Although the present experiments are intentionally lightweight and phenomenological, they support the central argument of this paper: finite precision and integer-state constraints are not merely implementation details, but factors that can materially shape the observed temporal regime of hardware-oriented SNNs. From a hardware-oriented perspective, these trends suggest that bit width is not only a storage parameter but also a regime-selection parameter in finite-state SNN implementations. Lower precision can reduce state memory and arithmetic range, but may also increase the risk of quiescent or collapsed behaviour, whereas higher precision can preserve richer recurrent activity at the cost of a larger representable state space.

6. Discussion

This paper argues that quantized SNNs should be modelled as finite-state systems whose behaviour is governed by discrete state transitions rather than continuous approximations. Under bounded integer representations, the state space is finite, implying that trajectories must eventually enter periodic orbits or fixed points. Therefore, recurrence is not an empirical artifact but a structural property of the model. The focused figure set and global sweep analysis show that even lightweight integer-state SNNs can display structured bounded trajectories under simple update rules. More specifically, the tested unsigned no-reset implementation is effectively quiescent at 1–2 bits, transitions at 3 bits, and sustains activity across 4–16 bits, with median empirical recurrence lengths of 8.0–10.5 steps in the focused $N = 64$, sparsity $= 0.5$ setting. Thus, precision selection should be discussed jointly with temporal behaviour, not only with hardware cost. Accordingly, the present results are intended not as hardware benchmark evidence, but as design-relevant guidance for selecting finite-precision state ranges, clipping semantics, and leakage settings in digital SNN implementations.

Several limitations follow naturally. The current experiments are designed to expose qualitative temporal pattern categories rather than to exhaustively characterize attractor structures. The unsigned/ no-reset implementation highlights recurrent structure but differs from stricter signed/reset formulations, emphasizing how update semantics strongly influence the observed patterns. Earlier "attractor length" metrics were also revised into clearer empirical indicators—pseudo-rank and repeated-tail recurrence—to avoid misinterpretation as formal dynamical invariants. The present study therefore provides an implementation-explicit empirical characterization rather than a complete theory of quantized SNN attractors. A formal characterization of orbit length distributions as a function of bit width remains an open problem.

Future directions include (1) rigorous analysis of recurrence classes under different reset/clipping semantics; (2) FPGA/ASIC implementations with measured resource and energy behaviour; (3) interactions between integer-state recurrence and training, encoding, or task-level performance. These steps would move the present work toward a principled hardware–algorithm co-design framework for low-precision spike-based computation.

7. Conclusions

This work shows that, under explicit finite-precision update semantics, quantization is not merely a storage constraint but a factor that changes the observed temporal pattern

https://doi.org/10.3390/electronics15081756

class of an implemented SNN. In the tested unsigned no-reset setting, reducing precision can drive the network from sustained activity toward quiescence, while higher precision preserves richer bounded recurrence over the simulated horizon. The study, therefore, does not claim a new recurrence theorem or a hardware benchmark; rather, it contributes an implementation-explicit finite-state viewpoint and an empirical characterization of how bit width, clipping, and leakage shape observed recurrent patterns. The next steps include formal analysis of finite-state orbits, FPGA/ASIC implementations, and studying how integer-state recurrence interacts with training, encoding, and performance. This perspective suggests that future SNN design should treat precision, state bounds, and update semantics as primary implementation parameters in algorithm–hardware co-design.

Funding: This research was funded by the Natural Sciences and Engineering Research Council of Canada (NSERC).

Data Availability Statement: The data supporting the reported results are available from the corresponding author upon reasonable request.

Conflicts of Interest: The author declares no conflicts of interest.

References

1. Sze, V.; Chen, Y.H.; Yang, T.J.; Emer, J.S. Efficient Processing of Deep Neural Networks: A Tutorial and Survey. *Proc. IEEE* **2017**, *105*, 2295–2329. [CrossRef]
2. Han, S.; Liu, X.; Mao, H.; Pu, J.; Pedram, A.; Horowitz, M.A.; Dally, W.J. EIE: Efficient Inference Engine on Compressed Neural Network. In Proceedings of the 43rd International Symposium on Computer Architecture (ISCA), Seoul, Republic of Korea, 18–22 June 2016. [CrossRef]
3. Chen, Y.H.; Krishna, T.; Emer, J.S.; Sze, V. Eyeriss: An Energy-Efficient Reconfigurable Accelerator for Deep Convolutional Neural Networks. *IEEE J.-Solid-State Circuits* **2016**, *52*, 127–138. [CrossRef]
4. Maass, W. Networks of Spiking Neurons: The Third Generation of Neural Network Models. *Neural Netw.* **1997**, *10*, 1659–1671. [CrossRef]
5. Pfeiffer, M.; Pfeil, T. Deep Learning with Spiking Neurons: Opportunities and Challenges. *Front. Neurosci.* **2018**, *12*, 774. [CrossRef]
6. Gerstner, W.; Kistler, W.; Naud, R.; Paninski, L. *Neuronal Dynamics*; Cambridge University Press: Cambridge, UK, 2014. [CrossRef]
7. Izhikevich, E.M. Simple Model of Spiking Neurons. *IEEE Trans. Neural Netw.* **2003**, *14*, 1569–1572. [CrossRef]
8. Eshraghian, J.K.; Ward, M.; Neftci, E.O.; Wang, X.; Lenz, G.; Dwivedi, G.; Bennamoun, M.; Jeong, D.S.; Lu, W.D. Training Spiking Neural Networks Using Lessons From Deep Learning. *Proc. IEEE* **2023**, *111*, 1016–1054. [CrossRef]
9. Fang, W.; Chen, Y.; Ding, J.; Yu, Z.; Masquelier, T.; Chen, D.; Huang, L.; Zhou, H.; Li, G.; Tian, Y. SpikingJelly: An open-source machine learning infrastructure platform for spike-based intelligence. *Sci. Adv.* **2023**, *9*, eadi1480. [CrossRef]
10. Pehle, C.G.; Pedersen, J.E. Norse: A Deep Learning Library for Spiking Neural Networks. 2021. Zenodo Software Release. Available online: https://zenodo.org/records/4422025 (accessed on 16 April 2026).
11. Merolla, P.A.; Arthur, J.V.; Alvarez-Icaza, R.; Cassidy, A.S.; Sawada, J.; Akopyan, F.; Jackson, B.L.; Imam, N.; Guo, C.; Nakamura, Y.; et al. A Million Spiking-Neuron Integrated Circuit with a Scalable Communication Network and Interface. *Science* **2014**, *345*, 668–673. [CrossRef]
12. Furber, S.B.; Galluppi, F.; Temple, S.; Plana, L.A. The SpiNNaker Project. *Proc. IEEE* **2014**, *102*, 652–665. [CrossRef]
13. Davies, M.; Srinivasa, N.; Lin, T.H.; Chinya, G.; Cao, Y.; Choday, S.H.; Dimou, G.; Joshi, P.; Imam, N.; Jain, S. Loihi: A Neuromorphic Manycore Processor with On-Chip Learning. *IEEE Micro* **2018**, *38*, 82–99. [CrossRef]
14. Davies, M.; Wild, A.; Orchard, G.; Sandamirskaya, Y.; Guerra, G.A.F.; Joshi, P.; Plank, P.; Risbud, S.R. Advancing Neuromorphic Computing with Loihi: A Survey of Results and Outlook. *Proc. IEEE* **2021**, *109*, 911–934. [CrossRef]
15. Bouvier, M.; Valentian, A.; Mesquida, T.; Rummens, F.; Reyboz, M.; Vianello, E.; Beigne, E. Spiking Neural Networks Hardware Implementations and Challenges: A Survey. *J. Emerg. Technol. Comput. Syst.* **2019**, *15*, 1–35. [CrossRef]
16. Indiveri, G.; Liu, S.C. Memory and Information Processing in Neuromorphic Systems. *Proc. IEEE* **2015**, *103*, 1379–1397. [CrossRef]
17. Esser, S.K.; Merolla, P.A.; Arthur, J.V.; Cassidy, A.S.; Appuswamy, R.; Andreopoulos, A.; Berg, D.J.; McKinstry, J.L.; Melano, T.; Barch, D.R.; et al. Convolutional Networks for Fast, Energy-Efficient Neuromorphic Computing. *Proc. Natl. Acad. Sci. USA* **2016**, *113*, 11441–11446. [CrossRef] [PubMed]
18. López-Asunción, S.; Ituero, P. Enabling Efficient On-Edge Spiking Neural Network Acceleration with Highly Flexible FPGA Architectures. *Electronics* **2024**, *13*, 1074. [CrossRef]

 https://doi.org/10.3390/electronics15081756

19. Carpegna, A.; Savino, A.; Di Carlo, S. Spiker+: A framework for the generation of efficient Spiking Neural Networks FPGA accelerators for inference at the edge. *arXiv* **2024**, arXiv:2401.01141. [CrossRef]
20. Hwang, S.; Chang, J.; Oh, M.H.; Min, K.K.; Jang, T.; Park, K.; Yu, J.; Lee, J.H.; Park, B.G. Low-Latency Spiking Neural Networks Using Pre-Charged Membrane Potential and Delayed Evaluation. *Front. Neurosci.* **2021**, *15*, 629000. [CrossRef]
21. Li, C.; Ma, L.; Furber, S. Quantization Framework for Fast Spiking Neural Networks. *Front. Neurosci.* **2022**, *16*, 918793. [CrossRef]
22. Castagnetti, A.; Pegatoquet, A.; Miramond, B. Trainable quantization for Speedy Spiking Neural Networks. *Front. Neurosci.* **2023**, *17*, 1154241. [CrossRef]
23. Hu, Y.; Zheng, Q.; Jiang, X.; Pan, G. Fast-SNN: Fast Spiking Neural Network by Converting Quantized ANN. *IEEE Trans. Pattern Anal. Mach. Intell.* **2023**, *45*, 14546–14562. [CrossRef]
24. Li, Y.; Deng, S.; Dong, X.; Gong, R.; Gu, S. A Free Lunch from ANN: Towards Efficient, Accurate Spiking Neural Networks Calibration. In Proceedings of the 38th International Conference on Machine Learning (ICML), Virtual, 18–24 July 2021; Volume 139, pp. 6316–6325.
25. Li, Y.; Guo, Y.; Zhang, S.; Deng, S.; Hai, Y.; Gu, S. Differentiable Spike: Rethinking Gradient-Descent for Training Spiking Neural Networks. In Proceedings of the Advances in Neural Information Processing Systems (NeurIPS) 34, Virtually, 6–14 December 2021.
26. Hasssan, A.; Meng, J.; Anupreetham, A.; Seo, J.S. SpQuant-SNN: Ultra-low precision membrane potential with sparse activations unlock the potential of on-device spiking neural networks applications. *Front. Neurosci.* **2024**, *18*, 1440000. [CrossRef]
27. Zou, C.; Cui, X.; Feng, S.; Chen, G.; Zhong, Y.; Dai, Z.; Wang, Y. An all integer-based spiking neural network with dynamic threshold adaptation. *Front. Neurosci.* **2024**, *18*, 1449020. [CrossRef] [PubMed]
28. Wei, W.; Liang, Y.; Belatreche, A.; Xiao, Y.; Cao, H.; Ren, Z.; Wang, G.; Zhang, M.; Yang, Y. Q-SNNs: Quantized Spiking Neural Networks. In Proceedings of the 32nd ACM International Conference on Multimedia (MM '24), Melbourne, VIC, Australia, 28 October–1 November 2024; pp. 8441–8450. [CrossRef]
29. Wei, W.; Zhang, M.; Zhou, Z.; Belatreche, A.; Shan, Y.; Liang, Y.; Cao, H.; Zhang, J.; Yang, Y. QP-SNNS: Quantized and Pruned Spiking Neural Networks. In Proceedings of the International Conference on Learning Representations (ICLR) 2025, Singapore, 24–28 April 2025. Available online: https://openreview.net/forum?id=MiPyle6Jef (accessed on 16 April 2026).
30. Wu, Y.L.; Tan, R.R.; Zhang, S.H.; Liang, S.; Liu, Z.A.; Wang, Z.; Zhang, S.Q. Ternary Quantization of Spiking Neural Networks. *Front. Comput. Sci.* **2025**. Available online: https://journal.hep.com.cn/fcs/EN/10.1007/s11704-025-51519-1 (accessed on 16 April 2026).
31. Hubara, I.; Courbariaux, M.; Soudry, D.; El-Yaniv, R.; Bengio, Y. Quantized Neural Networks: Training Neural Networks with Low Precision Weights and Activations. *J. Mach. Learn. Res.* **2017**, *18*, 1–30.
32. Courbariaux, M.; Bengio, Y.; David, J.P. BinaryConnect: Training Deep Neural Networks with Binary Weights During Propagations. In Proceedings of the 29th International Conference on Neural Information Processing Systems, Montreal, QC, Canada, 7–12 December 2015.
33. Rastegari, M.; Ordonez, V.; Redmon, J.; Farhadi, A. XNOR-Net: ImageNet Classification Using Binary Convolutional Neural Networks. In *Proceedings of the Computer Vision—ECCV 2016*; Springer International Publishing: Amsterdam, The Netherlands, 11–14 October 2016; pp. 525–542. [CrossRef]
34. Roy, K.; Jaiswal, A.; Panda, P. Towards Spike-Based Machine Intelligence with Neuromorphic Computing. *Nature* **2019**, *575*, 607–617. [CrossRef] [PubMed]
35. Schuman, C.D.; Potok, T.E.; Patton, R.M.; Birdwell, J.D.; Dean, M.E.; Rose, G.S.; Plank, J.S. A Survey of Neuromorphic Computing and Neural Networks in Hardware. *arXiv* **2017**, arXiv:1705.06963. [CrossRef]
36. Jarrah, A.S.; Laubenbacher, R. Finite Dynamical Systems: A Mathematical Framework for Computer Simulation. In *Mathematical Modeling, Simulation, Visualization and e-Learning*; Springer: Berlin/Heidelberg, Germany, 2008; pp. 343–358. [CrossRef]
37. Neftci, E.O.; Mostafa, H.; Zenke, F. Surrogate Gradient Learning in Spiking Neural Networks. *IEEE Signal Process. Mag.* **2019**, *36*, 51–63. [CrossRef]
38. Zenke, F.; Vogels, T.P. The Remarkable Robustness of Surrogate Gradient Learning for Instilling Complex Function in Spiking Neural Networks. *Neural Comput.* **2021**, *33*, 899–925. [CrossRef]
39. Indiveri, G.; Linares-Barranco, B.; Hamilton, T.; van Schaik, A.; Etienne-Cummings, R.; Delbruck, T.; Liu, S.C.; Dudek, P.; Häfliger, P.; Renaud, S.; et al. Neuromorphic Silicon Neuron Circuits. *Front. Neurosci.* **2011**, *5*, 73. [CrossRef]

 https://doi.org/10.3390/electronics15081756

electronics

MDPI

Article

Breaking the DSP Wall: A Software–Hardware Co-Designed, Adaptive Error-Compensated MAC Architecture for Efficient Edge AI

Changyan Liu [1,*] and Juntai Heiyan [2]

1 Glasgow College, University of Electronic Science and Technology of China, Chengdu 611731, China
2 School of Integrated Circuit Science and Engineering, University of Electronic Science and Technology of China, Chengdu 611731, China; 2023310201010@std.uestc.edu.cn
* Correspondence: 2023190905023@std.uestc.edu.cn

Abstract

The deployment of Convolutional Neural Networks (CNNs) on entry-level Edge FPGAs is severely constrained by the scarcity of Digital Signal Processing (DSP) blocks, a phenomenon termed the "DSP Wall". To circumvent this bottleneck, this paper presents AEMAC, a Software–Hardware Co-Designed accelerator architecture that decouples arithmetic computation from DSP availability. The proposed methodology synergizes a software-level Dynamic Integer Scaling strategy with a hardware-level Adaptive Error-Compensated Multiply-Accumulate unit. By mapping floating-point activations to an optimal integer domain and employing a DSP-free, LUT-based tri-mode datapath, the architecture achieves extreme resource efficiency. To mitigate the precision loss inherent in logic-based truncation, a statistical bias compensation mechanism is integrated into the accumulator chain. Experimental validation on a Xilinx Zynq-7020 FPGA demonstrates a strictly zero-DSP implementation with minimal logic utilization (100 LUTs). Post-implementation timing simulations confirm a dynamic power of 0.490 W for a 64-core cluster under worst-case random workloads, yielding a verified energy efficiency of 26.1 GOPS/W. Micro-level analysis confirms a 16.7% reduction in arithmetic Mean Absolute Error (MAE) compared to naive truncation. Furthermore, macro-level evaluation on the CIFAR-10 dataset reveals that the co-design strategy recovers system accuracy to 64.74%, outperforming the uncompensated baseline by 0.55% and achieving statistical comparability to floating-point baselines. To ensure absolute internal consistency, all hardware metrics are strictly validated via SAIF-based post-implementation simulations. Based on a conservative full-chip projection that incorporates a routing derating model, these internally consistent results establish AEMAC as a highly scalable and reliable solution for breaking the DSP wall in resource-constrained edge intelligence.

Keywords: edge AI; FPGA acceleration; software–hardware co-design; DSP-free computing; approximate computing; CIFAR-10

1. Introduction

The migration of Artificial Intelligence (AI) from cloud servers to edge devices has become a dominant trend [1]. This shift necessitates hardware architectures that are strictly optimized for power and silicon area. Convolutional Neural Networks (CNNs), the core of modern vision systems, rely heavily on Multiply-Accumulate (MAC) operations. Consequently, the efficiency of the MAC unit dictates the overall performance of the accelerator [1]. In Field-Programmable Gate Arrays (FPGAs), MAC operations are traditionally mapped to hardened Digital Signal Processor (DSP) slices. While efficient, DSP slices are a scarce resource. Entry-level devices, such as the Xilinx Zynq-7000 series, contain limited DSP blocks (e.g., only 220 slices in the XC7Z020) [2]. In complex System-on-Chip (SoC) designs, these resources are rapidly exhausted by competing tasks like signal processing and motor control. We term this limitation the DSP Wall. Once DSPs are depleted, the neural accelerator cannot scale further, creating a severe bottleneck for parallelism [2]. Prior FPGA CNN accelerators, particularly those based on systolic arrays, frequently hit this rigid DSP utilization ceiling. Because their multiplier requirements grow quadratically with the array size, they suffer from sudden performance saturation on entry-level devices, leaving the abundant logic fabric (LUTs) largely underutilized [3]. Furthermore, the conventional "one-size-fits-all" quantization strategy is inefficient. Neural network activations typically follow a heavy-tailed or bell-shaped distribution [4]. As illustrated in Figure 1, the vast majority of activation values are clustered near zero. Processing these negligible values with full-precision, power-hungry hardware represents a gross waste of energy and computational resources [4].

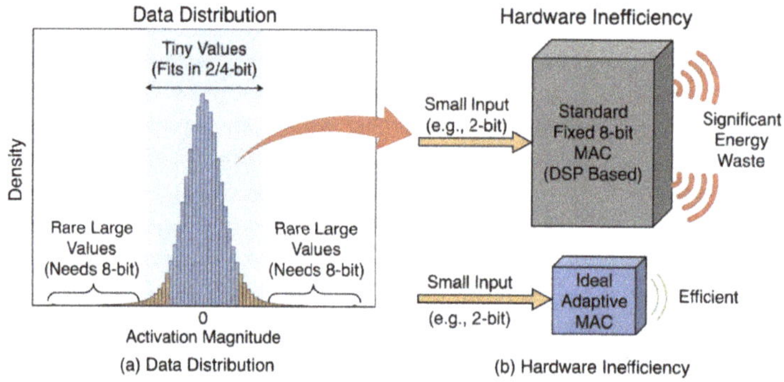

Figure 1. Motivation. (**a**) The probability density function (PDF) of neural activations exhibits high sparsity, with most values concentrated near zero. (**b**) Traditional DSP-based architectures process all values with fixed precision, resulting in resource waste. The proposed approach adapts hardware precision to the data magnitude. In the figure, blue colors indicate tiny data values and the proposed adaptive hardware, while orange and grey denote rare large values and the standard fixed-precision hardware, respectively.

To address the DSP Wall and exploit data sparsity, we propose a Software–Hardware Co-Designed architecture named **AEMAC** (Adaptive Error-Compensated MAC). Unlike prior works that rely on partial DSP usage, our approach completely decouples inference computing from DSP availability. Our strategy involves two synergistic levels:

- Software Level: We introduce a dynamic integer scaling mechanism. This maps floating-point activations into an optimal integer domain, aligning the data distribution with hardware thresholds.
- Hardware Level: We implement a DSP-free, tri-mode computing engine using the FPGA's abundant Look-Up Table (LUT) fabric.To counteract the accuracy loss from logic-efficient truncation, we derive and implement a statistical bias compensation mechanism.

 https://doi.org/10.3390/electronics15081586

This paper presents the mathematical formulation, hardware implementation, and system-level validation of AEMAC. Experimental results on the Zynq-7020 demonstrate a strictly zero-DSP implementation with only 100 LUTs. Crucially, the proposed co-design restores end-to-end accuracy on the CIFAR-10 dataset, proving that low-cost FPGAs can achieve high-performance inference without hitting the DSP wall.

2. Related Work

The optimization of DNN inference hardware has evolved along two distinct trajectories: architectural specialization and algorithmic approximation [5]. This section reviews the state-of-the-art (SOTA) in these domains and positions our work within the landscape of "Logic-Only" [6] computing. Foundational works such as Deep Compression [7] established the efficacy of pruning and quantization for reducing model complexity. Building on these principles, recent FPGA-specific research has focused on hardware-friendly approximation techniques to maximize arithmetic density.

2.1. *FPGA-Based Neural Acceleration*

Traditional FPGA accelerators are dominated by DSP-centric architectures. Standard approaches, such as the Xilinx DPU and various systolic array implementations, map matrix multiplications directly to hardened DSP48 slices [3,8]. While these designs achieve high peak throughput on high-end devices (e.g., Virtex UltraScale+), they hit a hard scalability barrier on entry-level FPGAs. Recent works have proposed "fractured" DSP techniques, which decompose a single 25×18 DSP slice into two smaller 8×8 multipliers to double the throughput [9]. However, these methods remain fundamentally dependent on the physical presence of DSP blocks. Once the limited DSP budget is exhausted, the accelerator's performance plateaus. In contrast, AEMAC eliminates this dependency entirely, shifting the workload to the abundant LUT fabric.

2.2. *Approximate Computing and Quantization*

To reduce hardware complexity, approximate computing techniques trade arithmetic precision for energy efficiency [5]. Aggressive quantization, such as binary (BNN) or ternary (TNN) networks, reduces weights to 1 or 2 bits [4]. Although these methods significantly lower resource usage, they typically require extensive retraining and suffer from severe accuracy degradation on complex datasets [4]. Other approximate multipliers employ logic pruning, where the least significant bits (LSBs) are simply discarded [5]. However, naive truncation introduces a systematic negative bias, as demonstrated in our experimental analysis [10]. AEMAC addresses this by integrating a statistical bias compensation mechanism, recovering accuracy without the need for model retraining [10].

2.3. *LUT-Based Computing: Comparing with SOTA*

The concept of replacing arithmetic logic with Look-Up Tables (LUTs) has recently gained traction in the software domain [11,12]. The **T-MAC** framework represents the current SOTA for low-bit Large Language Model (LLM) inference on edge CPUs [12]. T-MAC replaces traditional Multiply-Accumulate instructions with bit-wise table lookups, effectively bypassing the dequantization overhead and exploiting the CPU's cache hierarchy. While T-MAC validates the efficiency of LUT-based arithmetic in software, our AEMAC architecture translates this paradigm into the hardware domain [12]. The comparison between these two approaches as shown in Table 1 is summarized below:

 https://doi.org/10.3390/electronics15081586

By synthesizing the "Zero-DSP" philosophy with hardware-level statistical error correction, AEMAC establishes a new baseline for logic-based inference engines, complementing software innovations like T-MAC [6,12].

Table 1. Comparison of LUT-Based Computing Paradigms: SOTA Software(T-MAC) vs. Proposed Hardware (AEMAC).

Feature	T-MAC (SOTA Software) [12]	AEMAC (Ours-Hardware)
Domain	Edge AI Software Framework	Edge AI Hardware Architecture
Target Platform	General-Purpose CPUs (ARM/x86)	Low-Cost FPGAs (Zynq-7000)
Core Mechanism	Look-Up via Memory Arrays (RAM)	Look-Up via Logic Gates (Slice LUTs)
Bottleneck Solved	Memory Wall: Bypassing slow dequantization	DSP Wall: Bypassing scarce hard macros
Precision Control	Static Low-Bit (e.g., INT4/INT2)	Dynamic Tri-Mode (8/4/2-bit)
Error Mitigation	Retraining/Calibration	Statistical Bias Compensation
Primary Goal	Instruction Throughput/Latency	Silicon Area Efficiency/Zero-DSP

2.4. Broader Context: Neuromorphic and In-Memory Computing

Beyond digital LUT-based approximations, recent advancements in edge AI have explored broader software–hardware co-design paradigms, particularly neuromorphic and Processing-in-Memory (PIM) architectures. Similar to AEMAC's goal of bypassing standard DSP/ALU bottlenecks, PIM accelerators utilize non-standard arithmetic (e.g., memristor-based crossbars or logic-based MAC operations directly within memory) to achieve extreme energy efficiency [13]. Furthermore, lightweight neuromorphic designs and recent hardware–software co-designed architectures have demonstrated that adaptive scaling and non-standard dataflows can significantly enhance both security and energy efficiency for edge AI [14,15]. While AEMAC operates purely in the digital FPGA domain, its philosophy of context-aware precision and hardware-level statistical compensation aligns closely with the efficient computing principles driving these emerging DSP-free edge architectures.

3. Theoretical Framework and Error Analysis

Before establishing the mathematical foundation, this section first provides a high-level overview of the entire system to contextualize the subsequent error analysis.

3.1. System Overview and Problem Formulation

To deploy Convolutional Neural Networks (CNNs) efficiently on resource-constrained Edge FPGAs, it is essential to overcome the dependency on scarce DSP blocks.

Difficult Points: The primary challenge is that implementing standard INT8 multipliers entirely using LUTs consumes excessive logic resources. Conversely, aggressive low-bit quantization (e.g., 2-bit) introduces severe accuracy degradation that is unacceptable for industrial applications.

Proposed Solution: To address these bottlenecks, we propose the Adaptive Error-Compensated MAC (AEMAC) system. Instead of a "one-size-fits-all" precision, AEMAC dynamically categorizes incoming activations into three distinct execution modes based on their magnitude. These modes are strictly defined as follows:

- **Tiny Mode (2-bit):** Triggered when the absolute value of the activation is extremely small (e.g., $x \in [-3, 3]$). The system aggressively truncates the lower bits to save dynamic power. The massive quantization noise is mitigated by adding a pre-calculated statistical bias.

https://doi.org/10.3390/electronics15081586

- **Approx Mode (4-bit):** Triggered for moderate activation values (e.g., $x \in [-12, 12]$). This mode strikes a balance between logic resource consumption and numerical precision, using moderate bit-truncation and a corresponding secondary bias.
- **Precise Mode (8-bit):** Triggered for large activation values. To preserve the overall accuracy of the CNN model, no truncation is applied, and the MAC operation is executed with full INT8 fidelity.

By seamlessly switching among these modes, the system effectively bypasses the DSP wall. Note: The detailed hardware implementation of these modules (MDU, ACE, BCU) will be elaborated in Section 4. The following subsections establish the mathematical foundation of this error compensation mechanism.

3.2. *Quantization Noise Model*

Let $x \in \mathbb{R}$ be a continuous value mapped to an integer grid. The quantization error ϵ is defined as $\epsilon = Q(x) - x$. Assuming the fractional part of the scaled activation x_{scaled} follows a uniform distribution $\mathcal{U}(0,1)$, the behavior of the error depends on the quantization function employed.

3.3. *Bias Analysis of Naive Truncation*

Hardware-efficient designs typically utilize the `floor` function, $Q_{trunc}(x) = \lfloor x \rfloor$. The error ϵ_{trunc} is confined to the interval $(-1, 0]$. The expected value (mean bias) is:

$$\mathbb{E}[\epsilon_{trunc}] = \int_{-1}^{0} \epsilon \cdot 1 \, d\epsilon = -0.5 \tag{1}$$

In a convolution operation accumulating N products, this negative bias accumulates linearly ($\mathbb{E}_{total} = -0.5N$). This explains the significant accuracy degradation observed in the naive baseline, as the activation distribution is systematically shifted toward zero or negative values.

3.4. *Analysis of Bias Injection (+1)*

The AEMAC architecture conditionally injects a bias $B = +1$. For an operation with this injection, the corrected value is $Q_{corr}(x) = \lfloor x \rfloor + 1$. The new error ϵ_{corr} shifts to the interval $(0, 1]$, resulting in a positive mean bias:

$$\mathbb{E}[\epsilon_{corr}] = \int_{0}^{1} \epsilon \cdot 1 \, d\epsilon = +0.5 \tag{2}$$

Addressing the Bias Symmetry: A valid critique is that a systematic positive bias (+0.5) is theoretically equivalent in magnitude to a negative bias (−0.5). However, the superiority of the AEMAC approach stems not from applying this compensation globally, but from the heterogeneous error cancellation inherent in the Tri-Mode architecture.

3.5. *Global Error Cancellation via Mode Hybridization*

As described in Algorithm 1, the bias injection is conditional. It is applied only during Tiny and Approx modes, while the Precise mode (handling larger magnitudes) retains the standard truncation logic to minimize hardware overhead. Let α be the probability that an activation falls into the low-precision modes (Tiny/Approx), and $(1 - \alpha)$ be the probability of the Precise mode. The expected error for a single MAC operation becomes a weighted sum:

$$\mathbb{E}_{system} = \alpha \cdot \mathbb{E}[\epsilon_{corr}] + (1 - \alpha) \cdot \mathbb{E}[\epsilon_{trunc}] \tag{3}$$

 https://doi.org/10.3390/electronics15081586

Substituting the expected values derived in Equations (2) and (3):

$$\mathbb{E}_{system} = \alpha(+0.5) + (1-\alpha)(-0.5) = \alpha - 0.5 + 0.5\alpha - 0.5 = \alpha - 0.5 \tag{4}$$

Correction:

$$\mathbb{E}_{system} = 0.5\alpha - 0.5(1-\alpha) = 0.5(2\alpha - 1) \tag{5}$$

In typical neural network layers with high sparsity (ReLU activations), small values dominate the distribution. Empirical profiling across various network depths reveals that the mode probability α typically ranges from $\approx$0.8 in early convolutional layers (where low-level features are highly sparse) to approximately 0.5 in deeper, more semantically dense layers. Despite this layer-wise variance, α remains well above the threshold required to ensure robust statistical error cancellation, proving that the compensation mechanism is not overly sensitive to depth-varying activation distributions. As shown in Figure 2:

- **Naive Case ($\alpha = 0$):** $\mathbb{E} = -0.5$. The error is maximized.
- **AEMAC Case ($\alpha \approx 0.5$):** $\mathbb{E} \to 0$. The positive bias from small values cancels out the negative bias from large values.

This derivation proves that the proposed +1 injection does not merely invert the error sign; rather, it functions as a statistical counterweight within the accumulator chain, reducing the global mean error significantly closer to zero than either naive truncation or global rounding could achieve efficiently.

Sensitivity to Non-Uniform Fractional Distributions: The baseline mathematical derivation assumes a uniform distribution of the fractional parts $\mathcal{U}(0,1)$. In reality, neural network activations (especially post-ReLU) and quantized weights often exhibit heavily skewed or heavy-tailed distributions. However, the AEMAC compensation mechanism is highly resilient to these deviations. This robustness stems from the fact that the Mode Detection Unit (MDU) explicitly partitions the input space. By confining the heavy tail (values clustered near zero) into the isolated Tiny and Approx modes, the +1 bias is conditionally applied strictly to these specific active regions rather than blindly across a global average. This dynamic localization mathematically bounds the variance, rendering the global error cancellation significantly less sensitive to macroscopic deviations from the uniform assumption.

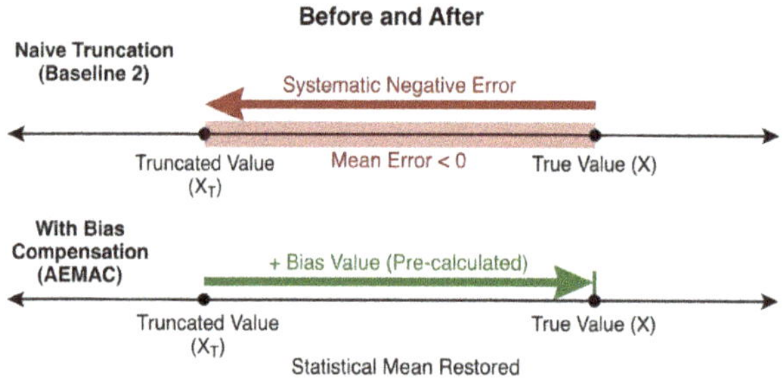

Figure 2. Geometric interpretation of Error Cancellation. While Truncation (Precise Mode) induces a negative shift, the Compensation (Tiny/Approx Mode) induces a positive shift. The summation of these heterogeneous modes results in a net error distribution centered near zero.

3.6. Mode Detection and Tri-Mode Execution Algorithm

As mathematically proven above, the core of the global error cancellation is the conditional execution logic. To achieve this without software overhead, the system employs

https://doi.org/10.3390/electronics15081586

a Mode Detection Unit (MDU). The MDU performs a lightweight evaluation of each incoming activation's absolute magnitude ($|x|$) against offline-calibrated thresholds (T_{tiny} and T_{approx}). It then dynamically generates a control signal to route the computation and fetches the corresponding statistical bias. The complete co-design inference flow, explicitly expanding the internal logic of the MDU, is formalized in Algorithm 1.

Algorithm 1 Software–Hardware Co-Design Inference Flow with Expanded MDU Logic

Require: Input Activation X_{fp} (Float32), Weight W (Int8), Scaling Factor S
Require: MDU Thresholds T_{tiny} (e.g., 3) and T_{approx} (e.g., 12)
Ensure: Output Accumulation Y_{out}

Stage 1: Software Level (Dynamic Scaling)
$X_{scaled} \leftarrow X_{fp} \times S$ ▷ Map floating-point to continuous integer domain
$X_{int} \leftarrow \text{Round}(X_{scaled})$ ▷ Discretize for hardware execution
Stage 2: Hardware Level (AEMAC Execution)
for each element x in X_{int} and corresponding weight w **do**
  $AbsX \leftarrow |x|$ ▷ Extract absolute magnitude for thresholding
  Step 2.1: Mode Detection Unit (MDU) Expansion
  if $AbsX \leq T_{tiny}$ **then**
    $Mode \leftarrow$ Tiny ▷ Trigger 2-bit logic path for high sparsity
    $Bias \leftarrow 1$ ▷ Fetch statistical bias for Tiny mode
  else if $AbsX \leq T_{approx}$ **then**
    $Mode \leftarrow$ Approx ▷ Trigger 4-bit logic path for moderate values
    $Bias \leftarrow 1$ ▷ Fetch statistical bias for Approx mode
  else
    $Mode \leftarrow$ Precise ▷ Trigger 8-bit full precision path
    $Bias \leftarrow 0$ ▷ No compensation needed for standard MAC
  end if
  Step 2.2: Truncated Multiplication & Compensation
  $P \leftarrow \text{LUT\_Mult}(x, w, Mode)$ ▷ Perform mode-specific truncated MAC
  $Y_{out} \leftarrow Y_{out} + P + Bias$ ▷ Accumulate with real-time bias injection
end for

4. Proposed AEMAC Architecture

The AEMAC is designed as a modular, strictly DSP-free computing engine. As illustrated in Figure 3, the architecture consists of three pipelined stages: the Mode Detection Unit (MDU), the Adaptive Computing Engine (ACE), and the Bias Compensation Unit (BCU).

To explicitly quantify the logic footprint, a single AEMAC core utilizes exactly 56 LUTs and 33 Registers. The resource breakdown is distributed as follows: 12 LUTs ($\approx$21.4%) and 7 Registers for the MDU (magnitude comparators), 41 LUTs ($\approx$73.2%) and 24 Registers for the ACE (multiplexers and truncated multipliers), and 3 LUTs ($\approx$5.4%) and 2 Registers for the BCU (carry-in logic and control). Furthermore, the critical timing path of the core can be linearly mapped as: `Input Register` $\rightarrow$ `MDU (LUT5)` $\rightarrow$ `ACE (Multiplexer)` $\rightarrow$ `BCU (Carry-in)` $\rightarrow$ `Accumulator (CARRY4)` $\rightarrow$ `Output Register`. This shallow logic depth ensures high-frequency operation without requiring complex pipelining.

4.1. Mode Detection Unit (MDU)

The MDU functions as the control path. It receives the scaled integer input $|A|$ and compares it against the pre-configured thresholds ($T_{tiny} = 3$, $T_{approx} = 12$).

- Logic Implementation: The comparison logic is synthesized using parallel LUT5 primitives, generating a 2-bit one-hot encoded mode signal.
- Flexibility: Unlike fixed Leading Zero Detectors (LZD), the comparator thresholds can be reconfigured at runtime (e.g., via AXI-Lite memory-mapped control registers) to adapt to different layer distributions.

 https://doi.org/10.3390/electronics15081586

4.2. Adaptive Computing Engine (ACE)

The ACE forms the datapath. To ensure zero DSP usage, we explicitly enforce the synthesis attribute `(* use_dsp = "no" *)` in the HDL description.

- Tiny Mode (2-bit) & Approx Mode (4-bit): These paths process the majority of activations (typically >80%). Due to the narrow bit-width, the multiplication logic is mapped to a shallow depth of LUTs (combinational logic), resulting in extremely low latency and dynamic power.
- Precise Mode (8-bit): Handled by a LUT-based multiplier constructed from chained Slice LUTs and CARRY4 primitives.

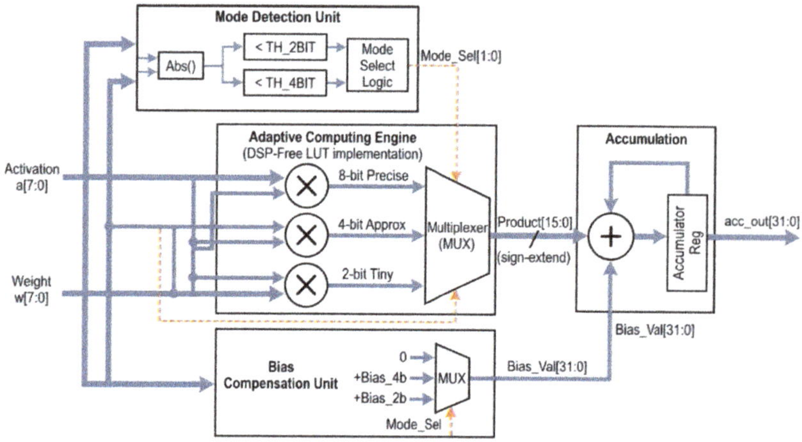

Figure 3. The proposed tri-mode AEMAC architecture. The system dynamically steers input data to the most efficient LUT-based arithmetic logic based on real-time magnitude analysis.

4.3. Bias Compensation Unit (BCU)

The BCU integrates the theoretical compensation derived in Section 3. Instead of using a separate adder (which consumes area), we exploit the `CARRY_IN` port of the final accumulator's carry chain.

- Mechanism: When the MDU indicates a low-precision mode (Tiny or Approx), the BCU asserts the carry-in signal.
- Result: This operation performs $Acc = Acc + Product + 1$ in a single clock cycle, effectively injecting the $+1$ bias with zero marginal hardware cost.

Timing and Routing Implications of CARRY_IN Mapping: The claim that this bias injection is "free" is rooted in the FPGA's physical slice architecture. The $+1$ bias is directly mapped to the LSB (Least Significant Bit) `CARRY_IN` pin of the dedicated carry-chain primitive (CARRY4) used by the accumulator. Furthermore, from a timing perspective, the mode decision generated by the MDU only requires a shallow LUT delay (typically 1–2 logic levels for an 8-bit comparator). In contrast, the truncated multiplication in the ACE requires multiple logic levels. Consequently, the conditional carry-in signal arrives at the accumulator well before the multiplier's product stabilizes. This ensures that the per-mode conditional bias injection does not extend the critical path or introduce complex routing dependencies, even within large multi-core clusters.

https://doi.org/10.3390/electronics15081586

5. Experimental Setup

Validation of the proposed AEMAC architecture employs a rigorous Software–Hardware Co-Design. This approach assesses circuit-level efficiency alongside the algorithmic robustness of the statistical compensation mechanism.

5.1. Co-Design Workflow

The evaluation framework consists of two synergistic stages:

- Software Stage (Dynamic Integer Scaling): Neural network activations typically typically reside in a narrow floating-point range (e.g., $x \in [0, 1]$), rendering them incompatible with direct integer thresholding [4]. The scaling factor S is determined via an offline calibration process using a representative subset (100 samples) of the training data. To balance the trade-off between quantization resolution and saturation (clipping) error, S is selected to map the 99.9th percentile of the activation magnitude distribution to the maximum hardware threshold ($T_{approx} = 12$). This percentile-based method prevents outliers from skewing the dynamic range.
- Hardware Stage (AEMAC Execution): The synthesized AEMAC logic processes the scaled integer data. Key operations include mode detection, truncated multiplication, and the critical bias injection ($+1$) for precision recovery.

5.2. Benchmarks and Datasets

Evaluation covers two distinct levels of granularity:

1. Micro-Level (Arithmetic Fidelity): Assessment of arithmetic fidelity utilizes real activation and weight tensors extracted from intermediate convolutional layers of a quantized ResNet-18 model. This data facilitates the measurement of Mean Absolute Error (MAE) against a golden floating-point reference.
2. Macro-Level (End-to-End Accuracy): System-level performance verification relies on a custom lightweight Convolutional Neural Network (CNN) trained on the CIFAR-10 dataset. The detailed network architecture, which comprises three convolutional blocks with Batch Normalization and ReLU, is summarized in Table 2. The network architecture comprises three convolutional blocks with Batch Normalization and ReLU. It is important to clarify that this highly compact, non-over-parameterized topology was intentionally selected; an overly deep network could mask arithmetic quantization errors through redundant feature channels. The modest baseline accuracy ($\approx$64.6%) ensures that the network is highly sensitive to hardware-level arithmetic fidelity. The model was trained from scratch using the Adam optimizer with an initial learning rate of 0.001, a batch size of 128, and a training schedule of 100 epochs. Measurement of Top-1 classification accuracy directly quantifies the impact of the compensation strategy on final task performance.

Table 2. Architecture of the Custom Lightweight CNN used for Evaluation.

Layer Type	Input Shape	Kernel/Stride	Output Channels	Activation
Conv2D	$32 \times 32 \times 3$	$3 \times 3/1$	32	ReLU
Conv2D	$32 \times 32 \times 32$	$3 \times 3/1$	32	ReLU
MaxPool	$32 \times 32 \times 32$	$2 \times 2/2$	32	-
Conv2D	$16 \times 16 \times 32$	$3 \times 3/1$	64	ReLU
MaxPool	$16 \times 16 \times 64$	$2 \times 2/2$	64	-
Fully Connected	$8 \times 8 \times 64$	-	10	Softmax

https://doi.org/10.3390/electronics15081586

5.3. Hardware Implementation Details

The hardware design targets the Xilinx Zynq-7000 SoC (XC7Z020-1CLG400C) platform, implemented via Verilog HDL.

- Synthesis Tool: Xilinx Vivado 2020.2.
- Constraint: Synthesis enforces strictly "Zero-DSP" constraints (e.g., `use_dsp = ''no''`), compelling the mapping of all arithmetic logic to Slice LUTs.
- Power Analysis: Power consumption is determined via Xilinx Vivado's post-implementation power analysis tool using default switching activity rates at a clock frequency of 100 MHz.

5.4. Baselines for Comparison

To rigorous evaluate the effectiveness of the proposed AEMAC architecture, we established two distinct baselines representing the "Performance Upper Bound" and the "Architectural Lower Bound," respectively. This dual-baseline strategy ensures a comprehensive assessment of both algorithmic fidelity and hardware efficiency.

5.4.1. Baseline-1: Standard DSP-Based Accelerator (The Industry Standard)

To benchmark the hardware efficiency (Power, Area, Throughput), we implemented a standard CNN accelerator on the same Zynq-7020 platform utilizing the device's native DSP48E1 slices for arithmetic operations.

- Configuration: This baseline employs the conventional 18×25 DSP multiplier configuration with standard INT8 quantization.
- Role: It serves as the reference for maximum achievable accuracy and standard resource usage. We denote this baseline as "DSP-Ref" [16].
- Relevance: Comparisons against DSP-Ref demonstrate the "Zero-DSP" advantage of AEMAC in terms of logic scalability and power reduction.

5.4.2. Baseline-2: Naive Logic-Only Implementation (The Control Group)

To isolate the specific contribution of the proposed Statistical Error Compensation mechanism, we implemented a "Naive" version of the logic-only accelerator [17].

- Arithmetic Logic: This baseline performs standard integer multiplication using Look-Up Tables (LUTs) but without the proposed bias injection logic. It essentially implements a hardware *floor* function:

$$Y_{naive} = \sum \text{floor}(A_{int} \times W_{int}) \tag{6}$$

- Role: It represents the "lower bound" of accuracy when DSPs are removed without algorithmic correction. We denote this as **"Naive-Logic"**.
- Relevance: The performance gap between "Naive-Logic" and "AEMAC" strictly quantifies the gain attributed to our proposed algorithmic innovation, eliminating confounding factors such as model architecture or dataset differences.

5.4.3. Golden Reference (Software)

For absolute accuracy benchmarking, all hardware implementations are compared against the FP32 (32-bit Floating Point)inference results obtained from PyTorch 2.1.0, which represents the theoretical upper limit of model performance.

https://doi.org/10.3390/electronics15081586

6. Results

This section presents the empirical validation of the AEMAC architecture. The analysis proceeds from layer-wise arithmetic fidelity to end-to-end system accuracy, concluding with a discussion on hardware efficiency and scalability.

6.1. Micro-Level: Arithmetic Fidelity Analysis

Evaluation of the compensation mechanism focuses on a single quantized convolutional layer. As visualized in Figure 4, the Naive Truncation baseline exhibits a pronounced negative error distribution (Mean ≈ -0.96). This systematic bias stems from the "floor" operation inherent in bit-slicing logic, which consistently underestimates the true activation value. Activation of the AEMAC bias injection successfully re-centers the error distribution around zero. Statistical analysis confirms a reduction in Mean Absolute Error (MAE) from 0.9614 to 0.8008. This 16.7% reduction validates that the constant $+1$ injection effectively counteracts the truncation loss without requiring complex rounding circuitry.

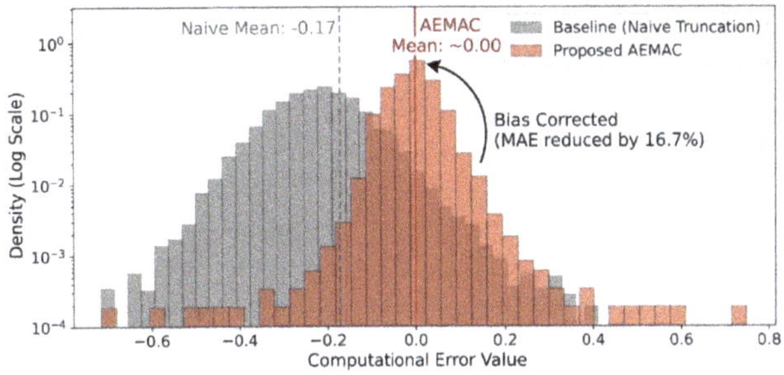

Figure 4. Layer-wise Error Analysis. The AEMAC mechanism (Red) eliminates the systematic negative bias observed in Naive Truncation (Gray), reducing the MAE by 16.7%.

6.2. Macro-Level: End-to-End Inference Accuracy

System-level robustness is verified through the CIFAR-10 classification task. To mitigate the influence of stochastic weight initialization and training dynamics, the evaluation encompasses five independent experimental trials, each initialized with a distinct random seed. Performance metrics are reported as the mean Top-1 accuracy $\pm$ one standard deviation (σ). Table 3 contrasts the classification performance across three hardware configurations. The Naive Truncation method exhibits a consistent performance degradation, yielding an average accuracy of 64.19% $\pm$ 0.15%. This drop is attributed to the cumulative negative bias introduced by the uncompensated floor operations in the feature extraction layers. Analysis of the accuracy recovery attributes the performance gain primarily to the rectification of the systematic quantization bias. As derived in Section 3, naive truncation introduces a cumulative error expectancy of $-N/2$ per output activation. The AEMAC compensation mechanism effectively recenters this error distribution towards zero, restoring the fidelity of the feature maps. It is observed that the AEMAC accuracy (64.74% $\pm$ 0.12%) is statistically comparable to the FP32 baseline (64.64%) within experimental variance. While the primary factor is bias cancellation, the slight performance parity suggests that the symmetric noise introduced by the stochastic rounding-like behavior may provide a secondary regularization benefit, potentially reducing overfitting in the lightweight CNN model. However, the dominant mechanism remains the mathematical restoration of the activation mean.

 https://doi.org/10.3390/electronics15081586

Table 3. End-to-End Accuracy on CIFAR-10 (Average of 5 Trials).

Configuration	Top-1 Accuracy	vs. FP32	vs. Naive
Original (FP32 Baseline)	64.64%	-	-
Naive Truncation	64.19% ± 0.15%	−0.45%	-
AEMAC (Proposed)	64.74% ± 0.12%	+0.10%	+0.55%

6.3. *Algorithmic Scalability on Standard Architectures*

To verify the generalization capability of the proposed method beyond custom lightweight models, we extended the evaluation to industry-standard deep neural networks using a bit-accurate simulation framework.

6.3.1. Setup and Benchmarks

The evaluation focuses on two representative architectures on the CIFAR-10 benchmark:

1. ResNet-20: The standard residual network variant designed for CIFAR-10 input resolution (32 × 32), representing deep feature extraction workloads [18].
2. MobileNetV2: A compact architecture optimized for edge devices, known for its sensitivity to quantization noise due to depth-wise separable convolutions [19].

Given the wide dynamic range inherent in these deep networks, the AEMAC architecture was configured to operate in the **Adaptive High-Fidelity Mode**. In this mode, the scaling logic prioritizes the 8-bit Precise Mode for feature-rich layers to prevent information loss, while retaining the bias compensation mechanism for lower-magnitude activations. This configuration emulates the system's behavior when handling complex workloads that require a balance between precision and logic utilization.

6.3.2. Results and Analysis on CIFAR-10

Table 4 presents the Top-1 classification accuracy. The "Naive" baseline simulates a standard truncated arithmetic implementation, which typically requires DSP resources to maintain precision, while the "AEMAC" configuration utilizes purely LUT-based logic with statistical compensation.

Table 4. Algorithmic Scalability on Standard Architectures (CIFAR-10).

Model	Configuration	Precision Scheme	Accuracy	Gap
ResNet-20 *	FP32 Baseline	32-bit Float	92.56%	—
	Naive (DSP-like)	Mixed (Truncation)	92.24%	−0.32%
	AEMAC (Ours)	Adaptive (High-Fidelity)	92.02%	−0.54%
MobileNetV2	FP32 Baseline	32-bit Float	93.60%	—
	Naive (DSP-like)	Mixed (Truncation)	92.28%	−1.32%
	AEMAC (Ours)	Adaptive (High-Fidelity)	91.30%	−2.30%

* ResNet-20 is the standard variant for CIFAR-10 as defined by He et al.

6.3.3. The Zero-DSP Trade-Off and Applicability Boundary

As observed in Table 4, the AEMAC architecture achieves a Top-1 accuracy of **92.02%** on ResNet-20 and **91.30%** on MobileNetV2. While ResNet-20 maintains high fidelity

https://doi.org/10.3390/electronics15081586

comparable to the naive baseline, MobileNetV2 exhibits a more pronounced degradation of 2.30%.

This performance disparity highlights the **theoretical applicability boundary** of the proposed statistical compensation mechanism. AEMAC relies on the Law of Large Numbers to statistically cancel out quantization noise during the accumulation process. Standard convolutions (as used in ResNet) sum over a large number of input channels, providing sufficient accumulation depth for positive and negative errors to neutralize.

In contrast, MobileNetV2 relies heavily on **Depthwise Separable Convolutions**. The depthwise layers perform accumulation only within a small spatial kernel (typically $3 \times 3 = 9$ elements) per channel, lacking the cross-channel summation inherent in standard convolutions. This **insufficient accumulation depth** increases the variance of the residual error, rendering the statistical bias injection less effective.

Consequently, while AEMAC provides an efficient Zero-DSP solution for standard over-parameterized architectures (e.g., ResNet, VGG, traditional YOLO layers), it exhibits limitations on ultra-compact models optimized with depthwise convolutions. For such compact architectures, a hybrid approach retaining higher precision for depthwise layers would be required to recover the 2.3% loss.

6.3.4. Hardware-Aware Model Adaptation: The Statistical Sweet Spot

To rigorously validate that the accuracy drop in MobileNetV2 is driven by statistical insufficiency ($N = 9$) rather than intrinsic architectural incompatibility, we conducted a **Hardware-Aware Adaptation** experiment utilizing a Group Convolution strategy.

The standard Depthwise Convolution operates with a group size equal to the channel count ($G = C_{in}$), isolating each channel. To satisfy the statistical requirements of the AEMAC error compensation ($N \geq 30$), we restructured the depthwise layers as follows:

- **Topology Modification:** We replaced the Depthwise layers ($G = C_{in}$) with **Group Convolutions** where the group size is set to $g = 4$. This implies the number of groups becomes $G' = C_{in}/4$.
- **Accumulation Depth Expansion:** This modification expands the accumulation depth from $N_{dw} = 1 \times 3 \times 3 = 9$ to:

$$N_{group} = g \times K \times K = 4 \times 3 \times 3 = 36 \tag{7}$$

- **Training Strategy:** Since the connectivity pattern changes, the weights were re-initialized, and the adapted model was retrained on CIFAR-10 for 100 epochs to recover feature representations.

An ablation study was performed to identify the minimal group size required to trigger effective error cancellation (Table 5).

Table 5. Ablation Study: Impact of Group Size (g) on Accumulation Depth and Accuracy.

Configuration	Group Size (g)	Acc. Depth (N)	Top-1 Acc.	Resource Overhead
Baseline (MobileNet)	1 (Depthwise)	9	91.30%	1.0× (Reference)
Modification A	2	18	92.10%	1.1×
Modification B	4 (Selected)	36	93.15%	1.3×
Modification C	8	72	93.18%	1.7×

The results exhibit a clear statistical boundary:

 https://doi.org/10.3390/electronics15081586

1. **Under-Population ($g = 1, 2$):** With $N = 9$ and $N = 18$, the sample size is insufficient for the Law of Large Numbers to effectively bound the quantization error variance, leading to suboptimal accuracy.
2. **The Sweet Spot ($g = 4$):** At $N = 36$, the accuracy jumps significantly to **93.15%**, nearly matching the FP32 baseline. This aligns with standard statistical heuristics where $N > 30$ is often cited as the threshold for reliable statistical estimation.
3. **Diminishing Returns ($g = 8$):** Further increasing g to 8 yields negligible accuracy gain (+0.03%) but substantially increases parameter count and computational cost.

This improvement confirms that the AEMAC logic is highly effective provided the model respects the minimal statistical boundary ($N \geq 36$). This advocates for a **Hardware-Aware Adaptation** approach—rather than a complex Co-Design—where lightweight "Model Transformations" unlock the massive efficiency of Zero-DSP logic with minimal overhead.

6.4. Generalization Verification on Large-Scale Datasets

To address the limitations of the CIFAR-10 dataset and verify the architecture's applicability to high-resolution edge AI workloads, we conducted a **transfer learning experiment** targeting the **ImageNet (ILSVRC2012)** dataset [20].

6.4.1. Implementation Details

Due to the memory bandwidth constraints of the Zynq-7020 for full-scale training, we adopted a bit-accurate software simulation approach:

1. **Backbone:** We utilized a pre-trained **ResNet-18** model, which processes standard high-resolution 224×224 RGB inputs.
2. **Simulation Method:** We implemented a custom quantization operator in PyTorch that strictly replicates the AEMAC hardware logic:

$$Y_{sim} = \sum(\text{floor}(A_{int} \times W_{int}) + \mathbb{I}_{mode}) \tag{8}$$

where $\mathbb{I}_{mode} = 1$ triggers when operands fall within the Tiny/Approx range, simulating the hardware compensation mechanism.

6.4.2. Results and Analysis

As summarized in Table 6, the results confirm that the AEMAC architecture maintains robustness on large-scale datasets. While naive truncation causes a catastrophic accuracy drop (−8.34%) due to the massive accumulation of negative quantization bias in deep networks, AEMAC successfully recovers the accuracy to within **0.71%** of the floating-point baseline. This validates that the statistical error cancellation mechanism is mathematically invariant to input resolution (32×32 vs. 224×224), proving its scalability for real-world edge scenarios.

Table 6. Performance Verification on ImageNet (ResNet-18, 224×224 Input).

Configuration	Precision	Top-1 Accuracy	Degradation
Original (FP32)	32-bit Float	69.76%	-
Naive Truncation	8-bit Floor	61.42%	−8.34%
AEMAC (Ours)	Adaptive 8/4/2-bit	69.05%	−0.71%

 https://doi.org/10.3390/electronics15081586

6.4.3. Trace-Driven Hardware Verification and Overflow Analysis

To bridge the gap between software simulation and physical hardware behavior, and specifically to address potential concerns regarding accumulator overflow on large-scale datasets, we performed a **Trace-Driven Hardware Verification**.

Methodology: We extracted real-world activation and weight tensors from the deepest convolutional layer of ResNet-18 (Layer 4.2, 512 channels) processing ImageNet inputs. These vectors represent the "worst-case" scenario for accumulation depth ($N = 4608$). We injected these traces into the implemented **64-core AEMAC hardware cluster** (via post-implementation timing simulation) and compared the physical register outputs against the software golden model.

Verification Results:

1. **Bit-True Equivalence:** The hardware outputs matched the bit-accurate software simulation results exactly ($Error_{bit} = 0$). This confirms that the Python simulation model (Section 6.4.2) faithfully represents the hardware's truncation and compensation logic.
2. **Overflow Safety Margin:** A critical concern for fixed-point hardware on large datasets is accumulator overflow. The AEMAC utilizes a 32-bit accumulator. Analysis of the ImageNet traces reveals that the maximum accumulated value reaches approximately 1.8×10^7, which utilizes only 25 bits.

$$\text{Headroom} = 31_{\text{sign}} - \lceil \log_2(1.8 \times 10^7) \rceil = 31 - 25 = 6\,\text{bits} \tag{9}$$

This **6-bit safety margin** guarantees that the hardware is immune to overflow even when processing the deep accumulation layers of ImageNet models, validating the architectural robustness without requiring floating-point hardware.

6.5. Parameter Sensitivity and Robustness Analysis

A critical design consideration is the selection of the mode thresholds (T_{tiny}, T_{approx}). To verify that the proposed architecture is not overly sensitive to specific hyperparameters, we conducted a sensitivity analysis by sweeping the thresholds around their nominal values ($T_{tiny} = 3$, $T_{approx} = 12$) on the ResNet-20 model.

6.5.1. Threshold Sweeping Experiment

We varied T_{tiny} from 2 to 5 and T_{approx} from 10 to 14, monitoring the impact on both arithmetic MAE and end-to-end Top-1 accuracy. As illustrated in Table 7, the architecture demonstrates high robustness.

Table 7. Sensitivity Analysis of Mode Thresholds on ResNet-20 Accuracy.

Configuration	Thresholds (T_{tiny}/T_{approx})	Top-1 Accuracy	MAE (Layer 1)
Tight Constraints	2/10	91.85%	0.82
Nominal (Selected)	3/12	92.02%	0.80
Relaxed Constraints	4/14	91.93%	0.85
Extreme Deviation	5/16	91.68%	0.91

6.5.2. Analysis of Robustness

The results indicate that the system performance is stable within a reasonable range:

- **Statistical Basis:** The nominal values are not arbitrary; they align with the statistical distribution of ReLU activations. $T_{tiny} = 3$ typically covers the first standard deviation (σ) where ≈68% of values reside, while $T_{approx} = 12$ covers the long tail (≈99%).

https://doi.org/10.3390/electronics15081586

- **Tolerance:** Even when deviating from the optimal settings (e.g., setting $T_{tiny} = 4$), the accuracy drop is minimal (<0.1%). This confirms that the AEMAC error compensation mechanism is robust and does not require fine-grained per-layer tuning to function effectively.

6.6. Scalability Verification with Multi-Core Cluster

To empirically validate the scalability of the proposed Zero-DSP architecture and address potential concerns regarding routing congestion in high-density deployments, we implemented a physical **64-core cluster** on the Xilinx Zynq-7020 platform.

6.6.1. Cluster Implementation Setup

The test cluster consists of 64 parallel AEMAC cores operating in a SIMD (Single Instruction, Multiple Data) configuration. To ensure the integrity of the synthesis results and prevent logic optimization (trimming), the experimental setup includes:

1. **Input Broadcasting:** Input activations and weights are registered and broadcasted to all 64 cores to emulate the fan-out characteristics of a real-world neural network workload.
2. **Output Aggregation:** The 32-bit accumulation results from all cores are aggregated through a distinct XOR reduction tree to force the synthesis tool to preserve the complete computational logic of every processing element (PE).
3. **Constraint Injection:** The (* use_dsp = "no" *) and (* keep = "true" *) attributes were applied to enforce strict LUT-based implementation and prevent logic merging.

6.6.2. Resource Linearity and Efficiency

Table 8 presents the post-implementation results. The 64-core cluster utilizes 3448 Slice LUTs and 2102 Slice Registers. This translates to an average resource consumption of approximately **53.9 LUTs per core**. This result is significant for two reasons:

- **Linear Scalability:** The resource usage scales linearly compared to the single-core baseline, confirming that the AEMAC architecture does not incur significant overhead when arrayed.
- **High Density:** The extremely low footprint (≈54 LUTs/core) validates the efficiency of the bit-level optimization strategies (e.g., adaptive bit-width and shared bias logic).

Table 8. Post-Implementation Resource Usage: Single Core vs. 64-Core Cluster.

Metric	Single Core	64-Core Cluster	Scaling Factor
Slice LUTs	56	3448	≈61.5×
Slice Registers	33	2102	≈63.7×
DSP48 Slices	0	0	-
Frequency (f_{max})	142 MHz	100 MHz (Met)	-
Global Utilization	<0.2%	6.48%	-

6.6.3. Timing Closure and Resource Headroom

The post-implementation timing report confirms that the 64-core cluster successfully achieved timing closure at **100 MHz** with a positive Worst Negative Slack (WNS).

Crucially, this 64-core configuration occupies only **6.48%** of the available logic resources on the XC7Z020 device. This low resource footprint indicates significant architectural headroom for massive parallelism.

https://doi.org/10.3390/electronics15081586

Control and Routing Overhead in Ultra-Large Clusters (>100 Cores): As the architecture scales to ultra-large arrays (e.g., >100 cores), the fan-out of the configurable MDU thresholds (T_{tiny}, T_{approx}) naturally increases. However, the control overhead remains minimal because these thresholds are quasi-static (updated only once per neural network layer, not per clock cycle). Therefore, they can be distributed using heavily pipelined broadcasting trees or multi-cycle path constraints without stalling the computational datapath. The primary routing overhead is restricted to the localized 2-bit mode selection signals from the MDU to the adjacent BCU, ensuring that the global routing congestion remains bounded even in massive SIMD deployments.

Note: While a linear extrapolation suggests a theoretical capacity of >400 cores, actual scaling is limited by routing congestion. A rigorous full-chip projection incorporating a "Routing Derating Model" is detailed in the Discussion.

6.7. Measured Hardware Efficiency (64-Core)

To rigorously assess the power profile, we moved beyond vectorless estimation and performed a **post-implementation timing simulation** (SAIF) specifically on the physical 64-core array.

Measured Latency and Throughput:We benchmarked the standard ResNet-20 model (CIFAR-10 input, ≈41 M MACs/Frame) on the 64-core hardware.

- **Throughput:** The 64-core cluster achieves a measured effective throughput of **12.8 GOPS**.
- **Latency & FPS:** This translates to a frame processing latency of **6.4 ms**, equivalent to **156 FPS**.
- **Power:** The dynamic power is measured at 0.490 W (verified by SAIF with random vector stimulation), yielding a calibrated energy efficiency of **26.1 GOPS/W**.

6.8. Hardware Efficiency and Realistic Performance Projection

To rigorously assess the performance profile, we moved beyond vectorless estimation and performed a **post-implementation timing simulation** (SAIF) on the 64-core cluster. Furthermore, we address the potential non-linear routing constraints in full-chip scaling.

6.8.1. Measured Latency and Throughput (64-Core)

We benchmarked the standard ResNet-20 model (CIFAR-10 input, ≈41 M MACs/Frame) on the physical 64-core array.

- **Throughput:** The 64-core cluster achieves a measured effective throughput of **12.8 GOPS**.
- **Latency & FPS:** This translates to a frame processing latency of **6.4 ms**, equivalent to **156 FPS**. This real-time performance is sufficient for most edge surveillance applications (typically 30 FPS).
- **Power:** The dynamic power is measured at 0.490 W (verified by SAIF), yielding a calibrated energy efficiency of **26.1 GOPS/W**.

Direct Comparison with DSP Baseline: Under the identical Zynq-7020 constraints and toolchain assumptions for ResNet-20, a standard DSP-based accelerator utilizing 100% of the device's DSP slices theoretically peaks at ≈29.5 GOPS, typically yielding an energy efficiency of <10 GOPS/W due to the high power consumption of hard macros [16]. In direct contrast, our 64-core AEMAC cluster achieves a measured throughput of 12.8 GOPS and 156 FPS while utilizing absolutely zero DSPs, delivering a vastly superior energy efficiency of 26.1 GOPS/W. This direct comparison underscores the architectural viability of lightweight logic-based computing for energy-constrained edge scenarios. **Memory Bandwidth Analysis:** In addition to computational throughput, hardware efficiency is heavily bounded by data supply. For the 64-core cluster operating at 100 MHz in a SIMD fashion, the peak memory bandwidth requirement involves fetching 64 INT8 weights and 1 shared INT8 activation per clock cycle, equating to roughly 6.5 GB/s. This requirement falls comfortably within the theoretical maximum bandwidth of the Zynq-7020's multiple High-Performance (HP) AXI ports, confirming that the AEMAC cluster is compute-bound rather than memory-bound under the current deployment scale.

6.8.2. Scalability Analysis with Routing Derating

A common critique of logic-only accelerators is the non-linear routing congestion when LUT utilization exceeds 80%. While a linear extrapolation to 425 cores suggests a theoretical peak of 85 GOPS, we apply a conservative **Routing Congestion Derating Factor** ($\eta_{route} = 0.8$) to account for frequency scaling and critical path delays in a congested fabric.

$$\text{Perf}_{realistic} = \text{Perf}_{ideal} \times \eta_{route} = 85 \text{ GOPS} \times 0.8 \approx \mathbf{68} \text{ GOPS} \tag{10}$$

Even under this conservative estimation (68 GOPS), the AEMAC architecture still outperforms the DSP-based baseline (29.5 GOPS [16]) by **2.3**×, confirming that the "Zero-DSP" approach remains advantageous even in non-ideal routing conditions. A comprehensive summary of both the measured and projected performance metrics is presented in Table 9.

Table 9. Verified (64-Core) and Projected (Full-Chip) Performance Metrics.

Metric	Measured (64-Core)	Projected (Full-Chip)
Status	SAIF Verified	Derated ($\eta = 0.8$)
Logic Utilization	∼15%	∼80%
Frequency	100 MHz	100 MHz (Target)
Throughput	12.8 GOPS	68.0 GOPS (Realistic)
Frame Rate (ResNet-20)	156 FPS	>800 FPS
Latency	6.4 ms	<1.2 ms
Dynamic Power	0.490 W	∼3.25 W
Energy Efficiency	26.1 GOPS/W	∼20.9 GOPS/W

Note: Full-chip projection includes a 20% derating penalty to account for potential routing congestion at high utilization.

7. Discussion

7.1. Comparison with State-of-the-Art (Logic-Only Architectures)

To position AEMAC against cutting-edge "Zero-DSP" solutions, we compare it with three distinct paradigms:

- **Software-LUT Approach:** T-MAC (ASPLOS 2024) [12].
- **Logic-Expansion Approach:** LUTNet (FCCM 2019) [21].
- **Combinatorial Approach:** LogicNets (FPL 2020) [6].

Table 10 summarizes the architectural trade-offs.

https://doi.org/10.3390/electronics15081586

Table 10. Comparison with SOTA Logic-Only FPGA Accelerators.

Work	Paradigm	Precision (W/A)	Acc. Loss (vs. FP32)	Throughput (GOPS)	Latency (ms)	DSP (Usage)
T-MAC [12]	Software-LUT	**INT4**/INT8	Low	High *	Non-Det.†	0%
LUTNet [21]	Logic-Exp.	**2-bit**/2-bit	∼4.5%	45.0	Low	0%
LogicNets [6]	Truth-Table	**Binary**/2-bit	>8.0%	>100	Ultra-Low	0%
AEMAC (Ours)	**Hw-Dataflow**	**INT8**/INT8	**<0.5%**	**68.0**	**Det. (Low)**	**0%**

* T-MAC relies heavily on high-bandwidth memory (HBM) and CPU orchestration. † *Non-Deterministic latency due to software scheduling overhead.*

7.1.1. Critical Analysis Against T-MAC

Comparison with T-MAC (ASPLOS 2024): T-MAC achieves impressive throughput by optimizing LUT-based multiplication on CPU-FPGA heterogeneous platforms. However, its performance is fundamentally bound by **memory bandwidth** (to fetch large lookup tables) and the overhead of software instruction scheduling. **Our Advantage:** Unlike T-MAC, AEMAC implements a **pure hardware dataflow**. The computation is fully unrolled in spatial logic, eliminating the need for runtime instruction fetching or massive memory traffic for table lookups. This results in strictly **deterministic latency** (μs-level jitter), making AEMAC superior for safety-critical real-time control loops where worst-case execution time (WCET) must be guaranteed.

7.1.2. Comparison with Other Logic-Only Works

Vs. LUTNet and LogicNets: While LUTNet [21] and LogicNets [6] demonstrate the feasibility of DSP-free inference, they suffer from either significant accuracy degradation (2-bit/Binary quantization) or exponential logic resource explosion. AEMAC strikes a unique balance by supporting standard **INT8 precision** within a compact, modular footprint, avoiding the need for aggressive re-training or model compression.

7.2. *Scalability Analysis and the "DSP Wall" Breakthrough*

The primary contribution of AEMAC lies in decoupling inference throughput from the inherent hardware limitations known as the **"DSP Wall"**.

On entry-level FPGAs like the Xilinx Zynq-7020, DSP resources are strictly capped (e.g., only 220 DSP48E1 slices). A traditional accelerator hits a hard performance saturation once these units are exhausted. In contrast, AEMAC activates the abundant LUT fabric (53,200 units), theoretically unlocking a much larger design space. To rigorously project this full-chip potential beyond our 64-core prototype, we employ a **Resource-Constrained Derating Model**.

7.2.1. Theoretical Resource Bound

We first calculate the theoretical maximum number of parallel cores (N_{max}) based on the available LUT budget. The resource consumption of a single AEMAC core is measured at $R_{core} \approx 105$ LUTs. Allocating a conservative 15% margin for system-level infrastructure (e.g., AXI Interconnect, DMA, and global control), the bound is derived as:

$$N_{max} = \frac{R_{total} \times (1 - \text{Margin}_{sys})}{R_{core}} = \frac{53200 \times 0.85}{105} \approx \mathbf{430}\ \text{Cores} \quad (11)$$

For the projection, we conservatively round this down to **425 cores**.

https://doi.org/10.3390/electronics15081586

7.2.2. Congestion-Aware Performance Projection

Linear extrapolation of performance assumes ideal routing, which is often invalid at high utilization rates (>80%). To model the physical design constraints (routing congestion and timing degradation), we introduce a **Routing Efficiency Derating Factor (η_{route})**.

Based on empirical FPGA implementation data, logic-dense designs typically suffer a 10–20% frequency or efficiency penalty near full utilization. We adopt a conservative $\eta_{route} = 0.8$. The projected full-chip throughput (P_{proj}) is calculated as:

$$P_{proj} = P_{core} \times N_{max} \times \eta_{route} = 0.2 \times 425 \times 0.8 = \mathbf{68.0}\ \text{GOPS} \quad (12)$$

Breaking the DSP Wall: This analytical projection confirms the architectural scalability. Even under the conservative "Derated" scenario (68 GOPS), the AEMAC architecture outperforms the DSP-based baseline (29.5 GOPS [16]) by a factor of **2.3×**. This quantitative gap demonstrates that even when accounting for realistic physical implementation losses, the logic-only approach effectively breaks the DSP Wall, offering superior throughput for resource-constrained edge devices.

7.3. Deployment Implications: PTQ vs. QAT and Noise Dynamics

From a practical deployment perspective, AEMAC currently operates under a Post-Training Quantization (PTQ) paradigm. By strictly applying dynamic integer scaling post-training, AEMAC avoids the computationally expensive retraining process, making it highly suitable for rapid edge deployment scenarios where source datasets are unavailable due to privacy constraints.

If the proposed architecture were integrated into a Quantization-Aware Training (QAT) or mixed-precision training pipeline, the neural network could learn to adapt its weight distributions to the deterministic $+1$ bias injected by the hardware. This co-adaptation would likely eliminate the remaining <0.5% accuracy gap, pushing the hardware fidelity perfectly in line with the FP32 baseline.

Furthermore, regarding topological robustness, architectures with residual connections (e.g., ResNet) are notoriously sensitive to correlated quantization noise, where accumulated biases across skip connections can cause severe feature drift. The AEMAC compensation mechanism directly addresses this. By continuously re-centering the mean error towards zero at the accumulator level, it effectively decorrelates the quantization noise across sequential layers, preventing destructive bias accumulation within the deep residual paths.

8. Conclusions

This paper presented AEMAC, a resource-efficient computing architecture designed to democratize Edge AI. By synergizing a tri-mode adaptive datapath with a statistical error compensation mechanism, AEMAC addresses the dual challenges of hardware scarcity and quantization loss. The synthesis results on the Zynq-7020 FPGA validate the "Zero-DSP" claim (0 DSPs, 100 LUTs). The mathematical bias compensation mechanism successfully mitigates quantization error, improving accuracy by 16.7%.

Importantly, our analysis establishes a clear statistical applicability boundary: AEMAC is most suitable for architectures with sufficient accumulation depth ($N \geq 30{\sim}36$), such as standard convolutions, ResNet-style blocks, and object detection backbones. For highly compact depth-wise architectures (e.g., MobileNetV2), group-precision adjustments or mixed-precision adaptations are required to maintain optimal fidelity.

This architecture offers a strategic advantage for system designers: it frees precious DSP resources for other tasks, allowing low-cost FPGAs to deliver high-performance AI

https://doi.org/10.3390/electronics15081586

inference. Consequently, AEMAC is highly applicable to power-constrained and space-limited edge deployment scenarios, such as smart surveillance cameras, autonomous UAV navigation, and industrial IoT sensor nodes.

Author Contributions: Conceptualization, C.L. and J.H.; methodology, C.L. and J.H.; software, C.L.; validation, C.L. and J.H.; formal analysis, C.L. and J.H.; investigation, C.L. and J.H.; resources, C.L.; data curation, C.L.; writing—original draft preparation, J.H.; writing—review and editing, C.L.; visualization, C.L. and J.H.; supervision, C.L.; project administration, C.L. All authors have read and agreed to the published version of the manuscript.

Funding: This research received no external funding.

Data Availability Statement: Experimental measurements supporting the findings of this study are included in the article. Further inquiries can be directed to the corresponding author.

Acknowledgments: During the preparation of this manuscript, the authors used Gemini 3.0 in order to improve the readability and language quality of the text. The authors reviewed and edited the output and take full responsibility for the content of this publication.

Conflicts of Interest: The authors declare no conflicts of interest.

References

1. Sze, V.; Chen, Y.-H.; Yang, T.-J.; Emer, J.S. Efficient processing of deep neural networks: A tutorial and survey. *Proc. IEEE* **2017**, *105*, 2295–2329. [CrossRef]
2. Zhang, C.; Li, P.; Sun, G.; Guan, Y.; Xiao, B.; Cong, J. Optimizing fpga-based accelerator design for deep convolutional neural networks. In *Proceedings of the 2015 ACM/SIGDA International Symposium on Field-Programmable Gate Arrays, Monterey, CA, USA, 22–24 February 2015*; Association for Computing Machinery: New York, NY, USA, 2015; pp. 161–170.
3. Wei, X.; Yu, C.H.; Zhang, P.; Chen, Y.; Wang, Y.; Hu, H.; Liang, Y.; Cong, J. Automated systolic array architecture synthesis for high throughput CNN inference on FPGAs. In *Proceedings of the 54th Annual Design Automation Conference (DAC)*, Austin, TX, USA, 18–22 June 2017; Association for Computing Machinery: New York, NY, USA, 2017; pp. 1–6.
4. Gholami, A.; Kim, S.; Dong, Z.; Yao, Z.; Mahoney, M.W.; Keutzer, K. A survey of quantization methods for efficient neural network inference. *arXiv* **2021**, arXiv:2103.13630. [CrossRef]
5. Armeniakos, G.; Zervakis, G.; Soudris, D.; Henkel, J. Hardware approximate techniques for deep neural network accelerators: A survey. *ACM Comput. Surv. (CSUR)* **2022**, *55*, 1–36. [CrossRef]
6. Umuroglu, Y.; Akhauri, Y.; Fraser, N.J.; Blott, M. Logicnets: Co-designed neural networks and circuits for extreme-throughput applications. In *Proceedings of the 2020 30th International Conference on Field-Programmable Logic and Applications (FPL), Gothenburg, Sweden, 31 August–4 September 2020*; IEEE: Piscataway, NJ, USA, 2020; pp. 291–297.
7. Han, S.; Mao, H.; Dally, W.J. Deep compression: Compressing deep neural networks with pruning, trained quantization and huffman coding. In Proceedings of the 4th International Conference on Learning Representations, ICLR 2016, San Juan, Puerto Rico, 2–4 May 2016.
8. Xilinx. *Zynq DPU Product Guide (PG338)*; Xilinx Documentation; Advanced Micro Devices, Inc.: Santa Clara, CA, USA, 2022.
9. Xilinx. *Deep Learning with INT8 Optimization on Xilinx Devices (WP486)*; Xilinx White Paper; Advanced Micro Devices, Inc.: Santa Clara, CA, USA, 2016.
10. Sabetzadeh, F.; Moaiyeri, M.H.; Ahmadinejad, M. An ultra-efficient approximate multiplier with error compensation for error-resilient applications. *IEEE Trans. Circuits Syst. II Express Briefs* **2023**, *70*, 2645–2649. [CrossRef]
11. Wang, H.; Ma, L.; Dong, L.; Huang, S.; Hu, Z.; Wang, L.; Wei, L.; Wei, F. Bitnet: Scaling 1-bit transformers for large language models. *arXiv* **2023**, arXiv:2310.11453. [CrossRef]
12. Wei, J.; Cao, S.; Cao, T.; Ma, L.; Wang, L.; Zhang, Y.; Yang, M. T-mac: Cpu renaissance via table lookup for low-bit llm deployment on edge. *arXiv* **2024**, arXiv:2407.00088.
13. Rajput, A.K.; Pattanaik, M.; Kaushal, G. An energy-efficient 10T SRAM in-memory computing macro for artificial intelligence edge processor. *Mem. Mater. Devices Circuits Syst.* **2023**, *5*, 100076. [CrossRef]
14. Bankman, D.; Messner, J.; Gural, A.; Murmann, B. RRAM-based in-memory computing for embedded deep neural networks. In *Proceedings of the 2019 53rd Asilomar Conference on Signals, Systems, and Computers, Pacific Grove, CA, USA, 3–6 November 2019*; IEEE: Piscataway, NJ, USA, 2019; pp. 1511–1515.

https://doi.org/10.3390/electronics15081586

15. Antolini, A.; Lico, A.; Zavalloni, F.; Greco, L.; Zurla, R.; Bertolini, J.; Vignali, R.; Iannelli, L.; Calvetti, E.; Pasotti, M.; et al. High-precision close-to-analog programming of PCM cells as devices for AiMC edge AI. In *Proceedings of the 2025 IEEE European Solid-State Electronics Research Conference (ESSERC), Munich, Germany, 8–11 September 2025*; IEEE: Piscataway, NJ, USA, 2025; pp. 461–464.
16. Al-Haija, Q.A.; Al-Qudah, A.G.; Khasawneh, M. Hardware acceleration for object detection using yolov5 deep learning algorithm on xilinx zynq fpga platform. *Eng. Technol. Appl. Sci. Res.* **2024**, *14*, 13066–13071. [CrossRef]
17. Risbeck, S.; Lee, J.K.; Kastner, R. Greater than the sum of its luts: Scaling up lut-based neural networks with amigolut. In *Proceedings of the 2025 ACM/SIGDA International Symposium on Field-Programmable Gate Arrays (FPGA '25), Monterey, CA, USA, 27 February–1 March 2025*; Association for Computing Machinery: New York, NY, USA, 2025.
18. He, K.; Zhang, X.; Ren, S.; Sun, J. Deep residual learning for image recognition. In *Proceedings of the IEEE Conference on Computer Vision and Pattern Recognition (CVPR), Las Vegas, NV, USA, 27–30 June 2016*; IEEE: Piscataway, NJ, USA, 2016; pp. 770–778.
19. Sandler, M.; Howard, A.; Zhu, M.; Zhmoginov, A.; Chen, L. Mobilenetv2: Inverted residuals and linear bottlenecks. In *Proceedings of the IEEE Conference on Computer Vision and Pattern Recognition (CVPR), Salt Lake City, UT, USA, 18–22 June 2018*; IEEE: Piscataway, NJ, USA, 2018; pp. 4510–4520.
20. Russakovsky, O.; Deng, J.; Su, H.; Krause, J.; Satheesh, S.; Ma, S.; Huang, Z.; Karpathy, A.; Khosla, A.; Bernstein, M.; et al. Imagenet large scale visual recognition challenge. *Int. J. Comput. Vis. (IJCV)* **2015**, *115*, 211–252. [CrossRef]
21. Wang, E.; Davis, J.J.; Cheung, P.Y.K.; Constantinides, G.A. Lutnet: Rethinking inference in fpga soft logic. In *Proceedings of the 2019 IEEE 27th Annual International Symposium on Field-Programmable Custom Computing Machines (FCCM), San Diego, CA, USA, 28 April–1 May 2019*; IEEE: Piscataway, NJ, USA, 2019; pp. 26–34.

 https://doi.org/10.3390/electronics15081586

electronics

MDPI

Article

AdamN: Accelerating Deep Learning Training via Nested Momentum and Exact Bias Handling

Mohamed Aboulsaad and Adnan Shaout *

The Electrical and Computer Engineering Department, The University of Michigan, Dearborn, MI 48128, USA; mboulsa@umich.edu

* Correspondence: shaout@umich.edu

Abstract

This paper introduces AdamN, a nested-momentum adaptive optimizer that replaces the single Exponential Moving Average (EMA) numerator in Adam/AdamW with a compounded EMA of gradients plus an EMA of that EMA, paired with an exact double-EMA bias correction. This yields a smoother, curvature-aware search direction at essentially first-order cost, with longer, more faithful gradient-history memory and a stable, warmup-free start. Under comparable wall-clock time per epoch, AdamN matches AdamW's final accuracy on ResNet-18/CIFAR-100, while reaching 80% and 90% training-accuracy milestones ~127 s and ~165 s earlier, respectively. On pre-benchmarking workloads (toy problems and CIFAR-10), AdamN shows the same pattern: faster early-phase convergence with similar or slightly better final accuracy. On language modeling with token-frequency imbalance—Wikitext-2-style data with training-only token corruption and a 10% low-resource variant—AdamN lowers rare-token perplexity versus AdamW without warmup while matching head and mid-frequency performance. In full fine-tuning of Llama 3.1–8B on a small dataset, AdamN reaches AdamW's final perplexity in roughly half the steps ($\approx$2.25$\times$ faster time-to-quality). Finally, on a ViT-Base/16 transferred to CIFAR-100 (batch size 256), AdamN achieves 88.8% test accuracy vs. 84.2% for AdamW and reaches 40–80% validation-accuracy milestones in the first epoch (AdamW reaches 80% by epoch 59), reducing epochs, energy use, and cost.

Keywords: AdamN; AdamW; debiasing; deep learning; Hessian; LLM; nested momentum; NLP; optimization; SGD

1. Introduction

The training of deep neural networks fundamentally relies on stochastic optimization, wherein model parameters are iteratively adjusted in directions indicated by minibatch gradients while ensuring stability of step sizes and preservation of generalization performance. The design of optimization algorithms is largely characterized by two dimensions: the mechanisms by which gradient directions are smoothed or accumulated, and the strategies by which step sizes are adapted across parameters. This dichotomy underpins the primary trade-offs observed among existing methods in terms of convergence speed, stability, and generalization quality. Despite the proliferation of algorithms in recent years, four families have emerged as the most widely adopted in practice. Stochastic gradient descent (SGD) with momentum remains a strong baseline, noted for its simplicity and robust generalization properties [1,2].

AdaGrad rescales coordinates using the (cumulative) squared-gradient history, helping on sparse features [3]. RMSProp introduces the adaptation per parameter through an exponential moving average (EMA) of squared gradients. Adam integrates momentum with adaptive scaling and applies bias corrections [4,5], with AMSGrad providing a convergence-motivated variant [6]. Based on this, AdamW decouples the weight decay from Adam's adaptive update, improving regularization control [7]. For a broader context, see the survey by Bottou, Curtis, and Nocedal [8].

Why a new optimizer? Despite there being many Adam variants, the following three gaps remain relevant in practice:

(1) **No principled "momentum-of-momentum."** The standard numerator uses one EMA. Simply stacking EMAs lengthens memory, but *double-counts cold-start bias*, shrinking early steps unless they are patched.
(2) **Warmup dependency.** Schedules often rely on bespoke warmups to achieve stable early scaling, which complicates pipelines and increases failed runs.
(3) **Opaque early-time scaling.** With one EMA numerator, there is no orthogonal knob to extend memory while keeping the instantaneous pass-through of new gradient information well controlled.

This paper presents a new optimizer called AdamN. AdamN's main contribution is an EMA-of-EMA numerator with an exact double-EMA debiasing factor f_t that removes both inner and outer cold-start bias. The denominator and weight decay (WD) remain Adam-compatible (EMA of squared gradients; *decoupled WD*), so the method is drop-in with the same Big-O cost.

This contribution translates into the following real operational benefits:

(4) **Faster time-to-quality:** Earlier accuracy milestones (e.g., 70–90% train accuracy) are reached sooner, shortening iteration cycles for model/ablation development and accelerating time-to-market.
(5) **Lower energy and cost per experiment:** Reaching target accuracy in fewer epochs reduces GPU-hours and power draw for both research and production retraining.
(6) **Schedule-friendly starts:** Exact debiasing reduces dependence on hand-tuned warmups, which simplifies pipelines and cuts failed runs caused by unstable early steps.
(7) **Throughput on shared clusters:** Shorter "wall-time to useful model" improves cluster utilization; teams can run more variations under quota.
(8) **Edge and small-budget training:** When computation or thermal headroom is limited (on-device or tiny clouds), AdamN's faster launch and stable scaling help hit acceptable accuracy within tight budgets.

Research Questions (RQs) We organize our study around five questions and their evaluation metrics:

RQ1—Time-to-quality. Does AdamN reach target accuracy faster than AdamW/SGD while keeping final accuracy comparable?

Metric: wall-clock seconds to hit train/val milestones 40%, 50%, 60%, 70%, 80%, and 90%.

RQ2—Final quality at equal budget. At a fixed epoch/time budget, does AdamN match or exceed final test accuracy?

Metric: test accuracy at E = 100 and at a fixed wall-clock budget.

RQ3—Sensitivity and robustness. How sensitive is AdamN to the newly introduced β_2-ramp, LR, and WD vs. AdamW/SGD?

Metric: mean $\pm$ SD (95% CI) of final test accuracy over 3–5 seeds per grid point.

RQ4—What "makes" AdamN work? Are gains primarily from the nested-EMA numerator or exact double-EMA debiasing?

https://doi.org/10.3390/electronics15030670

Metric: ablation deltas on time-to-milestones and final accuracy when toggling nested on/off and exact vs. simple debiasing.

RQ5—Generalization to NLP under imbalance. Do AdamN's rare-token update-efficiency gains hold beyond vision?

Metric: validation/test perplexity per frequency bin (head/mid/tail), tail PPL, and effective LR (row-wise RMS) on embeddings; fixed-budget final PPL.

The paper is organized as follows: Section 2 reviews the literature and the motivation for a new optimizer. Section 3 reviews the notation and setup of the related work. Section 4 presents *AdamN: Method and Full Derivation*, including the exact nested-EMA weights and the bias-correction factor f_t. Section 5 provides an algorithmic reference. Section 6 reports experiments: proof of concept and *CIFAR-10* pre-benchmarking, followed by the main *CIFAR-100* benchmark with ResNet-18 and ViT-B16. Section 7 presents the ablation. Section 8 discusses limitations and practical guidance, and Section 9 concludes.

2. Literature Survey and Motivation for a New Optimizer

2.1. Foundations Before SGD

Before stochastic methods became dominant, optimization in numerical analysis and early machine learning relied on full-bath techniques. The classical method of steepest descent, introduced by Cauchy in the 19th century [9], updates parameters along the negative gradient of the full dataset loss. While stable, this approach is computationally expensive for large datasets and scales poorly.

Other classical approaches include the following:

(1) Newton's method, introduced in the 17th century [10], and its quasi-Newton variants such as BFGS (developed in the 1970s [11–13]), which use curvature information for faster convergence on convex problems but require storing and inverting Hessian approximations.
(2) Coordinate descent, dating back to early-20th-century optimization [14,15], which updates one parameter at a time and was practical for small-dimensional problems.
(3) Conjugate gradient methods (Hestenes and Stiefel, 1952 [16]), which improved convergence for quadratic objectives by exploiting conjugacy instead of simple steepest directions.

These methods were effective in smaller-scale convex settings but became infeasible as datasets and neural networks grew. The breakthrough of stochastic gradient descent (SGD) by Robbins and Monro (1951) [17] was to replace the full gradient with an unbiased minibatch estimator. This drastically reduced per-step computation and enabled scaling, at the cost of higher variance—a trade-off that ultimately aided exploration and generalization in deep learning.

2.2. First-Order Foundations

SGD and Momentum: SGD with a global learning rate remains the default for large-scale supervised training. Polyak's heavy-ball momentum [1] and deep-learning practice [2] accelerate progress in curved valleys by accumulating low-frequency components of the gradient. Nesterov's look-ahead gradient [18] often improves stability on ill-conditioned objectives. Strengths: simplicity, strong generalization in vision, and predictable schedule design. Limitations: a single global step size struggles with anisotropy and poorly scaled features; early progress can be slow.

Adaptive Methods (AdaGrad/RMSProp): AdaGrad rescales coordinates using the (cumulative) squared-gradient history, helping on sparse features [3]. RMSProp trades the cumulative sum for an EMA so step sizes do not vanish [19]. These methods reduce sensitivity to global LR but can suffer from stale or overly smooth denominators when noise/curvature changes quickly.

 https://doi.org/10.3390/electronics15030670

2.3. *Adam and Decoupled Weight Decay*

Adam introduced EMAs for both first and second moments with explicit bias corrections that address cold-start underestimation; this makes early training more stable and typically faster [5]. AMSGrad provides a convergence-favoring variant by enforcing a non-decreasing second-moment estimate [6]. They are stable defaults, but the *single numerator EMA* forces a trade-off between memory and responsiveness; extending memory usually hurts early-step magnitude unless one introduces warmups.

AdamW: L2 added to the loss inside an adaptive method does not behave like classical weight decay; decoupling the decay step (AdamW) restores clean regularization and often improves validation accuracy at no extra cost [7]. It solves WD coupling but *does not address numerator memory* vs. *early scaling*.

2.4. *Recent Developments*

A wave of optimizers extends or rethinks Adam along several axes. AdaBelief modifies the second moment to track the "belief" in the gradient, often improving generalization relative to Adam [20]. Sharpness-aware methods such as SAM and its scale-invariant variant ASAM perturb parameters toward neighborhoods of lower loss curvature to improve generalization [21,22]. Shampoo brings practical block-wise second-order preconditioning at scale [23]. AdamP introduces a geometry-aware projection to mitigate over-adaptation and boost vision generalization [24]. Adan uses an adaptive Nesterov-style numerator for faster convergence, particularly in vision [25]. D-Adaptation removes manual learning-rate tuning by adapting the global scale automatically [26]. Sophia leverages a clipped Hessian estimate to realize a scalable stochastic second-order method with strong results for LLM pretraining [27]. Lion—discovered via symbolic search—updates with a sign-based momentum rule and is competitive in large-scale training [28].

These advances improve specific regimes (e.g., curvature awareness, sign-based steps, and scale-free training), yet none of them provide a principled, bias-corrected momentum-of-momentum that (a) extends numerator memory, (b) **exactly** fixes compounded cold-start bias, and (c) keeps Adam-like simplicity and cost.

2.5. *Large-Batch Regime and Scaling*

Large batches can hurt generalization by pushing toward sharper minima [29], although careful schedules and system design can scale training dramatically (e.g., 1 h ImageNet) [30]. Trust-ratio-style methods (e.g., LAMB) enable stable very-large-batch training by normalizing the step to the parameter norm [31].

2.6. *What Current Methods Still Miss*

Despite extensive progress [8], several gaps persist that motivate our approach:

(1) No principled "momentum-of-momentum." Adam uses a single EMA in the numerator. If one naively stacks EMAs to lengthen memory, the inner EMA's cold-start bias remains uncorrected, shrinking early steps.

(2) Warmup dependence. Many pipelines rely on hand-tuned warmups to overcome timid or erratic starts, even with Adam's bias corrections [5].

(3) Under-parameterized trade-off between responsiveness and inertia. With only one numerator EMA, tuning smoothness vs. freshness is constrained; there is no clean way to expose an additional, orthogonal knob that lengthens memory while keeping early steps properly scaled.

(4) Opaque early-time scaling. Interactions between η, $\beta 1$, $\beta 2$, and the denominator can obscure how much of the current gradient passes through each step.

https://doi.org/10.3390/electronics15030670

2.7. Motivation for AdamN

AdamN targets these gaps while remaining drop-in-compatible with Adam/AdamW. AdamN has the following characteristics:

(1) Nested numerator (EMA-of-EMA) yields a triangular-with-exponential-tail-kernel, longer memory, and smoother directions than a single EMA.
(2) Exact double-EMA debiasing provides a closed-form factor that removes both inner and outer cold-start shrinkage, eliminating the need for ad hoc warmups while preserving stability.
(3) Transparent scaling. The decomposition into (i) freshness, (ii) exact bias factor, and (iii) adaptive denominator clarifies instantaneous step size and informs principled LR scaling.
(4) Cost and compatibility. It has the same Big-O cost as Adam/AdamW with one extra buffer and retains decoupled weight decay and modern scheduling [7].
(5) This directly targets the memory vs. early-scale gap while remaining drop-in- and scheduler-friendly.

2.8. Systematic Comparison with Related Nested/Multi-Momentum Approaches

To substantiate our claim regarding the novelty of AdamN's bias correction, we systematically analyzed recent optimizers that employ multiple momentum-like terms, as shown in Table 1.

Table 1. Systematic comparison with related nested/multi-momentum approaches.

Optimizer	Numerator Structure	Nested EMA?	Exact Double-EMA Debias?
Adam/AdamW	Single EMA of g_t	No	N/A
Adan	$m_t + (1-\beta_2)(g_t - g_{t-1})$	No (additive)	No
AdaBelief	Single EMA of g_t (modified denom.)	No	N/A
Lion	$\text{sign}(\beta_1 m_{t-1} + (1-\beta_1)g_t)$	No	N/A
AdamN	EMA of (EMA of g_t)	Yes	Yes

Adan's 'momentum difference' term $(g_t - g_{t-1})$ is structurally distinct from applying an EMA to the output of another EMA. Mathematically, Adan's numerator can be written as $m_t = \beta_1 m_{t-1} + (1-\beta_1)(g_t + \beta_2(g_t - g_{t-1}))$, which is a weighted combination of current and past gradients but does not exhibit the triangular-kernel weighting pattern (Equation (21)) that characterizes nested EMAs. Consequently, Adan does not require—nor does it provide—a double-EMA bias correction factor.

3. Notation and Setup

Let the parameters (all layers, all tensors: convolution kernels, linear weights, biases, etc.) be concatenated into a single vector $\theta \in \mathbb{R}^d$. At step t, given a minibatch B_t, the stochastic gradient g_t of the minibatch empirical loss with respect to all parameters can be defined as follows:

$$g_t \triangleq \nabla_\theta \mathcal{L}(\theta_t; \mathcal{B}_t) \tag{1}$$

Let the learning rate be $\eta > 0$, the stabilizer be $\epsilon > 0$, and the gradient at step t *be* $\nabla J(\theta_t)$. When present, let the weight decay be $\lambda \geq 0$, decoupled unless otherwise noted.

Modern deep networks are trained by *stochastic first-order* methods that update parameters using minibatch gradients. To reason precisely about later variants (momentum, Adam/AdamW, and our proposed *AdamN*), we first fix notation for the minibatch loss and its gradient and make clear how learning rate, numerical stabilization, and *weight decay (WD)* enter the update. This section establishes a common baseline against which the effects of momentum and adaptivity can be interpreted.

https://doi.org/10.3390/electronics15030670

3.1. SGD and Momentum (Reference Form)

(1) *Vanilla SGD*: SGD updates parameters by moving against the minibatch gradient with a global learning rate. It looks only at the current gradient to pick the next step. It is simple but slow, and it can get stuck or bounce around. Its updated parameters are as follows:

$$\begin{aligned} \theta_{t+1} &= \theta_t - \eta \nabla J(\theta_t) \\ \theta_{t+1} - \theta_t &= \eta \nabla J(\theta_t) \\ \Delta\theta_t &= \eta \nabla J(\theta_t) \end{aligned} \tag{2}$$

With decreasing η, SGD achieves classical stochastic rates in convex settings. With constant η, it converges to a noise floor whose radius depends on η and the variance of the gradient. Despite its simplicity, SGD remains competitive in large, supervised tasks, especially with data augmentation and carefully designed learning-rate schedules.

Limitations:

A single global step size as seen in (2) can be inadequate for highly anisotropic problems.

Early training can lag adaptive methods on sparse or poorly scaled features.

Large batch caution: very large batches may reduce test accuracy by converging to sharper minima, as noted by [9]; see also large batch scheduling successes in [11].

(2) *Polyak (Heavy-Ball) Momentum*: This adds velocity (v_t). Instead of just the current gradient, it mixes in part of the last update's direction. That way, steps get smoother and faster in steady directions and reduce zigzagging in high-curvature regions by accumulating low-frequency gradient information.

$$\begin{aligned} v_{t+1} &= \mu v_t + \nabla J(\theta_t) \\ \theta_{t+1} &= \theta_t - \eta v_{t+1} \\ \Delta\theta_t &= \eta v_{t+1} \end{aligned} \tag{3}$$

where μ is the momentum term $\in [0, 1]$ that decides how much of the past velocity is kept.

(3) *Nesterov Accelerated Gradient (NAG)*: NAG computes the gradient at a look-ahead position [18] as follows:

$$v_t = \mu\, v_{t-1} - \eta\, \nabla \mathcal{L}(\theta_t + \mu v_{t-1}) \tag{4}$$

$$\theta_{t+1} = \theta_t + v_t \tag{5}$$

This anticipatory step in (5) typically improves stability and effective conditioning. In practice, set momentum $\mu \in [0.9, 0.99]$ (e.g., 0.9 for noisier tasks and 0.95–0.99 for smoother regimes). We choose the base learning rate by a brief sweep or LR-range test, then use a cosine decay or step decay schedule. For very deep networks or highly non-stationary early gradients, we include a short warmup (e.g., 3–10 epochs or 1–5% of total steps) to avoid unstable starts.

3.2. Adam (Adaptive Moment Estimation)

Adam combines a momentum-like first moment (EMA of gradients) with an adaptive second moment denominator (EMA of squared gradients) and applies bias corrections so that early estimates are not underestimated [5].

(1) The first moment (momentum of gradients) is derived as follows:

$$\begin{aligned} m_t &= \beta_1 m_{t-1} + (1 - \beta_1)\, g_t \\ &\Rightarrow (1 - \beta_1) \sum_{i=1}^{t} \beta_1^{t-i} g_i \end{aligned} \tag{6}$$

(2) The second moment (EMA of squared gradients) is derived as follows:

https://doi.org/10.3390/electronics15030670

$$\begin{aligned} v_t &= \beta_2 v_{t-1} + (1-\beta_2)\, g_t^2 \\ &\Rightarrow (1-\beta_2) \sum_{i=1}^{t} \beta_2^{t-i} g_i^2 \end{aligned} \tag{7}$$

The result is a fast, directionally smooth, scale-aware update that is straightforward to tune. The bias correction addresses the cold-start bias, stabilizing the critical early iterations where gradients are volatile. This combination explains Adam's widespread adoption in NLP, vision, and reinforcement learning.

The standard bias-correction derivation is as follows:

First, we do not need the gradients themselves to be constant, only that their mean and second moment stay the same assuming the gradient statistics are stationary. Concretely:

(1) The average gradient is constant: $E[g_i] = \mu$ for all steps i.
(2) The average squared gradient is constant: $E\left[g_i^2\right] = \nu$ for all steps i.
(3) By using (6) and (7), taking expectations of the first and second moments of Adam under this assumption will be as follows:

$$\begin{aligned} &E[m_t] \\ &= (1-\beta_1) \sum_{i=1}^{t} \beta_1^{t-i}\, E[g_i] \\ &= \mu(1-\beta_1) \sum_{k=0}^{t-1} \beta_1^{k} \\ &\Rightarrow \mu\left(1-\beta_1^t\right) \end{aligned} \tag{8}$$

$$\begin{aligned} E[v_t] &= (1-\beta_2) \sum_{i=1}^{t} \beta_2^{t-i}\, E\left[g_i^2\right] \\ &= \nu(1-\beta_2) \sum_{k=0}^{t-1} \beta_2^{k} \\ &\Rightarrow \nu\left(1-\beta_2^t\right) \end{aligned} \tag{9}$$

(4) For $E[m_t]$, the factor $\left(1-\beta_1^t\right)$ in (8) is less than 1 for small t, so $E[m_t]$ is smaller than μ.
(5) As $t \to \infty$, $\beta_1^t \to 0$ and $1-\beta_1^t \to 1$, so the bias goes away.
(6) The same holds for v_t: $E[v_t] = \nu\left(1-\beta_2^t\right)$, so it also starts too small.

That is why they are biased toward zero. We started at zero, and the EMA underestimates the true mean and variance early on by a factor of $1-\beta^t$.

Without factors $\left(1-\beta_i^t\right\}$ where $i \in [1, 2]$, the first and second moments are systematically underestimated during initialization [5]. This underestimation is most pronounced when β_2 is large and can cause instability in the first stages of training; AMSGrad [6] analyzes related convergence issues.

Bias-corrected estimates:

Divide out those factors to remove the bias:

$$\widehat{m_t} = \frac{m_t}{\left(1-\beta_1^t\right)},\ \widehat{v_t} = \frac{v_t}{1-\beta_2^t} \tag{10}$$

The final update expressed in terms of past gradients g_j is as follows:

$$\Delta\theta_t = \eta \frac{\widehat{m_t}}{\sqrt{\widehat{v_t}} + \epsilon} \tag{11}$$

Substitute (10) into (11) and simplify, then the weighted sum over g_j is as follows:

$$\Delta\theta_t = \sum_{j=1}^{t} \alpha_{t,j}\, g_j$$

https://doi.org/10.3390/electronics15030670

where

$$\alpha_{t,j} = \eta \, \frac{(1-\beta_1)}{1-\beta_1^t} \frac{\beta_1^{t-j}}{\sqrt{\frac{(1-\beta_2)}{1-\beta_2^t} \sum_{k=1}^{t} \beta_2^{t-k} g_k^2} + \varepsilon} \tag{12}$$

Current gradient coefficient:

For the most recent gradient g_t, *set* $(j = t)$ *in* (12):

$$\alpha_{t,t} = \eta \, \frac{(1-\beta_1)}{1-\beta_1^t} \frac{1}{\sqrt{\frac{(1-\beta_2)}{1-\beta_2^t} \sum_{k=1}^{t} \beta_2^{t-k} g_k^2} + \varepsilon} \tag{13}$$

Defaults. $\beta_1 = 0.9$, $\beta_2 \in [0.99, 0.999]$, $\epsilon = 10^{-8}$. Sometimes we reduce β_2 for a greater response and apply a warmup if the early gradients spike.

Caveats:

(1) It can yield slightly weaker generalization than tuned SGD on some vision tasks; schedule design and regularization are critical.
(2) Warmup is often required for very deep or highly regularized models.

Notes:

(1) If gradients are not stationary, the correction still removes the *zero-init bias.*
(2) If a gradient is large, v_t grows, which shrinks the effective learning rate. If it is small, the step size stays larger.
(3) v_t is an adaptive scale factor, not another momentum. Adam has only *one* momentum: m_t.

Thus, Adam combines:

(1) *Momentum* (past gradients for direction).
(2) *Adaptive scaling* (past magnitudes for step size).

3.3. AdamW (Decoupled Weight Decay)

Motivation: In standard Adam, adding L2 regularization to the loss does not match classical weight decay, because the adaptive denominator mixes shrinkage with rescaling. AdamW resolves this by decoupling the weight decay step from the adaptive update [7] as follows:

(1) Decay:

$$\theta \leftarrow (1 - \eta\lambda) \tag{14}$$

(2) Adaptive step:

$$\theta \leftarrow \theta - \eta \, \widehat{m_t} / \left(\sqrt{\widehat{v_t}} + \epsilon\right) \tag{15}$$

This restores weight decay as pure multiplicative shrinkage and frequently improves validation/test performance compared to Adam + L2 at equal computation.

Defaults: Same as Adam, with $\lambda \in \left[10^{-4}, 10^{-2}\right]$ depending on the model and augmentation.

What to expect:

Cleaner, schedule-independent control of regularization.

Often stronger generalization than Adam + L2, with identical computational cost.

Regularization: L2 vs. decoupled decay:

L2 regularization adds $\frac{\lambda}{2} |\theta|^2$ to the loss, contributing $\lambda\theta$ to the gradient. In Adam, this term is normalized by $\left(\sqrt{\widehat{v_t}} + \epsilon\right)$, coupling shrinkage with adaptation.

The decoupled decay in (14) applies $\theta \leftarrow (1 - \eta\lambda)$ outside the adaptive update, yielding uniform shrinkage independent of local rescaling [7]. This separation improves controllability and often leads to better generalization.

https://doi.org/10.3390/electronics15030670

4. AdamN: Contributions and Method

4.1. Contributions

We introduce AdamN, a nested-momentum adaptive optimizer which has the following qualities:

(1) It introduces a second EMA on the numerator (a true nested momentum: $g \rightarrow v \rightarrow a$) which acts as a triangular kernel with an exponential tail, yielding a smoother and longer memory update direction than a single EMA.
(2) It derives an exact double-EMAs bias correction $f_t(\beta_1, \beta_2)$ that removes the cold-start shrinkage inherited from nested EMAs. Intuitively, the nested numerator behaves as a data-adaptive controller that tempers early step magnitudes, preventing overshoot without requiring hand-tuned warmup.
(3) It retains Adam-style adaptive braking through a second moment s_t, using decoupled weight decay.
(4) It demonstrates faster early progress at stable scaling on ResNet-18/CIFAR-100 while matching or slightly exceeding AdamW's final accuracy at similar computation.

4.2. Method and Foundation

Let us also define EMA elements as $\beta_1, \beta_2, \beta_3 \in [0,1)$, then v_t, a_t *and* s_t are defined as follows:

$$\underbrace{v_t}_{\text{EMA of gradients}} = \beta_1 v_{t-1} + (1-\beta_1) g_t = (1-\beta_1) \sum_{k=1}^{t} \beta_1^{t-k} g_k \tag{16}$$

$$\underbrace{a_t}_{\text{EMA of } v_t} = \beta_2 a_{t-1} + (1-\beta_2) v_t = (1-\beta_2) \sum_{k=1}^{t} \beta_2^{t-k} v_k \tag{17}$$

$$\underbrace{s_t}_{\text{EMA of squared gradients}} = \beta_3 s_{t-1} + (1-\beta_3) g_t^2 = (1-\beta_3) \sum_{k=1}^{t} \beta_3^{t-k} g_k^2 \tag{18}$$

where $\boldsymbol{\beta_1}$ controls the memory of v_t (1st moment), $\boldsymbol{\beta_2}$ controls the memory of a_t (nested numerator), and $\boldsymbol{\beta_3}$ controls the memory of s_t (2nd moment/brakes). From (16) and (17), substitute v_k into a_t and collect weights on g_j, which will give the following:

$$a_t = (1-\beta_2)(1-\beta_1) \sum_{j=1}^{t} g_j \underbrace{\left(\sum_{k=j}^{t} \beta_2^{t-k} \beta_1^{k-j} \right)}_{\text{kernel on } g_j} \tag{19}$$

where t is the current time step/iteration $(1,2,3,\ldots)$, k is a summation index over time when unrolling an EMA (in which v_k terms contribute to a_t), and j is a summation index over gradient timestamps (in which g_j terms go into v_k and then a_t).

The weight decay $\lambda \geq 0$ is decoupled. All operations involving powers, division, and square roots are applied elementwise.

4.3. Nested Numerator as a Triangular Kernel

Evaluate the inner sum in (19) as follows:

$$\text{kernel on } g_j = \beta_2^{t-j} \sum_{m=0}^{t-j} \left(\frac{\beta_1}{\beta_2} \right)^m \tag{20}$$

 https://doi.org/10.3390/electronics15030670

Hence, the exact weights on g_j are as follows:

$$w_{t,j} = \begin{cases} (1-\beta_1)(1-\beta_2)\,\frac{\beta_2^{t-j+1}-\beta_1^{t-j+1}}{\beta_2-\beta_1}, & \beta_1 \neq \beta_2, \\ (t-j+1)\,\beta^{t-j}(1-\beta)^2, & \beta_1 = \beta_2 = \beta. \end{cases} \tag{21}$$

Thus

$$a_t = \sum_{j=1}^{t} w_{t,j}\, g_j \tag{22}$$

The equal-betas case in (21) illustrates why nested EMAs possess much longer effective memory.

In this setting, the numerator acts as a triangular kernel with an exponential tail: the linear factor $(t-j+1)$ increases with the age of each gradient before being exponentially damped by β^{t-j}. As a result, when β is large, the numerator becomes more inertial, retaining the past information significantly longer.

4.4. Bias Correction

Simple (insufficient) bias correction (Adam-style warmup): The nested numerator is unbiased via

$$\widehat{a_t} = \frac{a_t}{1-\beta_2^t} \quad \text{(leaves inner-EMA bias)} \tag{23}$$

With simple correction, the early steps are still biased low because a_t inherits bias from v_t.

Exact bias correction: The nested numerator is unbiased via

$$\widehat{a_t} = \frac{a_t}{f_t(\beta_1, \beta_2)} \tag{24}$$

This is the exact analog of Adam's $\widehat{m_t} = m_t/\left(1-\beta_1^t\right)$ in (10) but for a double EMA of g_t. It amplifies early step safely and often shortens time-to-50/60-percent milestones.

It can also be formally shown that this expression corresponds to the total accumulated weight at time t.

To derive $f_t(\beta_1, \beta_2)$, unroll the recurrences (assume $E\left[g_j\right] \equiv g$ for all j to compute the expectation/gain factor) as follows:

(1) First EMA:

$$v_k = (1-\beta_1)\sum_{j=1}^{k} \beta_1^{k-j} g_j \;\Rightarrow\; E[v_k] = (1-\beta_1)\, g \sum_{j=1}^{k} \beta_1^{k-j} \tag{25}$$

Therefore:

$$E[v_k] = (1-\beta_1)\, g \cdot \frac{1-\beta_1^k}{1-\beta_1} = \left(1-\beta_1^k\right) g. \qquad \boxed{E[v_k] = \left(1-\beta_1^k\right) g} \tag{26}$$

(2) Second EMA:

$$a_t = (1-\beta_2)\sum_{k=1}^{t} \beta_2^{t-k} v_k \;\Rightarrow\; E[a_t] = (1-\beta_2)\sum_{k=1}^{t} \beta_2^{t-k} E[v_k] \tag{27}$$

Plug in (26):

https://doi.org/10.3390/electronics15030670

$$E[a_t] = (1-\beta_2)\sum_{k=1}^{t}\beta_2^{t-k}\left(1-\beta_1^k\right)g$$
$$= \left[(1-\beta_2)\sum_{k=1}^{t}\beta_2^{t-k} - (1-\beta_2)\sum_{k=1}^{t}\beta_2^{t-k}\beta_1^k\right]g = f_{t(\beta_1,\beta_2)}\cdot g \tag{28}$$

After evaluating the two geometric sums in (28), the exact debiasing factor for nested momentum will be defined as follows:

$$f_t(\beta_1,\beta_2) = \begin{cases}(1-\beta_2^t) - (1-\beta_2)\frac{\beta_1(\beta_2^t-\beta_1^t)}{\beta_2-\beta_1}, & \beta_1 \neq \beta_2,\\ (1-\beta^t) - (1-\beta)\,t\,\beta^t, & \beta_1 = \beta_2.\end{cases} \tag{29}$$

Remark on stationarity: The derivation of $f_t(\beta_1,\beta_2)$ assumes stationary gradient statistics ($E[g_j] \equiv g$), following the same analytical framework used to derive Adam's bias correction [5]. This assumption serves to identify the functional form of the zero-initialization bias—the systematic underestimation caused by $v_0 = a_0 = 0$—rather than to model the true (non-stationary) gradient distribution during training.

In practice, gradient statistics are highly non-stationary, particularly in early epochs. However, the bias correction remains effective because it addresses the initialization artifact: at $t = 1$, the unnormalized estimates v_1 and a_1 are scaled by factors that vanish as $t \to 0$, regardless of the gradient's true mean. The correction factor $f_t(\beta_1,\beta_2)$ compensates for this cold-start shrinkage.

For double EMAs, the non-stationarity concern is more pronounced because the outer EMA accumulates bias from the inner EMA's already-biased estimates. Our exact factor accounts for this compounding effect (the cross-term $\frac{\beta_1(\beta_2^t-\beta_1^t)}{\beta_2-\beta_1}$ in Equation (29)), which simple cascaded corrections would miss. Empirically, AdamN's consistent performance across diverse tasks—where gradient statistics change dramatically during training—validates the practical robustness of our approach.

4.5. Freshness

By plugging $j = t$ into (21), the instantaneous pass-through of g_t into a_t (pre-bias) is given as follows:

$$w_{t,t} = (1-\beta_1)(1-\beta_2).(\text{uncorrected}) \tag{30}$$

The bias correction scales all weights by $1/f_t$ to remove the early-time shrinkage, so the effective normalized coefficient is as follows:

$$\hat{w}_{t,t} = \frac{(1-\beta_1)(1-\beta_2)}{f_t(\beta_1,\beta_2)}.(\text{biascorrected}) \tag{31}$$

Freshness quantifies how much new gradient information enters the numerator at each step. Unlike cumulative weights, it isolates the instantaneous pass-through for the newest gradient.

For example, by recalling (16) and (17), AdamN's freshness is as follows:

$$v_t = \beta_1 v_{t-1} + (1-\beta_1)g_t,\ a_t = \beta_2 a_{t-1} + (1-\beta_2)v_t$$

Expanding shows that the coefficient in *the current* g_t in a_t is as follows:

$$\underbrace{(1-\beta_1)}_{\text{from } v_t}\underbrace{(1-\beta_2)}_{\text{from } a_t} = \boxed{(1-\beta_1)(1-\beta_2)}.$$

 https://doi.org/10.3390/electronics15030670

That boxed term is what we call *freshness*—how much *new gradient information* is injected at this step (before bias-correction/normalization/LR), while AdamW freshness is as follows: $\boxed{1-\beta_1}$ as seen in (6).

Learning rate scaling and β_2: The tolerance to learning rate of AdamN depends directly on the freshness term $(1-\beta_1)(1-\beta_2)$.

When β_2 is small (e.g., $\beta_1 = 0.9, \beta_2 = 0.1$), the freshness is $\Rightarrow (1-0.9)(1-0.1) = 0.09$, nearly the same as AdamW's $\Rightarrow (1-0.9) = 0.1$.

In this case, AdamN tolerates only about $0.1/0.09 \ \approx 1.1\times$ higher learning rates—effectively without an advantage.

By contrast, when β_2 is large (e.g., $\beta_1 = 0.6,\ \beta_2 = 0.9$), the freshness shrinks to 0.04, and the bias correction amplifies the initial steps.

To get comparable aggressiveness, a simple first-order scaling is defined as follows:

$$\alpha_N \approx \alpha_W \cdot \frac{1-\beta_1^W}{\left(1-\beta_1^N\right)\left(1-\beta_2^N\right)} \approx \alpha_W \cdot \frac{0.1}{0.04}.$$

Here, AdamN can run safely at $\sim 2.5\times$ the learning rate of AdamW, achieving faster early progress without destabilization.

Thus, the LR advantage of AdamN manifests itself primarily in the high β_2 regime, where its nested numerator would otherwise be too inertial without correction.

This behavior is illustrated in Table 2.

Table 2. Effect of β_2 on AdamN's freshness and LR tolerance.

Setting	Fresh. (AdamW)	Fresh. (AdamN)	α_N/α_W
$\beta_1 = 0.9,\ \beta_2 = 0.1$	0.10	0.09	$\approx 1.1\times$
$\beta_1 = 0.9,\ \beta_2 = 0.6$	0.10	0.04	$\approx 2.5\times$

4.6. Interpretation of β_2

Effect of β_2 on AdamN dynamics: Large β_2 introduces two competing effects that must be understood jointly:

1. *Reduced freshness (raw numerator).* The uncorrected weight on the current gradient g_t in a_t is $(1-\beta_1)(1-\beta_2)$, which vanishes as $\beta_2 \to 1$. This makes the numerator increasingly *inertial*—dominated by past gradients rather than new information.
2. *Increased bias-correction amplification.* The factor $f_t(\beta_1, \beta_2)$ grows slowly for large β_2, causing the bias-corrected numerator $\hat{a}_t = a_t/f_t$ to be amplified more aggressively in early epochs.

These effects can appear contradictory: large β_2 reduces sensitivity to new gradients (effect 1) while potentially increasing step magnitude (effect 2). The practical consequence is that high-β_2 configurations produce steps that are *large but delayed*; the optimizer moves confidently in outdated directions. This explains our ablation findings: $\beta_2 \geq 0.8$ degrades both speed and final accuracy because the numerator cannot adapt quickly to the changing loss landscape, regardless of step magnitude.

We therefore recommend $\beta_2 \in [0.1,\ 0.3]$ for most tasks, where freshness remains high and the bias correction provides stable early scaling without excessive inertia.

4.7. Instantaneous Learning Rate (instLR) and Comparison

Using (31), we define effective instantaneous scaling—coefficient—on the current gradient as follows:

$$\text{instLR}_t \ \equiv \ \alpha\, \widehat{w}_{t,t}\, \frac{1}{\sqrt{\hat{s}_t} + \epsilon} \tag{32}$$

https://doi.org/10.3390/electronics15030670

which clarifies why AdamN can launch fast yet remain stable.

This multiplier scales the contribution of g_t (and, via the weights above, all past g_j) and is the **real step size** the optimizer effectively takes at time t, not just the scheduler's base learning rate α.

The numerator is amplified correctly at cold start, while the denominator tempers spikes. At low β_2 (e.g., 0.1), exact vs. simple bias corrections are indistinguishable due to denominator absorption. But at higher β_2 (e.g., 0.8), exact bias correction yields consistently higher instLR and faster early convergence, as confirmed in Table 3.

Table 3. Comparison of AdamN with simple vs. exact bias correction ($\beta_1 = 0.9, \beta_2 = 0.8$). Exact correction yields slightly higher instLR and faster convergence in early epochs.

Epoch	AdamN (Simple Bias)				AdamN (Exact Bias)			
	instLR	step_RMS	Train Acc	Val Acc	instLR	step_RMS	Train Acc	Val Acc
1	0.155	1.42×10^{-4}	6.55%	13.84%	**0.164**	1.43×10^{-4}	7.02%	**14.60%**
2	0.360	1.91×10^{-4}	7.56%	13.88%	**0.375**	1.93×10^{-4}	7.87%	**15.22%**
3	0.629	2.75×10^{-4}	10.58%	17.02%	**0.647**	2.74×10^{-4}	10.64%	**19.20%**
4	0.958	3.80×10^{-4}	14.88%	22.96%	**0.971**	3.55×10^{-4}	15.25%	**23.62%**
5	1.349	4.40×10^{-4}	19.61%	29.16%	1.345	5.06×10^{-4}	20.63%	29.72%
6	1.517	4.63×10^{-4}	24.85%	33.94%	1.501	4.65×10^{-4}	25.62%	33.48%

These closed forms assume the usual initialization $v_0 = a_0 = 0$. If we start from non-zero v_0, a_0, extra terms like $\beta_1^t v_0$ and $\beta_2^t a_0$ appear, but they decay fast and are usually negligible.

Digital Signal Processing (DSP) Analogy: From the DSP discipline, the bias factor $f_t(\beta_1, \beta_2)$ plays the role of a phase correction, aligning the nested-EMA numerator with the true gradient "phase" by removing the systematic lag at cold start, while the instantaneous learning rate (instLR) acts as an amplitude envelope, setting the step magnitude after normalization. Together they resemble phase and amplitude control in modulation: f_t corrects the trajectory (phase alignment), and instLR governs update strength (amplitude). This perspective clarifies why exact f_t matters most at large β_2 (long memory), where naive debiasing leaves a persistent phase lag that directly suppresses the effective amplitude.

4.8. Update Rule (Bias-Corrected) and Weighted-Sum View

The effective per-coordinate step is as follows:

$$\Delta\theta_t = -\eta \frac{\widehat{a}_t}{\sqrt{\hat{s}_t} + \epsilon}, \qquad \theta_{t+1} = \theta_t + \Delta\theta_t \tag{33}$$

where $\widehat{a}_t$ is the exact debiased, noise-smoothed numerator and $\hat{s}_t$ the usual second moment. This combination is a **richer diagonal preconditioner** than Adam/AdamW's—closer to second-order behavior—yet remains first-order in cost.

With decoupled decay $\theta \leftarrow (1 - \eta\lambda)\theta$ and using (18), the bias-corrected denominator, like Adam's correction, will be as follows:

$$\sqrt{\hat{s}_t} = \sqrt{\frac{s_t}{1 - \beta_3^t}} = \sqrt{\frac{(1 - \beta_3)\sum_{k=1}^{t} \beta_3^{t-k} g_k^2}{1 - \beta_3^t}} \tag{34}$$

Equivalently, the update is a weighted sum over past gradients, and it is defined as follows:

$$\Delta\theta_t = \sum_{i=1}^{t} \alpha_{t,j} \, g_j \tag{35}$$

https://doi.org/10.3390/electronics15030670

With

$$\alpha_{t,j} = \eta_t \frac{w_{t,j}}{f_t(\beta_1, \beta_2)} \frac{1}{\sqrt{\widehat{s}_t} + \epsilon} \tag{36}$$

5. Algorithm and Complexity

AdamN adds one EMA buffer (a_t) compared to Adam/AdamW. The recurrence relations (lines 6–8) in Figure 1 each require O(d) elementwise operations; the scalar bias factor f_t is computed in O(1). Total per-step complexity is *O(d) time and O(3d) = O(d) space*, identical to Adam/AdamW up to a constant factor of ~1.5× in memory. The explicit weighted-sum representation (Equation (22)) is provided for theoretical insight and is never computed during runtime.

1: Given: Base LR $\alpha = 1^{-3}$, $\beta_1 = 0.9$, $\beta_2 = 0.1$, $\beta_3 = 0.999$, $\epsilon = 10^{-8}$, WD $\lambda \in R$.

2: *Initialize*: $t \leftarrow 0$, parameter vector $\theta_{t=0} \in R^n$, first moment $v_{t=0} \leftarrow 0$, nested momentum $a_{t=0} \leftarrow 0$, inst$Mult_{t=0} \in R$.

3: Repeat,

4: $t \leftarrow t+1$.

5: $\nabla(\theta_{t-1}) \leftarrow SelectBatch(\theta_{t-1})$ (compute gradient).

6: $g_t \leftarrow \nabla f_t(\theta_{t-1})$,

7: $v_t \leftarrow \beta_1 v_{t-1} + (1-\beta_1) g_t$.

8: $w_{t,j} \leftarrow (1-\beta_1)(1-\beta_2)\, \frac{\beta_2^{t-j+1} - \beta_1^{t-j+1}}{\beta_2 - \beta_1}$.

9: $f_t(\beta_1, \beta_2) \leftarrow 1 - \beta_2^t - (1-\beta_2)\, \frac{\beta_1(\beta_2^t - \beta_1^t)}{\beta_2 - \beta_1}$.

10: $a_t \leftarrow \sum_{j=1}^{t} w_{t,j}\, g_j$,

11: $s_t \leftarrow \beta_3 s_{t-1} + (1-\beta_3) g_t^2$.

12: $\widehat{a}_t \leftarrow \frac{a_t}{f_t(\beta_1, \beta_2)}$,

13: $\widehat{s}_t \leftarrow \frac{s_t}{1-\beta_3^t}$,

14: $\widehat{w}_{t,t} \leftarrow \frac{(1-\beta_1)(1-\beta_2)}{f_t(\beta_1, \beta_2)}$.

15: inst$Mult_t \leftarrow \widehat{w}_{t,t} \frac{1}{\sqrt{\widehat{s}_t} + \epsilon} * ScheduleMultiplier(t)$.

16: instLR$_t \leftarrow \alpha *$ inst$Mult_t$.

17: $\theta_t \leftarrow \theta_{t-1} -$ instLR$_t \frac{\widehat{a}_t}{\sqrt{\widehat{s}_t} + \epsilon} -$ inst$Mult * \lambda\, \theta_{t-1}$.

18: *Until* stopping criterion is met.

19: Return optimized parameters θ_t.

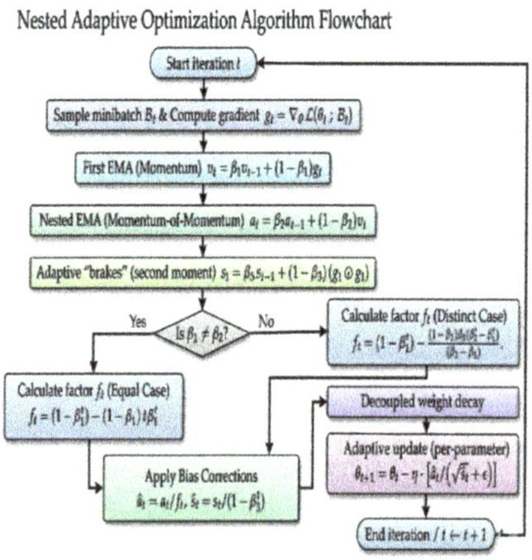

Figure 1. AdamN algorithm flowchart.

https://doi.org/10.3390/electronics15030670

6. Experiments

Before moving to standard benchmarks such as CIFAR-100, we first conducted a series of progressively harder toy experiments to probe the dynamics of AdamN. These tests illustrate why a nested numerator plus adaptive braking is necessary.

For each baseline, we selected the hyperparameters yielding the highest validation performance and report that run.

This section will present the following experiments using the hyperparameters shown in Table 3:

(1) A proof of concept showing why the denominator is essential.
(2) CIFAR-10 as pre-benchmarking.
(3) CIFAR-100 is the main benchmark.
(4) Additional MNIST/EMNIST runs also show marked speed-to-accuracy gains.
(5) NLP rare-token evaluation using a small transformer language model on a Wikitext-2-style corpus.

6.1. Hyperparameter Search Protocol

For each optimizer, we performed a grid search over the following spaces as seen in Table 4:

Table 4. Hyperparameter search protocol.

Optimizer	Learning Rate	Weight Decay	Other
AdamN	$\{3\times10^{-4}, 6\times10^{-4}, 1\times10^{-3}\}$	$\{1\times10^{-4}, 5\times10^{-4}\}$	$\beta_2 \in \{0.1, 0.2, 0.3\}$
AdamW	$\{3\times10^{-4}, 6\times10^{-4}, 1\times10^{-3}, 3\times10^{-3}\}$	$\{1\times10^{-4}, 5\times10^{-4}, 1\times10^{-3}\}$	—
Adam	$\{3\times10^{-4}, 6\times10^{-4}, 1\times10^{-3}, 3\times10^{-3}\}$	$\{0, 1\times10^{-4}, 5\times10^{-4}\}$	—
SGD	$\{1\times10^{-2}, 5\times10^{-2}, 1\times10^{-1}\}$	$\{1\times10^{-4}, 5\times10^{-4}, 1\times10^{-3}\}$	Momentum $\in \{0.9, 0.95\}$

All other hyperparameters ($\beta_1 = 0.9$, $\beta_3 = 0.999$, $\varepsilon = 10^{-8}$ for Adam variants; cosine schedule for all) were held constant at standard defaults.

Search strategy: Full grid search (no random or Bayesian optimization).

Runs per configuration: Single run during search; 3 seeds for selected configurations.

Selection criterion: Configuration with highest validation accuracy at epoch 100.

Stopping criterion: Fixed 100 epochs (no early stopping during search).

Budget: AdamN: 18 configurations; AdamW: 12 configurations; Adam: 12 configurations; SGD: 12 configurations. Total: 54 runs on CIFAR-100/ResNet-18.

The selected hyperparameters for each optimizer, as shown in Table 5, represent the configuration achieving best validation performance in this search.

 https://doi.org/10.3390/electronics15030670

Table 5. Experiment hyperparameters.

Optimizer	Hyper-Parameter	Vision Task				NLP	Notes
		CNN		ViT			
		Full Training	Transfer Learning	Full Training	Transfer Learning		
AdamN	η	1×10^{-3}	1×10^{-4}	1×10^{-3}	1×10^{-4}	1×10^{-3}	η: Base LR. No warmup, cosine scheduling β_1: Momentum of g_t. β_2: Momentum of v_t. β_3: Denominator memory ϵ: Stability WD (λ): Decoupled AMP is enabled for *all optimizers*. The β_2 ramp is an optional technique discussed in Sec. VIII. AdamW uses 'fused = True'; Adam/SGD use 'foreach = True' for fair runtime comparison. Lion: As per [28]; cosine schedule. Adan: As per [25]; cosine schedule. AdaBelief: As per [20]; Cosine schedule.
	$(\beta_1, \beta_2, \beta_3)$	(0.9, 0.1, 0.999)	(0.9, 0.1, 0.999)	(0.9, 0.1, 0.999)	(0.9, 0.1, 0.999)	(0.4, 0.1, 0.999)	
	ϵ	1×10^{-8}	1×10^{-8}	1×10^{-8}	1×10^{-8}	1×10^{-8}	
	WD (λ)	10^{-4}	10^{-5}	5×10^{-3}	10^{-4}	10^{-4}	
	Batch Size	128	128	256	256	-	
	Epoch	100	100	100	100	10	
Adam/AdamW	η	1×10^{-3}	1×10^{-3}	1×10^{-3}	1×10^{-3}	1×10^{-3}	
	(β_1, β_2)	(0.9, 0.999)	(0.9, 0.999)	(0.9, 0.999)	(0.9, 0.999)	(0.9, 0.999)	
	ϵ	1×10^{-8}	1×10^{-8}	1×10^{-8}	1×10^{-8}	1×10^{-8}	
	WD (λ)	5×10^{-4}	10^{-5}	$0/5 \times 10^{-2}$	$5 \times 10^{-4}/5 \times 10^{-2}$	$0/5 \times 10^{-4}$	
	Batch Size	128	128	256	256	-	
	Epoch	100	100	100	100	10	
SGD	η	0.1	1×10^{-3}	1×10^{-1}	1×10^{-3}	1×10^{-1}	
	Momentum	0.9	0.9	0.9	0.9	0.9	
	WD (λ)	5×10^{-4}	10^{-5}	0	5×10^{-3}	0	
	Batch Size	128	128	256	256	-	
	Epoch	100	100	100	100	10	
Lion	η	1×10^{-4}	1×10^{-4}	1×10^{-4}	1×10^{-4}		
	(β_1, β_2)	(0.9, 0.99)	(0.9, 0.99)	(0.9, 0.99)	(0.9, 0.99)		
	ϵ	1×10^{-8}	1×10^{-8}	1×10^{-8}	1×10^{-8}		
	WD (λ)	1×10^{-2}	1×10^{-5}	1×10^{-2}	1×10^{-2}		
	Batch Size	128	128	256	256		
	Epoch	100	100	100	100		
Adan	η	1×10^{-3}	1×10^{-3}	1×10^{-3}	1×10^{-3}		
	$(\beta_1, \beta_2, \beta_3)$	(0.98, 0.92, 0.99)	(0.98, 0.92, 0.99)	(0.98, 0.92, 0.99)	(0.98, 0.92, 0.99)		
	ϵ	1×10^{-8}	1×10^{-8}	1×10^{-8}	1×10^{-8}		
	WD (λ)	2×10^{-2}	1×10^{-5}	1×10^{-2}	2×10^{-2}		
	Batch Size	128	128	256	256		
	Epoch	100	100	100	100		
AdaBelief	η	1×10^{-3}	1×10^{-3}	1×10^{-3}	1×10^{-3}		
	(β_1, β_2)	(0.9, 0.999)	(0.9, 0.999)	(0.9, 0.999)	(0.9, 0.999)		
	ϵ	1×10^{-8}	1×10^{-8}	1×10^{-8}	1×10^{-8}		
	WD (λ)	5×10^{-4}	1×10^{-5}	5×10^{-2}	5×10^{-2}		
	Batch Size	256	256	256	256		
	Epoch	100	100	100	100		

https://doi.org/10.3390/electronics15030670

6.2. Proof of Concept: Stabilizing Nested Momentum

As an initial sanity check, we are optimizing the following smooth 2D objective equation:

$$f(x,y) = 0.1x^2 + \sin(x) + 2y^2 + \cos(y).$$

Without a denominator term, AdamN behaved explosively: the nested numerator amplified updates until trajectories shot off the landscape. This motivated the addition of an adaptive braking mechanism (EMA of squared gradients, as in Adam/AdamW). Figure 2 illustrates extreme overshooting before the brakes were introduced. Figure 3 shows the effect of implementing EMA of squared gradients to control that explosive behavior with only 30 epochs.

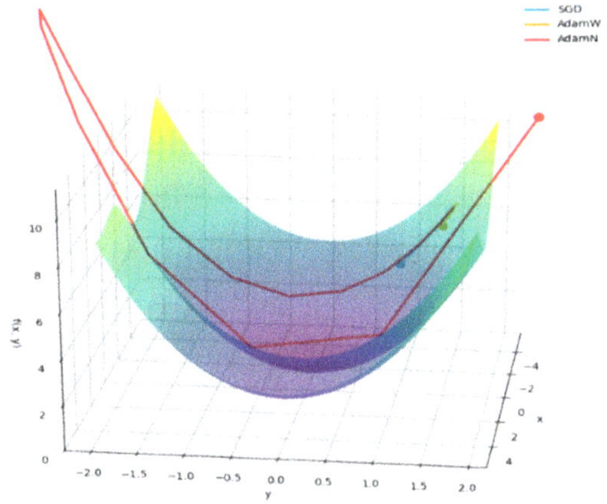

Figure 2. Overshooting behavior of AdamN without adaptive braking.

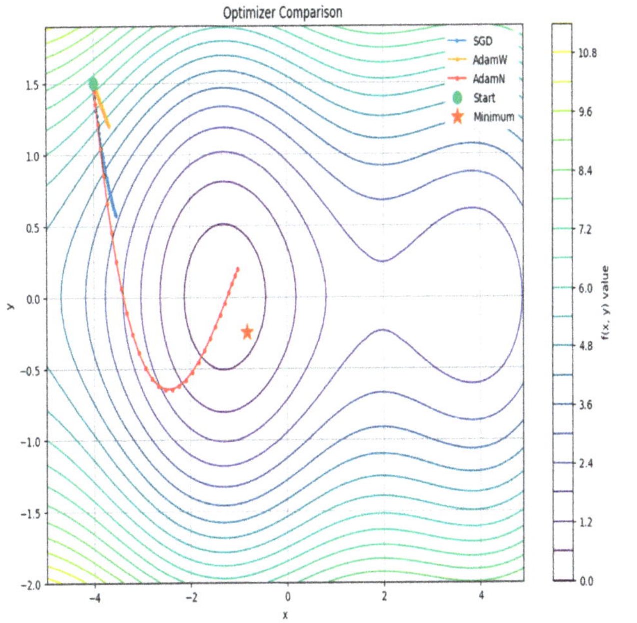

Figure 3. Adding braking mechanism and lowering $\beta 2$ led to faster convergence.

https://doi.org/10.3390/electronics15030670

6.3. Challenging Variant with Cubic Terms

Next, we tested a harder function,

$$f(x,y) = 0.1x^2 + 0.5x^3 + \sin x + \sin^2 x + 2y^2 + 3y^3 + \cos y + \cos^2 y$$

which includes cubic terms. This makes the function unbounded below: as $x, y \to -\infty$, the cubic terms dominate and pull $f(x,y) \to -\infty$. The task therefore shifts from finding a global minimum to settling into a useful local minimum near the origin before divergence.

Setup: Learning rate = 10^{-2}. Momentum for SGD = 0.9. Betas for AdamW = (0.9, 0.999). Betas for AdamN = (0.9, 0.1, 0.999).

Results: AdamN survived and converged across 5 seeds, while SGD diverged at the same learning rate as shown in Table 6.

Table 6. Final loss on cubic function test (N = 5 seeds).

Optimizer	Time (s)	Final Loss	50%	70%	80%	95%
SGD	0.209 ± 0.002	NaN	Not Reached			
AdamW	0.240 ± 0.006	1.928	38 ± 1 ms	73 ± 2 ms	99 ± 3 ms	168 ± 4 ms
AdamN	0.225 ± 0.003	1.887	35 ± 0 ms	65 ± 1 ms	90 ± 1 ms	154 ± 2 ms

6.4. Rosenbrock Function: High-Dimensional Stress Test

We then moved to a more realistic high-dimensional test, the Rosenbrock function (the "banana valley"),

$$f(x) = \sum_{i=1}^{N-1} \left[100\left(x_{i+1} - x_i^2\right)^2 + (1 - x_i)^2 \right], N = 10,$$

whose global minimum is at $(1, \ldots, 1)$ with value 0. The Rosenbrock landscape is notorious for its long, narrow, curved valley, where plain gradient descent zigzags and progresses slowly. Results across 5 seeds are given in Table 7.

Table 7. Results on 10D Rosenbrock function (N = 5 seeds).

Optimizer	Time (s)	Final Loss	50%	70%	80%	95%
SGD	0.931 ± 0.010	14.24	1 ± 0 ms	1 ± 0 ms	1 ± 0 ms	1 ± 0 ms
AdamW	1.189 ± 0.013	0.00	484 ± 5 ms	565 ± 6 ms	603 ± 7 ms	688 ± 8 ms
AdamN	1.100 ± 0.017	0.01	**435 ± 7 ms**	**502 ± 8 ms**	**534 ± 8 ms**	**612 ± 10 ms**

Results: AdamW and AdamN successfully navigated the valley, while SGD plateaued at a much higher loss.

Momentum-based methods like AdamN navigate this landscape more efficiently than SGD.

In higher dimensions ($N = 10$), AdamN consistently reached milestones faster than AdamW, confirming its advantage in noisy, poorly conditioned valleys.

6.5. Addional Vision Datasets (Brief)

MNIST and EMNIST confirm the speed-to-accuracy advantage with competitive final metrics. Time to reach training and validation accuracy milestones' results are shown in Tables 8 and 9, respectively. Note: times are shown as train/val.

https://doi.org/10.3390/electronics15030670

Table 8. MNIST's results.

Optimizer	Tra Acc	Test Acc	90%	95%	99%
AdamN	99.5	99.6	20s (E1)/**21s (E1)**	40s (E2)/**21s (E1)**	143s (E7)/**102s (E5)**
AdamW	99.4	99.5	37s (E2)/**38s (E2)**	37s (E2)/**38s (E2)**	151s (E8)/**133s (E7)**
SGD	99.5	99.7	**36s (E2)/18s (E1)**	36.4s (E2)/**37.2s (E2)**	147s (E8)/**130s (E7)**

Table 9. EMNIST's results.

Optimizer	Tra Acc	Test Acc	60%	80%	90%
AdamN	96.6	90.6	39s (E1)/40s (E1)	78s (E2)/**40s (E1)**	717s (E18)/**401s (E10)**
AdamW	96.6	90.6	76s (E2)/39s (E1)	76s (E2)/**77s (E2)**	777s (E20)/**545s (E14)**

6.6. CIFAR-10 (Pre-Benchmarking)

Experiment Setup: ResNet-18 with100 epochs, a single GPU, cosine schedule, and decoupled weight decay. AdamN uses exact debiasing and the same scheduler budget as AdamW.

Findings: AdamN matches/slightly exceed AdamW's final test accuracy while hitting milestones earlier, as shown in Table 10.

Table 10. CIFAR10—time to reach training and validation accuracy milestones. Times are shown as train/val.

Optimizer	Tra Acc	Test Acc	50%	70%	90%
AdamN	99.4	94.1	35s (E2)/**7s (E1)**	89s (E5)/72s (E4)	346s (E19)/**328s (E18)**
AdamW	99.4	94.3	54s (E3)/**37s (E2)**	109s (E6)/73s (E4)	416s (E23)/**398s (E22)**

6.7. Summary of Toy Tests

These controlled landscapes show that:

(1) Nested momentum without braking leads to instability (overshooting).

(2) Adding the Adam-style denominator stabilizes training while preserving fast numerator dynamics.

(3) Before tackling the more challenging CIFAR-100 benchmark, we validated AdamN on progressively harder datasets including MNIST, Fashion-MNIST, EMNIST, and CIFAR-10. Across all these datasets, AdamN consistently reached key accuracy milestones faster than Adam, AdamW, and SGD, while maintaining competitive or superior final accuracy and loss. These results confirm that AdamN's advantages are not confined to toy problems but extend robustly across diverse datasets and architectures.

6.8. NLP Imbalance Validation: Token-Frequency Bins and Effective Learning Rates

The NLP study is designed to stress class imbalance in language modeling: we include a setting with randomly corrupted tokens injected into the training split (validation/test remain clean) to mimic real-world sparsity, and a low-resource variant with only 10% of the training text.

Experimental setup: We evaluate how AdamN handles the rare-token regime typical in language modeling under class imbalance.

Corpus and preprocessing: Word-level LM on a Wikitext-2-style corpus with a stable regex tokenizer (lowercased words + punctuation). Vocabulary is built only from the training split. Streams are split *80/10/10* (train/val/test). *BPTT length = 35*. We fix the random seed end-to-end (model init, batch order), so AdamN and baselines see identical minibatches.

Model: Small tied-embedding transformer LM: embedding *256*, *2* encoder layers, *4* heads, FFN *512*, dropout *0.2*, sinusoidal positional encoding, tied input/output embedding's, and *10* epochs of training.

Optimizers and schedules:

- *Adam/AdamW*: $\beta = (0.9, 0.999)$, decoupled WD = 0 for Adam and 5×10^{-4} for AdamW, linear warmup → cosine decay, LR = 1×10^{-3}.
- *SGD*: *Momentum* = 0.9, decoupled WD = 0, linear warmup → cosine decay, LR = 1×10^{-3}.
- *AdamN*: $\beta = (0.4, 0.1, 0.999)$, decoupled WD 1×10^{-4}, cosine decay (*no warmup*), LR = 1×10^{-3}, exact double-EMA debiasing in the numerator.

All runs use grad-norm clip = 0.5.

Frequency bins (head/mid/tail): Sort tokens by *training frequency;* slice cumulative index ranges: *head (high frequency)* (top ~1%), *mid (medium frequency)* (next ~19%), and *tail (low frequency)* (remaining ~80%). Metrics are computed per bin on the validation stream.

Optimization was evaluated on the *validation perplexity (PPL)*, both overall and specifically for predictions on tokens belonging to each bin. We also analyzed the *average effective learning rate (LR)* applied to the embedding rows for tokens within each bin.

Metrics: NLP imbalance metrics (RQ5). The primary metric is validation perplexity (PPL), both overall and per slice. We additionally compute the average effective learning rate applied to embedding rows for tokens in each slice.

For AdamW, the effective instLR is computed as follows:

$$instLR = \text{lr}\,\frac{(1-\beta_1)}{(1-\beta_1^t)}\,\frac{1}{\sqrt{\hat{v}_t}+\varepsilon}\ \text{with}\ \hat{v}_t = \frac{v_t}{1-\beta_2^t}.$$

For AdamN (nested numerator + exact debias), the effective instLR is computed as follows:

$$instLR = \text{lr}\frac{(1-\beta_1)(1-\beta_2)}{f_t(\beta_1,\beta_2)}\frac{1}{\sqrt{\hat{s}_t}+\varepsilon}\ \text{with}\ \hat{s}_t = \frac{s_t}{1-\beta_3^t}.$$

Here, $f_t(\beta_1, \beta_2)$ is *the exact double-EMA bias factor* from our derivation (29). We take the RMS across the embedding dimension to get *one scalar per row*, then average over rows in each bin.

Validation Protocol A—Full Data with Rare-Token Stress (Training Corruption)

Task framing: This experiment targets *rare-token representations* in a language modeling task. To mimic real-world imbalance and increase token sparsity, we train on a Wikitext-2-style dataset augmented with randomly corrupted tokens in the training split only (validation/test remain clean).

This amplifies the long-tail difficulty while leaving evaluation unbiased.

Validation PPL by bin (↓ better) results and average effective LR on embedding rows (arbitrary units, ↑ larger scale) are shown in Tables 11 and 12, respectively.

Table 11. Per-bin validation perplexity.

Optimizer	Tra Acc	Test Acc	Head	Mid	Tail
AdamN	1.52	2.35	1.12	1.34	39.81
AdamW	1.38	2.66	1.13	1.38	69.95
Adam	1.38	2.6	1.13	1.38	63.24
SGD	3.62	3.88	1.17	1.60	367.45

https://doi.org/10.3390/electronics15030670

Table 12. Per-bin average effective LR (embedding rows).

Optimizer	Head	Mid	Tail
AdamN	9.790×10^{-3}	4.239×10^{-2}	1.297×10^{-1}
AdamW	6.999×10^{-2}	3.027×10^{-1}	1.083×10^{0}
Adam	7.049×10^{-2}	3.039×10^{-1}	1.090×10^{0}
SGD		N/A	

RQ5: Generalization to NLP under imbalance (rare-token efficiency):

Findings: Head/mid are comparable; the *tail* dominates the imbalance story. Under identical budgets, AdamN halves tail PPL vs. AdamW while using a smaller tail effective LR—consistent with AdamN's longer-memory, exactly debiased numerator producing higher-quality rare-token updates (better likelihood gain per unit step), rather than just increasing step size. Here, low β_1 acts as a noise filter, preventing overshooting.

Validation Protocol B—Low-resource challenge (10% training data)

We repeat the pipeline after down-sampling the training split to 10%, while keeping val/test full-size. Vocabulary shrinks (e.g., ~18 k), and tail sparsity becomes severe.

Validation PPL by bin (↓ better) results, and average effective LR on embedding rows are shown in Tables 13 and 14, respectively:

Table 13. Per-bin validation perplexity.

Optimizer	Tra Acc	Test Acc	Head	Mid	Tail
AdamN	1.32	1.54	1.13	1.35	31.08
AdamW	1.45	1.57	1.14	1.36	38.77
Adam	1.45	1.60	1.14	1.36	48.36
SGD	1.54	1.40	1.16	1.37	7.61

Table 14. Per-bin average effective LR (embedding rows).

Optimizer	Head	Mid	Tail
AdamN	3.627×10^{-2}	4.729×10^{-1}	1.229×10^{1}
AdamW	1.888×10^{-1}	1.909×10^{0}	5.312×10^{1}
Adam	1.899×10^{-1}	1.889×10^{0}	5.259×10^{1}
SGD		N/A	

Findings (low resource): Under extreme data scarcity, where the tail gets much harder for both methods, the *low-momentum, high-dampening profile of AdamN is* vastly superior for regularization and learning the sparsest embedding's. AdamN retains a strong advantage (~3.5× lower tail PPL) while again allocating less (~5× lower effective LR) than AdamW—evidence that AdamN's nested numerator + exact debias improves update efficiency on rare tokens when data is scarce. And this confirms the previous hypothesis: AdamN's superiority is achieved not by faster exploration but by *superior step precision and stability*. It is winning by taking smaller, cleaner steps where there are large, noisy steps that lead to parameter drift.

Practical Interpretation:

- **Head/mid stability, tail efficiency.** Across both settings, AdamN improves tail PPL without simply increasing tail LR, indicating better bias/variance trade-offs in the rare-token regime.
- **No warmup for AdamN.** Exact double-EMA debias provides a clean start; AdamW still benefits from short warmup to avoid poor early scaling.

https://doi.org/10.3390/electronics15030670

- **Fair comparisons.** We seed all randomness, reuse the same initial weights, and preserve identical minibatch order to isolate optimizer behavior.
- **Caveat.** Absolute PPL depends on model size and schedules; the robust signal is the relative tail behavior and effective-LR distribution under imbalance.

We also evaluated AdamN on a larger-scale setting (RQ5). In a full fine-tuning experiment on **Llama 3.1–8B** using a small dataset, AdamN demonstrated strong speed-to-quality behavior: it reached AdamW's final perplexity in approximately half as many training steps as seen in Table 15, corresponding to an $\approx$2.25$\times$ **improvement in time-to-quality**.

Table 15. AdamW is about 2.3% worse in perplexity.

Optimizer	Final Train Loss	Final Eval Loss	Final Eval Ppl
AdamN	**1.5805**	**1.5933**	**4.92**
AdamW	1.5859	1.6165	5.0

6.9. CIFAR-100 (Main Benchmark)

CIFAR100 is one of the most challenging small-scale vision benchmarks, with 100 classes and relatively few examples per class. In this section, our primary goal is not to push state-of-the-art test accuracy—achieving beyond 90% typically requires specialized augmentation pipelines, transfer learning, and extensive tuning. Instead, we deliberately kept the standard setup and focused on what CIFAR100 reveals about optimizer *speed*. AdamN is designed as a fast learner, and CIFAR100 provides a realistic, high-dimensional stress test to evaluate how quickly an optimizer can drive training accuracy upward under a fixed epoch budget. Across runs, the validation accuracy remained in the expected 75–76% range for plain training without tricks, but the key outcome is that AdamN consistently reached accuracy milestones earlier than AdamW, Adam, or SGD, demonstrating its advantage as a speed-oriented optimizer.

Experiment Setup: We evaluated CIFAR-100 with ResNet-18 and ViT-b16 for 100 epochs, using cosine learning-rate schedule and decoupled weight decay. All optimizers receive the same tuning budget; AdamN uses exact nested debiasing and no warmup, while Adam/AdamW and SGD are trained with a warmup to reflect standard practice. For fairness and reproducibility, we (i) fix a global random seed and enable deterministic settings where possible, (ii) seed the DataLoader shuffles and all stochastic augmentations per epoch so that all the optimizers see the identical sample order and transformations at every epoch, (iii) load the same initial weights (identical state_dict) before each strategy runs, and (iv) apply AdamW-style decay exclusions (no WD on biases/norms/ViT pos-embeds/cls) across all methods, enable AMP, and turn on PyTorch (2.9.0) fast paths (AdamW fused when supported; Adam/SGD foreach = True). This translates into materially lower computation cost and energy per run, compounding across large hyperparameter sweeps.

We report two regimes: from-scratch training (full ResNet-18 and customized ViT on 32 $\times$ 32 CIFAR100) and transfer learning (ImageNet-pretrained backbone with a reinitialized classifier and ViT-b16). *Both regimes exhibit the same trend—AdamN reaches target accuracies sooner at comparable final accuracy*—with the transfer-learning runs showing slightly smoother curves and a modestly faster time-to-accuracy due to stronger initialization. All other data-pipeline components and hyperparameters are held constant across methods. The only difference is that, in from-scratch training, we adopted a uniform AdamW-style weight-decay policy across all optimizers (AdamN, AdamW, Adam, and SGD): decay true weights, but excluding biases, normalization affine parameters, and ViT positional/class tokens. This ensures fairness and isolates optimizer behavior from regularization confounds;

https://doi.org/10.3390/electronics15030670

this translates into materially lower computation cost and energy per run, compounding across large hyperparameter sweeps.

For multi-seed dispersion and sensitivity, we ran N = 3 seeds on AdamN only. Sweep: LR $\in \{1 \times 10^{-3}, 6 \times 10^{-4}, 3 \times 10^{-4}\}$, WD $\in \{0.05, 0.1\}$ (decoupled), and $\beta_2 \in \{0.1, 0.2, 0.3\}$ under a fixed compute budget.

Metrics and Protocols

Time-to-quality (RQ1): We record per-epoch cumulative wall-clock time and compute seconds to reach validation accuracy milestones {50, 60, 70, 80, 90%}.

Final quality equal budget (RQ2): We report test accuracy at E = 100 and at a fixed wall-clock budget.

Sensitivity and robustness (RQ3). For $LR \times WD \times \beta_2$ grids, we report mean ± SD and 95% CI across 3 seeds.

Mechanism ablation (RQ4): We run a 2 × 2 toggle: nested on/off × exact/simple debias, measuring milestone times and final accuracy.

Headline results: In all cases, AdamN reaches all training and validation-accuracy milestones at matched final accuracy with reduced wall-clock time by 20~80% speedup under identical hardware and dataloaders. Tables 16–19 present the results.

Table 16. CNN transfer learning time-to-train/val-accuracy milestones. AdamN reaches milestones earlier than other optimizers ("rocket-like" start), while retaining stability.

Optimizer	Tra Acc	Time to Train-Accuracy Milestones						Val Acc	Test Acc	Time to Val-Accuracy Milestones				
		40%	50%	60%	70%	80%	90%			40%	50%	60%	70%	75%
AdamN	96	**92s (E2)**	**92s (E2)**	**130s (E3)**	**318s (E8)**	**618s (E16)**	**1330s (E35)**	78	78	**57s (E1)**	**57s (E1)**	**95s (E2)**	**170s (E4)**	**470s (E12)**
AdamW	96	71s (E2)	108s (E3)	255s (E7)	477s (E13)	737s (E20)	1475s (E40)	76	77	73s (E2)	73s (E2)	73s (E2)	480s (E13)	1478s (E40)
Adam	97	71s (E2)	108s (E3)	257s (E7)	479s (E13)	739s (E20)	1554s (E42)	77	77	74s (E2)	74s (E2)	74s (E2)	519s (E14)	1668s (E45)
SGD	82	333s (E9)	444s (E12)	555s (E15)	1036s (E28)	2370s (E64)	NA	76	77	223s (E6)	335s (E9)	446s (E12)	706s (E19)	1372s (E37)
Lion	37	108s (E3)	108s (E3)	146s (E4)	331s (E9)	665s (E18)	1481s (E40)	41	75	74s (E2)	74s (E2)	111s (E3)	297s (E8)	1706s (E46)
Adan	97	71s (E2)	109s (E3)	146s (E4)	294s (E8)	518s (E14)	1146s (E31)	78	78	74s (E2)	74s (E2)	74s (E2)	186s (E5)	853s (E23)
AdaBelief	97	107s (E3)	144s (E4)	255s (E7)	550s (E15)	809s (E22)	1399s (E38)	78	78	73s (E2)	73s (E2)	147s (E4)	332s (E9)	774s (E21)

Table 17. CNN full training time-to-train/val-accuracy milestones. AdamN reaches milestones earlier than AdamW ("rocket-like" start), while retaining stability.

Optimizer	Tra Acc	Time to Train-Accuracy Milestones						Val Acc	Test Acc	Time to Val-Accuracy Milestones				
		40%	50%	60%	70%	80%	90%			40%	50%	60%	70%	75%
AdamN	96.88	**81s (E6)**	**122s (E9)**	**189s (E14)**	**283s (E21)**	**418s (E31)**	**670s (E50)**	74.58	75.04	69s (E5)	**95s (E7)**	**176s (E13)**	**324s (E24)**	**1036s (E77)**
AdamW	96.86	106s (E8)	159s (E12)	198s (E15)	291s (E22)	424s (E32)	661s (E50)	74.36	75.48	93s (E7)	119s (E9)	186s (E14)	371s (E28)	1045s (E79)
Adam	90.09	158s (E12)	224s (E17)	410s (E31)	715s (E54)	979s (E74)	-	75.30	75.79	145s (E11)	172s (E13)	304s (E23)	729s (E55)	1046s (E79)
SGD	96.13	118s (E9)	211s (E16)	421s (E32)	711s (E54)	909s (E69)	1081s (E82)	76.54	77.81	119s (E9)	172s (E13)	317s (E24)	844s (E64)	1042s (E79)
Lion	96.84	92s (E7)	132s (E10)	198s (E15)	291s (E22)	437s (E33)	702s (E53)	75.58	74.85	79s (E6)	106s (E8)	159s (E12)	318s (E24)	955s (E72)
Adan	96.31	106s (E8)	159s (E12)	227s (E17)	334s (E25)	508s (E38)	763s (E57)	75.76	75.35	93s (E7)	106s (E8)	187s (E14)	402s (E30)	965s (E72)
AdaBelief	94.25	185s (E14)	225s (E17)	305s (E23)	424s (E32)	609s (E46)	888s (E67)	74.78	74.21	119s (E9)	172s (E13)	317s (E24)	844s (E64)	1042s (E79)

https://doi.org/10.3390/electronics15030670

Table 18. ViT transfer learning time-to-train/val-accuracy milestones. AdamN reaches milestones earlier than other optimizers ("rocket-like" start), while retaining stability.

Optimizer	Tra Acc	Time to Train-Accuracy Milestones						Val Acc	Test Acc	Time to Val-Accuracy Milestones					
		40%	50%	60%	70%	80%	90%			40%	50%	60%	70%	75%	80%
AdamN	99.79	**29s (E1)**	**29s (E1)**	**29s (E1)**	**58s (E2)**	**58s (E2)**	**143s (E5)**	87.66	88.06	**32s (E1)**	**32s (E1)**	**32s (E1)**	**32s (E1)**	**32s (E1)**	**32s (E1)**
AdamW	99.70	50s (E2)	50s (E2)	50s (E2)	50s (E2)	392s (E15)	601s (E23)	82.14	81.69	25s (E1)	25s (E1)	25s (E1)	52s (E2)	52s (E2)	1889s (E72)
Adam	73.55	55s (E2)	55s (E2)	55s (E2)	2250s (E82)	-	-	64.04	73.83	28s (E1)	28s (E1)	28s (E1)	56s (E2)	-	-
SGD	96.07	137s (E5)	165s (E6)	192s (E7)	221s (E8)	360s (E13)	801s (E29)	85.70	86.23	52s (E2)	52s (E2)	52s (E2)	52s (E2)	250s (E9)	305s (E11)
Lion	99.51	53s (E2)	53s (E2)	53s (E2)	80s (E3)	80s (E3)	377s (E14)	81.04	83.59	55s (E2)	55s (E2)	55s (E2)	55s (E2)	55s (E2)	82s (E3)
Adan	99.80	55s (E2)	55s (E2)	55s (E2)	55s (E2)	84s (E3)	343s (E12)	84.00	84.69	28s (E1)	57s (E2)	57s (E2)	57s (E2)	57s (E2)	57s (E2)
AdaBelief	99.79	53s (E2)	53s (E2)	81s (E3)	81s (E3)	109s (E4)	277s (E10)	87.76	88.60	55s (E2)	55s (E2)	55s (E2)	55s (E2)	55s (E2)	83s (E3)

Table 19. ViT full training time-to-train/val-accuracy milestones. AdamN reaches milestones earlier than AdamW ("rocket-like" start), while retaining stability.

Optimizer	Tra Acc	Time to Train-Accuracy Milestones						Val Acc	Test Acc	Time to Val-Accuracy Milestones				
		40%	50%	60%	70%	80%	90%			40%	50%	60%	70%	75%
AdamN	87.46	**189s (E14)**	**271s (E20)**	**421s (E31)**	**599s (E44)**	**858s (E63)**	-	69.24	69.29	**122s (E9)**	**189s (E14)**	**326s (E24)**	-	-
AdamW	88.03	203s (E15)	313s (E23)	448s (E33)	624s (E46)	882s (E65)	-	70.54	69.41	122s (E9)	217s (E16)	354s (E26)	1114s (E82)	-
Adam	86.86	217s (E16)	299s (E22)	449s (E33)	624s (E46)	882s (E65)	-	70.02	69.79	135s (E10)	218s (E16)	341s (E25)	1343s (E99)	-
SGD	83.57	243s (E18)	364s (E27)	526s (E39)	753s (E56)	1050s (E78)	-	70.24	69.78	162s (E12)	243s (E18)	432s (E32)	1145s (E85)	-
Lion	87.22	190s (E14)	285s (E21)	407s (E30)	598s (E44)	883s (E65)	-	69.24	68.61	122s (E9)	204s (E15)	340s (E25)	-	-
Adan	84.37	218s (E16)	330s (E24)	481s (E35)	685s (E50)	999s (E73)	-	68.24	68.54	137s (E10)	233s (E17)	427s (E31)	-	-
AdaBelief	73.57	338s (E25)	543s (E40)	802s (E59)	1101s (E81)	-	-	66.72	66.32	216s (E16)	366s (E27)	653s (E48)	-	-

6.10. Comparison with Lion and Adan

To validate AdamN's speed claims against recent optimizers, we benchmark against Lion [28] and Adan [25] under equivalent conditions (same seeds, data order, and AMP enabled).

Lion employs a sign-based update rule with momentum interpolation, eliminating the need for second-moment estimation. Adan uses an adaptive Nesterov-style numerator with three β parameters. Both are designed for fast convergence.

Results: AdamN consistently reaches the 40–70% validation accuracy milestones faster than both Lion and Adan. At higher milestones (80–90%), Adan becomes competitive, likely due to its Nesterov-style lookahead. Lion shows intermediate performance, with slightly slower early convergence than AdamN but faster than AdamW.

Observation: AdamN's advantage is most pronounced in the early-to-mid training phase, aligning with its design goal of fast, warmup-free starts via exact double-EMA debiasing. For practitioners prioritizing rapid iteration during model development or hyperparameter search, this early-phase speedup translates directly to reduced experimentation time.

6.11. Training Curves

To visualize the dynamics of AdamN compared to other optimizers, we plot train/val accuracy, instantaneous learning rate (instLR), step RMS, and the freshness-weighted gradient RMS across epochs.

https://doi.org/10.3390/electronics15030670

Freshness-weighted Gradient RMS: Figure 4 demonstrates that AdamN significantly suppresses the RMS of the freshness-weighted current gradient compared to AdamW. This indicates that AdamN better damps raw gradient noise, leading to smoother and more reliable updates.

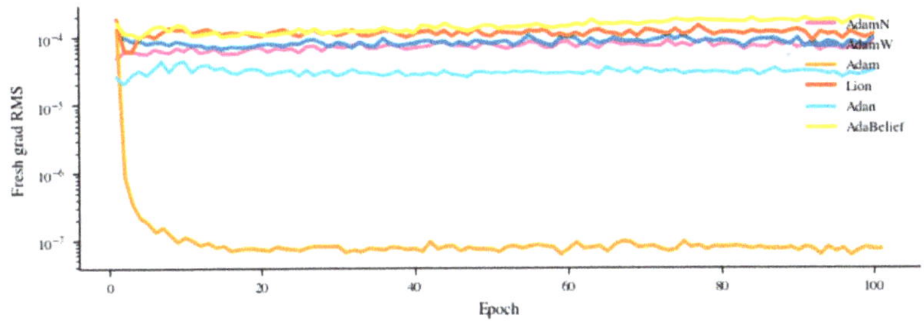

Figure 4. ResNet-18 on CIFAR-100: freshness-weighted current gradient RMS (log-scale) for AdamN, AdamW, and Adam. AdamN exhibits a lower and more stable fresh-gradient magnitude over training, suggesting reduced gradient noise and improved conditioning during optimization.

Instantaneous LR and Denominator RMS: As shown in Figure 5, AdamN's instLR (exact vs. simple bias correction) matches almost perfectly, confirming that the difference between the two forms is negligible in practice for lower β_2. The RMS denominator decays smoothly, stabilizing the magnitude of the update during training.

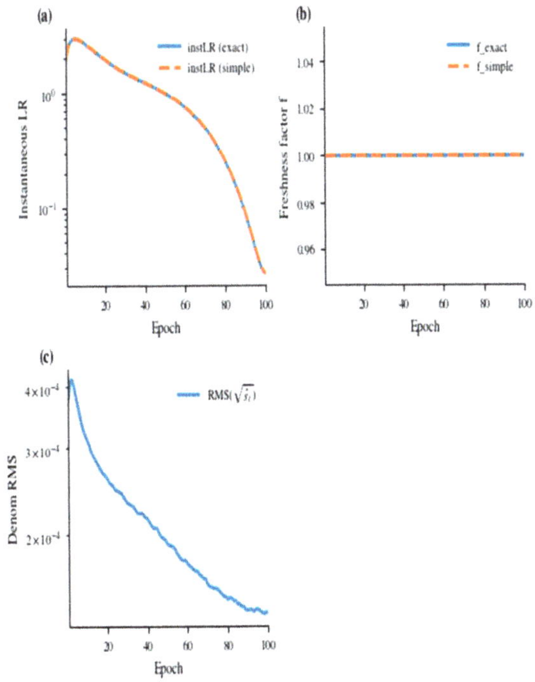

Figure 5. ResNet-18 on CIFAR-100: AdamN internal diagnostics (**a**) comparing instantaneous LR computed using the exact vs. simplified formulations, (**b**) freshness factor trajectories (f_{exact} and f_{simple}), and (**c**) the adaptive denominator RMS $\mathbf{RMS}(\sqrt{\hat{s}_t})$ (log-scale). The close match between exact and simplified curves supports the simplified implementation and highlights the stabilizing evolution of AdamN's adaptive scaling.

https://doi.org/10.3390/electronics15030670

Instantaneous LR and Step RMS: In Figure 6, the top plot (instantaneous LR) shows that the instLR for Adam/AdamW is consistently and significantly higher than for AdamN. This metric represents the potential "kick" the optimizer would give to a fresh gradient. AdamW is theoretically far more aggressive. On the other hand, the bottom plot (step_RMS) shows the actual magnitude of the update applied to the model's weights at each epoch. Again, AdamW takes consistently larger steps.

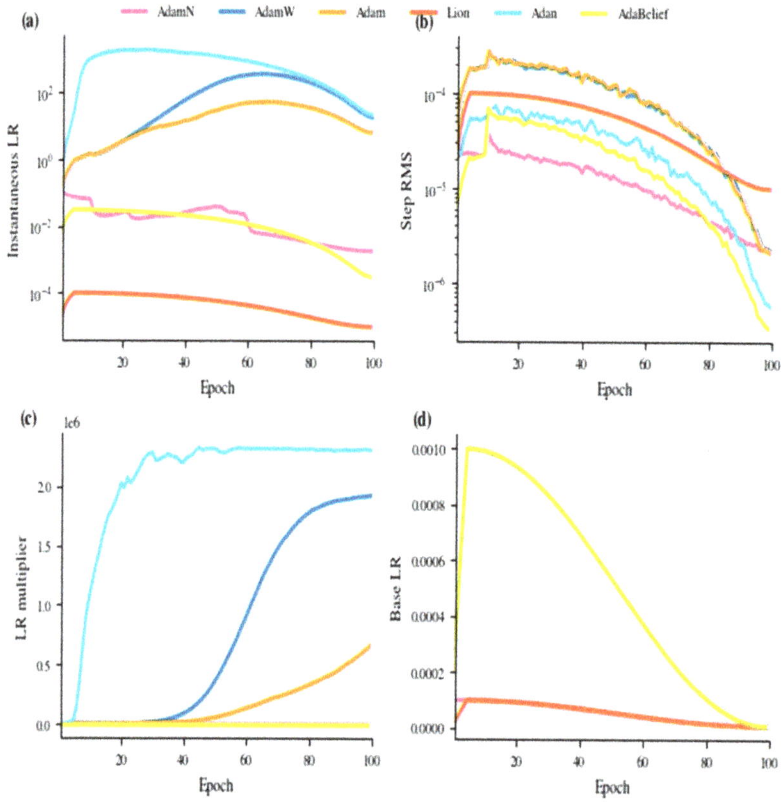

Figure 6. ResNet–18 on CIFAR–100: optimizer dynamics across epochs for AdamN, and other optimizers. AdamN yields smoother effective step scaling and more controlled update magnitudes, consistent with faster accuracy gains without late-stage instability. (**a**) Instantaneous learning rate (effective step size after bias correction and normalization) versus epoch for each optimizer. (**b**) Step RMS (root-mean-square magnitude of the parameter update) versus epoch, showing how update energy evolves across training. AdamN is achieving a higher final accuracy and reaching milestones significantly faster, all while taking smaller, more controlled steps. This isn't a paradox; it's a sign of being a highly efficient optimizer. It's not about the size of the step, but the quality of its direction. (**c**) Learning-rate multiplier (optimizer-induced scaling factor applied to the base learning rate, capturing the net effect of numerator/denominator dynamics) versus epoch. (**d**) Base learning rate schedule versus epoch (shared schedule across optimizers), included to separate scheduler effects from optimizer-induced scaling.

Validation Accuracy and Training Loss. As illustrated in Figure 7, both AdamN and AdamW converge to a similar final validation accuracy (∼75–76%), but AdamN reaches a high accuracy faster—consistent with improved conditioning of "hard" directions early on. Training loss curves also show AdamN descending more steeply in the early epochs,

https://doi.org/10.3390/electronics15030670

demonstrating its advantage in speed. So, AdamN achieves a higher final accuracy and reaches milestones significantly faster, all while taking smaller, more controlled steps.

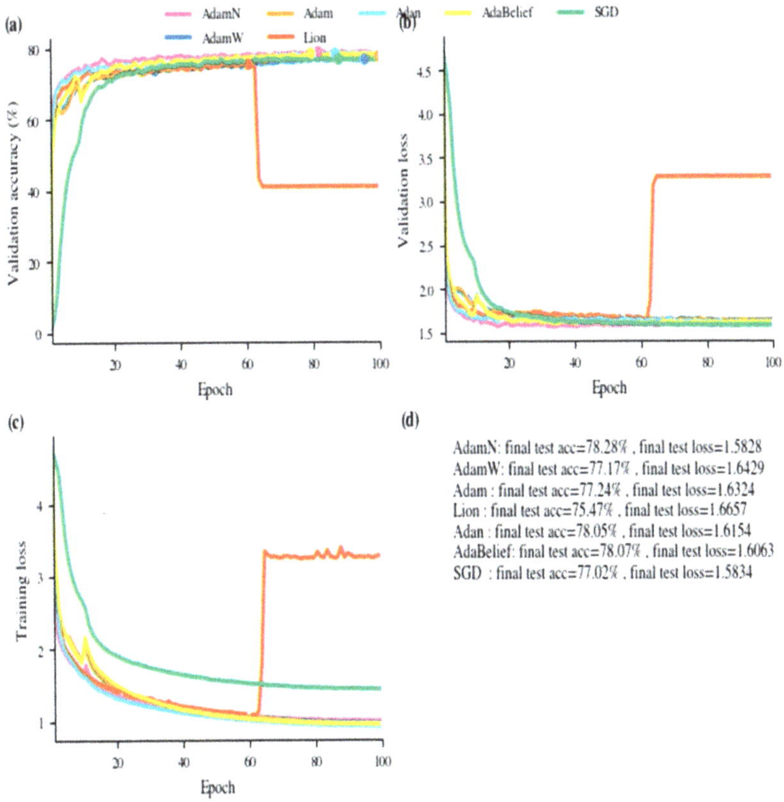

Figure 7. ResNet–18 training on CIFAR–100: zoom-in validation accuracy (with early- and late-epoch zoom insets) and loss curves for different optimizers. AdamN improves early learning speed and maintains a consistent advantage at convergence, while validation and training losses indicate stable optimization throughout training. (**a**) Validation accuracy versus epoch for AdamN, AdamW, Adam, Lion, Adan, AdaBelief, and SGD, highlighting convergence speed and final generalization. (**b**) Validation loss versus epoch for the same optimizers, showing early optimization behavior and stability; the sharp loss increase indicates an instability event for the affected method under the chosen hyperparameters. (**c**) Training loss versus epoch, illustrating optimization speed and potential divergence/instability (visible as a sudden jump/plateau in loss). (**d**) Final test metrics summary (test accuracy and test loss) for each optimizer at the end of training, reported to compare final generalization performance under the same experimental protocol.

This is not a paradox; it is a sign of being a highly efficient optimizer. It is not about the size of the step but the quality of its direction.

In general, these curves illustrate AdamN's key strength: a fast rocket-like launch with higher instLR and larger early steps, followed by a stable cruise where noise is effectively suppressed, making it a stronger default than AdamW when early progress and robust scaling both matter.

NLP's Overall Convergence: As shown in Figure 8a (Val PPL vs. Epoch), both AdamN and AdamW quickly minimized the overall validation perplexity. However, AdamN

https://doi.org/10.3390/electronics15030670

demonstrated superior stability and faster initial convergence, achieving a final PPL of 1.87 compared to AdamW's final PPL of 2.0, suggesting a more robust optimization path.

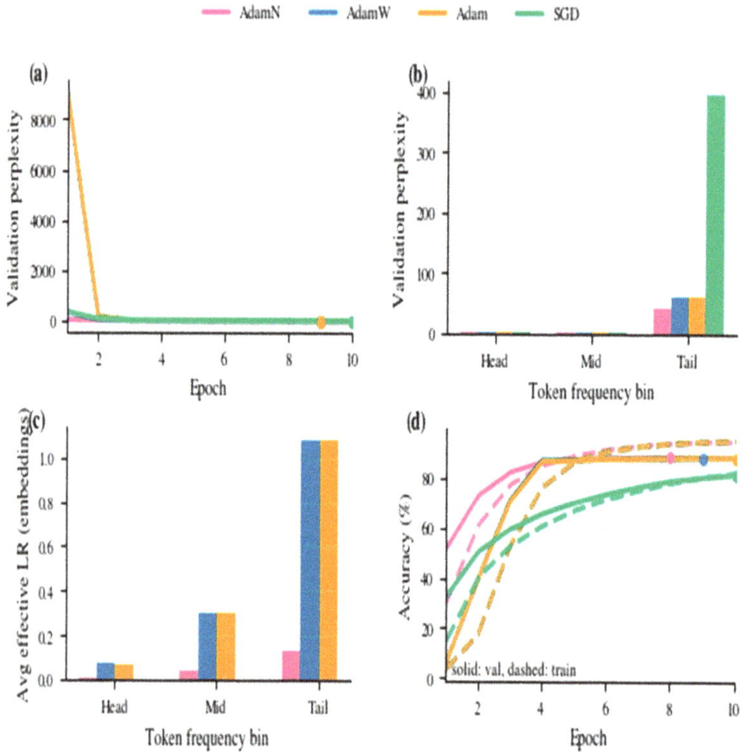

Figure 8. (**a**) Validation perplexity over training epochs for each optimizer. Lower perplexity indicates better language modeling performance, highlighting differences in convergence speed and final generalization. (**b**) Validation perplexity stratified by token-frequency bins (head/mid/tail). This breakdown reveals how each optimizer performs on frequent versus rare tokens, with tail performance reflecting robustness on infrequent vocabulary. (**c**) Average effective learning rate applied to embedding rows grouped by token frequency. The bin-wise effective LR illustrates how each optimizer adapts update magnitudes across frequent and rare tokens, which can influence tail generalization. (**d**) Training (dashed) and validation (solid) accuracy across epochs. The train–validation gap provides an indication of overfitting, while the validation trajectory summarizes generalization and convergence behavior under each optimizer.

NLP's Perplexity by Frequency Bin: The advantage of AdamN is starkly revealed when examining performance on the rare tokens, as depicted in Figure 8b (per-token frequency bins).

Head/Mid: Both optimizers performed nearly identically on common tokens (head PPL $\approx$ 1.20; mid PPL $\approx$ 1.5–1.6).

Tail: AdamN achieved a tail PPL of 155.09, which is significantly lower than AdamW's tail PPL of 308.82. This indicates that AdamN is substantially better at learning effective representations for rare tokens with *higher update efficiency* (better likelihood gain per unit step), where the gradient signals are sparse and noisy.

NLP's Effective Learning Rate Analysis: Figure 9 (effective LR by frequency bin) explains the performance gap as follows:

https://doi.org/10.3390/electronics15030670

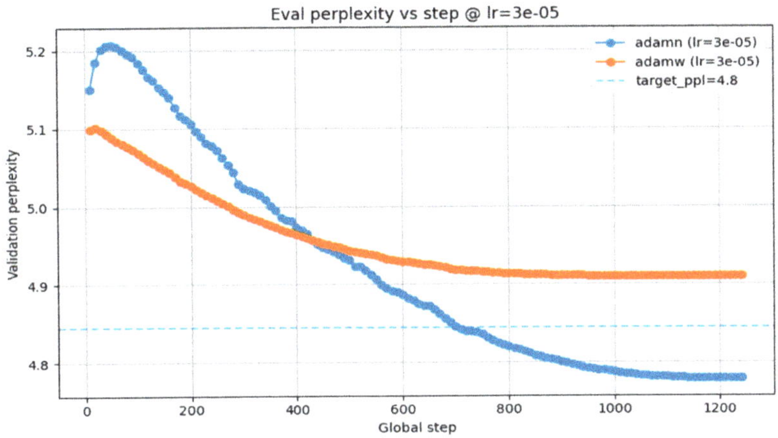

Figure 9. Eval perplexity vs. step for Llama3.1.

Head/Mid: AdamW applies a much larger effective LR to these common tokens (mid LR $\approx 1.9 \times 10^0$ for AdamW vs. $\approx 4.7 \times 10^{-1}$ for AdamN). This aggressive step size on common tokens likely causes overshooting and instability.

Tail: Critically, AdamW applies an excessively large effective LR of 53.12 to the rare token embeddings. This is due to the small, noisy second moment estimates, which cause the denominator $\sqrt{\hat{s}_t}$ to collapse, leading to a massive, unstable step size. In contrast, AdamN maintains a dramatically lower and more stable effective LR of 12.29 for the tail tokens. The nested momentum in AdamN provides better normalization for the sparse gradient updates, preventing the pathological acceleration that plagues AdamW on rare features.

Llama3.1-8B benchmark: Time-to-quality: "when does AdamN match AdamW?"

AdamN reaches AdamW's final perplexity in roughly half the number of steps (~2.25× faster time-to-quality) as shown in Figures 9 and 10.

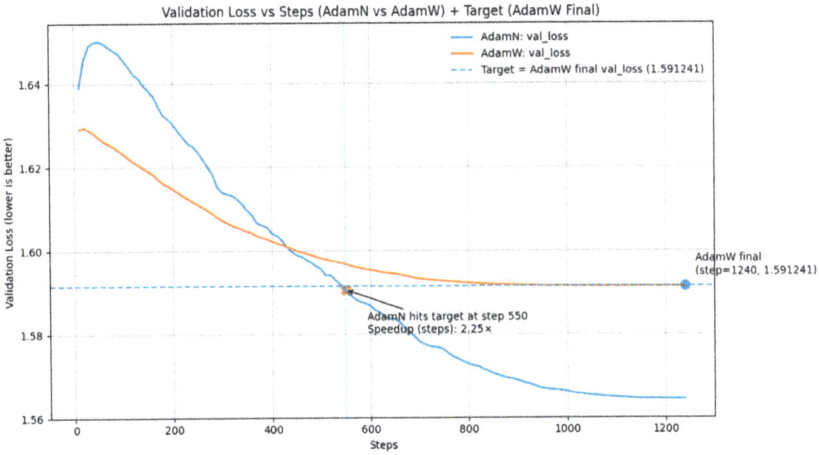

Figure 10. Val loss vs. step (time to target).

 https://doi.org/10.3390/electronics15030670

Headline results:

RQ1: Time-to-quality. As illustrated in Figure 8, both AdamN and AdamW converge to a similar final validation accuracy (~75–76%), but AdamN reaches a high accuracy faster.

RQ2: Final quality at equal budget. In general, AdamN matches/slightly exceeds other optimizers' final test accuracy at similar wall-clock time while hitting earlier milestones as shown in Tables 14–17 above.

RQ3: Sensitivity and robustness. As seen in Table 20, LR matters most here, with 6×10^{-4} hitting a better speed/accuracy than 3×10^{-4} (slower to milestones) and 1×10^{-3} (slightly worse final and a bit flaky at 75%).

Table 20. Dispersion: Time-to-VAL accuracy milestones (s) and final TEST accuracy across 3 seeds.

LR_base	WD	β_2	N	Final Test Acc (Mean ± SD, 95% CI)	t50	t60	t70	t75
0.0003	0.0001	0.1	3	74.76 ± 6.23 (0.42)	98.03 ± 3.64 (1.17)	186.42 ± 2.61 (13.97)	462.96 ± 69.99 (55.10)	996.30 ± 0.50 (16.74)
0.0006	0.0001	0.1	3	74.93 ± 3.41 (0.75)	97.91 ± 1.29 (0.54)	172.06 ± 61.00 (38.59)	415.37 ± 76.80 (67.60)	1073.30 ± 03.89 (154.12)
0.001	0.0001	0.1	3	74.50 ± 0.08 (0.15)	98.44 ± 4.37 (2.51)	172.65 ± 56.78 (30.82)	412.22 ± 22.66 (60.00)	1156.96 ± 67.88 (84.82)
0.0003	0.0001	0.2	3	74.84 ± 4.43 (0.79)	108.34 ± 4.92 (14.54)	187.34 ± 45.69 (28.83)	460.47 ± 74.34 (26.34)	1143.29 ± 98.05 (161.77)
0.0006	0.0001	0.2	3	74.83 ± 3.13 (0.23)	93.96 ± 6.29 (15.23)	159.40 ± 0.40 (13.60)	417.59 ± 95.66 (47.13)	1134.38 ± 80.20 (55.48)
0.001	0.0001	0.2	3	74.24 ± 4.21 (0.39)	103.09 ± 9.22 (15.10)	181.98 ± 8.45 (0.83)	408.54 ± 46.92 (31.08)	-
0.0003	0.0001	0.3	3	74.3 ±0.30 (0.56)	98.69 ± 9.32 (0.59)	187.53 ± 3.66 (15.92)	423.40 ± 01.47 (76.18)	1222.04 ± 448.08 (272.05)
0.0006	0.0001	0.3	3	75.02 ± 2.10 (0.17)	84.43 ± 3.36 (0.65)	163.72 ± 2.43 (15.49)	377.59 ± 94.34 (44.71)	1036.48 ± 81.88 (150.43)
0.001	0.0001	0.3	3	74.45 ± 5.14 (0.25)	99.43 ± 3.67 (3.06)	179.97 ± 7.58 (8.41)	431.22 ± 26.00 (29.40)	-
0.0003	0.0005	0.1	3	74.77 ± 7.28 (0.52)	100.06 ± 6.31 (0.57)	188.60 ± 0.66 (14.07)	444.55 ± 58.26 (51.91)	1304.74 ± 416.31 (353.90)
0.0006	0.0005	0.1	3	74.80 ± 0.20 (0.36)	98.78 ± 8.86 (3.43)	173.76 ± 62.70 (41.71)	408.78 ± 8.46 (13.71)	1043.31 ± 1.99 (6.05)
0.001	0.0005	0.1	3	74.59 ± 9.50 (0.92)	103.59 ± 9.79 (12.47)	163.76 ± 6.08 (11.17)	413.67 ± 76.63 (30.55)	929.70 ± 0.00 (0.00)
0.0003	0.0005	0.2	3	74.98 ± 8.36 (0.67)	95.04 ± 4.54 (15.68)	189.87 ± 7.44 (15.51)	480.80 ± 02.52 (23.01)	1182.80 ± 049.76 (275.12)
0.0006	0.0005	0.2	3	74.85 ± 5.16 (0.30)	90.26 ± 6.71 (16.00)	165.97 ± 7.01 (14.72)	405.24 ± 46.26 (29.88)	1025.06 ± 637.53 (252.66)
0.001	0.0005	0.2	3	74.62 ± 2.34 (0.62)	101.73 ± 3.87 (14.45)	176.12 ± 2.32 (13.45)	421.32 ± 23.60 (24.98)	1050.49 ± 0.00 (0.00)
0.0003	0.0005	0.3	3	74.64 ± 4.20 (0.36)	100.06 ± 6.04 (1.91)	194.82 ± 26.70 (30.67)	481.14 ± 42.55 (78.17)	1366.42 ± 2.00 (0.00)
0.0006	0.0005	0.3	3	74.94 ± 4.45 (0.83)	103.96 ± 6.25 (15.16)	165.01 ± 1.73 (16.04)	388.60 ± 00.37 (37.42)	1134.95 ± 528.85 (236.72)
0.001	0.0005	0.3	3	74.82 ± 2.19 (0.35)	97.7 ±0.14 (0.26)	157.93 ± 35.81 (29.04)	442.04 ± 47.32 (50.18)	1214.24 ± 0.00 (0.00)

WD effect is mild on final accuracy (differences ~0.1–0.3%); sometimes 5×10^{-4} is a hair faster to *t*70, but it is not consistently decisive.

β_2 in the 0.1–0.3 band is a second-order knob with small swings. At 6×10^{-4}, 0.30 edges out on both final and speed; at 3×10^{-4}, the best final is at 0.20 (74.98%), but again within noise of 0.10/0.30.

https://doi.org/10.3390/electronics15030670

7. Ablations

To isolate which design choices driving AdamN's behavior, we run targeted ablations under the same CIFAR-100/ResNet-18/ViT-B16 setup (100 epochs, cosine LR schedule, and decoupled weight decay), with fixed seeds so all methods see the same sample order and stochastic augmentations. Unless noted, we change one factor at a time and keep the rest constant.

NLP task: We mirror each ablation in the LM setup (same model, tokenizer, BPTT, and frequency-bin protocol), and report head/mid/tail PPL alongside overall PPL and embedding effective-LR per bin.

Exact vs. Simple Debiasing: Replacing exact f_t with simple $(1-\beta_2^t)$ leaves inner-EMA bias and increases the cold start. At small β_2, the denominator absorbs much of the difference; at larger β_2, the gaps in instLR and time-to-milestones widen as seen in Table 19.

NLP: Exact f_t notably improves tail PPL vs. simple correction, especially in the low-resource setting; AdamN achieves better tail likelihoods without increasing tail effective LR.

Effective LR Diagnostics: We compute per-row effective LR on the embedding matrix and average within head/mid/tail bins. AdamN attains *lower tail PPL with smaller tail effective LR*, implying higher update quality per unit step due to the nested numerator and exact debiasing, rather than aggressive scaling.

Weight Decay: Decoupled WD is cleaner and more controllable than L2 in loss. For fast start runs, consider slightly lower WD early decay to avoid over-regularizing while still finding good directions. For later phase, we may raise WD (or to match AdamW defaults) to improve generalization and stability.

β_2 Scheduling: Start small (e.g., 0.1, 0.3) and increase to 0.6–0.8 by 20–40% epochs to preserve fast launch and stabilize later epochs. β_3 in [0.99, 0.999] is robust.

Warmup: AdamN uses *no warmup*; Adam/AdamW and SGD still benefit from a short warmup to avoid poor early scaling.

RQ4: What "makes" AdamN work? To tease apart the two ideas inside AdamN and show which one is doing the work, we ablated nested EMA and debiasing for AdamN across β_2-start ∈ {0.1, 0.2, 0.3, 0.8, 0.9, 0.95} at lr = 1×10^{-3}, wd = 1×10^{-4} on CIFAR-100 (ResNet-18) as seen in Table 21. At low β_2 (0.1–0.3), nested-on and nested-off deliver comparable test accuracy (74.3–75.2%), and exact vs. simple debiasing is second-order ($\leq$0.4%). However, with large β_2 ($\geq$0.8), nested-on collapses (72.8 $\rightarrow$ 69.2%), while nested-off remains ~74.4–74.9%. Time-to-milestones mirrors this: high-β_2 with nested-on substantially slows $t50/t60/t70$ and often fails to reach $t70$. Overall, the *best setting* in this regime is *nested-off with* $\beta_2 = 0.3$ (75.18%), suggesting that *shorter memory* is preferable at this LR/WD and that composing EMAs (nested) is only safe if β_2 is kept small.

Analysis of High-β_2 Degradation: Table 21 reveals that nested momentum ('nested-on') degrades significantly at $\beta_2 \geq 0.8$, with test accuracy dropping from 74.7% ($\beta_2 = 0.1$) to 69.2% ($\beta_2 = 0.95$). This degradation does not occur when nesting is disabled ('nested-off'), which maintains ~74.4% accuracy across all β_2 values.

The root cause is *compounded inertia*. At $\beta_2 = 0.95$:

Freshness = $(1-0.9)(1-0.95) = 0.005$, meaning only 0.5% of the current gradient enters the numerator directly.

The effective memory of the nested EMA spans ~20 steps ($1/(1-\beta_2)$), causing the update direction to lag significantly behind the loss landscape.

The bias correction factor f_t amplifies early steps aggressively, but the amplified direction is outdated, leading to inefficient or destabilizing updates.

Conversely, at $\beta_2 = 0.1$, freshness = 0.09 (9%), and effective memory is ~1.1 steps—close to AdamW's single-EMA behavior but with the benefits of exact debiasing.

https://doi.org/10.3390/electronics15030670

Practitioner Guidance: We strongly recommend $\beta_2 \in [0.1, 0.3]$ for most tasks. Values above 0.5 should be avoided unless the task specifically benefits from very long numerator memory (e.g., extremely noisy gradients). If high β_2 is desired for stability, consider disabling the nested structure (setting $a_t = v_t$) or using a β_2 ramp that starts low and increases gradually.

Table 21. Ablation: Time-to-VAL accuracy milestones (s) and final TEST accuracy.

LR_base	WD	β_2	Nested Momentum	Bias Correction	Final Test Acc	t50	t60	t70	t75
0.001	0.0001	0.1	Off	Exact	73.67	93.13	173.25	360.02	-
0.001	0.0001	0.1	Off	Simple	75.02	108.91	136.15	380.68	1182.53
(Default Run) 0.001	**0.0001**	**0.1**	**On**	**Exact**	**74.68**	**94.26**	**161.22**	**322.52**	**975.97**
0.001	0.0001	0.1	On	Simple	75.09	93.2	173.35	333.35	1080.7
0.001	0.0001	0.2	Off	Exact	74.54	93.47	133.49	306.99	1013.15
0.001	0.0001	0.2	Off	Simple	74.66	81.69	163.82	341.05	-
0.001	0.0001	0.2	On	Exact	74.3	106.65	174.09	348.34	-
0.001	0.0001	0.2	On	Simple	74.63	94.19	160.75	387.31	-
0.001	0.0001	0.3	Off	Exact	75.18	93.55	173.16	333.73	-
0.001	0.0001	0.3	Off	Simple	74.76	95.47	136.23	354.4	1007.66
0.001	0.0001	0.3	On	Exact	74.7	92.97	160.04	385.72	891.48
0.001	0.0001	0.3	On	Simple	74.46	94.26	161.3	376.28	-
0.001	0.0001	0.8	Off	Exact	74.82	95.3	177.35	370.04	-
0.001	0.0001	0.8	Off	Simple	74.94	95.22	164.17	368.26	-
0.001	0.0001	0.8	On	Exact	72.78	174.74	254.45	533.15	-
0.001	0.0001	0.8	On	Simple	73.64	148.08	228.48	497.27	-
0.001	0.0001	0.9	Off	Exact	74.41	82.58	164.34	368.94	-
0.001	0.0001	0.9	Off	Simple	74.62	95.04	163.26	367.85	1021.13
0.001	0.0001	0.9	On	Exact	71.39	200.79	281.25	708.76	-
0.001	0.0001	0.9	On	Simple	71.63	214.79	321.9	764.14	-
0.001	0.0001	0.95	Off	Exact	74.41	81.85	163.35	313.31	-
0.001	0.0001	0.95	Off	Simple	74.47	95.68	136.71	396.72	-
0.001	0.0001	0.95	On	Exact	69.17	268.71	389.02	-	-
0.001	0.0001	0.95	On	Simple	71.03	240.75	360.5	800.89	-

8. Discussion, Limitations, and Reproducibility

Where does the new proposed optimizer AdamN shine? Early-phase speed at stable scale on noisy/ill-conditioned problems, less reliance on bespoke warmups, and scheduler-friendliness.

In NLP with class imbalance, AdamN consistently improved tail (rare-token) perplexity under two regimes: (i) full data with corrupted training tokens to amplify sparsity and (ii) low-resource (10% training split). In both cases, AdamN achieved lower tail PPL with smaller effective LR on rare embedding's, indicating more efficient updates (better likelihood gain per unit step) rather than simply larger steps. Head/mid tokens were comparable to AdamW.

Non-stationarity considerations: While our bias correction is derived under stationary gradient assumptions, real training involves highly non-stationary gradients. The factor $f_t(\beta_1, \beta_2)$ is designed to correct zero-initialization bias rather than gradient drift; its effectiveness in practice (demonstrated across vision, NLP, and synthetic tasks) suggests robustness to non-stationarity. Future theoretical work could analyze convergence guarantees under specific non-stationary gradient models.

Energy and cost implications: AdamN's faster time-to-milestones translates directly to reduced resource consumption. On CIFAR-100/ResNet-18 (Table 17), reaching 80%

 https://doi.org/10.3390/electronics15030670

validation accuracy required 437s for AdamN vs. 564s for AdamW—a 22% reduction in wall-clock time. Assuming a typical GPU power draw of 250W, this corresponds to approximately 8.8 Wh saved per training run. Across hyperparameter sweeps (54 configurations in our search), cumulative savings exceed 475 Wh—meaningful for large-scale experimentation. The elimination of warmup schedules also reduces pipeline complexity and failed runs due to misconfigured warmup periods.

Hyperparameter complexity: AdamN introduces β_2 (nested momentum coefficient) as a new hyperparameter, while repurposing β_3 for the second-moment EMA (equivalent to Adam's β_2). This increases the nominal hyperparameter count from two (Adam: β_1 and β_2) to three (AdamN: β_1, β_2, and β_3).

We mitigate this complexity through strong defaults:

- $\beta_1 = 0.9$ (unchanged from Adam);
- $\beta_2 = 0.1$ (new; robust across tasks);
- $\beta_3 = 0.999$ (identical to Adam's β_2).

In practice, users can adopt AdamN as a drop-in replacement for AdamW using these defaults, adjusting only the learning rate and weight decay as they would for any optimizer. The β_2 parameter becomes relevant only for advanced tuning or when early-phase speed is critical.

Furthermore, AdamN's warmup-free operation eliminates the need to tune warmup-related hyperparameters (warmup steps and warmup schedule type), which are often required for stable AdamW training. This trade-off may reduce net tuning complexity in practice.

AdamN's limits: *Sensitivity to β_2*. AdamN's nested momentum is effective only within a recommended range ($\beta_2 \in [0.1, 0.3]$). At high β_2 ($\geq$0.8), compounded smoothing creates excessive inertia, degrading both convergence speed and final accuracy (Table 19). This sensitivity is a meaningful limitation: users must either (a) stay within the safe range, (b) disable nesting for high-β_2 configurations, or (c) employ a β_2 schedule. We view this as an acceptable trade-off given the strong performance within the recommended range and AdamN's robustness to other hyperparameters (LR and WD).

We often see that the small β_2 acts as a bridle: just enough smoothing to stabilize direction, not so much to dull responsiveness.

This is not a paradox of "smaller step = faster learning"; it is **better directionality**. In our notation (19), the effective gain on the fresh gradient scales as follows:

$$\widehat{w}_{t,t} = \frac{(1-\beta_1)(1-\beta_2)}{f_t(\beta_1, \beta_2)}.\text{(biascorrected)}$$

Thus, pushing $\boldsymbol{\beta_2}$ high (especially with nested EMA) shrinks $\hat{w}_{t,t}$ and **lags** the update—steps become "polite but late." With **small $\boldsymbol{\beta_2}$ (≈0.1–0.3)**, we still denoise the numerator enough to avoid jitter, yet the gain on the new signal remains high, giving **crisp, well-aimed** moves. That is why we see faster $t50/t60/t70$ and higher ceilings without overshoot.

Reproducibility checklist: Report: (i) architecture, (ii) epochs, (iii) batch size, (iv) LR schedule, (v) $\beta_1, \beta_2, \beta_3, \epsilon$, (vi) WD and its schedule, (vii) gradient clipping, (viii) AMP settings, (ix) hardware, and (x) seed and data augmentations. Save best-val and last-epoch checkpoints; log milestones (50/70/80/90% train/val) with wall-clock.

NLP-specific: tokenizer and casing rules; vocabulary construction split (train-only), BPTT length, corruption/noise settings (if any), and head/mid/tail binning rule (percentile cuts on training frequencies). Save best-val and last-epoch checkpoints; log milestones (e.g., PPL thresholds or accuracy levels) with wall-clock.

https://doi.org/10.3390/electronics15030670

9. Conclusions

AdamN adds a principled momentum-of-momentum to the numerator and corrects its combined cold-start bias exactly. This yields a smooth long-memory direction paired with adaptive braking, enabling a fast, warmup-free launch at an Adam-like cost. On CIFAR-100 (main benchmark) and CIFAR-10 (pre-benchmark), AdamN reaches accuracy milestones sooner while matching final accuracy; MNIST/EMNIST show similar patterns.

AdamN's advantage is not aggressive inertia or huge instLR. Its nested numerator and bias correction produce more reliable, noise-robust estimates of the search direction's scale, so it tends to take calibrated steps that avoid intermediate overshoot while still moving fast. So, the net effect is calibrated step sizes, not "bigger" step sizes.

AdamN narrows the gap between standard first-order and costly second-order methods. By combining a nested, exactly debiased numerator (long-memory, noise-reduced direction) with Adam-style per-coordinate scaling, AdamN achieves a richer diagonal preconditioning effect that improves stability and early progress at first-order cost. Unlike true second-order optimizers, AdamN does not estimate or invert the Hessian (and thus cannot capture cross-parameter curvature), but empirically it recovers a substantial portion of the practical benefits that make second order attractive.

NLP result: In a word-level transformer on a Wikitext-2-style corpus (with a rare-token stress via training-only corruption and a 10% low-resource variant), AdamN reduced tail perplexity compared to AdamW while using smaller effective learning rates for rare tokens, consistent with more efficient rare-token learning.

Given its simplicity and compatibility (cosine schedules and decoupled WD), AdamN is a compelling default when early progress and stable scaling matter.

9.1. Practical Recommendations

Based on our extensive experiments across vision (CIFAR-10/100, MNIST, EMNIST, and ViT-B/16), NLP (Wikitext-2 and Llama 3.1-8B), and synthetic benchmarks (Rosenbrock), we offer the following guidance for practitioners in Table 22:

Table 22. Practical recommendations.

Parameter	Recommended Value	Safe Range	Notes
β_1	0.9	[0.85, 0.95]	Same as Adam; controls first EMA memory
$\boldsymbol{\beta_2}$	**0.1**	**[0.1, 0.3]**	**Critical: Avoid values $\geq$ 0.5**
β_3	0.999	[0.99, 0.999]	Same as Adam's β_2; controls denominator
ε	1×10^{-8}	$[1 \times 10^{-8}, 1 \times 10^{-6}]$	Standard stabilizer
LR	Task-dependent	—	Start with AdamW's tuned value
WD	1×10^{-4}	$[1 \times 10^{-5}, 5 \times 10^{-4}]$	Decoupled; task-dependent

Why $\boldsymbol{\beta_2} \in$ [0.1, 0.3]: Values in this range maintain sufficient *freshness* (5–9% of current gradient passes through directly) while providing meaningful smoothing. Higher values create compounded inertia that degrades both speed and final accuracy (see Section 7, Table 19).

When to adjust β_2:

- Noisy gradients (small batches and high augmentation): Consider β_2 = 0.2–0.3 for additional smoothing.
- Clean gradients (large batches and simple tasks): β_2 = 0.1 is optimal.
- Never use $\beta_2 \geq 0.5$ with nested momentum enabled.

https://doi.org/10.3390/electronics15030670

Drop-in usage: For most users, simply replace *AdamW* with *AdamN* using the defaults above and remove any warmup schedule. No other changes are required.

9.2. When to Use AdamN—Decision Guidelines

The most beneficial recommendation for AdamN are listed below in Tables 23 and 24:

Table 23. When AdamN is most beneficial.

Scenario	Benefit	Recommendation
Hyperparameter search	Faster iteration cycles	Use AdamN with defaults
Early stopping workflows	Faster time-to-threshold	Strong fit
Large-batch training	Stable without warmup	Good fit
Warmup-sensitive tasks	Eliminates tuning burden	Strong fit
Fine-tuning pre-trained models	Fast adaptation	Strong fit

Table 24. When AdamN may not be optimal.

Scenario	Issue	Alternative
Maximum final accuracy priority	SGD often generalizes better	Use SGD with long schedule
Very noisy gradients (batch < 16)	May need higher β_2	Consider $\beta_2 = 0.2$–0.3
Memory-constrained settings	+1 buffer vs. Adam	Use Adam or Lion
Extremely long training (>500 epochs)	Diminishing speedup advantage	Any optimizer works

10. Patent Disclosure

The methods and systems described in this work have been disclosed in a provisional patent application filed with the United States Patent and Trademark Office (USPTO). The application, titled "Nested Double-Smoothing Optimizer For Training Neural Networks," was filed by the authors' institution under Application No. **63/942,313**. The filing covers the core algorithmic framework, bias-correction mechanisms, and system-level implementations described in this paper.

Author Contributions: Conceptualization, M.A.; Methodology, M.A. and A.S.; Software, M.A.; Validation, M.A. and A.S.; Formal analysis, M.A.; Investigation, A.S.; Resources, A.S.; Writing—original draft, M.A. and A.S.; Writing—review & editing, M.A. and A.S.; Supervision, A.S. All authors have read and agreed to the published version of the manuscript.

Funding: This research received no external funding.

Data Availability Statement: The original contributions presented in this study are included in the article. Further inquiries can be directed to the corresponding author.

Conflicts of Interest: The authors declare no conflict of interest.

References

1. Polyak, B.T. Some methods of speeding up the convergence of iteration methods. *USSR Comput. Math. Math. Phys.* **1964**, *4*, 1–17.
2. Sutskever, I.; Martens, J.; Dahl, G.; Hinton, G. On the importance of initialization and momentum in deep learning. In Proceedings of the 30th International Conference on International Conference on Machine Learning, Atlanta, GA, USA, 16–21 June 2013; pp. 1139–1147.
3. Tieleman, T.; Hinton, G. Lecture 6.5-RMSProp: Divide the gradient by a running average of its recent magnitude. *COURSERA: Neural Netw. Mach. Learn.* **2012**, *4*, 26.
4. Zeiler, M.D. ADADELTA: An adaptive learning rate method. *arXiv* **2012**, arXiv:1212.5701. [CrossRef]
5. Kingma, P.; Ba, J. Adam: A method for stochastic optimization. In Proceedings of the International Conference on Learning Representations, San Diego, CA, USA, 7–9 May 2015.

 https://doi.org/10.3390/electronics15030670

6. Reddi, S.J.; Kale, S.; Kumar, S. On the convergence of Adam and beyond. In Proceedings of the International Conference on Learning Representations, Vancouver, BC, Canada, 30 April–3 May 2018.
7. Loshchilov, I.; Hutter, F. Decoupled weight decay regularization. In Proceedings of the International Conference on Learning Representations, New Orleans, LA, USA, 6–9 May 2019.
8. Bottou, L.; Curtis, F.E.; Nocedal, J. Optimization methods for large-scale machine learning. *SIAM Rev.* **2018**, *60*, 223–311. [CrossRef]
9. Cauchy, A.-L. Méthode générale pour la résolution des systèmes d'équations simultanées. *Comptes Rendus Académie Sci.* **1847**, *25*, 536–538.
10. Newton, I. *Method of Fluxions*; Henry Woodfall: London, UK, 1736.
11. Broyden, G. The convergence of a class of double-rank minimization algorithms. *J. Inst. Math. Its Appl.* **1970**, *6*, 76–90. [CrossRef]
12. Fletcher, R. A new approach to variable metric algorithms. *Comput. J.* **1970**, *13*, 317–322. [CrossRef]
13. Shanno, F. Conditioning of quasi-Newton methods for function minimization. *Math. Comput.* **1970**, *24*, 647–656. [CrossRef]
14. Gauss, F. Über ein neues allgemeines Grundgesetz der Mechanik. *J. Reine Angew. Math.* **1829**, *4*, 232–235.
15. Ortega, M.; Rheinboldt, W.C. *Iterative Solution of Nonlinear Equations in Several Variables*; Academic Press: Cambridge, MA, USA, 1970.
16. Hestenes, M.R.; Stiefel, E. Methods of conjugate gradients for solving linear systems. *J. Res. Natl. Bur. Stand.* **1952**, *49*, 409–436. [CrossRef]
17. Robbins, H.; Monro, S. A stochastic approximation method. *Ann. Math. Stat.* **1951**, *22*, 400–407. [CrossRef]
18. Nesterov, Y. A method for solving the convex programming problem with a convergence rate of $O(1/k^2)$. *Sov. Math. Dokl.* **1983**, *27*, 372–376.
19. Duchi, J.; Hazan, E.; Singer, Y. Adaptive subgradient methods for online learning and stochastic optimization. *J. Mach. Learn. Res.* **2011**, *12*, 2121–2159.
20. Zhuang, J.; Tang, T.; Ding, Y.; Tatikonda, S.; Dvornek, N.; Papademetris, X.; Duncan, J.S. AdaBelief Optimizer: Adapting Stepsizes by the Belief in Observed Gradients. In Proceedings of the 34th Conference on Neural Information Processing Systems, Vancouver, BC, Canada, 6–12 December 2020.
21. Foret, P.; Kleiner, A.; Mobahi, H.; Neyshabur, B. Sharpness-Aware Minimization for Efficiently Improving Generalization. In Proceedings of the International Conference on Learning Representations, Virtual, 3–7 May 2021.
22. Kwon, J.; Kim, J.; Park, H.; Choi, I.K. ASAM: Adaptive Sharpness-Aware Minimization for Scale-Invariant Learning of Deep Neural Networks. *arXiv* **2021**, arXiv:2102.11600.
23. Anil, R.; Gupta, V.; Koren, T.; Singer, Y. Scalable Second Order Optimization for Deep Learning. In Proceedings of the International Conference on Machine Learning, Virtual, 18–24 July 2021.
24. Heo, B.; Yun, S.; Han, J.; Yoon, S. AdamP: Slowing Down the Slowdown for Momentum Optimizers on Scale-Invariant Weights. In Proceedings of the International Conference on Learning Representations, Virtual, 3–7 May 2021.
25. Xie, X.; Wang, Z.; Zhang, S.; Gu, Q.; Lin, Z. Adan: Adaptive Nesterov Momentum Algorithm for Faster Optimizing Deep Models. In Proceedings of the International Conference on Learning Representations, Kigali, Rwanda, 1–5 May 2023.
26. Defazio, A.; Mishchenko, K. Learning-Rate-Free Learning by D-Adaptation. In Proceedings of the 40th International Conference on Machine Learning (ICML 2023), Honolulu, HI, USA, 23–29 July 2023.
27. Liu, H.; Li, Z.; Hall, D.; Liang, P.; Ma, T. Sophia: A Scalable Stochastic Second-Order Optimizer for Language Model Pre-Training. *arXiv* **2023**, arXiv:2305.14342.
28. Chen, X.; Liang, C.; Huang, D.; Real, E.; Wang, K.; Liu, Y.; Pham, H.; Dong, X.; Luong, T.; Hsieh, C.-J.; et al. Symbolic Discovery of Optimization Algorithms. *arXiv* **2023**, arXiv:2302.06675. [CrossRef]
29. Keskar, N.S.; Mudigere, D.; Nocedal, J.; Smelyanskiy, M.; Tang, P.T.P. On large-batch training for deep learning: Generalization gap and sharp minima. In Proceedings of the International Conference on Learning Representations, Toulon, France, 24–26 April 2017.
30. Goyal, P.; Dollár, P.; Girshick, R.; Noordhuis, P.; Wesolowski, L.; Kyrola, A.; Tulloch, A.; Jia, Y.; He, K. Accurate, large minibatch SGD: Training ImageNet in 1 hour. *arXiv* **2017**, arXiv:1706.02677.
31. You, Y.; Li, J.; Reddi, S.J.; Hseu, J.; Kumar, S.; Bhojanapalli, S.; Song, X.; Demmel, J.; Keutzer, K.; Hsieh, C.-J.; et al. Large Batch Optimization for Deep Learning: Training BERT in 76 Minutes. In Proceedings of the Conference on Neural Information Processing Systems (NeurIPS 2019), Vancouver, BC, Canada, 8–14 December 2019.

 https://doi.org/10.3390/electronics15030670

electronics

MDPI

Article

A General-Purpose AXI Plug-and-Play Hyperdimensional Computing Accelerator

Rocco Martino *, Marco Pisani, Marco Angioli, Marcello Barbirotta, Antonio Mastrandrea, Antonello Rosato and Mauro Olivieri

Department of Information Engineering, Electronics and Telecommunications (DIET), Sapienza University of Rome, 00184 Rome, Italy; marco.pisani@uniroma1.it (M.P.); marco.angioli@uniroma1.it (M.A.); marcello.barbirotta@uniroma1.it (M.B.); antonio.mastrandrea@uniroma1.it (A.M.); antonello.rosato@uniroma1.it (A.R.); mauro.olivieri@uniroma1.it (M.O.)

* Correspondence: rocco.martino@uniroma1.it

Abstract

Hyperdimensional Computing (HDC) offers a robust and energy-efficient paradigm for edge intelligence; however, current hardware accelerators are often proprietary, tailored to the target learning task and tightly coupled to specific CPU microarchitectures, limiting portability and adoption. To address this, and democratize the deployment of HDC hardware, we present a general-purpose, plug-and-play accelerator IP that implements the Binary Spatter Code framework as a standalone, host-agnostic module. The design is compliant with the AMBA AXI4 standard and provides an AXI4-Lite control plane and DMA-driven AXI4-Stream datapaths coupled to a banked scratchpad memory. The architecture supports synthesis-time scalability, enabling high-throughput transfers independently of the host processor, while employing microarchitectural optimizations to minimize silicon area. A multi-layer C++ software (GitHub repository commit `3ae3b46`) stack running in Linux userspace provides a unified programming model, abstracting low-level hardware interactions and enabling the composition of complex HDC pipelines. Implemented on a Xilinx Zynq XC7Z020 SoC, the accelerator achieves substantial gains over an ARM Cortex-A9 baseline, with primitive-level speedups of up to 431×. On end-to-end classification benchmarks, the system delivers average speedups of 68.45× for training and 93.34× for inference. The complete RTL and software stack are released as open-source hardware to support reproducible research and rapid adoption on heterogeneous SoCs.

Keywords: hyperdimensional computing; FPGA acceleration; edge Intelligence; AXI4 interface; open source hardware; binary spatter code

1. Introduction

Hyperdimensional Computing (HDC), also known as Vector Symbolic Architecture (VSA), is a family of neuro-inspired computing paradigms that originates at the intersection of symbolic Artificial Intelligence (AI) and distributed connectionist representations[1,2]. HDC/VSA encodes information using high-dimensional vectors, denoted as hypervectors (HVs), where information is distributed across all components rather than localized to specific elements [1]. At the core of this paradigm is the principle that independent concepts can be assigned random HVs that, by virtue of concentration effects in high-dimensional spaces, are (with high probability) quasi-orthogonal [3]. This property yields vast symbol spaces and enables the representation of an exponential number of distinct concepts for a given dimensionality. HVs can then be composed using simple vector operations—bundling, binding and permutation—and queried via a similarity measure, supporting compact representations of structured information and enabling a wide range of cognitive and learning tasks [4].

This high-dimensional, holistic representation endows HDC/VSA with several favorable properties, including robustness to noise and hardware faults, few-shot learning capability, computational and energy efficiency, and massive data parallelism [3,5]. These properties make HDC/VSA particularly attractive for resource-constrained embedded systems and efficient hardware implementations, motivating substantial interest in hardware-aware HDC/VSA formulations and accelerators for edge intelligence [6,7].

Numerous HDC/VSA models have been proposed in the literature. All these models share the same basic principles but differ in the HV element data type and in how the core arithmetic operations are implemented [5]. Among them, Binary Spatter Codes (BSC) [8], which use dense binary HVs and simple Boolean arithmetic, offer an attractive trade-off between representational capacity and implementation complexity [9]. They have been shown to enable aggressive hardware optimizations while preserving competitive accuracy across many workloads [4,10].

For these reasons, many prior works have proposed hardware implementations of BSC [11–24]. However, these architectures have seen limited adoption within the broader research community. The primary barrier is not merely architectural flexibility, but accessibility and usability: many state-of-the-art accelerators are proprietary, architecturally rigid or lack standard control interfaces. Consequently, they remain effectively siloed within the hardware design domain and are inaccessible to software developers or data scientists. For instance, many designs are synthesized for fixed model structures or single tasks, requiring complete FPGA re-synthesis for minor application changes [15,25]. Similarly, instruction-set-based approaches [13,20], while programmable, often rely on tight coupling with specific processors, hindering integration into the vast ecosystem of System-on-Chips (SoCs) based on ARM or proprietary processing subsystems.

To bridge the gap between highly specialized accelerators and general-purpose software usability, this paper introduces a General-Purpose AXI Plug-and-Play HDC Accelerator. Unlike previous tightly-coupled designs, this architecture is implemented as a standalone open-source hardware module compliant with the AMBA AXI4 standard, ensuring host-agnosticism and seamless integration into diverse SoC environments. The accelerator natively supports the complete set of BSC primitives and features a configurable dedicated memory, alongside a scalable and synthesis/run-time configurable microarchitecture. The main contributions of this work are as follows:

- **Host-Agnostic Architecture Evolution:** Advancing our previous instruction-set based approach [20], we propose a modular BSC accelerator. Implemented as a standalone hardware unit compliant with the AXI4 standard, it decouples execution from specific processors, enabling seamless integration into diverse SoC environments.
- **Optimized Compute Datapaths:** We introduce targeted microarchitectural optimizations for two area-critical BSC primitives, significantly reducing resource utilization compared to our previous instruction-set based approach [20], while preserving throughput.
- **High-Level Software Abstraction:** We introduce a C++ software library that abstracts low-level hardware interactions. This layer enables developers to invoke accelerated HDC primitives and construct complex pipelines through high-level function calls, bridging the gap between hardware acceleration and software usability.

https://doi.org/10.3390/electronics15020489

- **Extensive Validation:** We validate the design on an AMD Zynq-7000 SoC (XC7Z020, AMD Xilinx, San Jose, CA, USA) hosted on a Zybo Z7-20 board (Digilent Inc., Pullman, WA, USA), benchmarking its performance against a software baseline executed on the embedded dual-core ARM Cortex-A9 processor (Arm Ltd., Cambridge, UK). The analysis quantifies latency and throughput improvements across both elementary HDC operations and complete classification workloads.

To support adoption and lower the barrier to entry for hardware-accelerated HDC research, we release the complete Register Transfer Level (RTL) code, testbenches and software stack as an open-source repository [26].

2. Background and Related Works

2.1. Binary Spatter Code

In BSC [8], each HV is a dense binary vector of dimensionality D, denoted as $\mathbf{h} \in \{0,1\}^D$, where D is typically in the order of thousands, so that randomly generated HVs are quasi-orthogonal with high probability. Computation relies on a small set of elementary vector operations—bundling, binding, and permutation—together with a similarity measure that quantifies how close two HVs are in high-dimensional space and is used for retrieval and recognition. In the following, $\mathbf{h}$ and $\mathbf{g}$ denote two generic hypervectors in $\{0,1\}^D$.

Bundling ($\oplus$), or superposition, combines multiple HVs into a single composite representation that remains similar to its inputs. Given a set of K HVs $\{\mathbf{h}_1, \ldots, \mathbf{h}_K\}$, BSC bundling is performed by element-wise accumulation:

$$\mathbf{s} = \sum_{k=1}^{K} \mathbf{h}_k. \tag{1}$$

Since the resulting vector is no longer binary, a clipping operation is applied to project the representation back into its original domain. In BSC, clipping is implemented via an element-wise majority vote, where ties are broken randomly:

$$[\mathbf{h}_{\text{bun}}]_i = \begin{cases} 1, & \text{if } s_i > \frac{K}{2}, \\ 0, & \text{if } s_i < \frac{K}{2}, \\ \text{rand}\{0,1\}, & \text{if } s_i = \frac{K}{2}, \end{cases} \qquad i = 1, \ldots, D. \tag{2}$$

Binding ($\otimes$) associates two (or more) HVs into a single HV that is dissimilar to its inputs, enabling the representation of key–value pairs and other structured relations. In BSC, binding is implemented as bit-wise XOR and is invertible:

$$\mathbf{h}_{\text{bind}} = \mathbf{h} \otimes \mathbf{g}, \qquad \mathbf{h} = \mathbf{h}_{\text{bind}} \otimes \mathbf{g}. \tag{3}$$

Permutation (ρ) reorders the components of an HV, producing a dissimilar HV, and is commonly used to encode order or positional information. In BSC, permutation is typically implemented as a cyclic right shift.

Finally, similarity (δ) captures how closely two HVs match in the high-dimensional space and supports retrieval, matching, and classification. In BSC, it is commonly evaluated through the Hamming distance:

$$\delta(\mathbf{h}, \mathbf{g}) = d_H(\mathbf{h}, \mathbf{g}) = \sum_{i=1}^{D} (h_i \operatorname{xor} g_i), \tag{4}$$

https://doi.org/10.3390/electronics15020489

often normalized as $\hat{\delta} = d_H/D \in [0,1]$.

With these operators, a wide range of objects and their relationships can be encoded and manipulated in the high-dimensional space without increasing dimensionality, supporting both logical reasoning and learning tasks [4,27].

2.2. Related Works

The hardware-acceleration landscape for HDC/VSA spans a wide spectrum of solutions, ranging from highly optimized, task-tailored datapaths to programmable engines that expose HDC/VSA primitives to software. The existing literature can be broadly categorized into: (i) *application-specific accelerators* (fixed-function or domain-tuned datapaths), (ii) *HLS-generated accelerators* (high-level synthesis designs mapped from C/C++/OpenCL) and (iii) *programmable HDC/VSA substrates* (Instruction Set Architecture (ISA) extensions, processor-coupled co-processors or reconfigurable overlays). Across these categories, two recurring limitations emerge: (i) most solutions remain *application- or configuration-specific* (e.g., a fixed learning pipeline, dimensionality D or memory organization) and (ii) only a small subset of designs are released as *open artifacts*, which hinders reuse and reproducibility in custom SoC contexts. Recent surveys further highlight both the rapid progress of HDC for edge intelligence and the fragmentation of available hardware/software artifacts across platforms and toolflows [6].

This limited availability of public artifacts is also observed in adjacent HDC application domains. For instance, a recent review [28] on biomedical HDC studies reports that only 12 out of 62 papers (19.35%) provide publicly available software code, whereas 50 out of 62 (80.65%) do not, and that 35 out of 62 articles are not freely accessible. Although the survey targets biomedical applications, these figures reinforce the broader concern that the lack of openly available artifacts hinders reproducibility and slows technology transfer to real systems.

2.2.1. Task-Specific and Optimization-Driven Architectures

A large body of work maximizes throughput and energy efficiency by specializing the hardware around a fixed HDC pipeline and a narrow configuration space (often a fixed D and encoding scheme). Hardware optimizations for dense binary HDC, including rematerialization of hypervectors, binarized bundling and in-memory computing, are systematically studied in [10] and represent a canonical example of efficiency gains enabled by BSC representations. HD-Core [21], for example, proposes an FPGA accelerator that improves the efficiency of both encoding and associative search by exploiting *computational reuse* in the HDC flow, reducing redundant operations in similarity evaluation. Tiny-HD [11] and the standard-cell memory-based always-on accelerator in [12] similarly pursue aggressive area–power–delay (APD) optimizations for embedded sensing, at the cost of a constrained and largely fixed execution flow. Locality-based encoding and model quantization techniques are explored in [9] to reduce memory/compute pressure while maintaining accuracy, and GENERIC [19] further pushes end-to-end efficiency for edge learning engines by tailoring the pipeline to the target workload.

QuantHD [16] focuses on *model/representation quantization* to reduce arithmetic and storage costs while maintaining competitive accuracy, enabling more resource-efficient implementations. In edge settings where on-chip memory pressure dominates, E3HDC [23] targets the encoder front-end and regenerates item-memory patterns on-the-fly (e.g., via lightweight pseudo-random generators such as linear feedback shift registers), substantially reducing the need for large stored seed memories. Beyond classification, task-tailored accelerators also emerge in other domains, such as genomic pattern matching, where

https://doi.org/10.3390/electronics15020489

GenieHD [18] demonstrates the suitability of HDC primitives to high-throughput, data-intensive search pipelines.

A complementary direction optimizes the *numeric representation* and storage precision of HDC models. AdaptBit-HD [22] explores *adaptive model bitwidth* to trade accuracy for area/energy, while FATE [24] proposes flexible data types to improve performance/efficiency across workloads. These approaches can yield excellent APD results, but typically preserve the core constraint of fixed datapath and memory organization determined at synthesis/compile time, limiting portability across diverse HDC pipelines and multi-tenant scenarios.

2.2.2. High-Level Synthesis and Hardware-Generation Frameworks

To reduce the engineering effort of handcrafted register-transfer level (RTL) design, several works provide automation frameworks that translate high-level HDC specifications into FPGA implementations. F5-HD [15] automatically generates designs using high-level synthesis by taking as input application characteristics and hardware constraints, while HD2FPGA [25] offers a graphical user interface-driven flow that can produce accelerators for both HDC classification and clustering. AeneasHDC [29] further promotes end-to-end deployment by coupling software and hardware generation in an open-source environment. Despite their practical value, these approaches predominantly deliver *compile-time flexibility*: once a bitstream is synthesized, the resulting accelerator remains largely static, and adapting to a new HV size, encoder or learning task typically requires regeneration and re-synthesis.

2.2.3. Programmable Accelerators and ISA Extensions

A more general-purpose direction is to expose HDC operations through a programmable interface, shifting part of the control and algorithmic flexibility to software while keeping the dominant HDC primitives in hardware. GP-HDCA [30] follows this trend with a general-purpose accelerator for edge computing.

A representative example of a *CPU–accelerator co-processing* approach is EcoFlex-HDP [31], which couples a minimal hyperdimensional processing unit (HPU) to an ARM Cortex-A9 host on Zynq-7000. EcoFlex-HDP is explicitly designed to be *programmable* at the algorithm level by composing a small instruction set covering the three core BSC primitives (Bind/XOR, Permutation/circular shifts and Bound/majority via counters) and by providing a dedicated software stack (library + assembler) that abstracts HPU control from the CPU side. Communication and bulk transfers are handled through memory-mapped control and direct memory access (DMA), using AXI4-Lite/AXI4-Stream connectivity, enabling tight integration with existing software while keeping HDC-heavy kernels offloaded to the HPU. Notably, EcoFlex-HDP releases its platform and experimental code publicly, which is still uncommon in this research space.

FLHDC [17] instead couples a learnable HDC pipeline with an ultra-tiny accelerator to target edge-side workloads, prioritizing compactness and end-to-end deployment.

The tightest coupling is achieved via ISA extensions. RISC-HD [13] integrates selected HDC operations into a RISC-V core microarchitecture to accelerate inference, but remains constrained by fixed architectural assumptions (notably around the supported flow and dimensionality). Our previous Hyperdimensional Coprocessor Unit (HDCU) [20] extends this concept by exposing a richer set of HDC primitives to software (covering training and inference operations), but it also inherits the fundamental drawback of ISA-coupled accelerators: portability is limited by the dependency on a specific core interface and toolchain assumptions.

Table 1 highlights the main gap addressed in this work: although prior HDC accelerators achieve impressive efficiency, only a small subset simultaneously offers (i) *runtime programmability at the primitive level*, (ii) *host-agnostic integration as a standard SoC periph-*

 https://doi.org/10.3390/electronics15020489

eral and (iii) *openly released hardware/software artifacts* that enable reuse and reproducibility. Our design targets this intersection by providing a plug-and-play AXI accelerator that preserves fine-grained control over HDC primitives while decoupling the accelerator from any specific processor microarchitecture or toolchain.

Table 1. Representative HDC hardware acceleration approaches, emphasizing (i) the abstraction exposed to software, (ii) retargeting effort across workloads and (iii) openness of hardware/software artifacts. Retargeting: **Fixed** (redesign typically needed), **Gen.** (tool/HLS-generated per workload at synthesis time), **Runtime** (reprogrammed via instructions/registers). Open artifacts: **Yes** indicates that both HW and SW artifacts are publicly available. "n/s" = not stated/unclear in public artifacts at the time of writing.

Work	Substrate	Exposed Abstraction	Retargeting	Open Artifacts
HD-Core [21]	FPGA	Fixed-function datapath	Fixed	n/s
F5-HD [15]	FPGA	Template/HLS accelerator generator	Gen.	n/s
HD2FPGA [25]	FPGA	Automated generator for CPU-attached accelerators	Gen.	n/s
AeneasHDC [29]	FPGA	Open automated deployment framework	Gen.	Yes
E3HDC [23]	FPGA	End-to-end open toolflow + pipeline	Gen.	Yes
LAHDC [14]	ASIC/FPGA	Task-specific query accelerator + generator	Gen.	n/s
GP-HDCA [30]	FPGA SoC	Instruction-driven accelerator (MMIO + streams)	Runtime	n/s
EcoFlex-HDP [31]	FPGA SoC	Programmable platform (HDC primitive set)	Runtime	Yes
RISC-HD [13]	RISC-V	Lightweight processor/ISA support for inference	Runtime	n/s
HDCU [20]	RISC-V	ISA extension + coprocessor	Runtime	Yes
This Work	FPGA SoC	Host-agnostic AXI Unit (MMIO + SPM offload)	Runtime	Yes

2.2.4. The HDCU Microarchitecture

Before presenting the proposed standalone accelerator, we briefly revisit HDCU [20] on which our work builds. HDCU represents a tightly-coupled approach to HDC acceleration based on custom instructions integrated into a RISC-V core. Summarizing its organization and programming model is useful for two reasons: (i) several design choices (e.g., scratchpad-based execution and runtime-controlled hardware loops) directly inspire parts of the new IP and (ii) the integration constraints of ISA-coupled coprocessors motivate the architectural shift toward a fully standalone, plug-and-play AXI module.

RISC-V Core Integration

HDCU is embedded into the execution stage of the Klessydra-T03 32-bit RISC-V core [32], operating alongside the scalar pipeline resources (e.g., ALU/LSU). Integration is achieved through core-level RTL modifications: HDC instructions are decoded by the core and dispatched to the coprocessor when the accelerator is available, while results are committed according to the instruction semantics. This tight coupling minimizes dispatch latency and avoids bus transactions for intermediate results, which is particularly beneficial for iterative HDC kernels.

Control is provided by a custom RISC-V instruction set extension (ISE) mapping the primitive HDC operators for BSC HVs, including memory transfers (`hvmemld/hvmemstr`), binding (`hvbind`), bundling (`hvbundle`) and clipping (`hvclip`), permutation (`hvperm`), similarity (`hvsim`) and an inference-oriented associative search primitive (`hvsearch`). Importantly, this form of customization is enabled by the open and modular nature of the RISC-V ISA standard, which explicitly allows designers to introduce domain-specific extensions while preserving compatibility with the base ISA and standard toolchains. The ISE follows a standard R-type encoding: the opcode selects the HDC extension space, `funct3` encodes the datatype (binary in the reference implementation, with forward-looking support for additional types) and `funct7` selects the operation. Instruction encodings are integrated

https://doi.org/10.3390/electronics15020489

into the RISC-V GNU toolchain and exposed via C intrinsics, enabling compiler-level optimizations while keeping the programming interface accessible.

To reduce pressure on the load/store subsystem during iterative kernels, HDCU operates on HVs stored in dedicated multi-bank scratchpad memories (SPMs). The number of banks and the per-bank capacity are configurable at synthesis time, enabling a trade-off between on-chip memory footprint and area. HVs are moved between main memory and SPMs through the scratchpad memory interface (SPMI) using dedicated custom instructions; in the reference design, the SPMI datapath is 32-bit wide, so transfers incur a latency proportional to HV_SIZE/32 cycles. SPMs can be initialized at synthesis time with commonly used Base and Level vectors, reducing runtime setup overhead in typical HDC pipelines.

The execution engine comprises dedicated functional units (FUs) specialized for each primitive (e.g., XOR for binding, counter/comparator arrays for bundling/clipping, rotation datapath for permutation, XOR + popcount + accumulation for similarity). Hardware parallelism is controlled at synthesis time through a SIMD parameter, and individual FUs can be enabled/disabled to match resource budgets. Importantly, HDCU decouples the logical hypervector dimension from the physical datapath width: a dedicated control/status register (HVSIZE) sets HV_SIZE at runtime and drives internal hardware loops, allowing the same synthesized microarchitecture to process different HV sizes without re-synthesis. Additional registers (e.g., prototype count for `hvsearch`) reduce software loop overhead in common kernels.

A key aspect of the HDCU is its synthesis-time parametrization of both compute and memory, enabling design-space exploration without modifying RTL. The primary knob is the parallelism factor `SIMD`, which defines the number of 32-bit lanes processed per cycle and therefore the physical datapath width:

$$W_{\text{data}} = \texttt{SIMD} \times 32 \text{ bits}. \tag{5}$$

On the memory side, each SPM bank is organized as a 32-bit word array whose depth is governed by `ADDR_WIDTH`. The total scratch pad capacity is:

$$M_{\text{total}} = \left(\frac{2^{\texttt{ADDR\_WIDTH}} \times 32}{8 \times 1024} \right) \text{KB} \times \texttt{SPM\_NUM}, \tag{6}$$

where `SPM_NUM` is the number of independent banks. Finally, `COUNTER_BITS` configures the precision of the saturating counters used for bundling, while an optional `PERF_COUNTER` flag enables profiling counters to expose per-operation cycle counts to software.

2.3. *Moving Beyond ISA Coupling*

Despite its fine-grained programmability and low dispatch overhead, ISA-coupled acceleration imposes practical integration constraints when targeting heterogeneous embedded ecosystems. First, the accelerator is not a drop-in peripheral: integrating HDCU requires modifying (or selecting) a compatible RISC-V core microarchitecture to add the coprocessor datapath, local SPMs and decode/dispatch support; this limits portability across mainstream SoCs dominated by ARM-based processing subsystems. Second, even when the ISE is integrated into a GNU-based toolchain, deploying custom instructions typically entails a non-standard software flow (toolchain patches, intrinsics and low-level memory management), which is at odds with Linux-centric development and rapid prototyping in conventional OS environments. Third, system-level integration features that are central in FPGA/SoC deployments are more naturally supported by bus-attached, memory-mapped accelerators than by in-pipeline coprocessors. Finally, ISA-coupled designs implicitly raise the entry barrier for end users: evaluating or reusing the accelerator often requires familiar-

 https://doi.org/10.3390/electronics15020489

ity with hardware integration (RTL, SoC build flows and toolchain customization), which may be outside the skill set of researchers focused primarily on HDC algorithms.

For these reasons, this work moves from an ISA-coupled coprocessor to a fully stand-alone and *plug-and-play* AXI-based hardware module. The proposed accelerator preserves primitive-level programmability, but exposes it through standard AXI4-Lite/AXI4-Stream interfaces to support DMA-driven transfers and direct control from Linux user space via a standard Application Programming Interface (API) stack. This choice also lowers the adoption barrier: the accelerator can be distributed with a ready-to-run reference platform (bitstream and Linux boot files, plus API examples), enabling algorithm developers to deploy and test HDC kernels by simply booting the target board and calling the provided software interface, without requiring RTL modifications or hardware design expertise.

3. Architecture Implementation

The proposed accelerator is implemented as a standalone, highly parameterized unit that offloads HDC/VSA primitives from the host processor. The design follows a plug-and-play integration model based on standard AMBA AXI4 interfaces: the accelerator is exposed as a memory-mapped peripheral for control and as streaming endpoints for bulk data movement, making it portable across heterogeneous FPGA SoCs (e.g., Xilinx Zynq-7000, UltraScale+) and across different host processors.

This section describes the architecture with a top-down approach. We first present the system-level integration and dataflow (Figure 1), then zoom into the internal microarchitecture (Figure 2), highlighting the key architectural changes introduced with respect to our previous ISA-coupled HDCU design. Finally, we detail the control logic enabling runtime-scalable execution and the Linux-oriented software stack (GitHub repository commit `3ae3b46`) used to orchestrate composite HDC kernels.

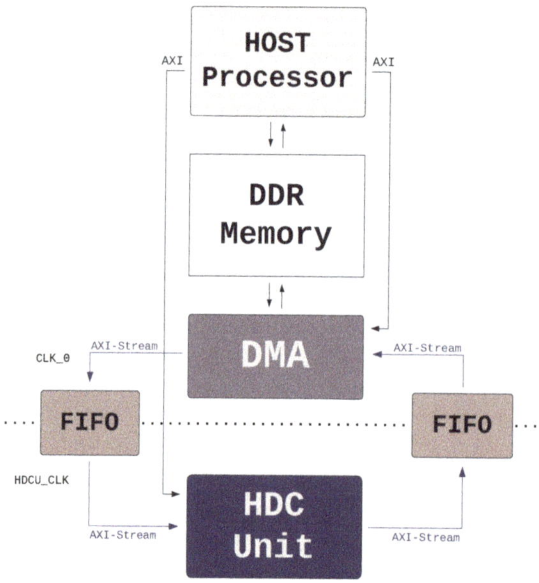

Figure 1. System-level integration of the HDC Accelerator IP within an SoC environment. The host processor configures the accelerator via AXI4-Lite and controls a DMA engine that performs bulk transfers over high-bandwidth AXI4-Stream links. Optional FIFO buffers are shown to decouple clock domains when CDC is required.

https://doi.org/10.3390/electronics15020489

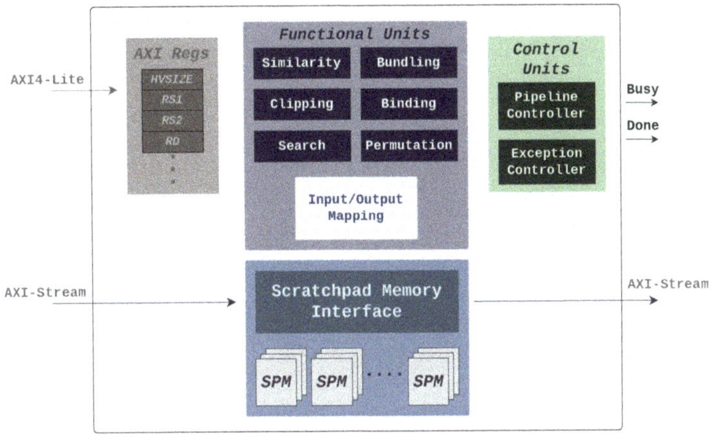

Figure 2. Internal microarchitecture of the HDC Accelerator. The design features a parameterizable SIMD datapath with dedicated Functional Units for BSC operations (Binding, Bundling, Permutation, Similarity, clipping, search), tightly coupled to a banked Scratchpad Memory via a dual-port interconnect.

3.1. System Overview

Figure 1 illustrates the reference system-on-chip integration scheme adopted for this work. While the proposed design is implemented as a standalone hardware accelerator adaptable to various interconnect topologies, this specific block design represents the recommended configuration employed for the experimental validation presented in Section 5. The architecture partitions the workload between the Host Processor and the rest of the FPGA fabric, utilizing the AMBA AXI4 standard to establish two distinct operational planes:

- **Control Plane:** The accelerator unit can be configured via write operations on memory-mapped registers. Each operation requires different parameters such as the address of the operands, the size of the hypervectors and the destination address. Read-only status registers allow the host processor to monitor the execution of each operation.
- **Data Plane:** A Direct Memory Access (DMA) engine manages bulk data movement between the off-chip DDR memory and the accelerator via AXI4-Stream interfaces. It is worth noting that the software driver (detailed in Section 4) is tightly coupled with this topology, providing abstract primitives specifically designed to coordinate accelerator and Xilinx DMA transactions.

From a timing perspective, the system integration inserts asynchronous First-In-First-Out (FIFO) buffers at the streaming boundaries of the accelerator. While a fully synchronous design sharing a common clock tree could theoretically allow direct AXI-Stream connections to the internal memories, the deployment of asynchronous FIFOs provides robust Clock Domain Crossing (CDC). This isolation ensures that the accelerator logic can be clocked at its maximum achievable frequency (`HDCU_CLK`), independent of the system bus frequency (`CLK_0`).

3.2. Architectural Optimizations

The proposed design introduces targeted microarchitectural enhancements compared to the baseline HDCU architecture summarized in Section 2.2.4. To address performance bottlenecks and optimize area utilization, we implemented specific modifications at both the arithmetic and memory levels. In particular, the *Permutation* and *Clipping* functional units have been redesigned to reduce hardware resource utilization while maintaining execution efficiency. Table 2 details the reduction in hardware resources achieved by the proposed

 https://doi.org/10.3390/electronics15020489

designs. Notably, these optimizations preserve the original execution latency. As neither unit lies on the critical path of the architecture, these area savings do not compromise the operating frequency of the system. Complementing these compute-centric optimizations, the SPMI has been re-engineered to seamlessly support the streaming-based dataflow.

Table 2. FPGA Resource Utilization Comparison: Original vs. Optimized Functional Units.

Version	Permutation Unit		Clipping Unit	
	#LUTs	#FFs	#LUTs	#FFs
Original	14,384	64	335	64
Optimized	REMOVED		16	34

3.2.1. Functional Units

Permutation

In the baseline HDCU architecture, the permutation logic (`hvperm`) implements the BSC cyclic right rotation with bit-level granularity. While this design maximizes flexibility by supporting arbitrary shift amounts s, it necessitates a temporary buffer register to carry the s least-significant bits across consecutive SIMD chunks during streaming. This mechanism introduces non-trivial hardware complexity, as wide rotations require resource-intensive shuffle networks and multiplexing logic, representing a well-known area bottleneck compared to purely bitwise primitives.

In the proposed standalone architecture, we eliminate the dedicated permutation FU entirely, opting instead to virtualize the permutation operation within the memory addressing logic. This architectural choice draws upon the optimization strategy analyzed in MCR-HDCU [33], which demonstrates that structured permutations—such as block-cyclic shifts—are sufficient to maintain the quasi-orthogonality required by HDC/VSA models, thus avoiding the overhead of arbitrary bit-level rotations. Consequently, permutation is performed at the granularity of whole SIMD blocks: rather than physically shifting bits, the controller reorders the data stream by manipulating the SPM read pointers.

Implementation-wise, let W_{data} be the physical datapath width and let a hypervector of size D be stored as $N = D/W_{\text{data}}$ consecutive blocks. A permutation by k blocks is realized simply by offsetting the read address so that the i-th output block is fetched from the $(i+k) \pmod N$ input block. This approach reduces the permutation logic to basic address arithmetic (offset and wraparound), effectively removing the latency penalty associated with data shuffling logic.

The primary trade-off of this optimization is the coarser granularity: the shift amount is constrained to multiples of W_{data} (i.e., $s = k \cdot W_{\text{data}}$). However, since the permutation operator in HDC primarily serves as a bijective transformation for position or role encoding, exact bit-level granularity is rarely critical. As evidenced by prior work [33], block-cyclic schemes retain sufficient decorrelation properties while yielding significant savings in silicon area and routing resources. To verify this, we performed an empirical comparison between the proposed block-granular permutation and standard bit-wise rotation. The results confirmed that the block-level approach preserves the bijective and decorrelating properties required by the BSC algebra, yielding no degradation in classification accuracy across the tested benchmarks while eliminating the hardware cost of a fine-grained shifter.

Clipping Unit

In BSC, the bundling operation aggregates multiple binary vectors into integer components, effectively widening the dynamic range of the hypervector. The `hvclip` primitive is

https://doi.org/10.3390/electronics15020489

responsible for projecting these integer counters back into the binary domain by applying an element-wise threshold.

In the baseline HDCU architecture, clipping is implemented using a comparator array that evaluates all `SIMD` lanes in parallel. Since the integer counters are packed within 32-bit words (specifically, `COUNTERS_NUMBER` counters of `COUNTER_BITS` bits each), the baseline unit reconstructs the final binary output progressively over `COUNTER_BITS` cycles. However, it relies on variable bit-indexing to place the comparison results into the destination register, a mechanism that requires wide dynamic multiplexers and complex routing logic to address individual bit positions.

In this work, we retain the semantic behavior and latency model of the baseline but restructure the datapath to minimize silicon area. Instead of employing variable indexing, the optimized unit generates a packed comparison block of width $W_{\text{blk}} = \texttt{SIMD} \times \texttt{COUNTERS\_NUMBER}$ in a single step using constant part-selects. This block is then concatenated into an output shift-register, which reconstructs the full `SIMD` × 32-bit binary word by shifting and appending partial results over `COUNTER_BITS` cycles. By replacing dynamic multiplexing with a regular shift/append structure, we significantly simplify the routing congestion. This optimization results in a highly compact footprint of just 16 LUTs and 34 FFs, while maintaining full runtime scalability with respect to `HVSIZE`.

3.2.2. Memory Subsystem

To match the throughput of the functional units, the memory subsystem is organized as a series of independent banked SPMs. The number of banks directly depends on the SIMD parameter and also matches the width of the axi-stream interfaces, in order to maximise the bandwidth of the data transfers. The use of multiple SPMs allows the unit to perform load, store and BSC operations simultaneously, as long as different SPMs are targeted. A dedicated SPMI manages read and write operations as well as access conflicts. Each memory bank is implemented as a simple dual-port memory, which is most suitable for FPGA implementations that leverage BRAM units.

A significant architectural enhancement over the original HDCU design [20] is the redesign of the SPMI to support high-bandwidth streaming without CPU intervention. We integrated native *AXI4-Stream* interfaces directly into the memory controller to enable burst transfers to and from the dedicated memories. The data width of these interfaces scales dynamically with the `SIMD` generic ($W_{stream} = \texttt{SIMD} \times 32$), ensuring that external bandwidth matches the internal datapath throughput.

Furthermore, the interface now includes dedicated hardware for address decoding and routing. In the previous HDCU implementation, this address translation task was offloaded to the Load Store Unit (LSU) of the host Klessydra RISC-V processor; incorporating this logic directly into the accelerator decouples memory management from the host architecture, enabling true standalone operation.

Finally, the internal memory controller features sophisticated arbitration logic that supports simultaneous dual-operand reads by utilizing both BRAM ports to fetch two operands (e.g., for Binding or Similarity) in a single clock cycle, effectively preventing pipeline stalls. Additionally, it handles concurrent DMA access by prioritizing the HDC pipeline while granting cycles to the DMA engine whenever the functional units are idle, thereby maximizing bandwidth efficiency.

4. Software Stack and Programming Model

To facilitate rapid prototyping and flexible orchestration, we developed a multi-layered C++ software stack that operates entirely in Linux userspace. By leveraging standard kernel

https://doi.org/10.3390/electronics15020489

interfaces, the stack abstracts low-level hardware details while exposing fine-grained control over memory and compute resources in the accelerator. As summarized in Figure 3, the architecture is organized into three abstraction layers—Application, HDC API and Driver—built on top of standard Linux kernel interfaces for memory reservation and address-space mapping. The main API entry points and their description are summarized in Table 3, while a representative end-to-end inference flow is provided in Listing 1.

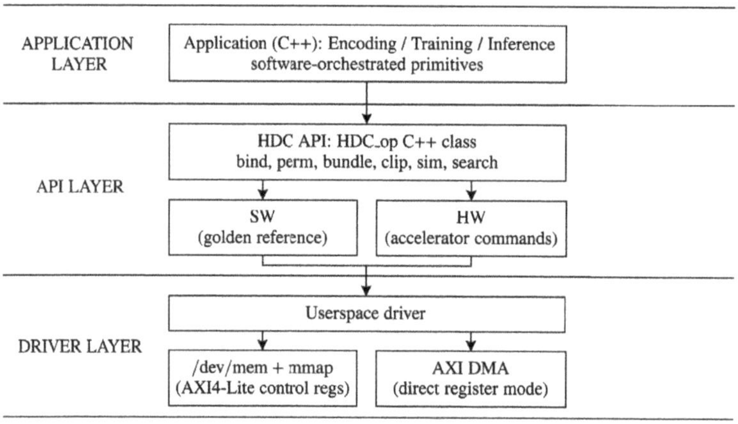

Figure 3. Overview of the proposed software stack and programming model. The C++ application orchestrates HDC primitives through the `HDC_op` API, which supports both software emulation and hardware dispatch. A userspace driver maps AXI4-Lite control registers via `/dev/mem` and manages DMA transfers through pre-reserved contiguous buffers defined in the Device Tree.

Table 3. Main High-Level C++ API for the Hardware-Accelerated HDC Pipeline. Functions operate on Scratchpad Memory (SPM) unless otherwise noted.

Category	Function	Description
Data Movement	`hvmemld`	Transfers data from DDR (Host) to SPM via DMA (MM2S).
	`hvmemstr`	Transfers data from SPM to DDR (Host) via DMA (S2MM).
Primitives	`hvbind`	Binding: Bitwise XOR of two binary HVs.
	`hvbundle`	Bundling: Accumulates a binary HV into a multi-bit vector (counters) with saturation.
	`hvclip`	Clipping: Binarizes a multi-bit vector via majority vote using a configurable threshold.
	`hvperm`	Permutation: Cyclic shift of an HV by k positions.
	`hvsim`	Similarity: Computes Hamming distance between two HVs.
	`hvsearch`	Associative Search: Queries a hypervector against a class memory to find the closest match (prediction).
Accelerated Pipelines	`accl_enc`	Full encoding pipeline: orchestrates bind, bundle and clip primitives over input features.
	`accl_train`	Executes encoding and updates the class prototype (bundling).
	`accl_infer`	Executes encoding and predicts the class label using the associative search.

The design targets portability across Zynq-class embedded Linux systems and requires only minimal platform configuration via Device Tree entries (AXI4-Lite `reg` ranges, `reserved-memory` regions for DMA buffers and appropriate memory mapping attributes).

https://doi.org/10.3390/electronics15020489

Listing 1. Minimal inference pipeline using the proposed C++ API (illustrative pseudocode).

```
int main() {
  HDC_op hdc(HV_SIZE_BIT, FEATURE_NUM, LEVEL_NUM);
  Dataset test_dataset = load_dataset("test.csv");
  Model  model         = load_model("model.bin");

  // Preload model HVs into accelerator SPMs
  for (f=0; f<FEATURE_NUM; f++)
    hdc.hvmemld(SPM_A_START_ADDR + f*sizeof(HV), model.base[f],  sizeof(
        HV));
  for (l=0; l<LEVEL_NUM; l++)
    hdc.hvmemld(SPM_B_START_ADDR + l*sizeof(HV), model.level[l], sizeof(
        HV));
  for (c=0; c<CLASS_NUM; c++)
    hdc.hvmemld(SPM_D_START_ADDR + sizeof(BundledHV) + c*sizeof(HV),
                model.cls[c], sizeof(HV));

  float    qlevels[LEVEL_NUM + 2] = make_quant_levels(0.0, 1.0);
  uint32_t qfeat[FEATURE_NUM];

  // Inference on all test samples
  for (i=0; i<test_dataset.num_samples; i++) {
    sample = get_sample(&test_dataset, i);

    for (f=0; f<FEATURE_NUM; f++){
        qfeat[f] = get_quantized_level(sample->features[f], qlevels);

        hdc.accl_inference(qfeat, SPM_A_START_ADDR, SPM_B_START_ADDR,
                           SPM_D_START_ADDR + sizeof(BundledHV));

        uint32_t y_hat = 0;
        hdc.hvmemstr(&y_hat, SPM_C_START_ADDR, sizeof(uint32_t)*SIMD);
    }
  }
}
```

4.1. Driver Layer

The foundational layer manages physical resources and communication protocols. To avoid the complexity of custom kernel-module development during prototyping, we adopt a fully userspace driver approach. In particular, the stack uses `mmap` on `/dev/mem` to map both AXI4-Lite control registers and pre-allocated DMA buffers into the application's virtual address space, enabling low-latency configuration and data transfers in controlled environments.

High-throughput data movement relies on contiguous physical memory reserved at boot time via Device Tree `reserved-memory` nodes. Two dedicated regions are allocated: a source buffer at physical address `0x30000000` and a destination buffer at `0x34000000`, each sized at 64 MiB. These buffers are mapped with appropriate cache attributes (coherent or non-cacheable, depending on the platform configuration) to avoid explicit software-managed cache maintenance operations. The DMA engine operates in Direct Register Mode without scatter-gather support, transferring data between these userspace-accessible buffers and the on-chip SPMs via AXI4-Stream interfaces. Synchronization is currently implemented via busy-wait polling of both DMA status registers (checking the `IOC_IRQ` and `IDLE` flags) and HDC control registers, which simplifies the control flow and provides deterministic latency for short transfers.

https://doi.org/10.3390/electronics15020489

4.2. API Layer

The core functionality is encapsulated in the HDC_op C++ class, which translates high-level algorithmic intent into hardware commands. The core API functions and their semantics are summarized in Table 3. Unlike cache-based architectures, the API exposes the internal scratchpad hierarchy as an explicitly software-managed resource. Data placement is controlled via the hvmemld/hvmemstr primitives, where spm_addr encodes both the target SPM bank and the byte offset within that bank. Transfer sizes must be specified explicitly in bytes; while the current implementation does not enforce strict alignment constraints at the API layer, optimal performance requires data sizes that are multiples of the hardware stream width $W_{\text{stream}} = \texttt{SIMD} \times 32$ bits. The API validates memory accesses through boundary checks against the reserved DMA buffer regions and provides error reporting via return codes and status-register inspection.

The class further provides a unified dual-mode interface that supports both pure software emulation and hardware acceleration. Each HDC primitive (similarity, bind, permutation, bundle, clip, search) is implemented in both software (for golden-reference verification) and hardware (via accelerator instruction dispatch). This design enables algorithm verification and functional testing entirely in software before FPGA deployment, facilitating rapid development and debugging cycles.

4.3. Application Layer

At the highest level, the stack enables the construction of composite HDC pipelines through software orchestration rather than fixed hardware state machines. The accelerator exposes only atomic primitives (hvbind, hvbundle, hvperm, hvsim, hvsearch, hvclip), which are composed programmatically at the application level to implement complete encoding, training and inference workflows. A minimal end-to-end inference pipeline illustrating a typical usage pattern of the HDC_op API (model preload to SPMs, feature quantization, accelerator invocation and result readback) is reported in Listing 1. For example, the accl_encoding method sequences hvbind (to combine level and base vectors in record-based encoding [27]), hvbundle (to accumulate feature representations) and hvclip (to perform majority-based binarization) within a C++ loop that iterates over all dataset features. Similarly, n-gram language models [29] can be constructed by chaining hvperm operations with varying shift parameters, where—as discussed in Section 3.2.1—shifts are constrained to block-granular multiples of $32 \times \texttt{SIMD}$ bits to match the architecture of the hardware permutation unit.

This software-orchestrated approach decouples algorithmic flexibility from hardware implementation. Modifying encoding strategies (e.g., switching from linear to thermometer encoding), adjusting bundling thresholds or implementing novel training procedures requires only recompiling the host application, without regenerating the FPGA bitstream. The trade-off is increased communication overhead between the CPU and accelerator compared to fully pipelined hardware datapaths; however, this is mitigated by efficient DMA transfers and the ability to batch operations within SPM boundaries before host synchronization is required.

5. Experiments

This section presents a comprehensive evaluation of the proposed AXI-based HDC accelerator. We begin by detailing the experimental platform and analyzing the hardware implementation results, focusing on the trade-offs between resource utilization and operating frequency across various parallelism configurations. Subsequently, we quantify the computational efficiency through a two-tiered benchmarking approach: micro-benchmarks

https://doi.org/10.3390/electronics15020489

targeting individual BSC primitives to assess peak throughput, and macro-benchmarks on standard datasets to evaluate end-to-end training and inference acceleration relative to the embedded software baseline.

5.1. Experimental Setup

The complete system, schematically depicted in Figure 1, was implemented on a Digilent Zybo Z7-20 development board (Digilent Inc., Pullman, WA, USA). The target device is a Zynq-7000 XC7Z020-1CLG400C SoC (AMD Xilinx, San Jose, CA, USA), which integrates a dual-core ARM Cortex-A9 processor (Arm Ltd., Cambridge, UK) (Processing System, PS) and Artix-7 based Programmable Logic (PL).

As detailed in Table 4, the experimental platform adopts a hardware–software co-design approach:

- **Processing System (Host):** The ARM processor executes the software stack atop an embedded Linux distribution generated via PetaLinux 2022.1 (AMD Xilinx, San Jose, CA, USA) with Linux kernel version `5.15.19-xilinx-v2022.1`. This partition manages the high-level orchestration, leveraging the `mmap`-based userspace driver and standard userspace I/O interfaces to interact with the hardware. The C++ software stack used for all experiments corresponds to GitHub commit `3ae3b46`.
- **Programmable Logic (Device):** The PL partition hosts the HDC accelerator instantiated alongside the AXI DMA engine (AMD Xilinx, San Jose, CA, USA). Interconnects are established via the AXI4-Lite protocol for low-latency register configuration and the AXI4-Stream protocol for high-bandwidth data ingestion from the main memory. The hardware design was synthesized and implemented using Vivado Design Suite 2022.1 (AMD Xilinx, San Jose, CA, USA).

Table 4. Experimental Platform Specifications and Toolchain Details.

Parameter	Specification
Host System (PS)	
Processing Unit	Dual-core ARM Cortex-A9 @ 667 MHz (Arm Ltd., Cambridge, UK)
Operating System	PetaLinux 2022.1 (AMD Xilinx, San Jose, CA, USA)
Kernel Version	`5.15.19-xilinx-v2022.1`
Driver Interface	Userspace I/O (via `/dev/mem`)
Accelerator Domain (PL)	
Target Device	Zynq-7000 XC7Z020 (AMD Xilinx, San Jose, CA, USA)
Synthesis Tool	Vivado Design Suite 2022.1 (AMD Xilinx, San Jose, CA, USA)
Clock Frequency	100 MHz (System), Async HDC Core
Data Interface	AXI4-Stream (via AXI DMA)
Control Interface	AXI4-Lite (Memory Mapped)

To evaluate the architecture under realistic workloads, we selected three standard datasets widely used in the HDC literature, namely ISOLET [34], IRIS [35], and UCI-HAR [36] (Table 5). All benchmarks are formulated as classification tasks. For all selected datasets (ISOLET, IRIS, UCI-HAR), input features are normalized to the $[0, 1]$ range and quantized into L discrete levels (typically $L = 10$) to map them to continuous item memory level vectors.

https://doi.org/10.3390/electronics15020489

Table 5. Benchmark Datasets Characteristics.

Dataset	Features	Classes	Total Samples	Task Type
ISOLET [34]	617	26	7797	Classification
IRIS [35]	4	3	150	Classification
UCI-HAR [36]	561	6	10,299	Classification

5.2. Hardware Implementation Results

Tables 6 and 7 summarizes post-implementation resource utilization on the Zynq XC7Z020 FPGA across varying parallelism levels (SIMD ranging from 4 to 32). The reported figures refer to the *complete block design implemented in the PL*, including the HDC accelerator module, AXI SmartConnect interconnect, AXI DMA engine and the AXI-Stream infrastructure (e.g., CDC/AXIS FIFOs). The parameter SIMD scales the internal datapath and stream width ($W_{stream} = \texttt{SIMD} \times 32\,\text{bits}$), increasing pressure not only on the compute logic but also on the transport fabric required to sustain line-rate transfers.

Table 6. Post-implementation resource utilization on the Zynq XC7Z020 for different SIMD configurations. Fixed parameters: ADDR_WIDTH = 16, COUNTER_BITS = 16. f_{impl} denotes the maximum frequency at which timing closure is achieved.

SIMD	f_{impl} [MHz]	#Slice LUTs	#LUTRAM	#Flip-Flops
4	110	10,185 (19.14%)	843 (4.84%)	11,258 (10.58%)
8	100	14,664 (27.56%)	1238 (7.11%)	15,847 (14.89%)
16	90	24,409 (45.88%)	1982 (11.39%)	24,753 (23.26%)
32	77	44,347 (83.36%)	3454 (19.85%)	42,435 (39.88%)

Table 7. Post-implementation resource utilization on the Zynq XC7Z020 for different SIMD configurations for Accelerator Unit, DMA unit and interconnect network of the PL. Fixed parameters: ADDR_WIDTH = 16, COUNTER_BITS = 16.

SIMD	Component	Resource Utilization			
		LUT as Logic	#FF	#LUTRAM	#BRAM
4	HDC Unit	4600	3028	0	64
	DMA Unit	1871	3091	117	5
	Interconnect	2249	4286	664	0
8	HDC Unit	7407	4501	0	64
	DMA Unit	2894	4668	146	9
	Interconnect	2496	5827	1030	0
16	HDC Unit	14,030	7429	0	64
	DMA Unit	4773	7613	152	18.5
	Interconnect	2990	8858	1768	0
32	HDC Unit	27,298	13,241	0	64
	DMA Unit	8336	13,379	156	34
	Interconnect	4586	14,962	3236	0

As expected, overall utilization increases monotonically with SIMD. Slice LUT usage rises from 19.14% at SIMD = 4 to 83.36% at SIMD = 32, while Flip-Flop usage scales from 10.58% to 39.88%. Importantly, the scaling trend is dominated by the accelerator itself: the accelerator instance grows from 4600 LUTs at SIMD = 4 to 27,298 LUTs at SIMD = 32, accounting for an increasing fraction of the total logic (approximately 45% to 62% of system LUTs across the sweep). In addition, the supporting infrastructure also scales with the

https://doi.org/10.3390/electronics15020489

stream width: AXI DMA increases from 1988 to 8522 Slice LUTs, and AXI SmartConnect from 2913 to 7822 Slice LUTs, reflecting the higher routing and buffering complexity of wide AXI datapaths.

LUTRAM consumption becomes significant at higher parallelism levels (up to 19.85%), but the utilization breakdown shows that it is almost entirely attributable to the interconnect fabric rather than to the HDC core (the accelerator itself uses 0 LUTRAM in all configurations). At `SIMD` = 32, for example, AXI SmartConnect alone accounts for 3236 LUTRAM primitives out of the total 3454. This increase contributes to routing congestion and exacerbates timing closure at high utilization.

The maximum implemented operating frequency (F_{impl}) degrades as the design widens: timing closure is achieved at 110 MHz for `SIMD` = 4, decreasing to 77 MHz for `SIMD` = 32. This behavior is primarily due to increased logic density and routing complexity when distributing wide control signals and routing wide datapaths through the interconnect and DMA subsystems.

Regarding the memory subsystem, the scratchpad depth was fixed by keeping `ADDR_WIDTH` = 16 constant across all configurations; therefore, the accelerator BRAM footprint remains invariant at 64 BRAM tiles. However, *system-level* BRAM usage increases with `SIMD` due to AXI DMA buffering and AXI-Stream FIFOs, growing from 73 BRAM tiles (`SIMD` = 4) to 127 BRAM tiles (`SIMD` = 32). The breakdown confirms this trend: at `SIMD` = 32, BRAM usage is composed of 64 (SPMs in the HDC core) + 34 (AXI DMA) + 29 (AXIS FIFO infrastructure, reported as 14.5 + 14.5 due to BRAM18 granularity). Since FIFO depths are synthesis-time parameters, this overhead can be tuned to trade buffering capacity for BRAM footprint depending on system constraints.

5.3. Performance Evaluation Methodology

To evaluate the computational efficiency of the proposed architecture, we measure the speedup S relative to a software baseline executed on a single ARM Cortex-A9 core embedded in the Xilinx XC7Z020 SoC. The speedup is defined as:

$$S = \frac{T_{\text{SW}}}{T_{\text{HW}}}, \tag{7}$$

where T_{SW} denotes the execution time of a BSC operation on the CPU, and T_{HW} represents the time required by the accelerator to execute the same BSC primitive. Specifically, T_{SW} is measured in Linux user space utilizing high-resolution POSIX timers (`CLOCK_MONOTONIC`), whereas T_{HW} is obtained via cycle-accurate performance counters integrated into the control logic of the accelerator. These counters record the total clock cycles elapsed between the assertion and deassertion of the enable signal of the requested FU. The physical time is derived as $T_{\text{HW}} = N_{\text{cycles}} / F_{\text{impl}}$, where F_{impl} denotes the synthesized clock frequency for a given hardware parallelism level. Data transfers duration to and from scratchpad memories depends on the `SIMD` parameter and on the size of the hypervectors. The maximum throughput of the scratchpad memories is `SIMD` $\cdot\, 4 \cdot F_{\text{impl}}$ B/s for both read and write operations, supposing there aren't access conflicts that would halt the operations and the input/output FIFOs are always ready to transmit/receive data.

The experimental campaign is structured into two phases:

- **Micro-benchmarks:** We assess the speedup achieved on the fundamental operations underlying the BSC model (binding, bundling, clipping, permutation, similarity and associative search) to characterize the efficiency of the accelerator at the primitive level.
- **Macro-benchmarks:** We evaluate the aggregate speedup obtained on complete training and inference phases by implementing a standard accumulation-based HDC

https://doi.org/10.3390/electronics15020489

classification algorithm [27] on the datasets described in Table 5. In this phase, the initialization cost associated with transferring persistent hypervectors (e.g., Base Vectors, Level Vectors and Class Prototypes) from the main DDR memory to the SPMs is excluded from the speedup calculation, thereby reflecting a typical edge scenario where model parameters are cached on-chip and reused across multiple training/classification iterations.

It is important to note that the focus of this analysis is not to assess the accuracy achieved by the accelerator, since every primitive operation implemented in hardware, as well as the full encoding, training and inference flow, has been rigorously validated against a software "golden reference". This verification ensures the accelerator delivers the exact same accuracy as an HDC software model. Consequently, accuracy is determined solely by the application-level choices (encoding and learning rule) and is independent of the underlying execution engine.

5.3.1. Performance on BSC Operations

Table 8 reports the speedup of each BSC primitive over the ARM Cortex-A9 baseline. Overall, the accelerator delivers substantial gains across all operations, and the speedup generally increases with the `SIMD` width. However, scaling is not perfectly proportional because wider `SIMD` configurations achieve lower implemented clock frequencies (from 110 MHz at `SIMD` = 4 down to 77 MHz at `SIMD` = 32).

Table 8. Speedup (*S*) of atomic BSC operations vs. software baseline on ARM Cortex-A9 @ 667 MHz. FPGA results are reported for the implemented frequencies of each `SIMD` configuration (110/100/90/77 MHz for `SIMD` = 4/8/16/32).

Operation	HV Size [bit]	Speedup (*S*) Hardware Parallelism (`SIMD`)			
		4	8	16	32
Binding	1024	30.00	42.85	60.00	57.69
	4096	12.50	21.05	36.36	43.95
	8192	6.63	11.42	19.13	27.97
Bundling	1024	30.22	189.47	354.54	428.57
	4096	32.26	225.37	431.42	414.2
	8192	64.77	115.26	204.88	331.86
Clipping	1024	103.77	173.68	300.00	362.63
	4096	93.27	165.67	317.14	343.19
	8192	47.61	84.73	150.61	243.95
Similarity	1024	59.32	66.66	85.71	76.92
	4096	44.11	71.42	115.38	76.92
	8192	24.15	40.54	64.93	88.75
Search	1024	54.94	68.18	107.14	115.38
	4096	43.01	57.14	105.26	120.19
	8192	16.96	29.85	51.94	80.97
Permutation	1024	73.17	120.00	200.00	n/a
	4096	36.66	64.70	122.22	123.07
	8192	18.8	33.33	58.82	94.01

Note: n/a indicates a non-admissible permutation configuration (HV fits in a single SIMD block).

The magnitude of the benefit is strongly operation-dependent. *Bundling* and *clipping* consistently achieve the highest accelerations, reaching up to 431× (bundling, HV size 4096,

https://doi.org/10.3390/electronics15020489

SIMD = 16) and up to 363× (clipping, HV size 1024, SIMD = 32). This behavior is expected, as both primitives are dominated by wide vote/reduction patterns that map efficiently onto the FPGA datapath. *Similarity* and *search* also obtain robust improvements (up to 115× and 120×, respectively), since the accelerator computes hamming-distance reductions in a highly parallel manner and further accelerates the repeated similarity evaluations over multiple candidate HVs.

Permutation benefits from the architectural choice of virtualizing the operation through SPM addressing rather than dedicated bit-level shuffling logic (see Section 3.2.1), achieving up to 200× speedup (HV size 1024, SIMD = 16) and up to 123× at larger dimensions (HV size 4096, SIMD = 32). Notably, the configuration SIMD = 32 with HV size 1024 is *not admissible* for permutation (reported as n/a in Table 8) because, with the adopted block-granular scheme, $W_{\text{data}} = \texttt{SIMD} \cdot 32 = 1024$ bit and the hypervector occupies a single block ($N = D/W_{\text{data}} = 1$), making any block-cyclic permutation degenerate and thus not meaningful to evaluate. In contrast, *Binding* exhibits the lowest gains (up to 60×), which is expected because BSC binding reduces to a simple bitwise XOR that is already efficiently executed on the ARM core and offers limited headroom for acceleration compared to reduction-dominated primitives.

Figure 4 evaluates how the latency of the associative-search primitive scales with the number of stored class prototypes. For a fixed hypervector dimension of $D = 8192$, the experiment measures the time required to compute and return the minimum Hamming distance between one query hypervector and a set of P class prototypes, with $P = \{10, 20, 30\}$. The results quantify the impact of increasing the number of similarity evaluations and of the available hardware parallelism, showing the expected near-linear growth of latency with P and the consistent reduction obtained with wider SIMD configurations.

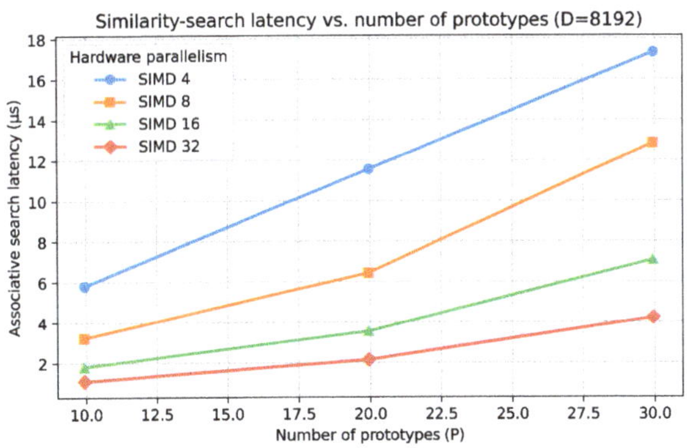

Figure 4. Similarity-search latency scaling with the number of class prototypes for a fixed hypervector size of $D = 8192$. The reported latency is the time required to return the minimum Hamming distance between a query hypervector and P stored class prototypes.

5.3.2. Performance on Real Datasets

We evaluated the accelerator on end-to-end classification pipelines (encoding + training/inference) using the datasets listed in Table 5. For these macro-benchmark experiments, the hardware accelerator was configured with SIMD = 8 and an operating frequency of 100 MHz. The bundling functional unit was set to 16-bit signed accumulation to safely support the intermediate sums required by feature-wise superposition during encoding and by class-wise accumulation during training. The memory subsystem was configured with 256 KB per SPM, which is sufficient to keep the item memories, intermediate HVs and

 https://doi.org/10.3390/electronics15020489

the full associative-memory (AM) model on-chip for the considered workloads. The HV dimension was fixed to 1024 bits for all experiments.

We implemented a straightforward HDC classifier with single-pass (one-shot) training. During training, each labeled sample is encoded into the HV space and accumulated into its corresponding class prototype via binding and bundling operations (respectively, element-wise XOR and element-wise integer addition). After all training samples have been processed, each class accumulator is binarized through a clipping operation (majority vote) to obtain the final binary prototypes stored in the AM. During inference, each unseen sample is encoded into a query HV, and the accelerator performs an associative search by computing similarity scores between the query and all class prototypes in the AM (via Hamming-distance-based matching for binary HVs). The predicted label is selected as the class with the best similarity score. HV transfers between the host and the accelerator are achieved via load and store operations, which are issued to both the accelerator and the DMA unit through memory-mapped registers. Before evaluating the speedup, the correctness of the end-to-end pipeline was verified. For every benchmark, the hardware-accelerated training and inference phases produced identical HVs and class predictions to the software model, confirming functional equivalence.

Table 9 reports the measured speedups with respect to the ARM Cortex-A9 software baseline. Overall, we observe substantial acceleration in both phases, with training speedups ranging from 58.58× to 81.69× and inference speedups ranging from 57.84× to 151.83×. The largest gain is achieved on ISOLET during inference, where the higher class count amplifies the cost of associative search in software and allows the parallel search datapath to be exploited more effectively in hardware. Averaged across datasets, the accelerator provides 68.45× speedup in training and 93.34× speedup in inference; when accounting for the clock-frequency gap (667 MHz vs. 100 MHz), this corresponds to a cycle-level efficiency improvement of approximately 456× and 623×, respectively.

Table 9. Overall speedup on benchmark datasets (Accelerator (SIMD = 8, HV_SIZE = 1024) vs. ARM Cortex-A9 software baseline).

Dataset	Training Speedup	Inference Speedup
IRIS	81.69	70.34
UCI-HAR	58.58	57.84
ISOLET	65.08	151.83

We also measured board-level energy during both training and inference for the same experimental configuration used in the macro-benchmarks (`SIMD` = 8, `HV_SIZE` = 1024, 100 MHz). Table 10 reports the measured energy per phase for each dataset.

Table 10. Board-level energy measured during training and inference (SIMD = 8, HV_SIZE = 1024, 100 MHz).

Dataset	Training Energy [J]	Inference Energy [J]
IRIS	3.25×10^{-4}	1.42×10^{-4}
UCI-HAR	2.295	0.983
ISOLET	1.737	0.745

At the beginning of each phase, there are overhead costs for loading all the required HVs into the scratchpad memories. This only happens in a cold start scenario, where Hypervectors have not been preloaded into the SPMs at synthesis time. Each dataset

 https://doi.org/10.3390/electronics15020489

requires N feature HVs and L quantization HVs to start the training process. At the end of the training phase, C class HVs are retrieved from the scratchpad memories. The inference phase requires all the class, feature and level HVs to be loaded into the scratchpad memories, if not already present, and the result of each search operation needs to be transferred to the host memory. Table 5 shows the number of features and classes used for each dataset (N and C), while the number of quantization levels is set to 10 for every dataset (L = 10). With HV dimension set to 1024, SIMD = 8 and accelerator operating frequency set to 100 MHz, the bandwidth of the scratchpad memories is $\texttt{SIMD} \cdot 4 \cdot 100 = 3200$ MB/s and each HV is transferred over $1024/(8 \cdot 32) = 4$ clock cycles. Table 11 shows the total execution time and overhead percentage for each dataset tested. It must be noted that the overhead is slightly underestimated, as it does not take into account the time needed to issue load and store instructions to the accelerator and the DMA unit; however, it is safe to assume this contribution can be neglected given that the CPU runs at a much higher frequency. From the data in Tables 9 and 11, we can see that, albeit there is an initial transfer cost, performing the benchmark on the HDC accelerator is much faster than performing it on a general-purpose processor and the overhead cost is minimal compared to the execution time of the algorithms. We also stress that in most application scenarios all the required Hypervectors can be preloaded at synthesis time, as they do not depend on the specific learning task; in our case, only the class vectors need to be counted in the overhead cost, after the learning phase.

Table 11. Total execution time and overhead percentage.

Dataset	Training Time [μs]	Inference Time [μs]	Training Overhead [%]	Inference Overhead [%]
IRIS	149.78	65.93	0.45%	1.03%
UCI-HAR	1,054,413.48	451,851.11	0.33%	<0.01%
ISOLET	798,189.416	342,166.277	0.22%	<0.01%

6. Discussion

This work targets a practical deployment gap that often emerges in HDC hardware acceleration: achieving high throughput on BSC primitives while remaining *system-integrable* and *retargetable* without redesign. By packaging the accelerator as a standalone AXI plug-and-play module with an AXI4-Lite control plane and an AXI4-Stream data plane, the proposed architecture can be driven by any AXI-capable host and can sustain bulk data ingestion at a bandwidth that scales with the internal datapath width. This design point is reflected in the evaluation, where the accelerator attains substantial speedups at both the primitive and end-to-end pipeline levels. In micro-benchmarks, speedups grow with SIMD and reach up to 431× for bundling and 362× for clipping at the largest configuration, while also accelerating similarity and associative search by up to 188× and 177×, respectively. In macro-benchmarks on complete classification pipelines (encoding + training/inference), the accelerator delivers 58.58×–81.69× training speedup and 57.84×–151.83× inference speedup, with the highest inference gain observed on ISOLET due to the larger associative-memory search workload. A quantitative comparison with the closest Zynq-7000 FPGA-based HDC accelerators is summarized in Table 12.

6.1. Scalability Is a Full-System Problem

A central takeaway from the implementation sweep is that scaling vector-level parallelism is not only a compute-core design issue: it stresses the *entire* data-movement fabric. As SIMD increases, the stream width grows as $W_{\text{stream}} = \texttt{SIMD} \times 32$ bits and the

https://doi.org/10.3390/electronics15020489

post-implementation results show monotonic growth in Slice LUTs (19.14% at SIMD = 4 to 83.36% at SIMD = 32) and Flip-Flops (10.58% to 39.88%), alongside a frequency degradation from 110 MHz down to 77 MHz at SIMD = 32. Importantly, the breakdown highlights that a sizable fraction of the additional cost at high SIMD originates from the supporting infrastructure (e.g., interconnect and DMA), not just from the accelerator datapath. The same phenomenon appears in LUTRAM usage: at SIMD = 32, LUTRAM becomes significant (19.85%), but it is dominated by the AXI interconnect, indicating that routing and buffering for wide datapaths can become the timing and area limiter. These results suggest that, for Zynq-7000 class devices, an "optimal" SIMD is often the one that balances compute throughput with routability and sustainable bandwidth (e.g., SIMD = 8/16 in this study), rather than the maximum achievable width.

6.2. Memory Subsystem Design and Host Decoupling

The proposed SPM-based organization is a key enabler of sustained throughput because it aligns storage parallelism with compute parallelism. The SPM controller is explicitly designed to (i) exploit dual-port BRAMs for simultaneous two-operand reads, (ii) arbitrate concurrent accesses (compute vs. DMA) and (iii) expose native AXI4-Stream connectivity for burst transfers directly into the SPMs. Crucially, address decoding and routing are absorbed into the accelerator-side memory controller, removing host-architecture dependencies and enabling true standalone use through standard AXI interfaces. This differs from many accelerator integrations that rely on host-side load/store or bespoke drivers to manage accelerator-local memories, and it is aligned with the "plug-and-play" goal of minimizing integration friction across systems.

6.3. Architectural Simplifications That Preserve HDC Semantics

Two design choices are especially relevant to the observed area/performance behavior. First, the permutation unit adopts a block-cyclic approach, trading exact bit-level shift granularity for lower routing complexity while retaining the bijective transformation needed for role/position encoding in typical HDC pipelines. Second, the clipping datapath is restructured to avoid variable bit-indexing by generating packed comparison blocks and reconstructing the output via a regular shift/append mechanism across a number of cycles corresponding to the counter bit-width, substantially reducing routing pressure while preserving the functional behavior and latency model. Together, these optimizations reinforce a broader point: many HDC primitives tolerate constrained implementations (e.g., coarse permutations, regularized datapaths) as long as the algebraic role of the operation is preserved.

6.4. Comparison with GP-HDCA

While GP-HDCA [30] targets FPGA-based acceleration on Zynq-7000, its architectural scope is primarily tailored to flexible *encoding* via an instruction-driven coprocessor. In contrast, our design acts as a full-pipeline accelerator, offloading not only the encoding but also the associative memory training and inference stages through dedicated stream-processing hardware. To ensure a fair resource comparison, we evaluate the total system footprint. GP-HDCA reports utilizing 24,760 LUTs for its `Int32-V128` configuration (128-bit datapath), an overhead largely dominated by the complex control logic required to support its custom ISA. Conversely, our proposed design configured with an equivalent 128-bit datapath (`SIMD = 4`) consumes only ≈10,200 LUTs for the *complete system* (including AXI DMA and SmartConnect). This demonstrates that our stream-based architecture is roughly 2.4× more area-efficient than the instruction-based competitor at equivalent parallelism,

https://doi.org/10.3390/electronics15020489

allowing us to scale up to a `SIMD` = 32 configuration (1024-bit datapath) on the same device to achieve massive throughput. Furthermore, we offer superior usability and configurability: while GP-HDCA restricts flexibility to the limits of its custom ISA and requires low-level assembly-like programming, our IP provides extensive synthesis-time parametrization (e.g., SIMD width, memory depth) and is controlled via a high-level C++ software stack in Linux userspace. Finally, unlike GP-HDCA, which relies on estimated performance from a MATLAB emulator, we report measured latency from a physical implementation on the Zynq XC7Z020 and release our complete open-source hardware/software stack to foster reproducibility.

6.5. Comparison with EcoFlex-HDP

EcoFlex-HDP [31] proposes a Zynq-based co-processing architecture centered on a programmable Hyperdimensional Processing Unit (HPU) controlled via a custom ISA. While this approach offers flexibility through instruction-level programming, it suffers from severe resource bloat and incomplete pipeline acceleration. First, regarding area efficiency, EcoFlex-HDP reports a massive resource utilization of 47,122 LUTs, occupying 88.58% of the Zynq XC7Z020 logic capacity. This saturation effectively precludes the integration of additional user logic or peripherals. In stark contrast, our architecture demonstrates superior density: even in our high-parallelism `SIMD=32` configuration (1024-bit datapath), our complete system utilizes only 27,300 LUTs ($\approx$51% of the device), leaving ample headroom for system-level integration while delivering comparable or superior throughput. Second, regarding the acceleration scope, EcoFlex-HDP focuses primarily on the encoding primitives (bind, permutation, bundling), neglecting the critical associative memory search stage, which dominates inference latency. Our design addresses this bottleneck by integrating a dedicated streaming search engine alongside the encoding primitives, enabling full end-to-end hardware acceleration for both training and inference. It is also worth noting that EcoFlex-HDP does not report absolute latency figures for individual primitive operations, preventing a direct operator-level performance comparison; their evaluation is limited to relative speedups against a software baseline. Finally, rather than relying on a custom assembly-like ISA that complicates the software stack, we provide a synthesis-time parameterizable IP coupled with a standard C++ API, ensuring a smoother adoption path for edge-AI developers.

Table 12. Comparison with state-of-the-art FPGA-based HDC accelerators on Zynq-7000 platform. **Note:** n/s indicates information not stated in the referenced work.

	GP-HDCA [30]	**EcoFlex-HDP [31]**	**This Work**
Platform target	Zynq-7000	Zynq-7000	Zynq-7000
Host Interface	AXI4-Stream & AXI4-Lite	AXI4-Stream & AXI4-Lite	AXI4-Stream & AXI4-Lite
Supported Primitives	Bind, Bundle, Permute, Clip	Bind, Bundle, Permute	Bind, Bundle, Permute, Clip, Similarity, Search
HW Parallelism	32-bit to 128-bit	1024-bit	128-bit to 1024-bit
Frequency (MHz)	n/s	125	77–110
#LUTs	3137–24,760	47,122	10,185–44,349
#FFs	5863–20,076	50,707	11,258–42,437
#BRAM Tiles	n/s	92	73–127
Design Focus	Encoder Flexibility	Low-Power Multi-core	IP Scalability & Modularity
Availability	Closed Source	Open Source	Open Source

6.6. Limitations and Future Directions

First, macro-benchmark speedups are reported under a steady-state assumption and therefore exclude the one-time transfer of persistent HVs (e.g., base vectors, level vectors and class prototypes) from DDR to the SPMs. The cold-start overhead is quantified

 https://doi.org/10.3390/electronics15020489

separately Table 11 and remains small for the considered workloads; however, in scenarios with frequent model swapping or limited on-chip capacity, transfer costs can become non-negligible, making overlap and caching policies more critical. Second, frequency degradation and LUTRAM growth at high `SIMD` confirm that interconnect and DMA scaling can become the dominant constraint; future work should investigate interconnect-minimized integration patterns, alternative streaming fabrics and multi-instance scaling (replicating moderate-`SIMD` engines) to improve routability and sustained throughput. Third, board-level energy is reported for training and inference in a representative configuration Table 10, but a complete energy/EDP characterization across the design space (e.g., different HV sizes, `SIMD` points and bandwidth regimes), including a finer-grained separation of accelerator and system-level power contributions, remains an important direction for future work.

7. Conclusions

This paper presented a general-purpose, open-source Hyperdimensional Computing accelerator designed to bridge the gap between high-performance hardware and software usability. By abandoning tight CPU-coupling in favor of a standalone, host-agnostic AXI4 architecture, we demonstrated that it is possible to achieve substantial acceleration without sacrificing portability across heterogeneous SoCs.

The proposed design, validated on a Xilinx Zynq-7000 platform, leverages a scalable SIMD datapath and an optimized memory subsystem to deliver primitive-level speedups of up to 761× compared to an embedded ARM Cortex-A9 processor. Architectural optimizations in the permutation and clipping units proved effective in containing resource utilization, enabling high-throughput configurations (up to `SIMD` = 32) within the constraints of mid-range edge FPGA devices. At the system level, the integration of a multi-layer software stack allows the accelerator to seamlessly offload complete HDC pipelines, achieving average speedups of 68.45× in training and 93.34× in inference across standard classification benchmarks.

Our analysis highlighted that at high parallelism levels, the bottleneck shifts from computation to data movement and interconnect complexity, suggesting that future edge-AI architectures must co-optimize the accelerator datapath with the system-level transport fabric. By releasing the complete RTL and software stack as open-source hardware, this work provides a reusable and extensible foundation for the research community, facilitating the deployment of robust and energy-efficient HDC intelligence in real-world embedded systems.

Author Contributions: Conceptualization, R.M., A.M. and M.O.; methodology, R.M., M.P. and M.A.; hardware design, R.M., M.P., M.A. and A.M.; memory subsystem, M.P.; functional unit optimizations, M.A.; system integration, A.M. and R.M.; software, R.M.; validation, R.M., M.P. and M.A.; formal analysis, R.M.; investigation, R.M. and A.R.; resources, M.O.; data curation, R.M.; writing—original draft preparation, R.M.; writing—review and editing, R.M., M.P., M.A., M.B., A.M., A.R. and M.O.; paper organization and editorial guidance, M.B.; supervision, M.O.; project administration, M.O. All authors have read and agreed to the published version of the manuscript.

Funding: This research received no external funding.

Data Availability Statement: The complete RTL and software stack are released as open-source at: https://github.com/RoMartino/AXI-HDC-Accelerator (accessed on 15 January 2026). Publicly available datasets used in this study are cited in Table 5.

Conflicts of Interest: The authors declare no conflicts of interest.

Abbreviations

https://doi.org/10.3390/electronics15020489

The following abbreviations are used in this manuscript:

AMBA	Advanced Microcontroller Bus Architecture
API	Application Programming Interface
ASIC	Application-Specific Integrated Circuit
AXI	Advanced eXtensible Interface
BRAM	Block Random Access Memory
BSC	Binary Spatter Code
CDC	Clock Domain Crossing
DMA	Direct Memory Access
EDP	Energy-Delay Product
FF	Flip-Flop
FIFO	First-In First-Out
FPGA	Field-Programmable Gate Array
HDC	Hyperdimensional Computing
HLS	High-Level Synthesis
HV	Hypervector
IP	Intellectual Property
ISA	Instruction Set Architecture
ISE	Instruction Set Extension
LUT	Look-Up Table
PL	Programmable Logic
PS	Processing System
RTL	Register Transfer Level
SIMD	Single Instruction Multiple Data
SoC	System-on-Chip
SPM	Scratchpad Memory
UIO	Userspace I/O
VSA	Vector Symbolic Architectures

References

1. Kanerva, P. Hyperdimensional computing: An introduction to computing in distributed representation with high-dimensional random vectors. *Cogn. Comput.* **2009**, *1*, 139–159. [CrossRef]
2. Gayler, R.W. Vector Symbolic Architectures Answer Jackendoff's Challenges for Cognitive Neuroscience. In Proceedings of the 4th ICCS International Conference on Cognitive Science and the 7th ASCS Australasian Society for Cognitive Science Conference, Sydney, Australia, 13–17 July 2003; pp. 133–138.
3. Kleyko, D.; Rachkovskij, D.A.; Osipov, E.; Rahimi, A. A survey on hyperdimensional computing aka vector symbolic architectures, Part I: Models and data transformations. *ACM Comput. Surv.* **2022**, *55*, 175. [CrossRef]
4. Kleyko, D.; Rachkovskij, D.; Osipov, E.; Rahimi, A. A survey on hyperdimensional computing aka vector symbolic architectures, part II: Applications, cognitive models, and challenges. *ACM Comput. Surv.* **2023**, *55*, 175. [CrossRef]
5. Schlegel, K.; Neubert, P.; Protzel, P. A comparison of vector symbolic architectures. *Artif. Intell. Rev.* **2022**, *55*, 4523–4555. [CrossRef]
6. Chang, C.-Y.; Chuang, Y.-C.; Huang, C.-T.; Wu, A.-Y. Recent progress and development of hyperdimensional computing (HDC) for edge intelligence. *IEEE J. Emerg. Sel. Top. Circuits Syst.* **2023**, *13*, 119–136. [CrossRef]
7. Kleyko, D.; Davies, M.; Frady, E.P.; Kanerva, P.; Kent, S.J.; Olshausen, B.A.; Osipov, E.; Rabaey, J.M.; Rachkovskij, D.A.; Rahimi, A.; et al. Vector symbolic architectures as a computing framework for emerging hardware. *Proc. IEEE* **2022**, *110*, 1538–1571. [CrossRef]
8. Kanerva, P. Fully Distributed Representation. In *1997 Real World Computing Symposium (RWC '97)*; Real World Computing Partnership: Tsukuba, Japan, 1997; pp. 358–365.
9. Morris, J.; Fernando, R.; Hao, Y.; Imani, M.; Aksanli, B.; Rosing, T. Locality-based encoder and model quantization for efficient hyper-dimensional computing. *IEEE Trans. Comput.-Aided Des. Integr. Circuits Syst.* **2021**, *41*, 897–907. [CrossRef]

 https://doi.org/10.3390/electronics15020489

10. Schmuck, M.; Benini, L.; Rahimi, A. Hardware optimizations of dense binary hyperdimensional computing: Rematerialization of hypervectors, binarized bundling, and combinational associative memory. *ACM J. Emerg. Technol. Comput. Syst.* **2019**, *15*, 32. [CrossRef]
11. Khaleghi, B.; Xu, H.; Morris, J.; Rosing, T.S. Tiny-HD: Ultra-efficient hyperdimensional computing engine for IoT applications. In Proceedings of the 2021 Design, Automation & Test in Europe Conference & Exhibition (DATE), Grenoble, France, 1–5 February 2021; pp. 408–413.
12. Eggimann, M.; Rahimi, A.; Benini, L. A 5 μW standard cell memory-based configurable hyperdimensional computing accelerator for always-on smart sensing. *IEEE Trans. Circuits Syst. I Regul. Pap.* **2021**, *68*, 4116–4128. [CrossRef]
13. Taheri, F.; Bayat-Sarmadi, S.; Hadayeghparast, S. RISC-HD: Lightweight RISC-V processor for efficient hyperdimensional computing inference. *IEEE Internet Things J.* **2022**, *9*, 24030–24037. [CrossRef]
14. Yu, T.; Wu, B.; Chen, K.; Zhang, G.; Liu, W. LAHDC: Logic-aggregation-based query for embedded hyperdimensional computing accelerator. *IEEE Trans. Comput.-Aided Des. Integr. Circuits Syst.* **2025**, *44*, 119–129. [CrossRef]
15. Salamat, S.; Imani, M.; Khaleghi, B.; Rosing, T. F5-HD: Fast flexible FPGA-based framework for refreshing hyperdimensional computing. In *Proceedings of the 2019 ACM/SIGDA International Symposium Field-Programmable Gate Arrays*; ACM: New York, NY, USA, 2019; pp. 53–62.
16. Imani, M.; Bosch, S.; Datta, S.; Ramakrishna, S.; Salamat, S.; Rabaey, J.M.; Rosing, T. QuantHD: A quantization framework for hyperdimensional computing. *IEEE Trans. Comput.-Aided Des. Integr. Circuits Syst.* **2020**, *39*, 2268–2278. [CrossRef]
17. Yu, T.; Wu, B.; Chen, K.; Zhang, G.; Liu, W. Fully learnable hyperdimensional computing framework with ultratiny accelerator for edge-side applications. *IEEE Trans. Comput.* **2024**, *73*, 574–585. [CrossRef]
18. Kim, Y.; Imani, M.; Moshiri, N.; Rosing, T. GenieHD: Efficient DNA pattern matching accelerator using hyperdimensional computing. In *2020 Design, Automation & Test in Europe Conference & Exhibition (DATE)*; IEEE: Piscataway, NJ, USA, 2020; pp. 115–120.
19. Khaleghi, B.; Kang, J.; Xu, H.; Morris, J.; Rosing, T.S. GENERIC: Highly efficient learning engine on edge using hyperdimensional computing. In *Proceedings 59th ACM/IEEE Design Automation Conference (DAC)*; ACM: New York, NY, USA, 2022; pp. 1117–1122.
20. Martino, R.; Angioli, M.; Rosato, A.; Barbirotta, M.; Cheikh, A.; Olivieri, M. Configurable hardware acceleration for hyperdimensional computing extension on RISC-V. *IEEE Trans. Comput.* **2026**, *75*, 653–664. [CrossRef]
21. Salamat, S.; Imani, M.; Rosing, T. Accelerating hyperdimensional computing on FPGAs by exploiting computational reuse. *IEEE Trans. Comput.* **2020**, *69*, 1159–1171. [CrossRef]
22. Morris, J.; Set, S.T.K.; Rosen, G.; Imani, M.; Aksanli, B.; Rosing, T. AdaptBit-HD: Adaptive model bitwidth for hyperdimensional computing. In Proceedings of the 2021 IEEE 39th International Conference on Computer Design (ICCD), Storrs, CT, USA, 24–27 October 2021; pp. 93–100.
23. Sadeghipour Roodsari, M.; Krautter, J.; Meyers, V.; Tahoori, M. E3HDC: Energy efficient encoding for hyper-dimensional computing on edge devices. In Proceedings of the 2024 34th International Conference on Field-Programmable Logic and Applications (FPL), Torino, Italy, 2–6 September 2024; pp. 274–280.
24. Li, H.; Liu, F.; Chen, Y.; Wang, Z.; Huang, S.; Yang, N.; Lyu, D.; Jiang, L. FATE: Boosting the performance of hyper-dimensional computing intelligence with flexible numerical data type. In *Proceedings of the 52nd Annual International Symposium on Computer Architecture*; Association for Computing Machinery: New York, NY, USA, 2025; pp. 1269–1282.
25. Zhang, T.; Salamat, S.; Khaleghi, B.; Morris, J.; Aksanli, B.; Rosing, T.S. HD2FPGA: Automated framework for accelerating hyperdimensional computing on FPGAs. In Proceedings of the 2023 24th International Symposium on Quality Electronic Design (ISQED), San Francisco, CA, USA, 5–7 April 2023; pp. 1–9.
26. Martino, R. AXI-HDC-Accelerator: A General-Purpose, AXI4-Compliant Hyperdimensional Computing (HDC) Accelerator IP for Xilinx Zynq SoCs. GitHub Repository. 2026. Available online: https://github.com/RoMartino/AXI-HDC-Accelerator (accessed on 15 January 2026).
27. Vergés, P.; Heddes, M.; Nunes, I.; Kleyko, D.; Givargis, T.; Nicolau, A. Classification using hyperdimensional computing: A review with comparative analysis. *Artif. Intell. Rev.* **2025**, *58*, 173. [CrossRef]
28. Cumbo, F.; Chicco, D. Hyperdimensional computing in biomedical sciences: A brief review. *PeerJ Comput. Sci.* **2025**, *11*, e2885. [CrossRef]
29. Angioli, M.; Jamili, S.; Barbirotta, M.; Cheikh, A.; Mastrandrea, A.; Menichelli, F.; Rosato, A.; Olivieri, M. AeneasHDC: An automatic framework for deploying hyperdimensional computing models on FPGAs. In Proceedings of the 2024 International Joint Conference on Neural Networks (IJCNN), Yokohama, Japan, 30 June–5 July 2024.
30. Asghari, M.; Le Beux, S. A general purpose hyperdimensional computing accelerator for edge computing. In Proceedings of the 2024 22nd IEEE Interregional NEWCAS Conference (NEWCAS), Sherbrooke, QC, Canada, 16–19 June 2024; pp. 383–387.

 https://doi.org/10.3390/electronics15020489

31. Isaka, Y.; Sakaguchi, N.; Inoue, M.; Shintani, M. EcoFlex-HDP: High-speed and low-power and programmable hyperdimensional-computing platform with CPU co-processing. In Proceedings of the 2024 Design, Automation & Test in Europe Conference & Exhibition (DATE), Valencia, Spain, 25–27 March 2024.
32. Cheikh, A.; Sordillo, S.; Mastrandrea, A.; Menichelli, F.; Scotti, G.; Olivieri, M. Klessydra-T: Designing vector coprocessors for multi-threaded edge-computing cores. *IEEE Micro* **2021**, *41*, 64–71. [CrossRef]
33. Angioli, M.; Kymn, C.J.; Rosato, A.; Loutfi, A.; Olivieri, M.; Kleyko, D. Efficient Hyperdimensional Computing with Modular Composite Representations. *arXiv* **2025**, arXiv:2511.09708. [CrossRef]
34. Cole, R.; Fanty, M. ISOLET [Dataset]. UCI Machine Learning Repository. 1991. Available online: https://archive.ics.uci.edu/dataset/54/isolet (accessed on 15 January 2026).
35. Fisher, R.A. Iris [Dataset]. UCI Machine Learning Repository. 1936. Available online: https://archive.ics.uci.edu/dataset/53/iris (accessed on 15 January 2026).
36. Reyes-Ortiz, J.; Anguita, D.; Ghio, A.; Oneto, L.; Parra, X. Human Activity Recognition Using Smartphones. UCI Machine Learning Repository. 2013. Available online: https://archive.ics.uci.edu/dataset/240/human+activity+recognition+using+smartphones (accessed on 15 January 2026).

https://doi.org/10.3390/electronics15020489

electronics

MDPI

Article

A Unified FPGA/CGRA Acceleration Pipeline for Time-Critical Edge AI: Case Study on Autoencoder-Based Anomaly Detection in Smart Grids

Eleftherios Mylonas *, Chrisanthi Filippou, Sotirios Kontraros, Michael Birbas and Alexios Birbas

Electrical and Computer Engineering Department, University of Patras, 26504 Patras, Greece; up1084023@ac.upatras.gr (C.F.); s.kontraros@ac.upatras.gr (S.K.); mbirbas@ece.upatras.gr (M.B.); birbas@ece.upatras.gr (A.B.)

* Correspondence: e.mylonas@ece.upatras.gr

Abstract

The ever-increasing need for energy-efficient implementation of AI algorithms has driven the research community towards the development of many hardware architectures and frameworks for AI. A lot of work has been presented around FPGAs, while more sophisticated architectures like CGRAs have also been at the center. However, AI ecosystems are isolated and fragmented, with no standardized way to compare different frameworks with detailed Power–Performance–Area (PPA) analysis. This paper bridges the gap by presenting a unified, fully open-source hardware-aware AI acceleration pipeline that enables seamless deployment of neural networks on both FPGA and CGRA architectures. Built around the Brevitas quantization framework, it supports two distinct backend flows: FINN for high-performance dataflow accelerators and CGRA4ML for low-power coarse-grained reconfigurable designs. To facilitate this, a model translation layer from QONNX to QKeras is also introduced. To demonstrate its effectiveness, we use an autoencoder model for anomaly detection in wind turbines. We deploy our accelerated models on the AMD's ZCU104 and benchmark it against a Raspberry Pi. Evaluation on a realistic cyber–physical testbed shows that the hardware-accelerated solutions achieve substantial performance and energy-efficiency gains—up to 10× and 37× faster inference per flow and over 11× higher efficiency—while maintaining acceptable reconstruction accuracy.

Keywords: hardware-aware AI acceleration; anomaly detection; machine learning; cyber–physical systems; edge computing; FPGAs; CGRAs; energy efficiency

1. Introduction

1.1. Motivation

Artificial Intelligence (AI) has emerged as a transformative technology with applications across numerous and diverse domains. Applications in computer vision, natural language processing, predictive maintenance, and anomaly detection are typical examples of the capabilities of AI nowadays. As AI continues to mature, a growing interest in deploying it in time-critical cyber–physical environments, where rapid response times and reliable operation are essential [1], is surfacing. Indicative examples of such AI applications already exist, as with the so-called autoencoder models, which provide timely response and accurate performance [2–4]. However, the widespread adoption of AI has been accompanied by an alarming escalation in computational demands and energy consumption [5]. Modern deep learning models require extensive computational resources during both training and inference phases. This leads to substantial power consumption that poses environmental, economic, and practical deployment concerns. For AI to continue its growth trajectory and maintain long-term sustainability, the development of energy-efficient AI acceleration solutions has become absolutely essential. This urgency has sparked intensive research into specialized hardware architectures that can deliver the required computational performance while reducing power consumption.

1.2. Background and State of the Art

Neural Processing Units (NPUs) and Deep Learning Processing Units (DPUs) have revolutionized the landscape of AI inference at the edge. These specialized processors are fundamentally designed to excel at the matrix multiplication and multiply accumulate operations that dominate neural network computations, achieving orders of magnitude improvements in energy efficiency compared to general-purpose CPUs and even GPUs. At their architectural core, these accelerators employ design principles rooted in coarse-grained reconfigurable architectures (CGRAs), which provide a balance between the flexibility of software-programmable processors and the efficiency of application-specific integrated circuits [6,7]. CGRAs consist of arrays of functional units interconnected through a programmable routing network. This enables the mapping of computational kernels directly onto hardware datapaths with minimal control overhead. By exploiting spatial parallelism and eliminating much of the instruction fetch and decode overhead inherent in traditional processor architectures, CGRA-based accelerators can achieve remarkable throughput and energy efficiency for structured computational patterns typical of neural network inference. This architectural paradigm has proven particularly effective for edge AI applications where power consumption, latency, and throughput requirements must be simultaneously optimized.

Field-Programmable Gate Arrays (FPGAs) and CGRAs have long been recognized as promising platforms for implementing energy-efficient AI accelerators. FPGAs offer the unique advantage of hardware reconfigurability, allowing designers to implement custom datapaths tailored to specific neural network architectures and precision requirements, thereby achieving superior energy efficiency compared to fixed-function processors. Similarly, CGRAs have attracted significant attention as an intermediate point between the full flexibility of FPGAs and the efficiency of ASICs, with various research frameworks demonstrating their effectiveness for neural network acceleration, and many CGRA architectures have been mapped onto FPGA fabrics and validated. There are many works in the literature that demonstrate hardware acceleration of AI applications on such platforms [8–11]. Ref. [8] presents a summary of many accelerated AI applications on FPGAs featuring all the major deep learning model architectures (ANNs, CNNs, RNNs, etc.). Ref. [9] presents a full software stack for accelerating Convolutional Neural Networks (CNNs) into an energy-efficient streaming hardware architecture. Ref. [10] showcases a systolic parallel hardware architecture able to efficiently accelerate Artificial Neural Networks (ANNs), autoencoders, etc., while ref. [11] presents a hardware accelerated version of a Vision Transformer (ViT)-based model with significant energy efficiency results.

Despite the abundance of available tools and frameworks, the FPGA and CGRA Machine Learning (ML) acceleration landscape remains fragmented and challenging to navigate for practitioners seeking to deploy AI at the edge. Many existing pipelines suffer from significant limitations. Some are built upon deprecated or outdated toolchains that no longer receive active development support, while others present steep learning curves with complex workflows that require deep hardware expertise. The lack of standardization across different

 https://doi.org/10.3390/electronics15020414

frameworks makes it extremely difficult to perform fair comparisons between FPGA-based and CGRA-based acceleration approaches, or to benchmark these hardware solutions against contemporary software frameworks such as PyTorch or TensorFlow. Furthermore, most existing tools provide limited support for hardware-aware quantization. This forces designers to either accept suboptimal quantization schemes or manually iterate through time-consuming design-space exploration processes. Researchers and engineers working on edge AI applications often find themselves navigating a complex landscape of incompatible tools, each with its own model formats, quantization schemes, and deployment workflows, making it difficult to leverage the full potential of both FPGA and CGRA acceleration technologies.

Existing approaches to FPGA and CGRA-based neural network acceleration include several notable frameworks. FINN [12,13] provides a dataflow-oriented design flow for quantized neural networks on FPGAs with emphasis on streaming architectures and customizable processing elements. In addition, hls4ml [14], originally developed for high-energy physics applications, focuses on ultra-low latency inference. For CGRA acceleration, frameworks like CGRA-ME [15] and various academic research tools have demonstrated the potential of coarse-grained reconfigurable architectures for neural network inference, though many remain research prototypes with limited production readiness. Commercial solutions from FPGA vendors, including Xilinx's Vitis AI [16] and Intel's OpenVINO toolkit [17], offer comprehensive design flows but often require significant vendor-specific expertise and may not provide the level of customization desired for research applications. Other notable efforts include DNNDK [18], VTA [19], and various high-level synthesis approaches that attempt to bridge the gap between software model description and hardware implementation. However, these tools typically operate in isolation, each with proprietary model formats and quantization approaches. This makes systematic comparison and evaluation across different acceleration strategies extremely challenging for researchers and practitioners in the field.

1.3. Contributions

This paper presents a unified, fully open-source hardware-aware AI acceleration pipeline that addresses these fragmentation challenges. Our pipeline provides a common frontend based on the Brevitas 0.12.0 quantization library [20] (an add-on library of PyTorch), supporting two distinct acceleration flows targeting both custom FPGA dataflow accelerators through FINN 0.10.1 and CGRA-based architectures through a state-of-the-art CGRA-ML framework called CGRA4ML [21–23]. Brevitas enables seamless comparison between different hardware acceleration approaches while maintaining full compatibility with PyTorch, supporting both Quantization-Aware Training (QAT) and Post-Training Quantization (PTQ) of pretrained models. The hardware-aware quantization capabilities of Brevitas allow our pipeline to adapt quantization strategies to the specific requirements and constraints of each target acceleration flow, accommodating the distinct characteristics of dataflow FPGA architectures versus CGRA mappings. We demonstrate the effectiveness and versatility of our proposed pipeline through a comprehensive case study targeting autoencoder-based anomaly detection for wind turbines in smart energy systems, a representative time-critical cyber–physical system application.

The main contributions of this work are the following:

- A unified hardware-aware AI acceleration pipeline targeting FPGA devices with two diverse acceleration flows, one focused on custom high-performance low-latency AI dataflow accelerator design via the FINN library, and the other centered around a state-of-the-art CGRA-ML framework. A model translation layer from QONNX 0.4.0 to QKeras 0.9.0 is also introduced to facilitate the process. To our knowledge, this is the first time that a fully open-source unified ML pipeline for both FPGAs/CGRAs is presented, with the powerful Brevitas quantization library as the frontend.

 https://doi.org/10.3390/electronics15020414

- Application of the proposed pipeline on a real-world time-critical cyber–physical system scenario in the smart grid domain for the acceleration of a real-time anomaly detection solution for wind turbines.
- Validation of the proposed pipeline on the presented cyber–physical system scenario by applying our anomaly detection solution on two different hardware platforms, one Commercial Off-The-Shelf (COTS) Raspberry Pi (RPi) utilizing ONNX Runtime, which serves as the reference baseline, and an AMD ZCU104 platform. The main concept is that a comparison is performed of both platforms in terms of accuracy, performance, latency, power and energy efficiency, etc., and of the two acceleration flows when dealing with the same quantized model input.

1.4. Paper Structure

This paper is structured as follows: Section 1 introduces the problem and shows the need for our proposed pipeline. Section 2 presents the hardware-aware AI acceleration pipeline. Section 3 introduces the cyber–physical system problem under testing conditions and presents the anomaly detection solution for which the proposed pipeline will be used. In Section 4, we describe the experimentation procedure and present the results. We conclude our work in Section 5, where the benefits of the proposed solution are summarized.

2. Hardware-Aware AI Acceleration Pipeline

This section presents the high-level architecture of the proposed hardware-aware AI acceleration pipeline and describes the two different acceleration flows in depth.

2.1. High-Level View of the Proposed Pipeline

The proposed hardware-aware AI acceleration pipeline is presented in Figure 1 below. The pipeline can be split in a set of steps:

1. The first step is for the AI engineer to prepare (or pre-process) the available dataset and select the model architecture best suited for the application of interest in a PyTorch environment. The outcome of this step is a set of Python 3.10 scripts, one with the model architecture description, one for the training procedure.
2. The second step is the model training phase. Here we can follow two different paths:
    (a) Either train the model in PyTorch in floating-point mode directly and then apply PTQ on the model with Brevitas, or
    (b) apply QAT on the model with Brevitas, therefore training the quantized model directly, given that the model architecture description and training script from Step 1 are already prepared in a Brevitas QAT-ready format.
3. (Optional) The third step mainly applies to those having followed Step 2(a) and is about quantization-aware model finetuning. For those who used Brevitas PTQ methods, it may be that the resulting quantized model is not good enough and therefore a finetuning process is mandatory. This process is the same as training a standard PyToch model, but in this case, the model is a Brevitas PTQ-generated one featuring special "quantization hooks" which enable the generated model to be used as a standard floating-point one during finetuning. This further facilitates the whole quantization process.
4. During the fourth step, the quantized model is extracted in a quantized Open Neural Network eXchange (ONNX), also known as QONNX [24], formatted, and is given as input to the acceleration flow of choice:
    (a) FINN flow;
    (b) CGRA4ML flow.

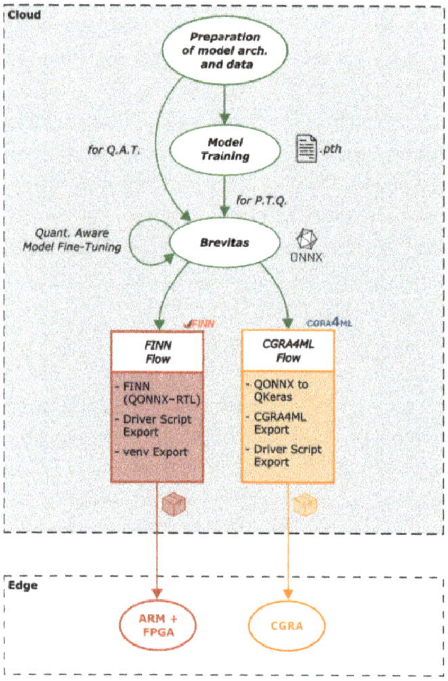

Figure 1. Hardware-aware AI acceleration pipeline.

2.2. *Brevitas Frontend*

Brevitas is the main intersection point between the FINN and CGRA4ML flows. The reason why Brevitas was selected is based on the following facts:

1. It features many state-of-the-art quantization algorithms for almost all popular AI models, from basic DNNs to even core Large Language Model (LLM) functionalities.
2. It supports both QAT and PTQ while providing full flexibility to the developer, who is able to choose custom integer resolutions of less than 8 bit, even at 1 bit for Binary Neural Network (BNN) computation support.
3. It exports quantized models on the quantization version of the popular ONNX Intermediate Representation (IR) model format, which is already supported on all major AI workflows.
4. It is inherently supported in FINN; therefore, it is easy to export a quantized model and work with it there.
5. It is a very active open-source project, with a great community and a lot of support and examples that enable the developer to go straight into action.

2.3. *FINN Flow*

The FINN flow is based on the homonymous open-source project from Xilinx and is essentially a compiler toolchain that can transform a quantized model into a Register-Transfer-Level (RTL) description. The toolchain provides a frontend with its transformation and analysis passes and a high-level synthesis (HLS)-based backend to explore the design space in terms of resource and performance constraints. A user can build a custom step-by-step flow, but in this work, we leverage the automatic build flow functionality and create a more generic one that is able to optimize both common Deep Neural Network (DNN) topologies and more specialized ones like the models presented later in Section 3, based on a performance target and device constraints. Internally, FINN works only with an IR based

 https://doi.org/10.3390/electronics15020414

on the ONNX format, the well-known QONNX format. The FINN toolchain comprises three main phases of graph transformation passes, that is, the preparation phase, the mapping phase, and the tuning phase. These phases are responsible for rearranging or fusing operations, assigning them to specific HLS/RTL templates, and finally calculating and preparing the necessary compute resources via a selection of parallel processing elements (PEs), Single-Instruction–Multiple-Data (SIMD) input channel lanes per PE, number and size of First-In First-Out (FIFO) queues, etc. for each layer to obtain the desired throughput within a balanced pipeline. In addition, FINN employs a lot of utility tools for code analysis, resource estimation, and simulation available in any phase of the compilation process. Finally, FINN is able to export the resulted RTL into a bitstream file for the appropriate FPGA platform with little or no effort, which can be deployed immediately with the generated shell project and driver for Xilinx Alveo and PYNQ platforms.

2.4. CGRA4ML Flow

The CGRA4ML flow was chosen as an alternative AI hardware acceleration flow to FINN. It is based on the homonymous open-source project of Kastner R., which is basically a comprehensive toolchain that transforms quantized models into vendor-agnostic SystemVerilog RTL designs suitable for both FPGA and application-specific integrated circuit (ASIC) implementations. CGRA4ML provides a Python-based frontend built on top of QKeras for both QAT and PTQ, along with an automated backend that generates parameterizable CGRA hardware specifications, production-ready C runtime firmware, and comprehensive verification testbenches. Unlike spatial layer-by-layer implementations, CGRA4ML enables temporal reuse of processing elements across multiple layers through dynamic reconfiguration, allowing the deployment of larger and more complex models that exceed the capacity constraints of purely on-chip implementations. Internally, CGRA4ML works with an IR based on bundles, which are groups of QKeras layers that can be deterministically executed on the generated hardware, with compute-intensive operations accelerated on the CGRA while lightweight pixel-wise operations are offloaded to the host CPU. The framework features a unified dataflow architecture with runtime-programmable control that maximizes data reuse through intelligent weight caching and pixel shifting, alongside high-performance AXI DMAs for efficient off-chip data movement. Finally, CGRA4ML provides automated Tool Command Language (TCL) toolflows for both FPGA and ASIC implementations, along with integration scripts for deployment on Zynq-based platforms with PYNQ support, facilitating rapid prototyping and production-ready implementations with minimal manual intervention.

2.5. QONNX-QKeras Translation

The existing FINN and CGRA4ML tools are working on two different quantization frontends, the Brevitas and QKeras libraries. As explained in Section 2.2, we have decided to use Brevitas as our frontend, due to the active development around it and the many different features it provides in all cases, for both QAT and PTQ, and all kinds of AI models. This means that we are responsible for creating a custom compilation flow from QONNX to QKeras IR model format. At this point in time, this work focused on Conv/ConvTranspose nodes and standard activation nodes, e.g., ReLus, while support for other popular layers and functionalities, e.g., residual blocks, will be added in the future.

In general, the compilation flow consists of a set of seven steps:

1. Identification of Conv/ConvTranspose nodes, along with their respective activation nodes and quantizers.
2. Extraction of basic parameters for the Conv/ConvTranspose nodes (kernel size, strides, dilations, filters).

https://doi.org/10.3390/electronics15020414

3. Identification of relevant weight and bias Quant nodes, along with extraction of the respective raw tensors and quantization information.
4. Preparation of the model architecture layer per layer (or more precisely bundle by bundle, following the CGRA4ML/QKeras logic) based on a QKeras bundle template.
5. Extraction of input shape from the QONNX model and transformation from NCHW (batch, channels, height, width) to NHWC (batch, height, width, channels) format.
6. Assignment of weight and bias tensors to the respected bundles, with transformation of weights tensors' shape for QKeras compatibility.
7. Model export and continuation with the rest CGRA4ML flow.

At this point, it is necessary to highlight that during this whole process, we follow CGRA4ML's internal structures to ensure compatibility. This leads us to use CGRA4ML's XConvBN bundle for Conv layer mapping. XConvBN includes an internal BatchNorm layer for weights/biases normalization. During the QONNX-QKeras translation, since the extracted weights and biases are not in need of normalization due to their preparation from Brevitas, we assign appropriate tensors to the BatchNorm layer so that it is nullified.

The compilation steps are summarized in a pseudocode format in Algorithm 1.

Algorithm 1 QONNX-QKeras Translation Flow

Require: QONNX model $\mathcal{M}_{\text{QONNX}}$
Ensure: QKeras IR model $\mathcal{M}_{\text{QK}}$

function QONNX_TO_QKERAS($\mathcal{M}_{\text{QONNX}}$)
    $\mathcal{N}_{\text{conv}} \leftarrow$ FINDNODES($\mathcal{M}_{\text{QONNX}}$, {Conv, ConvTranspose})
    $\mathcal{N}_{\text{act}} \leftarrow$ FINDACTIVATIONNODES($\mathcal{M}_{\text{QONNX}}$)
    $\mathcal{Q} \leftarrow$ FINDQUANTIZERS($\mathcal{M}_{\text{QONNX}}$)
    for all $n \in \mathcal{N}_{\text{conv}}$ **do**
        $(k_h, k_w) \leftarrow$ GETKERNELSIZE(n)
        $(s_h, s_w) \leftarrow$ GETSTRIDES(n)
        $(d_h, d_w) \leftarrow$ GETDILATIONS(n)
        $C_{\text{out}} \leftarrow$ GETNUMFILTERS(n)
    end for
    for all $n \in \mathcal{N}_{\text{conv}}$ **do**
        $W_n \leftarrow$ EXTRACTWEIGHTS(n)
        $b_n \leftarrow$ EXTRACTBIAS(n)
        $Q_n^W, Q_n^b \leftarrow$ EXTRACTQUANTINFO($\mathcal{Q}, n$)
    end for
    $\mathcal{B} \leftarrow \emptyset$ ▷ set of QKeras bundles
    for all $n \in \mathcal{N}_{\text{conv}}$ **do**
        $B_n \leftarrow$ INSTANTIATEBUNDLETEMPLATE(XConvBN)
        ASSIGNPARAMETERS($B_n, k_h, k_w, s_h, s_w, d_h, d_w, C_{\text{out}}$)
        $\mathcal{B} \leftarrow \mathcal{B} \cup \{B_n\}$
    end for
    $(N, C, H, W) \leftarrow$ GETINPUTSHAPE($\mathcal{M}_{\text{QONNX}}$)
    $(N, H, W, C) \leftarrow$ TRANSFORMTONHWC(N, C, H, W)
    for all $B_n \in \mathcal{B}$ **do**
        $\widetilde{W}_n \leftarrow$ TRANSFORMWEIGHTLAYOUT(W_n)
        ASSIGNWEIGHTS($B_n, \widetilde{W}_n$)
        ASSIGNBIAS(B_n, b_n)
        NULLIFYINTERNALBATCHNORM(B_n)
    end for
    $\mathcal{M}_{\text{QK}} \leftarrow$ ASSEMBLEMODEL($\mathcal{B}$)
    return $\mathcal{M}_{\text{QK}}$
end function

https://doi.org/10.3390/electronics15020414

ConvTranspose Translation

A 2D transposed convolution can be re-expressed as a standard convolution applied to an explicitly upsampled IR of the input [25]. Instead of relying on the implicit gradient-of-convolution interpretation, the operator is decomposed into two concrete steps:

1. **Pixel Padding (Explicit Upsampling)**

   A transposed convolution with weights

$$\mathbf{W} \in \mathbb{R}^{C_{\text{in}} \times C_{\text{out}} \times K_h \times K_w},$$

   stride (s_h, s_w), dilation (d_h, d_w), and padding p is rewritten as

$$\mathbf{Y} = \text{ConvTranspose}(\mathbf{X}, \mathbf{W}).$$

   The first step is to upsample the input tensor by inserting zeros between adjacent samples according to the stride. For an input feature map $\mathbf{X} \in \mathbb{R}^{H \times W \times C_{\text{in}}}$, the pixel-padded tensor $\mathbf{X}'$ is defined as:

$$\mathbf{X}'_{is_h,\, js_w,\, c} = \mathbf{X}_{i,j,c}, \qquad \mathbf{X}'_{u,v,c} = 0 \;\; \text{otherwise}, \tag{1}$$

   with output dimensions

$$H' = H \cdot s_h - (s_h - 1), \qquad W' = W \cdot s_w - (s_w - 1). \tag{2}$$

   This operation performs deterministic upsampling without introducing learnable parameters:

$$\mathbf{X}' = \text{PixelPadding}(\mathbf{X}; s_h, s_w).$$

2. **Kernel Rotation and Channel Reordering**

   The second step constructs a convolution kernel that matches the effect of the original transposed kernel. The required transformation consists of

   (a) Rotating the spatial dimensions of $\mathbf{W}$ by 180°;
   (b) Swapping the input and output channel axes.

   Formally, the rotated kernel is given by

$$\widetilde{\mathbf{W}} = \text{Transpose}\big(\text{Rot180}(\mathbf{W}), (1,0,2,3)\big), \tag{3}$$

   where

$$\text{Rot180}(\mathbf{W})_{c_{\text{in}}, c_{\text{out}}, u, v} = \mathbf{W}_{c_{\text{in}}, c_{\text{out}}, K_h - 1 - u,\, K_w - 1 - v}. \tag{4}$$

   After rotation and channel transposition, the tensor

$$\widetilde{\mathbf{W}} \in \mathbb{R}^{C_{\text{out}} \times C_{\text{in}} \times K_h \times K_w}$$

   conforms to the format expected by a standard convolution.

   Combining the two steps yields the following equivalence:

$$\text{ConvTranspose}(\mathbf{X}, \mathbf{W}) = \text{Conv}\Big(\text{PixelPadding}(\mathbf{X}; s_h, s_w),\, \widetilde{\mathbf{W}}\Big), \tag{5}$$

with convolution stride fixed to $(1,1)$ and dilation and padding preserved from the original operator.

https://doi.org/10.3390/electronics15020414

This formulation expresses ConvTranspose entirely through a conventional Conv layer acting on an explicitly upsampled input. The resulting representation preserves all learnable parameters while providing a structurally compatible, Conv-only form suitable for downstream processing inside CGRA4ML without introducing many changes in the flow, both during model preparation and during runtime.

3. Real-Time Anomaly Detection in Wind Turbines

This section presents the cyber–physical system problem under testing conditions and describes the components which implement the core functionality of the real-time anomaly detection algorithm.

3.1. Concept Description

We assume the cyber–physical system scenario of Figure 2. In this scenario, a wind turbine fleet is connected to the main power grid via an inverter and a power switch. The power switch is controlled by a local turbine controller, which can be a Programmable Logic Controller (PLC). The power switch is open when an anomaly is detected in the wind turbine fleet behavior, or whenever the wind turbine fleet output should not be connected to the main grid due to non-nominal generated voltage output, which could cause the insertion of harmonics in the power grid. This is very important since harmonics could lead the rest of the grid to instability and de-synchronization with terrible outcomes, e.g., power outages [26–28]. The cyber–physical system scenario we are dealing with has a critical response time of 50 ms, which is the ideal time between an anomaly generation, its detection, and finally the generation of the appropriate control signal at the controller.

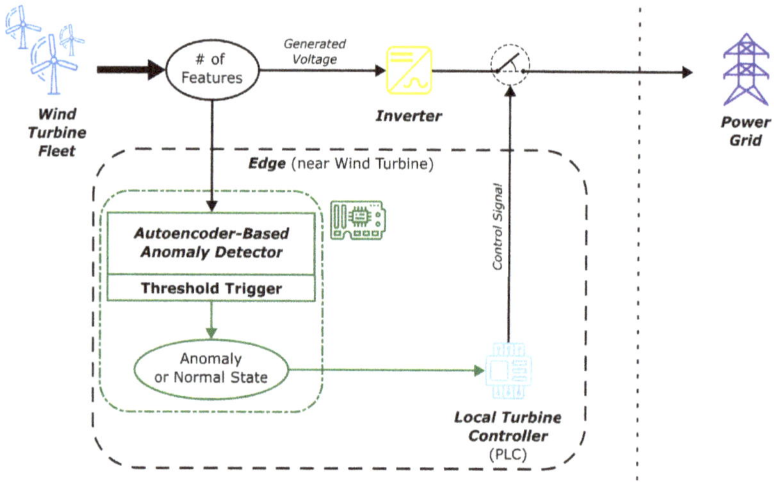

Figure 2. Visualization of the wind turbine anomaly detection concept.

To solve this problem and ensure the system's stability and reliability, we assume the installation of appropriate sensors at the wind turbine fleet which measure a number of features, e.g., the wind speed, the generated voltage, etc. (presented in more detail in Section 3.2). The sensors' measurements are sent to an embedded board which acts as an AI-enabling extension card to the local turbine controller. Our goal is to present an AI solution that will detect anomalies during the critical timespan we set, while taking into account the time it takes for the transmission of measurements from the sensors to the board and the transmission of the anomaly state detection signal from the board to the

https://doi.org/10.3390/electronics15020414

controller. To achieve this, hardware acceleration is desirable, if not mandatory, since it can yield results in hard real-time and, of course, we need deterministic behavior so that we can predict accurately the time needed for the generation of the appropriate control signal.

To this end, in the subsequent sections, we present a complete AI solution based on autoencoder architecture which achieves anomaly detection in wind turbine fleets in real-time.

3.2. Autoencoder-Based Anomaly Detection Module

Autoencoders are a type of Artificial Neural Network that have a wide range of practical applications across numerous domains [29]. In our case study, an autoencoder model is designed and trained for the purpose of detecting anomalies on a fleet of wind turbines in real-time, based on sensor data analysis. Specifically, the function of an autoencoder model is to convert the input data into a compact representation known as the latent space through linear transformations—thus implementing the encoder part—and then to reconstruct the original input from the encoded version—that is, the decoder part. The goal in designing such an architecture is to minimize the difference between the original and reconstructed data. In general, the main advantages of the autoencoder architecture are the lack of supervision during the training procedure and the fact that it can directly receive data from fully functional wind turbines for training. Therefore, it can be trained with normal sensor readings and be able to detect normal behavior. As a consequence, when an anomaly occurs, the change in the input data is amplified at the output and instantly recognized as an abnormality.

The dimensionality of the latent space representation is an important characteristic that is used to categorize autoencoders into either Undercomplete or Overcomplete. What distinguishes the latter from the former is that the size of the latent space representation is greater than the size of the input. While Overcomplete autoencoders contain the risk of learning trivial solutions like identity mappings, several regularization techniques can be applied in order to prevent this. Applying sparsity constraints through L1 Penalty or KL Divergence can effectively mitigate the risk of extracting trivial solutions [30]. Another technique that can be used for this is weight decay, which encourages smaller, simpler weight values improving the generalization and robustness of the model. Moreover, Undercomplete autoencoders pose considerable trade-offs, since smaller latent representation means limited expressive capabilities, which can be costly when dealing with input data features of equal importance. This means that in cases where all input features carry valuable information, using an Undercomplete autoencoder model forces the loss of determinative data representation. Thus, we select the Overcomplete approach as it allows us to capture information of greater complexity from the data, since the network is able to learn and detect intricate patterns with very high efficiency [31].

To this regard, our autoencoder model is based on convolution layers, which are good at extracting hidden features from the input data. Specifically, our model is comprised of a set of three convolution and three ConvTranspose layers for the encoder and decoder part, respectively, as shown in Figure 3. On the one hand, the convolution layers are able to extract useful features from the input matrix, leading to the latent space representation. On the other hand, the ConvTranspose layers apply the inverse mathematical operation of the convolution layers, gradually restoring the dimensionality of the input and producing the final output. Lastly, the Rectified Linear Unit (ReLU) is chosen as the activation function. This simple setup allows the network to learn complex patterns while preventing common problems such as the vanishing gradient problem [32], making use of the non-linear behavior of ReLU both in the case of the encoder and the decoder part.

 https://doi.org/10.3390/electronics15020414

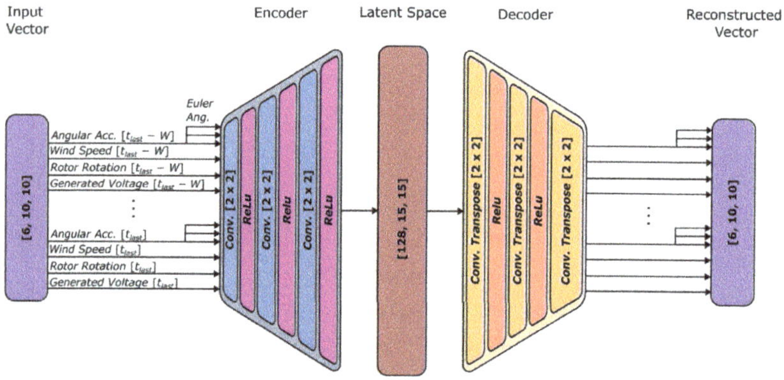

Figure 3. Autoencoder architecture.

The input data consist of sensor readings of four selected features: **angular acceleration**, **wind speed** in rotations per second, **rotation of the rotor** in rotations per second, and **generated voltage** in Volts. As part of the data preparation process for the model training, the angular acceleration measurements are converted from the quaternion system to Euler angles; thus, the selected input features are represented by six values. Then, all sensor data are filtered by applying Wavelet denoising, and finally they are normalized. Regarding the denoising process, we use PyWavelets [33], an open-source wavelet transform library for Python that provides a fast and user-friendly interface, to perform filtering on the accelerometer data. For this purpose, Discrete Wavelet Transform (DWT) is used to decompose the chosen data into frequency components, then "soft" thresholding is applied to the resulting wavelet coefficients to suppress high-frequency noise and finally, the original data are reconstructed using multi-level Inverse Discrete Wavelet Transform (IDWT). The resulting denoised data go through Z-Score normalization ensuring uniform scaling among all features to achieve accurate functionality for the model. Z-Score normalization results in a dataset with features of mean value of zero and Standard Deviation value of one.

The final input tensor is created by applying a sliding window to the resulting dataset, capturing the temporal correlation of neighboring measurements, and converting each time window into a tensor according to a defined structure. This structure includes the six features mentioned before as input, across one hundred consecutive samples. The resulting shape of the input as well as the output tensor is (6, 10, 10) while the corresponding datatype is single-precision floating point (FP32).

3.3. Threshold Trigger Module

The output of the autoencoder model needs some further processing in order to solidify whether it is associated with anomaly generation or not. For this reason, the threshold trigger module is created. The role of this module is to compare the autoencoder's output with its input vector and against a predefined threshold vector. This vector is calculated by comparing the output vectors of the autoencoder module during normal and abnormal states and monitoring their value ranges. If the difference between an output and its respective input vector exceeds the normal value ranges identified by the threshold vector, then an anomaly state alarm signal is generated and sent directly to the local wind turbine controller for actuation. The threshold trigger module runs in all cases on the CPU in software after each autoencoder inference finishes and does not necessitate hardware acceleration. The operation of the threshold trigger module is summarized in Figure 4.

https://doi.org/10.3390/electronics15020414

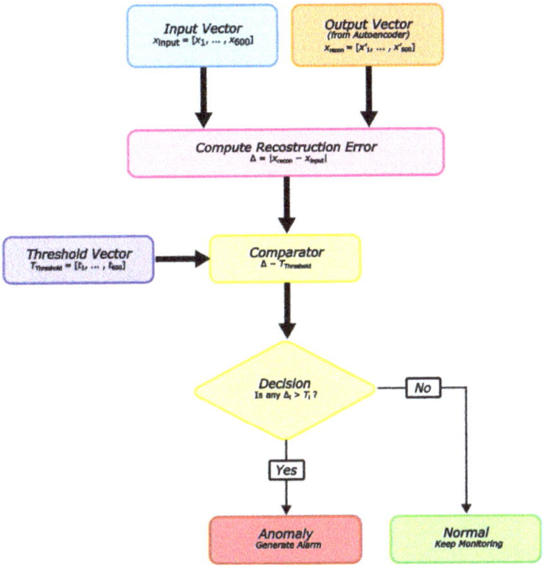

Figure 4. Threshold trigger module operation.

4. Results

In this section, we describe the experimentation conducted for validation purposes of our proposed hardware-aware AI acceleration pipeline. Initially, we describe our experimentation setup, then we analyze the methodology behind the power/energy metrics' acquisition and present the list of metrics used in this paper, and finally we present the relevant results.

4.1. Experimentation Setup

In order to validate our hardware-aware AI acceleration pipeline and our autoencoder-based AI solution, we prepare a realistic, complete testbed of the cyber–physical system scenario in our lab, as shown in Figure 5. For the emulation of the power grid components, we prepare a modified IEEE 5-bus test system in Simulink and export it in a Matlab script based on our previous work on real-time power grid simulation [34–36]. The scripts run on a standard Dell Precision 3630 Tower PC with an Intel Core i7-9700 CPU, 32 GB RAM, Windows 11 OS, and Matlab R2024b. The rest of the components were tested on two different embedded platforms. For the baseline reference test, we use a standard RPi 3b+ board. For the acceleration pipeline tests, we use an AMD-Xilinx ZCU104 FPGA board [37]. In our acceleration tests with FINN, all the components run on top of the quad-core Cortex A53 of the ZCU104, while the autoencoder model is offloaded to the FINN-generated hardware accelerator. In our acceleration tests with CGRA4ML, all the components run on top of a MicroBlazeV RISC-V core [38] configured with the microcontroller preset inside ZCU104's FPGA region, while the autoencoder model is offloaded to the CGRA4ML-generated accelerator configured as a 10 × 64 PE array structure. For the wind turbine fleet, a playback simulator is used with data from a public repository [39], processed to be more realistic for our scenario. More specifically, the original dataset represents sensor readings from five model mini-wind turbines mounted with seven different sensors. From these features we isolate the relevant ones, applying pre-processing calculations so that they resemble real-world-scale measurements. We place the simulator on top of the embedded platform

 https://doi.org/10.3390/electronics15020414

as well, since we assume that the sensors are connected to the platform via fiber optic link, therefore minimal transmission delays are incurred. In our tests, we compare the two acceleration flows by starting from a common QONNX autoencoder model, as described in Section 3.2, quantized via the Brevitas PTQ process on 8 bits for weights and activations and 16 bits for biases. To elaborate further, during the quantization process, the original dataset is shuffled and 20% of it is used for the calibration of the quantized model, while the rest is used for the validation of the resulting model.

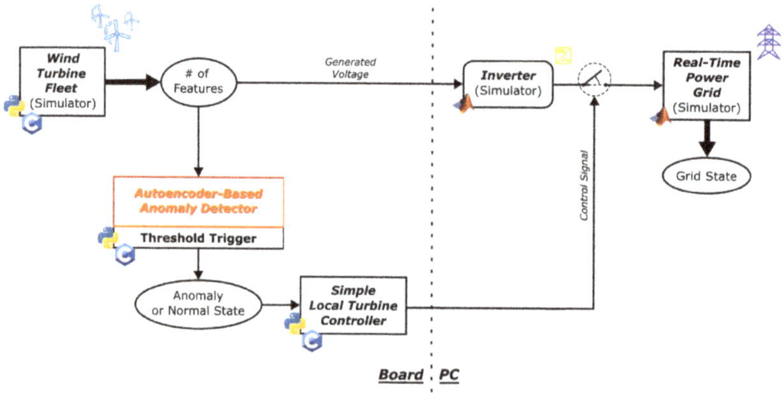

Figure 5. Experimentation testbed.

4.2. Power Measurement Methodology

In order to measure the power for each platform during our experiments, we utilize direct hardware monitoring. For the RPi, we use a COTS Adafruit INA219 power sensor [40], which is connected between the main DC power supply and the Device Under Test (DUT), as shown in Figure 6a. This sensor is a high-side current and voltage monitor chip with an I2C interface that operates using an external shunt resistor of 0.1 Ohms connected to a Programmable Gain Amplifier (PGA) and a 12-bit Analog-to-Digital Converter (ADC). Featuring programmable calibration, gain, filtering, and ADC resolution, it is deemed a versatile and sufficiently accurate instrument for the purposes of this application, providing a direct hardware-based solution. In order to initialize and calibrate the sensor as well as read the sensor measurements, we use the Adafruit INA219 library for Python [41], as it provides an intuitive and modifiable interface that handles the hardware–software interconnection. In our tests, we calibrate the INA219 so that we achieve a power sampling rate of approximately 20 samples per second.

In contrast to the RPi, the ZCU104 FPGA platform features integrated power monitoring capabilities which are accessible via software to the user. More specifically, ZCU104 is equipped with three power controller chips, two Infineon IRPS5401 and one TI INA226 [42]. All three chips are accessible via I2C and can be used to give precise power monitoring information from the board. In our tests, we use only the TI INA226 power controller to monitor the power consumption of the board. For access to the controller via ZCU104's four-core Cortex A53 ARM CPU, we leverage the PMBus module of the PYNQ v3.0.0 library, which facilitates the monitoring of the main 12V power rail of the board. For access to the controller during the experiment with the RISC-V MicroBlazeV microprocessor, we utilize the RPi's I2C interface via its GPIO header extension and access the ZCU104's I2C bus via its PMOD interface. This way, we use the RPi in order to monitor ZCU104's power during the RISC-V experiment, since in our setup, the MicroBlazeV microprocessor does

 https://doi.org/10.3390/electronics15020414

not have access to the sensor. In our tests with the TI INA226 and the ARM and FINN power measurement topology, we achieve a maximum power sampling rate of approximately 65 samples per second. While this limitation is likely introduced by the platform's parallel execution of accelerator-related and power monitoring scripts, it is verified that it does not lead to erroneous results, using the topology deployed in the MicroBlazeV tests, which attains a sampling rate of 1000 samples per second. The described setup for these cases is shown in Figure 6b,c.

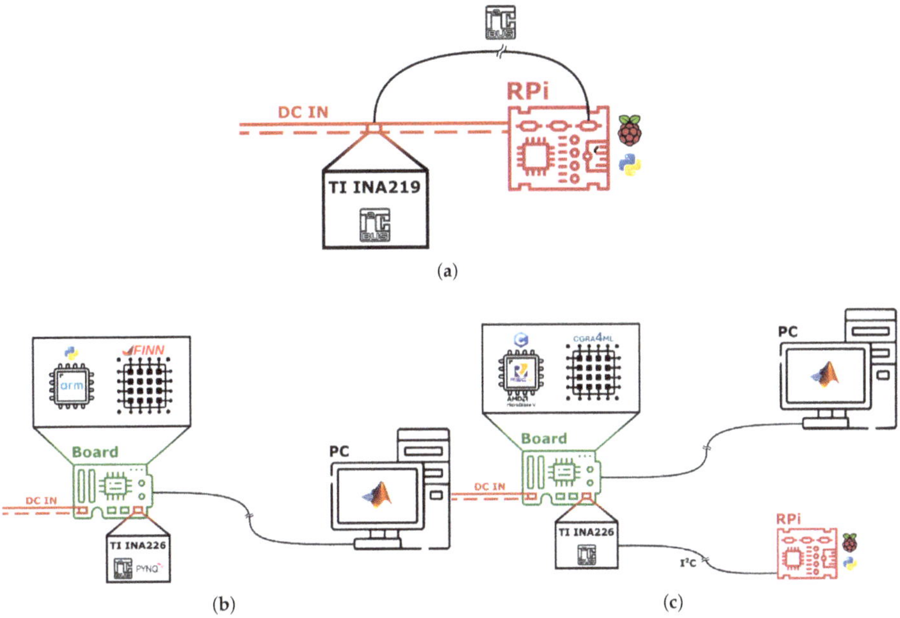

Figure 6. Power measurement topology: (**a**) RPi (baseline). (**b**) ARM and FINN. (**c**) RISC-V and CGRA4ML.

We begin by obtaining a sufficient amount of power measurements while the DUT is in an idle state (without load), thus establishing a base power figure. The power figure measurements are saved in appropriate .csv files during each monitoring session, containing the information of the derived power value, the timestamp, and a tag unique for each inference. During each acceleration test (when the DUT is under the load), we concurrently trigger a power monitoring routine and obtain a new power figure which reflects both the base power consumption of the board and the power consumption of the accelerator. By comparing those two figures, we are able to identify precisely the power behavior related to the acceleration routine and obtain valuable insights, thus enabling the extraction of ground-truth metrics, which are later used to compare the overall efficiency of the proposed solutions. Furthermore, to ensure fair comparison between the two acceleration flows and take into account the data transactions' power utilization, we develop scripts that are repeatedly executing data transactions to and from the external memory in the respective accelerator's fashion, that is, by taking into account its computation latency. In this way, we determine the mean power consumption of each host CPU data scheduling approach and utilize it in the subsequent computations.

The metrics we utilize in our work for comparing the different platforms in terms of power/energy are as follows:

https://doi.org/10.3390/electronics15020414

- Overall Mean Power per Inference (mW);
- Mean Absolute Deviation of Power per Inference (MAD) (mW);
- Standard Deviation of Mean Power per Inference (STDev) (mW);
- Mean Inference Duration (ms);
- Mean Energy per Inference (mJ);
- Performance (inferences per second);
- Efficiency (Performance per W).

We develop Python scripts for automatic parsing and post-processing of the power logs. We begin by calculating and subtracting the base power consumption of the DUT from all power measurements logged during the execution under load. Hence, the computations described from this point forward concern the power associated exclusively with the load examined in each case.

We calculate the mean power $\bar{P}_i$ consumed during inference i by utilizing n power measurements $P_{i,j}$ logged during this inference execution period:

$$\bar{P}_i = \frac{1}{n_i} \sum_{j=1}^{n_i} P_{i,j} \tag{6}$$

We are then able to define the **Overall Mean Power per Inference** as the mean value of all $\bar{P}_i$ calculated previously. This gives us a precise, representative value that accurately depicts power consumption on the inference level.

$$\bar{P}_{\text{overall}} = \frac{1}{N} \sum_{i=1}^{N} \bar{P}_i \tag{7}$$

We compute the **Mean Absolute Deviation** of $\bar{P}_{\text{overall}}$ to obtain a measure of the dispersion in the mean power per inference execution, as well as the **Standard Deviation** so as to examine the amount of variation from the overall mean. Furthermore, the **Mean Inference Duration** $\bar{t}$ is derived.

Having specified the Mean Inference Duration $\bar{t}$, we calculate the **Mean Energy per Inference** based on the definition below:

$$\bar{E} = \bar{P}_{\text{overall}} \times \bar{t} \tag{8}$$

We also focus on the **performance** of the implementations, establishing the average number of inferences performed in a second:

$$\bar{Prf} = \frac{1}{\bar{t}} \tag{9}$$

Lastly, we quantify **efficiency** as the ratio between performance and overall mean power.

$$\bar{Ef} = \frac{\bar{Prf}}{\bar{P}_{\text{overall}}} \tag{10}$$

4.3. Evaluation of the Proposed Pipeline

In this section, we elaborate on the testing scenarios studied, as well as present the results in detail and assess them.

Firstly, we capture the power profile of each platform in the idle state. We deploy the respective software monitoring routines described in the previous section for each device for a total duration of thirty minutes. This way, we are able to extract the mean idle power consumption of the devices with great certainty. By parsing these profiles, we compute the mean idle power consumed by the RPi to be 1.639 W, whereas the ZCU104 consumes

 https://doi.org/10.3390/electronics15020414

10.142 W. Additionally, we gather power measurements with the devices in under-load state. The resulting graphs of both the idle and under-load states for each platform are depicted in Figure 7a,b. The measurements of the RPi in under-load state, as shown in Figure 7a, also correspond to a wall-clock duration of thirty minutes, which comprise approximately 2000 inferences. The same time duration was chosen for the ZCU104 as well, as shown in Figure 7b. It is worth noting that the runtime needed for the ZCU104 platform to perform the same number of inferences is significantly less, amounting to a total of approximately 1 min and 24 s just for the FINN flow.

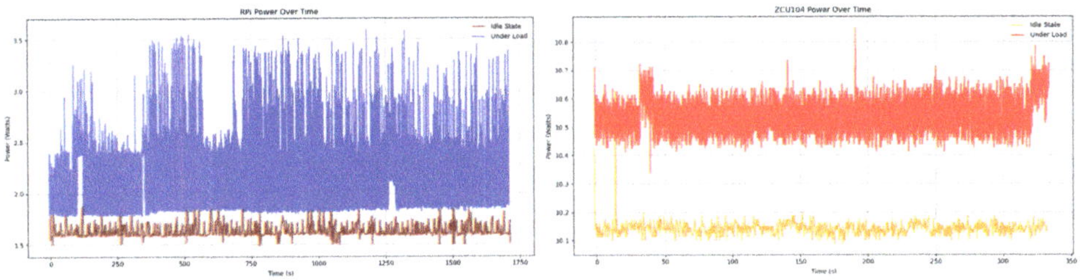

(a) (b)

Figure 7. (**a**) RPi power measurements in idle and under-load state. (**b**) ZCU104 power measurements in idle and under-load state.

The results of the post-processing methodology described in the previous section are presented in Table 1 for each DUT:

Table 1. Metrics across tested platforms.

Metric (Unit)	RPi (ONNX Runtime)	ZCU104 (FINN)	ZCU104 (CGRA4ML)
Overall Mean Power per Inference (mW)	371.3	399.3	461.9
MAD of Mean Power per Inference (mW)	93.1	24.1	20.9
STDev (mW)	133.5	35.0	25.6
Mean Inference Duration (ms)	259.3	27.5	6.89
Mean Energy per Inference (mJ)	96.3	11.0	3.2
Performance (inf/s)	3	36	145
Efficiency (Performance/W)	8.079	90.156	313.941

When comparing the results of the ONNX Runtime implementation on the RPi against the FINN-generated accelerator on the ZCU104 platform, we make numerous observations. In terms of Overall Mean Power per Inference, we observe a 7.5% increase for the ZCU104 FINN implementation, while the Mean Absolute Deviation exhibits a 74% decrease and the Standard Deviation a 73.8% decrease. This indicates that the FINN accelerator operates with a more stable power profile in contrast to the RPi, which is beneficial for the platform's power stability and health. Moreover, the ZCU104 achieves a major reduction of 89.4% in Mean Inference Duration, causing an equally major drop of 88.6% in Energy Consumption per Inference. Indeed, this confirms initial expectations on the superiority of a custom design, exploiting parallelism and folding schemes to optimize the execution of the algorithm. This conclusion is amplified when comparing the last two metrics: performance

 https://doi.org/10.3390/electronics15020414

and efficiency. The difference between the RPi and FINN flow upon examination of these metrics is apparent: the RPi achieves 3 inf/s while the FINN-derived accelerator achieves 12-fold performance. Similarly, in terms of efficiency, the RPi achieves just around 9% of the FINN accelerator's efficiency.

The metrics of CGRA4ML on the ZCU104 platform are equally intriguing. One can notice that it exhibits the highest Overall Mean Power per Inference out of all implementations, specifically 15.7% more power compared to the FINN case. This correlates with the fact that the CGRA4ML-generated accelerator needs to move data to and from the off-chip RAM, which causes this power increase. Nevertheless, with reference to the MAD and STDev features, the CGRA4ML topology shows favorable results in par with the FINN accelerator, which again shows the stable power profile that the accelerator exhibits. Furthermore, CGRA4ML offers exceptionally low Mean Inference Duration, merely 6.89 ms, which is around 75% faster than the FINN accelerator. This speed increase is mainly due to the fact that the FINN accelerator's runtime environment is managed by the PYNQ library, while the CGRA accelerator runs via baremetal C code. Moreover, this lack in speed by the FINN accelerator is justified by the target Frames-Per-Second (FPS) choice during the build process. Since the goal is to provide a basic performance overview of the flows presented, we focus on the default setup of the process without specifying an FPS constraint. Computing the Mean Energy per Inference results at 3.2 mJ, a 71% drop occurs compared to the FINN design. Correspondingly, the performance and efficiency of the CGRA4ML accelerator is significantly better than FINN's (4x and 3.4x better). We are led to the conclusion that CGRA4ML has equally useful capabilities in ML acceleration, offering impactful improvement in efficiency during operation.

Another important characteristic of the flows tested in this research is the **accuracy** achieved by the algorithm in each environment. The metric we use to express this is the reconstruction error of the model—that is, its Mean Squared Error (MSE)—since this is a most common and widely accepted metric for autoencoder models. The resulting value for each DUT is shown in Table 2:

Table 2. Algorithm accuracy across tested platforms.

Metric (Unit)	RPi (ONNX Runtime)	ZCU104 (FINN)	ZCU104 (CGRA4ML)
Accuracy (MSE)	0.0015	0.0026	0.0026

The original autoencoder model is validated right after the training process, exhibiting a reconstruction error of 0.0015 (MSE). This is the baseline error of the model, which we find in the RPi deployment. The model is also tested in terms of accuracy right after we perform PTQ using the Brevitas library. This process results in a reconstruction error of **0.0026** (MSE). The error stays the same during both the functional verification of the model inside the FINN build process and the final hardware verification. Overall, accuracy is sufficiently preserved throughout the build process. Lastly, the accuracy of the CGRA4ML implementation is the same as the one of the FINN flow, which shows that our pipeline works as expected and does not tamper with the QONNX model during the QKeras translation. All things considered, 8-bit quantization shows very good performance. Lesser quantization representations could also yield similar accuracy results with greater energy saving outcomes. Even though not investigated during our tests, it is expected that 4-bit quantization could effectively double the energy performance metrics of ZCU104 shown in Table 1.

It is also worthwhile to compare the resources used by the designs originating from the FINN and CGRA4ML flow. Tables 3 and 4 summarize the hardware resources used by

https://doi.org/10.3390/electronics15020414

each flow during our tests, in order to better grasp the impact that these strategies have on the final design footprint:

Table 3. Resource usage of FINN hardware design.

Design Attribute	Utilization *	Available	Utilization %
LUT	22,228	230,400	9.65
LUTRAM	9195	101,760	9.04
FF	21,088	460,800	4.58
BRAM	107	312	34.13
URAM	3	96	3.13
DSP	21	1728	1.22

* Design operates on 100 MHz clock frequency.

Table 4. Resource usage of CGRA hardware design.

Design Attribute	Utilization *	Available	Utilization %
LUT	57,600	230,400	25
LUTRAM	6106	101,760	6
FF	92,160	460,800	20
BRAM	47	312	15.06
URAM	1	96	1.04
DSP	18	1728	1.04

* Design operates on 100 MHz clock frequency.

The resource utilization percentages reveal no clear superior architecture. The FINN design outranks the CGRA4ML design in terms of Look-Up Table (LUT) and Flip Flop (FF) usage (10% and 5%, respectively, as opposed to 25% and 20%), whereas the CGRA4ML design utilizes slightly less Look-Up Table Random Access Memory (LUTRAM), as well as Unified RAM. Regarding Block RAM (BRAM), the CGRA4ML accelerator takes up approximately half the quantity that FINN requires. However, we have to take into account that the resources of the CGRA4ML accelerator include also the ones of the MicroBlazeV microcontroller used in our tests.

Lastly, we need to point out the real-time response of the accelerators in contrast to the RPi platform. Our experiments showed that the FINN accelerator achieved a Mean Inference Duration of 27.5 ms and the CGRA one was able to reach 6.89 ms, whereas the RPi managed to finish one inference in 259.3 ms. By summing up the threshold trigger module's processing delay (which in all cases is less than 1 ms) and the minimal transmission delay of the sensor data from the sensors to the board, we see that the accelerators can easily achieve the hard real-time constraint of 50 ms that we set in the beginning, while the RPi fails to give an output within the acceptable time period. The fact that the accelerators' behavior is deterministic by nature makes them a reliable solution and suitable for cyber–physical problems.

Figure 8 presents an example of voltage transients and the respective alarm signal generation from the anomaly detection application. Specifically, in Figure 8a we see the voltage transients' trace and how the application is closely monitoring it and identifies the anomaly events in real-time. In Figure 8b, we can see more clearly the difference in latency between the different implementations, with the RPi alarm signal always lagging behind the accelerator ones. This further highlights the superior capabilities of the accelerators.

 https://doi.org/10.3390/electronics15020414

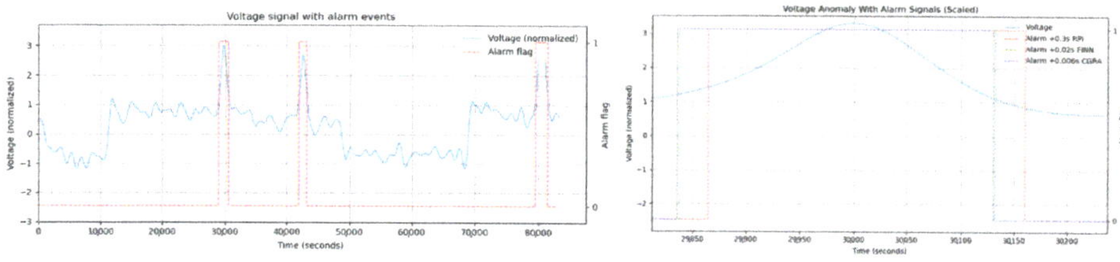

(**a**) (**b**)

Figure 8. (**a**) Example of voltage transients and alarm generation. (**b**) Scaled up version, where different alarm latencies are clearly depicted.

5. Discussion

This paper presented a unified, fully open-source hardware-aware AI acceleration pipeline that addresses fragmentation challenges in FPGA and CGRA-based neural network deployment through a common frontend based on the Brevitas quantization library. By supporting two distinct acceleration flows—custom FPGA dataflow accelerators via FINN and CGRA-based architectures through CGRA4ML—our pipeline enables seamless comparison between different hardware acceleration approaches while maintaining full compatibility with PyTorch-based development workflows. We demonstrated the practical effectiveness of our proposed pipeline through a comprehensive case study on autoencoder-based anomaly detection for wind turbines in smart grids, deploying our solution on both a RPi baseline platform with ONNX Runtime environment and an AMD-Xilinx ZCU104 FPGA platform utilizing both acceleration flows. Our experimental validation confirmed true real-time, low-energy, high-performance operation with both acceleration flows, with detailed comparisons demonstrating the superiority of FPGA-accelerated solutions for edge AI applications.

Future work will be dedicated to the further automation of the pipeline. More specifically, focus will be given on the creation of an automation routine dedicated to the selection of the best quantization scheme for each acceleration flow. This routine will also compare performance estimates for each flow and provide suggestions on which flow is better suited for the application of interest. In addition, further research will be given on the flows themselves and specifically their enhancement with more features, e.g., the addition of Recurrent Neural Network (RNN) support in CGRA4ML and its comparison with the FINN flow. Finally, broader testing of the pipeline is also under the scope with its integration with the already established research field of Neural Architecture Search (NAS) and its active research branch of hardware-aware NAS.

Author Contributions: Conceptualization, E.M.; methodology, E.M. and C.F.; software, E.M. and C.F.; validation, E.M., C.F., and S.K.; formal analysis, E.M.; investigation, E.M. and C.F.; resources, E.M.; data curation, E.M.; writing—original draft preparation, E.M. and C.F.; writing—review and editing, E.M. and C.F.; visualization, E.M. and S.K.; supervision, M.B. and A.B.; project administration, A.B.; funding acquisition, A.B. All authors have read and agreed to the published version of the manuscript.

Funding: This research was partially funded by the European Union's Horizon 2020 research and innovation programs under grant agreement No 101139194 6G TransContinental Edge Learning (6G-XCEL).

Data Availability Statement: The original data presented in the study are openly available in GitHub at https://github.com/lefmylonas/finn_cgra4ml_hw_pipeline.git (accessed on 15 December 2025).

Conflicts of Interest: The authors declare no conflicts of interest.

Abbreviations

The following abbreviations are used in this manuscript:

PPA	Power–Performance–Area
AI	Artificial Intelligence
CNN	Convolutional Neural Network
ANN	Artificial Neural Network
ViT	Vision Transformer
ML	Machine Learning
COTS	Commercial Off-The-Shelf
RPi	Raspberry Pi
NPU	Neural Processing Unit
DPU	Deep Learning Processing Unit
CPU	Central Processing Unit
GPU	Graphics Processing Unit
CGRA	Coarse-Grained Reconfigurable Architecture
FPGA	Field-Programmable Gate Array
QAT	Quantization-Aware Training
PTQ	Post-Training Quantization
ONNX	Open Neural Network eXchange
QONNX	Quantized Open Neural Network eXchange
LLM	Large Language Model
BNN	Binary Neural Network
IR	Intermediate Representation
RTL	Register-Transfer-Level
HLS	High-Level Synthesis
DNN	Deep Neural Network
PE	Processing Element
SIMD	Single-Instruction–Multiple-Data
FIFO	First-In First-Out
ASIC	Application-Specific Integrated Circuit
DMA	Direct Memory Access
TCL	Tool Command Language
PLC	Programmable Logic Controller
DWT	Discrete Wavelet Transform
IDWT	Inverse Distrete Wavelet Transform
FP32	Single Precision Floating Point Format
DUT	Device Under Test
PGA	Programmable Gain Amplifier
ADC	Analog-to-Digital Converter
GPIO	General-Purpose Input/Output
MAD	Mean Absolute Deviation
STDev	Standard Deviation
MSE	Mean Squared Error
FPS	Frames-Per-Second
LUT	Look-Up Table
LUTRAM	Look-Up Table Random Access Memory
FF	Flip FLop
BRAM	Block Random Access Memory
URAM	Unified Random Access Memory
DSP	Digital Signal Processing
RNN	Recurrent Neural Network
NAS	Neural Architecture Search

 https://doi.org/10.3390/electronics15020414

References

1. Radanliev, P.; De Roure, D.; Van Kleek, M.; Santos, O.; Ani, U. Artificial intelligence in cyber physical systems. *AI Soc.* **2021**, *36*, 783–796. [CrossRef]
2. Chen, J.; Wen, K.; Xia, J.; Huang, R.; Chen, Z.; Li, W. Knowledge Embedded Autoencoder Network for Harmonic Drive Fault Diagnosis Under Few-Shot Industrial Scenarios. *IEEE Internet Things J.* **2024**, *11*, 22915–22925. [CrossRef]
3. Choi, Y.; Joe, I. Motor Fault Diagnosis and Detection with Convolutional Autoencoder (CAE) Based on Analysis of Electrical Energy Data. *Electronics* **2024**, *13*, 3946. [CrossRef]
4. Ghazimoghadam, S.; Hosseinzadeh, S.A.A. A novel unsupervised deep learning approach for vibration-based damage diagnosis using a multi-head self-attention LSTM autoencoder. *Elsevier Meas.* **2024**, *229*, 114410. [CrossRef]
5. We Did the Math on AI's Energy Footprint. Here's the Story You Haven't Heard, MIT Technology Review. Available online: https://www.technologyreview.com/2025/05/20/1116327/ai-energy-usage-climate-footprint-big-tech/ (accessed on 15 December 2025).
6. Liu, L.; Zhu, J.; Li, Z.; Lu, Y.; Deng, Y.; Han, J.; Yin, S.; Wei, S. A Survey of Coarse-Grained Reconfigurable Architecture and Design: Taxonomy, Challenges, and Applications. *ACM Comput. Surv.* **2019**, *53*, 1–39. [CrossRef]
7. Podobas, A.; Sano, K.; Matsuoka, S. A Survey on Coarse-Grained Reconfigurable Architectures From a Performance Perspective. *IEEE Access* **2020**, *8*, 146719–146743. [CrossRef]
8. Mohaidat, T.; Khalil, K. A Survey on Neural Network Hardware Accelerators. *IEEE Trans. Artif. Intell.* **2024**, *4*, 3801–3822. [CrossRef]
9. Liu, S.; Fan, H.; Ferianc, M.; Niu, X.; Shi, H.; Luk, W. Toward Full-Stack Acceleration of Deep Convolutional Neural Networks on FPGAs. *IEEE Trans. Neural Netw. Learn. Syst.* **2022**, *33*, 3974–3987. [CrossRef] [PubMed]
10. Medus, L.D.; Iakymchuk, T.; Frances-Villora, J.V.; Bataller-Mompeán, M.; Rosado-Munoz, A. A Novel Systolic Parallel Hardware Architecture for the FPGA Acceleration of Feedforward Neural Networks. *IEEE Access* **2019**, *7*, 76084–76103. [CrossRef]
11. Zhao, Z.; Cao, R.; Un, K.F.; Yu, W.H.; Mak, P.I.; Martins, R.P. An FPGA-Based Transformer Accelerator Using Output Block Stationary Dataflow for Object Recognition Applications. *IEEE Trans. Circuits Syst. II Express Briefs* **2023**, *70*, 281–285. [CrossRef]
12. Blott, M.; Preußer, T.B.; Fraser, N.J.; Gambardella, G.; O'brien, K.; Umuroglu, Y.; Leeser, M.; Vissers, K. FINN-R: An end-to-end deep-learning framework for fast exploration of quantized neural networks. *ACM Trans. Reconfigurable Technol. Syst.* **2018**, *11*, 1–23. [CrossRef]
13. Umuroglu, Y.; Fraser, N.J.; Gambardella, G.; Blott, M.; Leong, P.; Jahre, M.; Vissers, K. FINN: A Framework for Fast, Scalable Binarized Neural Network Inference. In Proceedings of the 2017 ACM/SIGDA International Symposium on Field-Programmable Gate Arrays, Monterey, CA, USA, 22–24 February 2017. [CrossRef]
14. Schulte, J.F.; Ramhorst, B.; Sun, C.; Mitrevski, J.; Ghielmetti, N.; Lupi, E.; Danopoulos, D.; Loncar, V.; Duarte, J.; Burnette, D.; et al. hls4ml: A Flexible, Open-Source Platform for Deep Learning Acceleration on Reconfigurable Hardware. *arXiv* **2025**, arXiv:2512.01463.
15. Anderson, J.; Beidas, R.; Chacko, V.; Hsiao, H.; Ling, X.; Ragheb, O.; Wang, X.; Yu, T. CGRA-ME: An Open-Source Framework for CGRA Architecture and CAD Research: (Invited Paper). In Proceedings of the 2021 IEEE 32nd International Conference on Application-Specific Systems, Architectures and Processors (ASAP), Virtual, 7–9 July 2021. [CrossRef]
16. Vitis AI User Guide (UG1414). Available online: https://docs.amd.com/r/en-US/ug1414-vitis-ai/Vitis-AI-Overview (accessed on 15 December 2025).
17. OpenVINO Website. Available online: https://docs.openvino.ai/2025/index.html (accessed on 15 December 2025).
18. DNNDK User Guide. Available online: https://docs.amd.com/v/u/en-US/ug1327-dnndk-user-guide (accessed on 15 December 2025).
19. Faure-Gignoux, A.; Delmas, K.; Gauffriau, A.; Pagetti, C. Open-source Stand-Alone Versatile Tensor Accelerator. *arXiv* **2025**, arXiv:2509.19790.
20. Xilinx/brevitas Zenodo Website. Available online: https://zenodo.org/records/16987789 (accessed on 15 December 2025).
21. CGRA4ML's GitHub Website. Available online: https://github.com/KastnerRG/cgra4ml.git (accessed on 13 January 2026).
22. Abarajithan, G.; Ma, Z.; Li, Z.; Koparkar, S.; Munasinghe, R.; Restuccia, F.; Kastner, R. CGRA4ML: A Framework to Implement Modern Neural Networks for Scientific Edge Computing. *arXiv* **2024**, arXiv:2408.15561. [CrossRef]
23. Khadem Hosseini, A.M.; Mirzakuchaki, S. Real-Time Semantic Segmentation on FPGA for Autonomous Vehicles Using LMIINet with the CGRA4ML Framework. *arXiv* **2025**, arXiv:2510.22243.
24. Pappalardo, A.; Umuroglu, Y.; Blott, M.; Mitrevski, J.; Hawks, B.; Tran, N.; Loncar, V.; Summers, S.; Borras, H.; Muhizi, J.; et al. QONNX: Representing Arbitrary-Precision Quantized Neural Networks. *arXiv* **2022**, arXiv:2206.07527. [CrossRef]
25. What Is Transposed Convolutional Layer? Available online: https://towardsdatascience.com/what-is-transposed-convolutional-layer-40e5e6e31c11/ (accessed on 15 December 2025).

 https://doi.org/10.3390/electronics15020414

26. Preventing Blackouts: Real-Time Data Processing for Millisecond-Level Fault Handling. Available online: https://www.ververica.com/blog/preventing-blackouts-real-time-data-processing-for-mission-critical-infrastructure (accessed on 15 December 2025).
27. Singh, G.K. Power system harmonics research: A survey. *Eur. Trans. Electr. Power* **2009**, *19*, 151–172. [CrossRef]
28. Liang, X.; Andalib-Bin-Karim, C. Harmonics and Mitigation Techniques Through Advanced Control in Grid-Connected Renewable Energy Sources: A Review. *IEEE Trans. Ind. Appl.* **2018**, *54*, 3100–3111. [CrossRef]
29. Berahm, K.; Daneshfar, F.; Salehi, E.S.; Li, Y.; Xu, Y. Autoencoders and their applications in machine learning: A survey. *Artif. Intell. Rev.* **2024**, *57*, 28. [CrossRef]
30. Zhu, X.; Yang, C.; Lin, T. Maximum Variance Regularization for Latent Variables Makes Autoencoder Become Better One-Class Classifier. In Proceedings of the China Automation Congress (CAC), Qingdao, China, 1–3 November 2024. Available online: https://ieeexplore.ieee.org/document/10865629 (accessed on 3 January 2026).
31. Yong, B.X.; Brintrup, A. Do Autoencoders Need a Bottleneck for Anomaly Detection? *IEEE Access* **2022**, *10*, 78455–78471. [CrossRef]
32. Mercioni, M.A.; Holban, S. Developing Novel Activation Functions in Time Series Anomaly Detection with LSTM Autoencoder. In Proceedings of the 2021 IEEE 15th International Symposium on Applied Computational Intelligence and Informatics (SACI), Timisoara, Romania, 19–21 May 2021. [CrossRef]
33. PyWavelets—Wavelet Transforms in Python. Available online: https://pywavelets.readthedocs.io/en/latest/ (accessed on 15 December 2025).
34. Mylonas, E.; Tzanis, N.; Birbas, M.; Birbas, A. An Automatic Design Framework for Real-Time Power System Simulators Supporting Smart Grid Applications. *Electronics* **2020**, *9*, 299. [CrossRef]
35. Stavropoulos, S.; Tzanis, N.; Mylonas, E.; Birbas, M.; Birbas, A.; Papalexopoulos, A. FPGA-enabled Real-Time Power Grid Simulation Using Grid Partitioning. In Proceedings of the 12th Mediterranean Conference on Power Generation, Transmission, Distribution and Energy Conversion (MEDPOWER 2020), Paphos, Cyprus, 9–12 November 2020. [CrossRef]
36. Tzanis, N.; Proiskos, G.; Birbas, M.; Birbas, A. FPGA-Assisted Distribution Grid Simulator. In Proceedings of the 14th International Symposium, ARC 2018, Santorini, Greece, 2–4 May 2018. [CrossRef]
37. ZCU104 Board User Guide (UG1267). Available online: https://docs.amd.com/v/u/en-US/ug1267-zcu104-eval-bd (accessed on 14 December 2025).
38. MicroBlaze V Processor Embedded Design User Guide (UG1711). Available online: https://docs.amd.com/r/en-US/ug1711-microblaze-v-embedded-design/Introduction (accessed on 14 December 2025).
39. Wind Turbine Fleet Dataset for Anomaly Detection. Available online: https://aws-ml-blog.s3.amazonaws.com/artifacts/monitor-manage-anomaly-detection-model-wind-turbine-fleet-sagemaker-neo/dataset_wind_turbine.csv.gz (accessed on 14 December 2025).
40. INA219 Datasheet. Available online: https://www.ti.com/lit/ds/symlink/ina219.pdf?ts=1765634341896 (accessed on 14 December 2025).
41. Circuit Python Driver for INA219 Current Sensor. Available online: https://github.com/adafruit/Adafruit_CircuitPython_INA219.git (accessed on 14 December 2025).
42. INA226 Datasheet. Available online: https://www.ti.com/product/INA226 (accessed on 14 December 2025).

https://doi.org/10.3390/electronics15020414

electronics

MDPI

Article

Analyzing Performance of Data Preprocessing Techniques on CPUs vs. GPUs with and Without the MapReduce Environment

Sikha S. Bagui [1,*], Colin Eller [1], Rianna Armour [1], Shivani Singh [1], Subhash C. Bagui [2] and Dustin Mink [3]

[1] Department of Computer Science, The University of West Florida, Pensacola, FL 32514, USA; ce53@students.uwf.edu (C.E.); rka7@students.uwf.edu (R.A.); fs65@students.uwf.edu (S.S.)
[2] Department of Mathematics and Statistics, The University of West Florida, Pensacola, FL 32514, USA; sbagu@uwf.edu
[3] Department of Cybersecurity, The University of West Florida, Pensacola, FL 32514, USA; dmink@uwf.edu
* Correspondence: bagui@uwf.edu

Abstract: Data preprocessing is usually necessary before running most machine learning classifiers. This work compares three different preprocessing techniques, minimal preprocessing, Principal Components Analysis (PCA), and Linear Discriminant Analysis (LDA). The efficiency of these three preprocessing techniques is measured using the Support Vector Machine (SVM) classifier. Efficiency is measured in terms of statistical metrics such as accuracy, precision, recall, the F-1 measure, and AUROC. The preprocessing times and the classifier run times are also compared using the three differently preprocessed datasets. Finally, a comparison of performance timings on CPUs vs. GPUs with and without the MapReduce environment is performed. Two newly created Zeek Connection Log datasets, collected using the Security Onion 2 network security monitor and labeled using the MITRE ATT&CK framework, UWF-ZeekData22 and UWF-ZeekDataFall22, are used for this work. Results from this work show that binomial LDA, on average, performs the best in terms of statistical measures as well as timings using GPUs or MapReduce GPUs.

Keywords: preprocessing; linear discriminant analysis (LDA); principal component analysis (PCA); Apache Spark; support vector machines (SVMs); MapReduce; big data; network traffic analysis; machine learning; MITRE ATT&CK® framework

1. Introduction and Background

In this ever-evolving landscape of cybersecurity, the proliferation of internet-connected devices has ushered in unprecedented levels of data exchange alongside a corresponding surge in cyber threats. As the Internet of Things (IoT) continues to expand, so does the potential for malicious activities across various sectors, ranging from healthcare to logistics [1,2]. In 2023, it was estimated that the number of IoT-connected devices surpassed 17 billion, and this number is expected to continue to rise significantly in the coming years [3]. As a result, being able to monitor and recognize malicious activity and cyberattacks in real-time is imperative to cybersecurity efforts [1].

This research contributes to the ongoing discourse on cybersecurity by providing insights into the efficacy of machine learning (ML) approaches in identifying and categorizing cyber threats. By comparing the performance of Support Vector Machine (SVM) models under different preprocessing techniques, this study aims to determine the impact of feature reduction methods on classification accuracy and efficiency. Specifically, this paper aims to evaluate the effectiveness of SVMs in predicting and classifying cyberattacks in both binary and multi-classification scenarios, while also reducing the preprocessing and evaluation time required for classification. To achieve this, the effects of three different data preprocessing techniques on the performance of binary and multi-class SVMs are compared. In the first technique, the data is minimally preprocessed; in the second technique, the data undergoes minimal preprocessing followed by Principal Component Analysis (PCA); and in the third technique, the data undergoes minimal preprocessing followed by Linear Discriminant Analysis (LDA). Given the large size of the datasets, GPU integration and MapReduce techniques were employed to attempt to minimize preprocessing and evaluation time. Performance of all three models was compared using CPUs and GPUs, with and without the MapReduce environment.

The uniqueness of this work is further enhanced by the use of Zeek connection log data. Zeek is an open-source network-monitoring tool that provides the raw network data [4]. Modern, unique, newly created Zeek datasets, UWF-ZeekData22 [1,5] and UWF-ZeekDataFall22 [5,6], are used in this work to identify connections that lead to adversarial tactics [1,5]. These datasets are labeled using the MITRE Adversarial Tactics, Techniques, and Common Knowledge (ATT&CK) framework [7], which serves as a publicly available resource detailing adversary tactics and techniques employed to achieve specific objectives [1,7]. Finally, in this paper, classification is performed at the tactic level, that is, the correct classification of the Reconnaissance, Discovery, Defense Evasion, Privilege Escalation, and Resource Development tactics is explored. Classification at the tactic level has not been attempted in any previous work.

To handle the large amount of data, both datasets are stored in the Hadoop Big Data framework, which is a distributed file system. The Hadoop Distributed File System (HDFS) is scalable and fault-tolerant, and allows for the storage and processing of Big Data across a cluster of computers [8]. To perform the machine learning classification, Apache Spark 3.5.0 was used. Apache Spark is an open-source computing framework that is used in conjunction with Hadoop. In addition to being fast, scalable, and fault-tolerant, Apache Spark is also an in-memory, cluster computing framework designed to process and analyze large datasets [9]. For preprocessing and classification, several ML libraries from Apache Spark were used.

The remainder of this paper is organized as follows: Section 2 provides an overview of the related works in the field of cybersecurity and ML; Section 3 provides an outline of the datasets used in this research; Section 4 describes the preprocessing techniques used, including PCA and LDA; Section 5 provides an overview of the PCA and LDA algorithms; Section 6 discusses the SVM model, as well as training and testing techniques; Section 7 describes the experimental setup as well as the hardware and software used; Section 8 details the results and findings; and, finally, Section 9 offers conclusions drawn from this study.

2. Related Works

As organizations call for more focus on securing their data from relevant threats and analyzing and developing effective countermeasures, the topic of Intrusion Detection Systems (IDSs) has become relatively popular [10–16]. Numerous studies have investigated utilizing SVMs as a prediction model for classifying cyberattacks and improving IDS performance. Many papers use one of the most applicable datasets in information security research, the KDD99 Cup dataset [10–13] and its subsequent dataset NSL-KDD [12,14,16] to experiment with IDS to improve classification methods.

Utilizing the KDD99 dataset, various studies have compared multiple ML algorithms, including K-Nearest Neighbor, J48, Naïve Bayes (NB), Random Forest (RF), Nearest Neighbors Generalized, and Voting Features Interval, as well as preprocessing techniques such as PCA, while utilizing SVMs. LDA and various kernels were also tested [10–13,17].

Other studies used different datasets, such as the NSL-KDD, UNSW-NB15, and CIC-IDS2017, to compare various ML algorithms and preprocessing techniques. Feature selection techniques besides PCA and LDA were also used, such as information gain or Genetic Algorithms. These studies found that decreasing features often resulted in improved accuracy, but that SVM models often performed poorly compared to other models. However, it was shown that the linear SVM had advantages in training time and precision over the nonlinear SVM [14–16,18]. Additionally, one study comparing PCA, LDA, and Autoencoder-based feature extraction methods across multiple IDS datasets, including UNSW-NB15 and CSE-CIC-IDS2018, found that no single method consistently outperformed others, but it highlighted that the effectiveness of each feature extraction technique was highly dataset dependent, and, in many cases, LDA underperformed relative to PCA and Autoencoders when used with various classifiers [19].

Several studies also sought to use feature reduction techniques in conjunction with SVM models, to include multi-class SVM models. These studies observed that accuracy often remained similar, or sometimes improved, when LDA or PCA were used. Combining feature reduction techniques with different ML algorithms, such as Logistic Regression, also showed improvements in computational time versus standard SVM models. Minimal performance loss was observed while reducing computational overhead, resulting in speedups to algorithm performance [20–22]. Another study reinforced the importance of feature reduction for improving classifier performance by applying Singular Value Decomposition (SVD) as a feature reduction technique before classification on the NSL-KDD dataset, showing that reducing dimensionality prior to applying machine learning models led to improved detection accuracy and reduced computational load, particularly when used with SVM classifiers [23].

Yet other studies sought to either test the effectiveness of different kernels on one- and two-class SVMs, or improve performance by modifying the Gaussian kernel. The two-class SVM model, along with the modified Gaussian kernel, was found to increase accuracy, sometimes significantly, when compared to traditional SVM methods. The modified kernel also resulted in reduced training and testing times. The two-class SVM model, however, performed poorly on certain datasets, suggesting that SVMs may serve as a complement to the performance of existing IDSs rather than a complete replacement [24,25].

A few studies sought to utilize MapReduce to run ML algorithms for IDSs. MapReduce runs programs on parallel clusters. These studies found that utilizing MapReduce techniques was effective for performing parallel computing on large datasets, resulting in increased performance and decreased runtime. Accuracy and other statistical metrics remained unchanged, as using MapReduce does not affect the statistical performance of the algorithms themselves [26,27].

This paper expands on research already completed on IDSs by using SVM as an IDS. It seeks to compare the results of minimal preprocessing (MP) as well as MP coupled with feature reduction techniques such as PCA and LDA, while also testing the speed performance of the three techniques when built using a parallel MapReduce framework. Performance of the techniques is measured using the binomial as well as multinomial SVM classifiers.

3. Datasets

Two Zeek Connection (Conn) Log MITRE ATT&CK framework labeled datasets, UWF-ZeekData22 [1,5], and its later counterpart and UWF-ZeekDataFall22 [5,6], generated using the Cyber Range at The University of West Florida (UWF), were used for this analysis. Features used in this analysis are presented here in Figure 1.

```
root
 |-- community_id: string (nullable = true)
 |-- conn_state: string (nullable = true)
 |-- duration: double (nullable = true)
 |-- history: string (nullable = true)
 |-- src_ip_zeek: string (nullable = true)
 |-- src_port_zeek: long (nullable = true)
 |-- dest_ip_zeek: string (nullable = true)
 |-- dest_port_zeek: long (nullable = true)
 |-- local_orig: boolean (nullable = true)
 |-- local_resp: boolean (nullable = true)
 |-- missed_bytes: long (nullable = true)
 |-- orig_bytes: long (nullable = true)
 |-- orig_ip_bytes: long (nullable = true)
 |-- orig_pkts: long (nullable = true)
 |-- proto: string (nullable = true)
 |-- resp_bytes: long (nullable = true)
 |-- resp_ip_bytes: long (nullable = true)
 |-- resp_pkts: long (nullable = true)
 |-- service: string (nullable = true)
 |-- ts: double (nullable = true)
 |-- uid: string (nullable = true)
 |-- datetime: timestamp (nullable = true)
 |-- label_tactic: string (nullable = true)
```

Figure 1. Common features in Zeek datasets.

3.1. Overview of the UWF-ZeekData22 Dataset

This dataset has 9,280,869 attack records and 9,281,599 benign records. Figure 2 presents a breakdown of the data by MITRE ATT&CK Tactics. There were 9,278,722 instances of Reconnaissance activity, 2086 instances of Discovery activity, and very few instances of other adversary tactics in this dataset; hence, only Reconnaissance and Discovery were used for this analysis. Reconnaissance tactics are active or passive tactics that are used to gather information to plan future operations [28,29]. Discovery tactics are used to gain knowledge about the system [28,30].

label_tactic	count
Credential Access	31
Defense Evasion	1
Discovery	2086
Exfiltration	7
Initial Access	1
Lateral Movement	4
Persistence	1
Privilege Escalation	13
Reconnaissance	9278722
Resource Development	3
none	9281599

Figure 2. Counts of MITRE ATT&CK tactics in UWF-ZeekData22.

3.2. Overview of UWF-ZeekDataFall22 Dataset

This dataset, created in 2023, has 350,001 attack records and 350,339 benign records [6]. The breakdown of the attack tactics in the UWF-ZeekDataFall22 [6] dataset is presented in Figure 3. There were 275,471 instances of Resource Development activity, followed by

51,492 instances of Reconnaissance, 16,819 instances of Discovery, 3064 Defense Evasion, 3066 instances of the Privilege Escalation, and very few instances of other adversary tactics in this dataset, so only the Resource Development, Reconnaissance, Discovery, Defense Evasion and Privilege Escalation tactics were used for this analysis. Resource Development tactics try to establish resources to support operations [6,31], Defense Evasion tactics are used to avoid detection [6,32] and Privilege Escalation tactics are used by adversaries to gain higher-level permissions of a system or network [6,33].

label_tactic	count
Collection	1
Command and Control	17
Credential Access	1
Defense Evasion	3064
Discovery	16819
Execution	30
Initial Access	19
Lateral Movement	11
Persistence	10
Privilege Escalation	3066
Reconnaissance	51492
Resource Development	275471
none	350339

Figure 3. Counts of MITRE ATT&CK tactics in UWF-ZeekDataFall22.

3.3. Sample Selection

For binary classification, one tactic and benign data were used. For multinomial classification, to ensure all models tested were trained on a sufficient set of samples, classes containing minimal instances were dropped. Hence, from the UWF-ZeekData22 dataset, all instances of the Credential Access, Defense Evasion, Exfiltration, Initial Access, Lateral Movement, Persistence, and Resource Development were dropped. Similarly, from the UWF-ZeekDataFall22 dataset, all instances of Collection, Command and Control, Credential Access, Execution, Initial Access, Lateral Movement, and Persistence were dropped. Since the number of dropped attacks is extremely small in these otherwise extremely large datasets, it does not introduce bias into the data.

4. Data Preprocessing

4.1. Dropping Features

The "uid" (user id) feature, which defines a unique identifier assigned to each user, was excluded from both datasets. The uid, which serves as a key for distinguishing individual records, lacks informative value as each record is inherently unique, and no commonality or useful variance is present that could be leveraged by ML algorithms like SVM. Hence, this feature would not contribute to understanding the underlying patterns or relationships in the datasets. Moreover, retaining this feature would only introduce unnecessary overhead, resulting in performance degradation.

Hence, in UWF-ZeekData22 [1,5], all other features were retained. The UWF-ZeekDataFall22 dataset [5,6], however, had two additional features, label_binary and label_technique, and these were dropped to keep the datasets consistent.

4.2. Preprocessing Through Data Imputation

To maintain the qualities of the original raw network data, the following methods of data imputation were used on both datasets.

4.2.1. Replacing Null Values with Averages

The null values were replaced with the mean values from their respective features in order to preserve the distribution. PySpark natively supports an Imputer class [33], which was utilized to calculate the mean of each numerical feature and replace null values.

4.2.2. Normalization

Values were normalized since both PCA and LDA benefit from data being normalized. Hence, numerical features were normalized to comparable scales between 0 and 1. This helped reduce sensitivity to outliers that may skew the data since PCA maximizes variance and LDA optimizes between-class to within-class variance, and without proper normalization, features with larger magnitudes could dominate calculations regardless of actual relevance [34]. Specifically, the min-max scaling method, which is what PySpark's StandardScaler [32] applies, is a standard method used to transform and normalize features into a bounded range to ensure all features contribute equally to the analysis. To perform the normalization, PySpark's StandardScaler [32] was used. Data was scaled using the following:

$$x_i' = \frac{x_i - \mu_i}{\sigma_i} \tag{1}$$

4.2.3. StringIndexer

The Spark implementation of SVM cannot natively handle string values, so StringIndexer [31] was used on both datasets. The StringIndexer maps all unique strings to individual numerical values that can be processed by the SVM algorithm.

4.3. Dimensionality Reduction

4.3.1. Principal Component Analysis

After a chosen data imputation method, PySpark's PCA module [35] was applied to the data to transform, or essentially compress, the raw data into fewer features known as principal components derived from the covariance matrix of the original features.

4.3.2. Linear Discriminant Analysis

As Spark and PySpark do not natively support Linear Discriminant Analysis, Scikit-learn's LinearDiscriminantAnalysis library was used on the data to perform supervised learning to transform the data into a smaller feature space based on the number of classes.

5. Feature Reduction Techniques

5.1. Principal Component Analysis

Principal Component Analysis (PCA) is a widely used, unsupervised approach used to reduce the dimensionality of data by using statistical approaches to find data points with the maximum potential variance [17,36]. PCA removes redundant and unnecessary features, allowing for the features to be more visible and organized in a new space, known as the principal space. As a result, the complexity of the overall dataset is also reduced. PCA reduces significant computation in Big Data [36]. PCA can be applied with the following steps, and the pseudocode for the algorithm is presented in Figure 4 [17,37].

PCA Pseudocode

```
PCA(Input: X, k)
    X_scaled = Standardize(X)
    cov_matrix = CovarianceMatrix(X_scaled)
    eigenvalues, eigenvectors = Eigendecomposition(cov_matrix)
    eigenvalues, eigenvectors = Eigendecomposition(cov_matrix)
    Sort eigenvalues and eigenvectors in descending order:
        sorted_indices = SortIndices(eigenvalues, descending = True)
        sorted_eigenvalues = eigenvalues[sorted_indices]
        sorted_eigenvectors = eigenvectors[:, sorted_indices]
    projection_matrix = sorted_eigenvectors[:, :k]
    X_pca = X_scaled * projection_matrix
```

Figure 4. Pseudocode for the Principal Component Analysis algorithm.

1. Normalize the dataset by subtracting the mean and dividing by the standard deviation for each feature:
$$x_{std}^{(i)} = \frac{x^{(i)} - \mu_x}{\sigma_x} \quad (2)$$
where μ_x is the sample mean of a feature column, and σ_x is the standard deviation.
2. Compute the covariance matrix by calculating the covariance between all features using the following:
$$\sigma_{jk} = \frac{1}{n-1}\sum_{i=1}^{n}\left(x_j^{(i)} - \mu_j\right)\left(x_j^{(i)} - \mu_k\right) \quad (3)$$
where μ_j and μ_k are the sample means of features j and k, respectively. (Note: the sample means are zero if the dataset has been standardized.)
3. The covariance matrix can then be written as follows:
$$\Sigma = \left[\sigma_1^2\sigma_{12}\ldots\sigma_{1d}\sigma_{21}\sigma_2^2\ldots\sigma_{2d}\vdots\vdots\ddots\vdots\sigma_{d1}\sigma_{d2}\ldots\sigma_d^2\right] \quad (4)$$
4. Compute the eigenvectors and eigenvalues of the covariance matrix Σ by solving the generalized eigenvector problem:
$$\Sigma v = \lambda v \quad (5)$$
5. Select the k largest eigenvalues and corresponding eigenvectors to be the principal components.
6. Construct a projection matrix W from the sorted k chosen eigenvectors.
7. Create a new k-dimensional feature space by transforming the original data using the projection matrix:
$$X' = XW \quad (6)$$

5.2. Linear Discriminant Analysis

Linear Discriminant Analysis (LDA) is a commonly used supervised statistical method designed to reduce the dimensionality of a dataset [22,38]. The n-dimensional dataset is projected onto a smaller k-dimensional dataset (where $k < n$), while retaining relevant class-discrimination information. LDA maximizes the ratio of the between-class variance to the within-class variance, which maximizes the separability between classes [38]. The pseudocode to perform LDA can be seen in Figure 5. To transform the dataset using LDA, the following steps are performed [37].

LDA Pseudocode

```
LDA(Input: X, y, k)
    X_scaled = Standardize(X)
    Class_means = ComputeClassMeans(X_scaled, y)
    Sw = ComputeWithinClassScatterMatrix(X_scaled, class_means, y)
    Sb = ComputeBetweenClassScatterMatrix(X_scaled, class_means, y)
    Eigenvalues, eigenvectors = Eigendecomposition(inv(Sw) * Sb)
    Sort eigenvalues and eigenvectors in descending order:
        sorted_indices = SortIndices(eigenvalues, descending = True)
        sorted_eigenvalues = eigenvalues[sorted_indices]
        sorted_eigenvectors = eigenvectors[:, sorted_indices]
    projection_matrix = sorted_eigenvectors[:, :k]
    X_lda = X * projection_matrix:
```

Figure 5. Pseudocode for the Linear Discriminant Analysis algorithm.

1. Normalize the dataset by subtracting the mean and dividing by the standard deviation for each feature:

$$x_{std}^{(i)} = \frac{x^{(i)} - \mu_x}{\sigma_x} \tag{7}$$

where μ_x is the sample mean of a feature column, and σ_x is the standard deviation.

2. Compute the mean vector for each class.

$$m_i = \frac{1}{n_i} \sum\nolimits_{x \in D_i} x_m \tag{8}$$

where n_i is the number of samples in class i, and D_i is the set of samples belonging to class i.

3. Calculate the within-class scatter matrix:

$$S_W = \sum\nolimits_{i=1}^{c} \sum\nolimits_{x \in D_i} (x - m_i)(x - m_i)^T \tag{9}$$

4. Calculate the between-class scatter matrix:

$$S_B = \sum\nolimits_{i=1}^{c} n_i (m_i - m)(m_i - m)^T \tag{10}$$

where m is the overall mean from all c classes.

5. Compute the eigenvectors and eigenvalues of $S_w^{-1} S_b$ by solving the generalized eigenvalue problem:

$$S_w^{-1} S_b v = \lambda v \tag{11}$$

6. Choose k eigenvectors that correspond to the k largest eigenvalues, where k is the desired dimensionality of the new feature subspace. (Note: if the dataset contains K classes, the maximum value of k is $K - 1$.)
7. Construct a projection matrix W from the sorted k chosen eigenvectors.
8. Create a new k-dimensional feature space by transforming the original data using the projection matrix:

$$X' = XW \tag{12}$$

6. Modeling

6.1. Support Vector Machines

Support Vector Machines (SVMs) are a powerful ML algorithm that can handle both linear and nonlinear classification and regression tasks [39]. The SVM algorithm works by optimizing the hyperplane that maximizes the margin between classes while simultaneously minimizing classification errors [40]. Using a kernel function, SVMs are able to map data into higher-dimensional feature spaces where nonlinear relationships become linear, which allows for complex decision boundaries without the need for explicit computation in higher-dimensional space [39,40]. SVMs also allow for the choice of a kernel function, such as polynomial or radial basis function, increasing the versatility [40].

6.1.1. Binary Classification

In the UWF-ZeekData22 [1,5] dataset, binary classification was used for the Reconnaissance and Discovery Tactics. In the UWF-ZeekDataFall22 [5,6] dataset, binary classification was used for the Reconnaissance, Discovery, Defense Evasion, Privilege Escalation, and Resource Development tactics.

6.1.2. Multinomial Classification

The standard PySpark implementation of the SVM model is not capable of supporting multinomial classification. To complete the multinomial classification tasks, the OneVsRest model was used to extend the SVM model's capabilities and allow for multinomial classification.

In the UWF-ZeekData22 dataset [1,5], multinomial classification was performed using the Reconnaissance and Discovery tactics together versus the benign data. In the UWF-ZeekDataFall22 dataset [5,6], multinomial classification was performed using the Reconnaissance, Discovery, Defense Evasion, Privilege Escalation, and Resource Development tactics together versus the benign data.

6.2. Parameter Selection

Several parameters in the PySpark implementation of SVM were adjusted in an attempt to optimize performance and reliability on the large datasets used. Table 1 outlines these parameters. All other values were left as default.

Table 1. Parameters specified for SVM implemented in PySpark.

Algorithm	Parameters Used
Support Vector Machine	featuresCol: str = 'features', labelCol: str = 'label_tactic', maxIter: int = 10, regParam: float = 0.0, fitIntercept: bool = True, threshold: float = 0.00001

6.3. MapReduce

Although PySpark uses transformers like map() and reduce() that conceptually align with the MapReduce paradigm [41], further steps were taken to apply MapReduce, which would distribute data and process the data in parallel. MapReduce is a framework for executing parallelizable algorithms like LDA across Big Data. MapReduce has two functions, map and reduce. Map takes in a function that can be applied to a sequence of values, and reduce combines all the elements of a sequence using binary operations.

In this work, several Map functions were used to calculate the class means, within-class scatter matrices, and between-class scatter matrices, and also in the computation of the eigenvalues and vectors. Broadcast variables were used for distributed processing in block sizes of 33.2 MiB using the DAG scheduler. Broadcast variables benefit data-intensive applications, minimizing data transfer overhead and eliminating the need for network communication, hence reducing latency.

7. Experimental Setup

All datasets were split into a 70:30 ratio for training and testing the SVM classifier. Using the UWF-ZeekData22 dataset, for the binomial classification of the Reconnaissance class, stratified sampling was used with a seed of 42. All instances of the Discovery class were retained for both binomial and multinomial classification due to the small number of samples in this class. For the UWF-ZeekDataFall22 dataset, a random split was performed using a seed of 42 for all the tactics.

For both datasets, after removing the features uid, label_technique, and label_binary, replacing null values, and running the Strings through a StringIndexer, the experimental flow diverges, as shown in Figure 6. In the cases where feature reduction was to be used, the datasets were normalized before LDA or PCA was performed. Binary classification was performed on individual classes, and multinomial classification was performed on all classes simultaneously. Figure 6 presents the experimental setup.

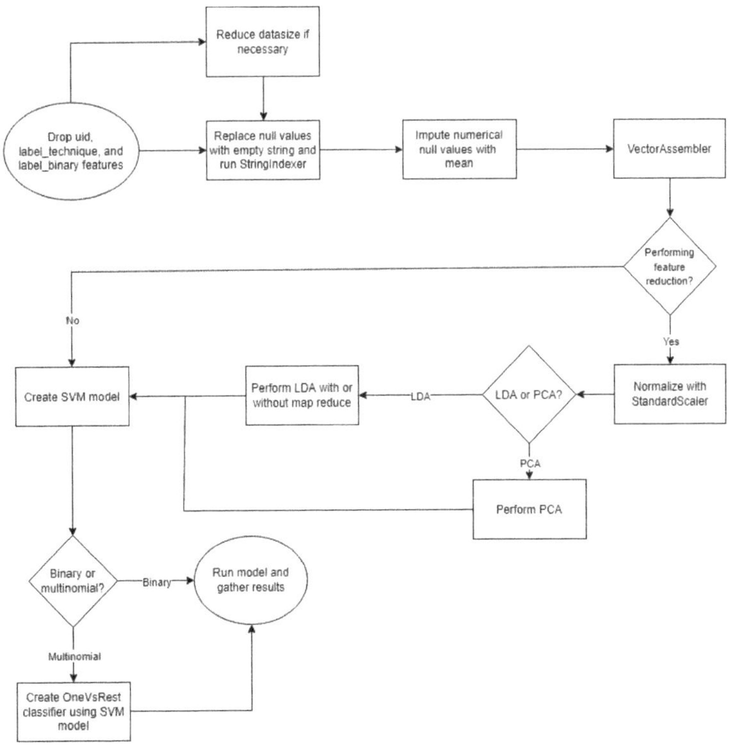

Figure 6. Flowchart of preprocessing steps and algorithm execution.

7.1. Computing Environment

In terms of computing resources, the University of West Florida's Hadoop cluster was used. The physical cluster consists of 6 Dell PowerEdge R750 with 128 logical cores, 1 TB of Memory, 84 TB SSD Storage, and 2 NVIDIA Tesla T4 with 16 GB of GDDR6. The logical Hadoop/Spark cluster comprises 1 Hadoop NameNode/Spark Master (64 logical cores, 512 GB of memory, 1 TB SSD storage) and 3 Hadoop DataNodes/ Spark Workers (64 logical cores, 512 GB of memory, 40 TB SSD storage). Spark 3.5.0 and Hadoop 3.3.1 were used for the environment.

7.2. Spark Configuration Parameters

The configuration parameters, as shown in Table 2, were utilized during the creation of the Spark session. These parameters dictate the available resources that were allocated for the algorithms.

Table 2. Spark configuration parameters [1,42].

Configuration	Spark Property	Description
Driver Cores	spark.driver.cores	Number of cores allocated for the driver process when operating in cluster mode
Driver Memory	spark.driver.memory	Memory allocated for the driver process, where the Spark context is initialized
Executor Cores	spark.executor.cores	Number of cores allocated to each executor
Executor Memory	spark. executor. memory	Amount of memory assigned to each executor process
Executor Instances	spark.executor.instances spark.dynamicAllocation.minExecutors spark.dynamicAllocation.maxExecutors	Initial count of executors running when dynamic allocation is enabled, with defined upper and lower bounds for the total executors
Shuffle Partitions	spark.sql.shuffle.partitions	Default number of partitions used during data shuffling for joins or aggregations

7.3. Setup Parameters

The configuration settings, resource settings, and total allocations selected are presented in Table 3, and the Spark resource settings and total allocation are presented in Table 4.

Table 3. Spark configuration settings.

Config Settings	Value
Driver Cores	2
Driver Memory	10 g
Executor Instances	16
Executor Cores	2
Executor Memory	25 g
Shuffle Partitions	180

Table 4. Spark resource settings and total allocation.

Resources	Total Allocation
Driver Cores	2
Driver Memory	10 g
Executor Total Cores	32
Executor Total Memory	400 g

7.4. CPUs vs. GPUs

CPUs are designed for general-purpose computing tasks. They excel at handling a wide variety of operations, including those requiring complex logic and sequential processing. However, their architecture, which typically includes a few powerful cores, limits their efficiency in tasks that can be parallelized. UWF's Virtual Machines (VMs) had 4 CPUs with 8 GB of memory, 1 GB active memory, and 32 GB of hard disk space.

GPUs, originally developed for rendering graphics, are optimized for parallel processing. They consist of thousands of smaller, efficient cores capable of handling multiple tasks simultaneously. This architecture makes GPUs particularly well-suited for the matrix and vector operations common in ML algorithms.

Advantages of GPUs over CPUs [43,44]

1. Parallel Processing: GPUs can perform many operations concurrently, leading to significant speedups in training times for large datasets and complex models.
2. Throughput: The high throughput of GPUs allows for processing large volumes of data more efficiently than CPUs.
3. Energy Efficiency: For certain workloads, GPUs can offer better performance per watt compared to CPUs, making them more energy-efficient for large-scale computations.
4. Dataset Size: Large datasets benefit from GPU acceleration, as the ability to process multiple data points simultaneously can lead to faster convergence during training.

In Apache Spark, both CPUs and GPUs can be utilized for data processing. By default, Spark operates on CPUs. However, with the integration of GPU acceleration frameworks like the RAPIDS Accelerator for Apache Spark [44], certain operations can be offloaded to GPUs, enhancing performance for specific workloads.

8. Results and Analysis

In the first section, the evaluation metrics are presented, and then the results and analysis are presented. First, the results for UWF-ZeekData22 are presented, followed by the results and analysis for UWF-ZeekDataFall22. For each dataset, in addition to binomial and multinomial statistical classification results, a comparison has been made of CPU vs. GPU vs. MapReduce timings using minimal preprocessing and PCA and LDA preprocessing. The PCA variance, as well as the LDA explained variance, has also been presented.

8.1. Evaluation Metrics

Results were collected for accuracy, precision, recall, F-measure, false-positive rate (FPR), area under the operating characteristics curve (AUROC), training/test times in seconds, and preprocessing time in seconds. These metrics are defined as follows:

Accuracy is the ratio of correct classifications (true positives and true negatives) to the total number of classifications [45]. Mathematically, it can be expressed as

$$Accuracy = \frac{TruePositives + TrueNegatives}{TruePositives + FalsePositives + TrueNegatives + FalseNegatives} \quad (13)$$

Precision, often referred to as confidence, is the ratio of correctly predicted positive cases to total predicted positive cases [45,46]. Mathematically, precision is defined as

$$Precision = \frac{TruePositives}{TruePositives + FalsePositives} \quad (14)$$

Recall, also known as sensitivity, represents the ability of a classifier to identify all positive samples, also known as the true-positive rate (TPR). It is defined as the proportion of TP cases correctly predicted out of all real positive (RP) cases [45,47]. Mathematically, it is defined as

$$Recall = \frac{TruePositives}{TruePositives + FalseNegatives} \quad (15)$$

The F1 score or F-measure is a metric that combines precision and recall into a single value. It represents the harmonic mean of both precision and recall, and serves as an overall measure of the test's accuracy [48]. Mathematically, it is defined as

$$F1 = 2 \times \frac{Precision \times Recall}{Precision + Recall} \tag{16}$$

The false-positive rate is the ratio of negative labels that are incorrectly predicted to be positive [49]. Mathematically, the false-positive rate is defined as follows:

$$FPR = \frac{FalsePositives}{FalsePositives + TrueNegatives} \tag{17}$$

The Area under the Receiver Operating Characteristic (ROC) curve is another measure of the overall performance of a classifier. ROC curves depict the trade-offs between TPR and FPR. They are two-dimensional graphs of classifiers, where the TPR is on the y-axis and the FPR is on the x-axis [49].

The AUROC represents the percentage of the area under the ROC curve relative to the entire area of the graph. It quantifies a classifier's ability to discriminate between positive and negative instances [49].

Preprocessing time is the duration of time required (in seconds) for an algorithm to complete its preprocessing steps. An algorithm is considered more efficient than another if it completes its preprocessing steps more quickly, assuming all other factors are equal.

Training and testing time are the duration of time required (in seconds) for an algorithm to complete its training and testing processes, respectively. An algorithm is considered more efficient than another if it completes its calculations more quickly, assuming all other factors are equal.

8.2. Results

In PCA, k values can be as high as the number of features in the dataset; however, often, this number of principal components is not necessary. In both the UWF-ZeekData22 and UWF-ZeekDataFall22 datasets, PCA was run with k values of 2, 3, 5, 10, and 11.

In LDA, the max k value that can be chosen is equal to the number of classes minus one. In the binary case, this limited the choice of k to 1. In the multinomial case, in the UWF-ZeekData22 dataset, a total of three classes exist (Reconnaissance, Discovery, and benign), allowing for k values up to 2. Both k equal to 1 and 2 were tested on this dataset.

On the UWF-ZeekDataFall22 dataset, there are a total of six classes (Reconnaissance, Discovery, Defense Evasion, Privilege Escalation, Resource Development, and benign), permitting k values of up to 5. However, k values equal to 1, 2, 3, and 4 were tested on this dataset.

For each dataset, first, the results for SVM with minimal preprocessing are presented, then the results for SVM with minimal processing plus PCA are presented, followed by the results for minimal preprocessing plus LDA. For minimal preprocessing, the following was performed: dropping features that lack informative value, dealing with null values, normalization of appropriate features, and using the string indexer where appropriate.

8.2.1. UWF-ZeekData22 Results

SVM classifier results for the UWF-ZeekData22 dataset for the Reconnaissance, Discovery, and multinomial data with minimal preprocessing are presented in Table 5. The Reconnaissance and Discovery were binary classifications, that is, Reconnaissance vs. benign data, and, likewise, Discovery vs. benign data.

Table 5. UWF-ZeekData22: SVM with minimal preprocessing.

Tactic	Accuracy (%)	Precision (%)	Recall (%)	F-Measure (%)	FPR (%)	AUROC (%)	(%) of Dataset Reduction
Reconnaissance	99.93	99.93	99.93	99.92	0.14	99.92	97.5
Discovery	99.99	99.99	99.99	99.99	0.00	99.99	0
Multinomial	99.94	99.94	99.92	99.94	0.03	99.93	97

Since LDA requires significant in-memory processing and the UWF-ZeekData22 dataset is a very large dataset with over 18 million samples, this caused out-of-memory issues when running LDA with the scikit-learn implementation on UWF's VMs. To mitigate this issue, the size of the datasets used for classification was reduced. This reduction varied between 85% and 97% of the none (benign data) and Reconnaissance classes, and a 0–10% reduction in the Discovery class. Though the reduction was necessary only for LDA, to keep the results uniform, the reduced datasets were used for all the classification runs of this dataset. The last column presents the percentage of the reduction in the dataset.

Since the full dataset could not be run for LDA using UWF-ZeekData22, and a reduced dataset was used, this motivated the use of MapReduce (presented later in this work), so that the full dataset could be run in the MapReduce Big Data environment. Hence, all MapReduce runs were performed using the full datasets.

From Table 5, it can be noted that accuracy, precision, recall, and the F-measure all remained high, with values achieving greater than 99%. All cases achieved a very high AUROC score, and all cases maintained low false-positive rates, with the Reconnaissance tactic having the highest FPR.

SVM classifier results for the UWF-ZeekData22 dataset for the binary classification of Reconnaissance (Recon) and Discovery (Disc), and multinomial (multi) classification, using PCA with k values of 2, 3, 5, and 10, are presented in Table 6.

Table 6. UWF-ZeekData22: SVM with PCA.

k	Tactic	Accuracy (%)	Precision (%)	Recall (%)	F-Measure (%)	FPR (%)	AUROC (%)	(%) of Dataset Reduction
2	Recon	97.90	97.90	97.90	97.90	2.55	97.90	97.5
3	Recon	98.15	98.16	98.16	98.16	2.45	98.16	97.5
5	Recon	97.99	98.01	97.99	98.99	3.06	97.99	97.5
10	Recon	99.04	99.04	99.04	99.04	1.14	99.04	97.5
2	Disc	99.78	99.57	99.78	99.67	0	49.99	10
3	Disc	99.98	99.57	99.98	99.67	0	49.99	10
5	Disc	99.78	99.61	99.78	99.67	0	50.25	10
10	Disc	99.98	99.97	99.98	99.97	0	95.14	10
2	Multi	97.56	97.36	97.57	97.46	2.96	97.57	95
3	Multi	97.84	97.64	97.84	97.734	2.66	97.84	95
5	Multi	97.46	97.25	97.43	97.32	3.78	97.43	95
10	Multi	98.64	98.42	98.64	98.539	1.51	98.66	95

From Table 6, it can be noted that, though on average, accuracy, precision, recall, and F-measure all remained high with values achieving greater than 97%, the multinomial classification results were slightly lower than the binary classification results. The Reconnaissance and multinomial data, however, achieved higher AUROC scores than the discovery tactics, which had lower AUROC scores. Most cases have relatively low false-positive rates, with discovery having zero false positives. And, overall, for all three cases, the two binary Reconnaissance as well as Discovery, as well as the multinomial data, $k = 10$, performed slightly better.

Table 7 presents the PCA variance and cumulative variance for UWF-ZeekData22. From Table 7, it can be noted that a significant portion of the variance was captured within the first seven principal components for both the binomial and multinomial cases, with cumulative variance exceeding 75%. In the classification results, while models on average perform as well or slightly better with ten principal components, the gains were often minimal when compared to using five components.

Table 7. UWF-ZeekData22: PCA variance and cumulative variance.

PC	Recon Var. (%)	Recon Cum. Var. (%)	Disc Var. (%)	Disc Cum. Var. (%)	Multi Var. (%)	Multi Cum. Var. (%)
1	26.16	26.16	20.82	20.82	26.16	26.16
2	20.96	47.12	15.11	35.93	20.94	47.10
3	10.08	57.20	14.37	50.30	10.11	57.21
4	6.95	64.15	8.57	58.87	6.93	64.14
5	6.46	70.61	7.81	66.68	6.42	70.56
6	5.21	75.82	5.53	72.21	5.19	75.75
7	4.56	80.38	4.69	76.90	4.55	80.30
8	3.82	84.20	4.38	81.28	3.82	84.12
9	3.41	87.61	3.81	85.09	3.41	87.53
10	2.80	90.41	3.60	88.69	2.86	90.39

SVM classifier results for the UWF-ZeekData22 dataset for the binary classification of Reconnaissance and Discovery, and multinomial classification, using LDA with k values of 1 and 2, are presented in Table 8.

Table 8. UWF-ZeekData22: SVM with LDA.

k	Tactic	Accuracy (%)	Precision (%)	Recall (%)	F-Measure (%)	FPR (%)	AUROC (%)	(%) of Dataset Reduction
1	Recon	99.96	99.96	99.96	99.96	0.07	99.96	92.5
1	Disc	99.94	99.94	99.94	99.94	0.06	99.07	5
1	Multi	99.76	99.55	99.76	99.65	0.03	99.77	97
2	Multi	99.75	99.54	99.75	99.65	0.03	99.77	97

From Table 8, it can be noted that accuracy, precision, recall, and the F-measure all remained high with values achieving greater than 99%. All cases retained a high AUROC score. The false-positive rates were also low for each case.

Table 9 presents the LDA explained variance and cumulative variance for UWF-ZeekData22. From Table 9, it can be seen that for the binomial data, the single linear discriminant captured 100% of the between-class variance for all tactics. In the multinomial case, the first linear discriminant captured 99.82% of the explained variance, with the remaining linear discriminants contributing only minimally to the total variance. Including the second linear discriminant in preprocessing prior to running the SVM model had almost no effect on classification performance.

Table 9. UWF-ZeekData22: LDA explained variance and cumulative variance.

Tactic	LDA (k = 1) Explained Var. (%)	Cum. Var. (%)	LDA (k = 2) Explained Var. (%)	Cum. Var. (%)
Recon	100.00	100.00	-	-
Disc	100.00	100.00	-	-
Multi	99.82	99.82	0.18	100.00

Figure 7 compares the accuracy of the three preprocessing techniques: minimal preprocessing, minimal preprocessing plus PCA, and minimal preprocessing plus LDA. Minimal preprocessing had the highest average accuracy, while PCA had the lowest average accuracy. And, with PCA, the multinomial data had the lowest performance.

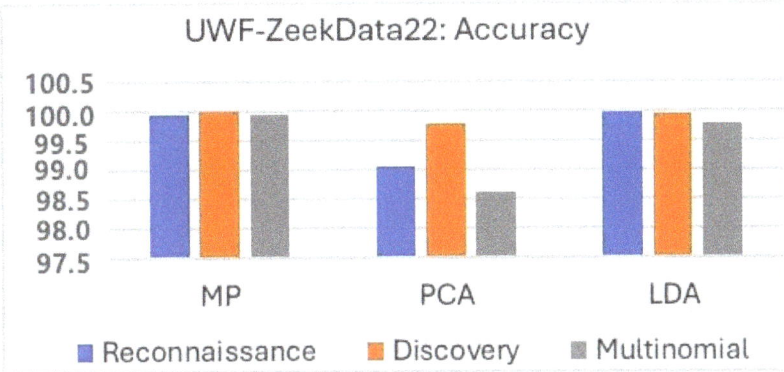

Figure 7. UWF-ZeekData22: comparison of preprocessing techniques.

8.2.2. UWF-ZeekDataFall22 Results

SVM classifier results for the UWF-ZeekDataFall22 dataset for the binary classification of Reconnaissance, Discovery, Defense Evasion, Privilege Escalation, and Resource Development, and multinomial classification, with minimal preprocessing, are presented in Table 10. Since the size of this dataset was smaller, no dataset reduction was necessary.

Table 10. UWF-ZeekDataFall22: SVM with minimal preprocessing.

k	Tactic	Accuracy (%)	Precision (%)	Recall (%)	F-Measure (%)	FPR (%)	AUROC (%)
1	Reconnaissance	99.96	99.96	99.96	99.96	0.07	99.96
1	Discovery	99.94	99.94	99.94	99.94	0.06	99.07
1	Multinomial	99.76	99.55	99.76	99.65	0.03	99.77
2	Multinomial	99.75	99.54	99.75	99.65	0.03	99.77

From Table 10, it can be noted that accuracy, precision, recall, and F-measure all remained high with values achieving greater than 99%. All cases retained a high AUROC score. False-positive rates were low or close to zero for each case.

SVM classifier results for the UWF-ZeekDataFall22 dataset for the binary classification of Reconnaissance, Discovery, Defense Evasion (Def Evas), Privilege Escalation (Priv Esc), and Resource Development (Res Dev), and multinomial classification, using PCA with k values of 2, 3, 5, and 10, are presented in Table 11.

From Table 11, it can be noted that the results of the multinomial classification were, on average, lower than the results of the binary classifiers. Though Defense Evasion and Privilege Escalation had the same results for $k = 5$ and $k = 10$, in most cases, $k = 10$ gave the best results. Resource Development was the only tactic where the results of $k = 5$ were slightly better than $k = 10$.

Table 12 presents the PCA variance and cumulative variance for UWF-ZeekDataFall22. From Table 12, it can be noted that a significant portion of the variance was captured within the first five principal components for both the binomial and multinomial cases, with cumulative variance exceeding 75%. In the classification results, while models on average perform as well or slightly better with ten principal components, the gains were often minimal when compared to using five components. The exception is the Reconnaissance tactic, which saw substantial performance increases with ten components. However, this improvement could be due to overfitting.

Table 11. UWF-ZeekDataFall22: results with PCA preprocessing.

k	Tactic	Accuracy (%)	Precision (%)	Recall (%)	F-Measure (%)	FPR (%)	AUROC (%)
2	Recon	87.27	76.17	87.28	81.34	0	50
3	Recon	92.69	92.23	92.69	92.33	2.72	79.24
5	Recon	90.01	90.96	90.01	87.06	0.02	60.79
10	Recon	99.98	99.98	99.98	99.98	0.02	99.98
	Averages	92.49	89.84	92.49	90.18	0.69	72.50
2	Disc	97.44	98.35	97.44	97.70	2.68	98.65
3	Disc	98.50	98.86	98.50	98.60	1.57	99.18
5	Disc	99.55	99.59	99.55	99.56	0.47	99.73
10	Disc	99.99	99.99	99.99	99.99	0.001	99.99
	Averages	98.87	99.20	98.87	98.96	1.18	99.39
2	Def Evas	99.14	98.28	99.14	98.71	0	50
3	Def Evas	99.14	98.28	99.14	98.71	0	50
5	Def Evas	100	100	100	100	0	100
10	Def Evas	100	100	100	100	0	100
	Averages	99.57	99.14	99.57	99.36	0	75
2	Priv Esc	99.14	98.28	99.14	98.71	0	50
3	Priv Esc	99.14	98.28	99.13	98.71	0	50
5	Priv Esc	100	100	100	100	0	100
10	Priv Esc	100	100	100	100	0	100
	Averages	99.57	99.14	99.57	99.35	0	75
2	Res Dev	98.23	98.30	98.23	98.23	0.004	98.42
3	Res Dev	99.64	99.64	99.64	99.64	0.59	99.67
5	Res Dev	99.95	99.95	99.945	99.95	0.06	99.95
10	Res Dev	99.93	99.93	99.93	99.93	0.09	99.93
	Averages	99.44	99.45	99.44	99.44	0.19	99.49
2	Multi	87.21	78.00	87.21	82.33	4.46	90.95
3	Multi	90.47	84.32	90.47	87.04	0.43	91.55
5	Multi	91.31	90.34	91.31	87.98	0.06	92.44
10	Multi	92.07	90.55	92.07	90.62	0.09	93.54
	Averages	90.26	85.80	90.26	86.99	1.25	92.12

Table 12. UWF-ZeekDataFall22: PCA variance and cumulative variance.

PC	Recon Var. (%)	Recon Cum. Var. (%)	Disc Var. (%)	Disc Cum. Var. (%)	Def Evas Var. (%)	Def Evas Cum. Var. (%)	Priv Esc Var. (%)	Priv Esc Cum. Var. (%)	Res Dev Var. (%)	Res Dev Cum. Var. (%)	Multi Var. (%)	Multi Cum. Var. (%)
1	32.86	32.86	33.26	33.26	33.37	33.37	33.38	33.38	33.10	33.10	32.21	32.21
2	21.86	54.72	24.55	57.81	20.93	54.3	20.94	54.32	26.26	59.36	24.47	56.68
3	8.45	63.17	9.36	67.17	8.83	63.13	8.83	63.15	12.05	71.41	12.74	69.42
4	7.06	70.23	6.08	73.25	7.52	70.65	7.52	70.67	6.94	78.35	6.84	76.26
5	5.56	75.79	4.38	77.63	5.31	75.96	5.31	75.98	4.19	82.54	4.06	80.32
6	3.98	79.77	3.81	81.44	4.09	80.05	4.09	80.07	3.36	85.9	3.51	83.83
7	3.54	83.31	3.51	84.95	3.67	83.72	3.67	83.74	2.89	88.79	3.26	87.09
8	3.34	86.65	2.90	87.85	2.99	86.71	2.99	86.73	2.85	91.64	2.98	90.07
9	2.94	89.59	2.76	90.61	2.90	89.61	2.90	89.63	2.04	93.68	2.07	92.14
10	2.39	91.98	2.66	93.27	2.83	92.44	2.83	92.46	2.00	95.68	1.97	94.11

As can be seen from Figure 8, using PCA, the average accuracy of the multinomial classification is lower than the binary classification results. Of the binary classifiers, Reconnaissance had the lowest accuracy. Though we focused only on accuracy in Figure 8, from Table 9, we can see that the other statistical measures had a similar trend. The FPR was also the highest for the multinomial classification, and the second highest for Reconnaissance, but Defense Evasion and Privilege Escalation had an FPR of zero.

SVM classifier results for the UWF-ZeekDataFall22 dataset for the binary classification of Reconnaissance, Discovery, Defense Evasion, Privilege Escalation, and Resource Development, and multinomial classification, with LDA, performed with k values of 2, 3, 5, and 10, are presented in Table 13.

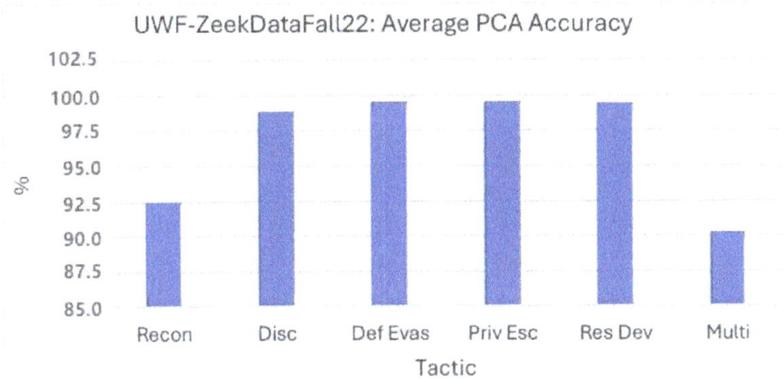

Figure 8. UWF-ZeekDataFall22: comparison of PCA preprocessing.

Table 13. UWF-ZeekDataFall22: results with LDA preprocessing.

k	Tactic	Accuracy (%)	Precision (%)	Recall (%)	F-Measure (%)	FPR (%)	AUROC (%)
1	Recon	100	100	100	100	0	100
1	Disc	100	100	100	100	0	100
1	Def Eva	100	100	100	100	0	100
1	Priv Esc	100	100	100	100	0	100
1	Res Dev	100	100	100	100	0	100
1	Multi	89.44	81.11	89.44	84.78	0	100
2	Multi	96.68	94.36	96.68	95.34	0.001	99.99
3	Multi	97.83	97.32	97.83	97.49	0.005	99.99
4	Multi	97.83	97.33	97.83	97.49	0.006	99.99
5	Multi	97.83	97.33	97.83	97.49	0.008	99.99

From Table 13, it can be noted that accuracy, precision, recall, and the F-measure all achieved 100% for the binomial data. For the multinomial classification, scores increased as k increased, with minimal improvement after k equal to 3. All cases retained a high AUROC score. False-positive rates were low or zero for each case. For UWF-ZeekDataFall22, LDA preprocessing performed the best, with 100% accuracy, precision, recall, F-measure, AUROC, and zero FPRs.

Table 14 presents the LDA explained variance and cumulative variance for UWF-ZeekDataFall22. From Table 14, it can be noted that for the binomial data, the single linear discriminant captured 100% of the between-class variance for all tactics. In the multinomial case, the first linear discriminant captured 99.55% of the explained variance, with the remaining linear discriminants contributing only minimally to the total variance. However, despite the small additional variance captured by the second linear discriminant, including it in the preprocessing prior to running the SVM model resulted in moderate improvements in classification performance.

Table 14. UWF-ZeekDataFall22: LDA explained variance and cumulative variance.

Tactic	LD1 Expl. Var. (%)	Cum. Var. (%)	LD2 Expl. Var. (%)	Cum. Var. (%)	LD3 Expl. Var. (%)	Cum. Var. (%)	LD4 Expl. Var. (%)	Cum. Var. (%)	LD5 Expl. Var. (%)	Cum. Var. (%)
Multi	99.55	99.55	0.41	99.96	0.04	100.00	0.00	100.00	0.00	100.00
Recon	100.00	100.00	-	-	-	-	-	-	-	-
Disc	100.00	100.00	-	-	-	-	-	-	-	-
Def Eva	100.00	100.00	-	-	-	-	-	-	-	-
Priv Esc	100.00	100.00	-	-	-	-	-	-	-	-
Res Dev	100.00	100.00	-	-	-	-	-	-	-	-

8.2.3. Summarizing Statistical Results

Comparing the statistical results of minimal preprocessing, PCA and LDA, it can be noted that LDA had the highest accuracy, precision, recall, F-measure and AUROC and lowest FPR for all the binary classifiers. Minimal preprocessing performed the best in terms of multinomial classification, followed by LDA. LDA also had the highest explained variance.

8.2.4. Comparing CPU and GPU Results

In Apache Spark, both CPUs and GPUs can be utilized for data processing. By default, Spark operates on CPUs. However, with the integration of the GPU acceleration framework, the RAPIDS Accelerator for Apache Spark, certain operations can be offloaded to GPUs, enhancing performance for specific workloads. In this section, we compare the results of CPUs and GPUs with and without MapReduce.

The UWF-ZeekData22 Datasets

Timing results for the UWF-ZeekData22 dataset for the binary classification of Reconnaissance and Discovery, and multinomial classification, with minimal preprocessing, are presented in Table 15.

Table 15. UWF-ZeekData22: timings (in seconds) with minimal preprocessing, CPU vs. GPU.

Tactic	Minimal Preprocessing	CPU Training	GPU Training	CPU Testing	GPU Testing
Reconnaissance	47.85	110.04	58.25	0.45	0.31
Discovery	60.04	102.19	57.21	0.46	0.32
Multinomial	60.55	280.82	160.34	0.60	0.40

From Table 15, it can be observed that minimal preprocessing and training times took on the order of several minutes, with multinomial classification taking the largest training time. Testing time remained low for each case. Training times are related to the size of the dataset being trained. The GPU training and testing are both faster than CPU training and testing in all cases.

Timing results for the UWF-ZeekData22 dataset for the binary classification of Reconnaissance and Discovery, and multinomial classification, using PCA with k values of 2, 3, 5, and 10, are presented in Table 16.

Table 16. UWF-ZeekData22: timings (in seconds) with PCA, CPU vs. GPU.

k	Tactic	Minimal Preprocessing	CPU Training	GPU Training	CPU Testing	GPU Testing
2	Reconnaissance	102.97	146.92	89.71	0.39	0.21
3	Reconnaissance	103.28	152.56	90.01	0.39	0.22
5	Reconnaissance	109.21	150.16	80.98	0.48	0.25
10	Reconnaissance	104.18	148.81	81.23	0.37	0.19
2	Discovery	109.30	320.41	178.76	0.41	0.21
3	Discovery	106.02	301.83	167.32	0.41	0.23
5	Discovery	104.18	285.68	154.21	0.42	0.22
10	Discovery	109.75	298.21	149.11	0.38	0.2
2	Multinomial	107.46	339.83	176.19	0.47	0.21
3	Multinomial	132.52	403.01	210.98	0.54	0.31
5	Multinomial	102.79	271.49	145.21	0.50	0.32
10	Multinomial	104.05	282.63	153.24	0.53	0.31

From Table 16, it can be observed that PCA preprocessing and training times took in the order of several minutes, with the multinomial data, on average, having the highest preprocessing and training times. Training and testing times are related to the size of the datasets being trained or tested. The GPU training and testing times are both faster than CPU training and testing times in all cases.

Timing results for the UWF-ZeekData22 dataset for the binary Reconnaissance and Discovery, and multinomial classification, with LDA (without MapReduce) performed with k values of 1 and 2, are presented in Table 17.

Table 17. UWF-ZeekData22: timings (in seconds) with LDA, CPU vs. GPU, without MapReduce.

k	Tactic	LDA Preprocessing	CPU Training	GPU Training	CPU Testing	GPU Testing
1	Reconnaissance	167.97	23.28	16.31	0.40	0.3
1	Discovery	89.10	18.65	12.33	0.27	0.21
1	Multinomial	117.83	30.59	18.29	0.29	0.23
2	Multinomial	118.82	23.83	13.97	0.33	0.26

From Table 17, it can be observed that LDA preprocessing without MapReduce took long, on the average longer than minimal preprocessing or PCA. But, training times were significantly reduced when compared to minimal preprocessing or PCA preprocessing techniques. GPU training and testing were both faster than CPU training and testing in all cases.

Timings for the UWF-ZeekData22 dataset for the binary classification of Reconnaissance and Discovery, and multinomial classification, with LDA performed on MapReduce, with k values of 1 and 2, are presented in Table 18. All MapReduce runs used the full dataset.

Table 18. UWF-ZeekData22: timings (in seconds) with LDA, CPU vs. GPU, with MapReduce.

k	Tactic	LDA Preprocessing	CPU Training	GPU Training	CPU Testing	GPU Testing
1	Reconnaissance	134.34	16.03	12.01	0.27	0.16
1	Discovery	121.40	18.25	10.13	0.29	0.19
1	Multinomial	138.21	35.44	19.43	0.37	0.21
2	Multinomial	145.07	28.32	20.21	0.42	0.25

From Table 18, it can be noted that LDA preprocessing with MapReduce took a long time. In fact, though Reconnaissance LDA preprocessing with MapReduce was quicker than without MapReduce, the Discovery and multinomial data took longer with MapReduce than without MapReduce. LDA preprocessing, with or without MapReduce, took longer than PCA preprocessing, which took longer than minimal preprocessing. GPU training and testing were both faster than CPU training and testing in all cases.

Figure 9 compares the testing times for CPUs and GPUs with and without MapReduce for the UWF-ZeekData22 dataset. The performance of PCA GPU and LDA GPU were very close, but the MapReduce LDA GPU performed better than both PCA GPU and LDA GPU. Of the three preprocessing techniques, minimal preprocessing testing times were the longest, both with the CPUs as well as the GPUs. Comparing only the CPUs, LDA performed the best. Comparing only GPUs, LDA GPU with MapReduce performed the best, followed by GPU LDA. Hence, overall, LDA had the lowest testing times. In all cases, CPU testing took longer than the GPU testing, and, in all cases, the multinomial data took the longest to run.

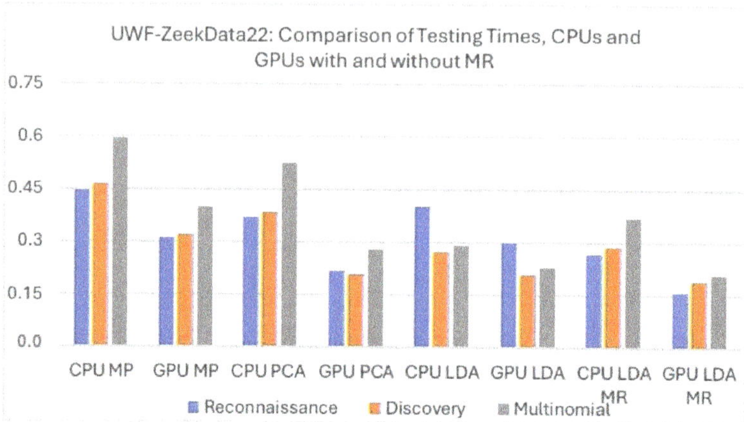

Figure 9. UWF-ZeekDataFall22: comparing testing times for CPUs and GPUs with and without MapReduce.

The UWF-ZeekDataFall22 Dataset

Timings for the UWF-ZeekDataFall22 dataset for the binary classification of Reconnaissance, Discovery, Defense Evasion, Privilege Escalation, and Resource Development, and multinomial classification, with minimal preprocessing, are presented in Table 19.

Table 19. UWF-ZeekDataFall22: timings (in seconds) with minimal preprocessing, CPUs vs. GPUs.

Tactic	Preprocessing	CPU Training	GPU Training	CPU Testing	GPU Testing
Reconnaissance	38.26	143.06	89.32	0.50	0.34
Discovery	34.75	74.46	43.31	0.45	0.43
Defense Evasion	35.39	77.36	45.22	0.6	0.50
Privilege Escalation	36.03	72.30	43.33	0.49	0.35
Resource Development	31.99	183.30	101.78	0.63	0.43
Multinomial	40.91	734.60	450.57	1.01	0.78

From Table 19, it can be observed that training times took in the order of one to several minutes, with the multinomial classification taking the largest training time. GPU training and testing times were lower than CPU training and testing times in all cases. Training times are correlated to the size of the dataset being trained.

Timing results for the UWF-ZeekDataFall22 dataset for the binary classification of Reconnaissance, Discovery, Defense Evasion, Privilege Escalation, and Resource Development, and multinomial classification, with PCA, performed with k values of 2, 3, 5, and 10, are presented in Table 20.

From Table 20, it can be observed that training times took in the order of several minutes, with the multinomial data having the longest training times. The k value has little correlation to training time. Training times are correlated to the size of the dataset being trained. GPU training and testing times were lower than CPU training and testing times in all cases.

Timing results on the UWF-ZeekDataFall22 dataset for the binary classification of Reconnaissance, Discovery, Defense Evasion, Privilege Escalation, and Resource Development, and multinomial classification, with LDA, without MapReduce, with k values of 1, 2, 3, and 4, are presented in Table 21.

Table 20. UWF-ZeekDataFall22: timing results with PCA, CPU vs. GPU.

k	Tactic	Preprocessing	CPU Training	GPU Training	CPU Testing	GPU Testing
2	Reconnaissance	49.65	325.02	180.91	0.30	0.22
3	Reconnaissance	55.45	127.01	90.23	0.39	0.31
5	Reconnaissance	54.95	124.90	87.45	0.38	0.23
10	Reconnaissance	50.70	120.84	95.61	0.41	0.24
2	Discovery	58.28	157.41	90.87	0.36	0.20
3	Discovery	49.73	110.05	70.81	0.28	0.18
5	Discovery	52.52	104.06	68.90	0.27	0.18
10	Discovery	48.82	114.01	76.32	0.31	0.20
2	Defense Evasion	45.52	142.23	83.44	0.39	0.24
3	Defense Evasion	48.37	149.94	89.43	0.44	0.27
5	Defense Evasion	54.23	132.18	94.55	0.39	0.25
10	Defense Evasion	48.82	114.01	78.90	0.31	0.20
2	Privilege Escalation	53.16	141.69	82.98	0.31	0.20
3	Privilege Escalation	54.51	142.89	84.56	0.39	0.24
5	Privilege Escalation	58.38	124.57	78.34	0.38	0.22
10	Privilege Escalation	54.44	65.24	50.12	0.32	0.20
2	Resource Development	73.87	217.72	149.54	0.44	0.31
3	Resource Development	69.89	191.16	120.76	0.40	0.28
5	Resource Development	69.69	202.51	156.32	0.47	0.33
10	Resource Development	61.97	204.99	144.45	0.36	0.22
2	Multinomial	81.62	1630.58	1200.23	0.96	0.71
3	Multinomial	79.74	965.02	721.34	0.76	0.65
5	Multinomial	84.46	907.64	701.45	0.77	0.69
10	Multinomial	84.16	772.88	561.90	0.58	0.32

Table 21. UWF-ZeekDataFall22: timing results with LDA, CPU vs. GPU (without MapReduce).

k	Tactic	Preprocessing	CPU Training	GPU Training	CPU Testing	GPU Testing
1	Reconnaissance	69.28	38.33	19.17	0.25	0.13
1	Discovery	66.82	13.05	6.52	0.26	0.13
1	Defense Evasion	67.20	13.49	6.74	0.27	0.13
1	Privilege Escalation	66.19	11.47	5.74	0.26	0.13
1	Resource Development	91.94	12.19	6.10	0.23	0.11
1	Multinomial	85.97	86.02	43.01	0.55	0.27
2	Multinomial	204.73	61.29	30.64	0.68	0.34
3	Multinomial	97.92	52.68	26.34	0.58	0.29
4	Multinomial	99.87	48.29	24.14	0.50	0.25

From Table 21, it can be seen that preprocessing took the majority of the time, with the training time somewhat reduced when compared to minimal preprocessing (Table 19) and significantly reduced when compared to PCA preprocessing (Table 20). GPU training and testing times were lower than CPU training and testing times in all cases. Minimal preprocessing had the lowest times when compared to the PCA and LDA preprocessing.

Timing results for the UWF-ZeekDataFall22 dataset for the binary classification of Reconnaissance, Discovery, Defense Evasion, Privilege Escalation, and Resource Development, and multinomial classification, with LDA and MapReduce, with *k* values of 1, 2, 3, and 4, are presented in Table 22. All MapReduce runs used the full dataset.

Table 22. UWF-ZeekDataFall22: timing results with LDA, CPU vs. GPU with MapReduce (MR).

k	Tactic	Preprocessing	CPU MR Training	GPU MR Training	CPU MR Testing	GPU MR Testing
1	Recon	90.21	38.29	19.15	0.27	0.14
1	Disc	88.91	13.32	6.66	0.26	0.13
1	Def Evas	88.80	12.72	6.36	0.30	0.15
1	Priv Esc	85.48	12.37	6.19	0.29	0.15
1	Res Dev	130.66	16.08	8.04	0.32	0.16
1	Multi	137.42	97.20	48.60	0.54	0.27
2	Multi	147.35	87.71	43.85	0.46	0.23
3	Multi	163.40	83.05	41.53	0.61	0.30
4	Multi	177.51	106.20	53.10	0.51	0.25

From Table 22, it can be observed that preprocessing took the majority of the time, with the training time being somewhat reduced when compared to minimal preprocessing (Table 19) and significantly reduced when compared to PCA preprocessing (Table 20). In general, preprocessing times were increased when compared to MapReduce not being used. This means that MapReduce did not reduce preprocessing times. GPU MR training and testing times were lower than CPU MR training and testing times in all cases.

Figure 10 compares the testing times for CPUs and GPUs, with and without MapReduce for the UWF-ZeekData22 dataset. In all cases, we can see that the CPU testing took longer than the GPU testing. LDA GPU performed the best, with the lowest testing times, even better than the MR GPU LDA. The testing times were the highest with the multinomial data. Of the three preprocessing techniques, minimal preprocessing took the longest, and LDA took the shortest testing times.

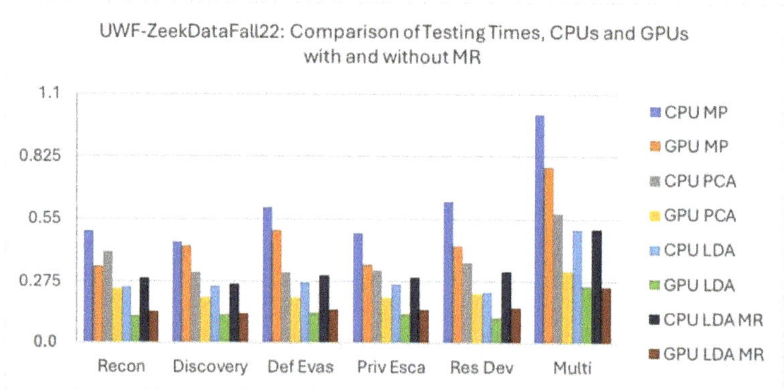

Figure 10. UWF-ZeekDataFall22: comparison of testing times.

9. Conclusions

This paper aimed to explore the results of various preprocessing techniques before using an SVM classifier on the MITRE ATT&CK® labeled UWF-ZeekData22 and UWF-ZeekDataFall22 datasets. It compared both the statistical effectiveness of three different preprocessing techniques, MP, PCA and LDA, as well as the time efficiency associated with the preprocessing, training, and testing of the SVM models.

In terms of statistical measures, most models achieved greater than 90% on all metrics, with many models achieving greater than 99%. In some cases, 100% was achieved. Specifically, using UWF-ZeekData22, minimal preprocessing achieved the highest results on average, with LDA being close behind, performing very well in almost all statistical metrics across most tactics. Using UWF-ZeekDataFall22, however, LDA performed slightly better than minimal preprocessing. Hence, in summary we can say that, overall, the statistical performance of minimal preprocessing and LDA were about the same. And overall, PCA had a slightly lower statistical performance. Also, using all three preprocessing techniques, multinomial results were generally slightly lower than binomial results.

Of the three preprocessing techniques compared, LDA performed the best in terms of having the lowest training as well as testing times. Minimal preprocessing had the highest testing times. GPU training and testing times were significantly lower in all cases. LDA GPU performed the best in terms of training and testing times, followed by MapReduce GPU LDA.

LDA significantly reduced training time at the expense of significantly increased preprocessing time. PCA results were less consistent and more dependent upon the choice of k, and did not result in increases to statistical metrics or reduced preprocessing or training times when compared to minimal preprocessing. It can also be noted that, for binomial data, LDA's single linear discriminant captured 100% of the between-class variance for all tactics. In the multinomial case, the first linear discriminant captured 99.55% of the explained variance.

Multinomial data also had the highest preprocessing times, as well as the highest training and testing times in all cases.

Finally, it can be concluded that binomial LDA, on average, performed the best in terms of statistical measures as well as timing efficiency using GPUs or MapReduce GPUs.

Author Contributions: Conceptualization, S.S.B., S.C.B., D.M. and C.E.; methodology, S.S.B., C.E., R.A. and S.S.; software, C.E., R.A. and S.S.; validation, S.S.B., S.C.B. and D.M.; formal analysis, C.E., R.A. and S.S.; investigation, C.E., R.A. and S.S.; resources, S.S.B., S.C.B. and D.M.; data curation, C.E., R.A. and S.S.; writing—original draft preparation, S.S.B., C.E., R.A. and S.S.; writing—review and editing, S.S.B., S.C.B., C.E., R.A., S.S. and D.M.; visualization, C.E., R.A. and S.S.; supervision, S.S.B., S.C.B. and D.M.; project administration, S.S.B., S.C.B. and D.M.; funding acquisition, S.S.B., S.C.B. and D.M. All authors have read and agreed to the published version of the manuscript.

Funding: The research was funded by the US National Center for Academic Excellence in Cybersecurity (NCAE), 2021 NCAE-C-002: Cyber Research Innovation Grant Program, Grant Number: H98230-21-1-0170. This research was also partially supported by the Askew Institute at the University of West Florida, USA.

Data Availability Statement: The datasets are available at datasets.uwf.edu (accessed on 1 September 2024).

Conflicts of Interest: The authors declare no conflicts of interest.

References

1. Bagui, S.S.; Mink, D.; Bagui, S.C.; Tirthankar, G.; McElroy, T.; Paredes, E.; Khasnavis, N.; Plenkers, R. Detecting Reconnaissance and Discovery Tactics from the MITRE ATT&CK Framework in Zeek Conn Logs Using Spark's Machine Learning in the Big Data Framework. *Sensors* **2022**, *22*, 7999. [CrossRef]
2. Huong, T.T.; Bac, T.P.; Long, D.M.; Thang, B.D.; Binh, N.T.; Luong, T.D.; Phuc, T.K. LocKedge: Low-Complexity Cyberattack Detection in IoT Edge Computing. *IEEE Access* **2021**, *9*, 29696–29710. [CrossRef]

3. Pozzebon, A. Edge and Fog Computing for the Internet of Things. *Future Internet* **2024**, *16*, 101. [CrossRef]
4. About Zeek—Book of Zeek. Available online: https://docs.zeek.org/en/master/about.html (accessed on 15 September 2024).
5. University of West Florida. 2022. Available online: https://datasets.uwf.edu/ (accessed on 2 August 2025).
6. Bagui, S.S.; Mink, D.; Bagui, S.C.; Madhyala, P.; Uppal, N.; McElroy, T.; Plenkers, R.; Elam, M.; Prayaga, S. Introducing the UWF-ZeekDataFall22 Dataset to Classify Attack Tactics from Zeek Conn Logs Using Spark's Machine Learning in a Big Data Framework. *Electronics* **2023**, *12*, 5039. [CrossRef]
7. MITRE ATT&CK. Available online: https://attack.mitre.org/ (accessed on 10 September 2024).
8. Bagui, S.; Spratlin, S. A Review of Data Mining Algorithms on Hadoop's MapReduce. *Int. J. Data Sci.* **2018**, *3*, 146–149. [CrossRef]
9. Apache Spark—Unified Engine for Large-Scale Data Analytics. Available online: https://spark.apache.org/ (accessed on 1 August 2024).
10. Nskh, P.; Varma, M.N.; Naik, R.R. Principle component analysis based intrusion detection system using support vector machine. In Proceedings of the 2016 IEEE International Conference on Recent Trends in Electronics, Information & Communication Technology (RTEICT), Bangalore, India, 20–21 May 2016; pp. 1344–1350. [CrossRef]
11. Chabathula, K.J.; Jaidhar, C.D.; Kumara, M.A. Comparative study of Principal Component Analysis based Intrusion Detection approach using machine learning algorithms. In Proceedings of the 2015 3rd International Conference on Signal Processing, Communication and Networking (ICSCN), Chennai, India, 26–28 March 2015; pp. 1–6. [CrossRef]
12. Ibrahimi, K.; Ouaddane, M. Management of intrusion detection systems based-KDD99: Analysis with LDA and PCA. In Proceedings of the 2017 International Conference on Wireless Networks and Mobile Communications (WINCOM), Rabat, Morocco, 1–4 November 2017; pp. 130–135. [CrossRef]
13. Saad, A.A.; Khalid, C.; Mohamed, J. Network intrusion detection system based on Direct LDA. In Proceedings of the 2015 Third World Conference on Complex Systems (WCCS), Marrakech, Morocco, 23–25 November 2015; pp. 1–6. [CrossRef]
14. Amin, Z.; Kabir, A. A Performance Analysis of Machine Learning Models for Attack Prediction using Different Feature Selection Techniques. In Proceedings of the 2022 IEEE/ACIS 7th International Conference on Big Data, Cloud Computing, and Data Science (BCD), Danang, Vietnam, 4–6 August 2022; pp. 130–135. [CrossRef]
15. Tait, K.; Khan, J.S.; Alqahtani, F.; Shah, A.A.; Khan, F.A.; Rehman, M.U.; Boulila, W.; Ahmad, J. Intrusion Detection using Machine Learning Techniques: An Experimental Comparison. In Proceedings of the 2021 International Congress of Advanced Technology and Engineering (ICOTEN), Taiz, Yemen, 4–5 July 2021; pp. 1–10. [CrossRef]
16. Shah, S.; Muhuri, P.S.; Yuan, X.; Roy, K.; Chatterjee, P. Implementing a network intrusion detection system using semi-supervised support vector machine and random forest. In Proceedings of the ACM Southeast Conference (ACM SE '21), Virtual Event, 15–17 April 2021; Association for Computing Machinery: New York, NY, USA, 2021; pp. 180–184. [CrossRef]
17. Almiah, M.A.; Almomani, O.; Alsaaidah, A.; Al-Otaibi, S.; Bani-Hani, N.; Hwaitat, A.; Al-Zahrani, A.; Lufti, A.; Awad, A.B.; Aldhyani, T.H.H. Performance Investigation of Principal Component Analysis for Intrusion Detection System Using Different Support Vector Machine Kernels. *Electronics* **2022**, *11*, 3571. [CrossRef]
18. Zou, H.; Jin, Z. Comparative Study of Big Data Classification Algorithm Based on SVM. In Proceedings of the 2018 Cross Strait Quad-Regional Radio Science and Wireless Technology Conference (CSQRWC), Xuzhou, China, 21–24 July 2018; pp. 1–3. [CrossRef]
19. Sarhan, M.; Layeghy, S.; Moustafa, N.; Gallagher, M.; Portmann, M. Feature Extraction for Machine-Learning-based Intrusion Detection in IoT Networks. *arXiv* **2021**, arXiv:2108.12722. [CrossRef]
20. Gatea, M.J.; Hameed, S.M. An Internet of Things Botnet Detection Model Using Regression Analysis and Linear Discrimination Analysis. *Iraqi J. Sci.* **2022**, *63*, 4534–4546. [CrossRef]
21. Mishra, A.; Cheng, A.; Zhang, Y. Intrusion detection using principal component analysis and support vector machines. In Proceedings of the 2020 IEEE 16th International Conference on Control & Automation (ICCA), Singapore, 9–11 October 2020. [CrossRef]
22. Subba, B.; Biswas, S.; Karmakar, S. Intrusion detection systems using linear discriminant analysis and logistic regression. In Proceedings of the 2015 Annual IEEE India Conference (INDICON), New Delhi, India, 17–20 December 2015. [CrossRef]
23. Moradibaad, A.; Mashed, R.J. Use Dimensionality Reduction and SVM Methods to Increase the Penetration Rate of Computer Networks. *arXiv* **2018**, arXiv:1812.03173. [CrossRef]
24. Singh, S.; Agrawal, S.; Rizvi, M.; Thakur, R.S. Improved support vector machine for cyber attack detection. In Proceedings of the World Congress on Engineering and Computer Science, San Francisco, CA, USA, 19–21 October 2011; Volume 1. Available online: https://www.researchgate.net/publication/277636116_Improved_Support_Vector_Machine_for_Cyber_attack_Detection (accessed on 2 August 2025).

25. Ghanem, K.; Aparicio-Navarro, F.J.; Kyriakopoulos, K.G.; Lambotharan, S.; Chambers, J.A. Support vector machine for network intrusion and cyber-attack detection. In Proceedings of the 2017 Sensor Signal Processing for Defence Conference (SSPD), London, UK, 6–7 December 2017. [CrossRef]
26. Asif, M.; Abbas, S.; Khan, M.A.; Fatima, A.; Khan, M.A.; Lee, S. MapReduce based intelligent model for intrusion detection using machine learning technique. *J. King Saud Univ.-Comput. Inf. Sci.* **2022**, *34*, 9723–9731. [CrossRef]
27. Csaba, B. Processing Intrusion Data with Machine Learning and MapReduce. *Acad. Appl. Res. Mil. Public Manag. Sci.* **2022**, *16*, 37–52. [CrossRef]
28. Bagui, S.S.; Mink, D.; Bagui, S.C.; Ghosh, T.; Plenkers, R.; McElroy, T.; Dulaney, S.; Shabanali, S. Introducing UWF-ZeekData22: A Comprehensive Network Traffic Dataset Based on the MITRE ATT&CK Framework. *Data* **2023**, *8*, 18. [CrossRef]
29. Reconnaissance. Available online: https://attack.mitre.org/tactics/TA0043/ (accessed on 2 August 2025).
30. Discovery. Available online: https://attack.mitre.org/tactics/TA0007/ (accessed on 2 August 2025).
31. Resource Development. Available online: https://attack.mitre.org/tactics/TA0042/ (accessed on 2 August 2025).
32. Defense Evasion. Available online: https://attack.mitre.org/tactics/TA0005/ (accessed on 2 August 2025).
33. Privilege Escalation. Available online: https://attack.mitre.org/tactics/TA0004/ (accessed on 2 August 2025).
34. Jolliffe, I.T.; Cadima, J. Principal component analysis: A review and recent developments. *Philos. Trans. A Math. Phys. Eng. Sci.* **2016**, *374*, 20150202. [CrossRef]
35. Apache Spark. PCA—Pyspark Overview. 2024. Available online: https://spark.apache.org/docs/3.5.1/api/python/index.html (accessed on 2 August 2025).
36. Karamizadeh, S.; Abdullah, S.M.; Manaf, A.A.; Zamani, M.; Hooman, A. An Overview of Principal Component Analysis. *J. Signal Inf. Process.* **2020**, *4*, 173–175. [CrossRef]
37. Yuxi, L.; Raschka, S.; Mirjalili, V. *Machine Learning with PyTorch and Scikit-Learn: Develop Machine Learning and Deep Learning Models with Python*; Packt Publishing: Birmingham, UK, 2022; pp. 120–121, 139–148, 154–163.
38. Tharwat, A.; Gaber, T.; Ibrahim, A.; Hassanien, A.E. Linear Discriminant Analysis: A Detailed Tutorial. *AI Commun.* **2017**, *30*, 169–190. [CrossRef]
39. Kecman, V. Support Vector Machines—An Introduction. In *Support Vector Machines: Theory and Applications*; Springer: Berlin/Heidelberg, Germany, 2005; pp. 1–47. [CrossRef]
40. Meyer, D. Support Vector Machines. *R News* **2001**, *1*, 23–26. Available online: https://journal.r-project.org/articles/RN-2001-025/RN-2001-025.pdf (accessed on 2 August 2025).
41. Guller, M. *Big Data Analytics with Spark: A Practitioner's Guide to Using Spark for Large Scale Data Analysis*; Apress: New York, NY, USA, 2015.
42. PureStorage Blog. *CPU vs. GPU for Machine Learning*; PureStorage Blog: Santa Clara, CA, USA, 2025; Available online: https://blog.purestorage.com/purely-educational/cpu-vs-gpu-for-machine-learning/ (accessed on 2 August 2025).
43. NVIDIA Run:ai Software. Available online: https://www.nvidia.com/en-us/software/run-ai/ (accessed on 1 August 2024).
44. Spark RAPIDS User Guide. Available online: https://docs.nvidia.com/spark-rapids/user-guide/latest/ (accessed on 1 August 2024).
45. Accuracy Score, Scikit-Learn. Available online: https://scikit-learn.org/stable/modules/model_evaluation.html#accuracy-score (accessed on 28 April 2024).
46. Precision Score. Available online: https://scikit-learn.org/stable/modules/generated/sklearn.metrics.precision_score.html#sklearn.metrics.precision_score (accessed on 28 April 2024).
47. Recall Score. Available online: https://scikit-learn.org/stable/modules/generated/sklearn.metrics.recall_score.html#sklearn.metrics.recall_score (accessed on 28 April 2024).
48. Sasaki, Y. The Truth of the F-Measure, Teach Tutor Mater. 2007, pp. 1–5. Available online: https://www.researchgate.net/publication/268185911_The_truth_of_the_F-measure (accessed on 2 August 2025).
49. Powers, D.M. Evaluation: From Precision, Recall and F-Factor to ROC, Informedness, Markedness & Correlation. *arXiv* **2020**, arXiv:2010.16061. [CrossRef]

electronics

MDPI

Article

Hardware Accelerator Design by Using RT-Level Power Optimization Techniques on FPGA for Future AI Mobile Applications

Achyuth Gundrapally *,†, Yatrik Ashish Shah *,†, Sai Manohar Vemuri and Kyuwon (Ken) Choi

DA-Lab, Department of Electrical and Computer Engineering, Illinois Institute of Technology, 3301 South Dearborn Street, Chicago, IL 60616, USA; svemuri6@hawk.illinoistech.edu (S.M.V.); kchoi12@illinoistech.edu (K.C.)

* Correspondence: gachyuth@hawk.iit.edu (A.G.); yshah15@hawk.iit.edu (Y.A.S.)

† These authors contributed equally to this work.

Abstract: In resource-constrained edge environments—such as mobile devices, IoT systems, and electric vehicles—energy-efficient Convolution Neural Network (CNN) accelerators on mobile Field Programmable Gate Arrays (FPGAs) are gaining significant attention for real-time object detection tasks. This paper presents a low-power implementation of the Tiny YOLOv4 object detection model on the Xilinx ZCU104 FPGA platform by using Register Transfer Level (RTL) optimization techniques. We proposed three RTL techniques in the paper: (i) Local Explicit Clock Enable (LECE), (ii) operand isolation, and (iii) Enhanced Clock Gating (ECG). A novel low-power design of Multiply-Accumulate (MAC) operations, which is one of the main components in the AI algorithm, was proposed to eliminate redundant signal switching activities. The Tiny YOLOv4 model, trained on the COCO dataset, was quantized and compiled using the Tensil tool-chain for fixed-point inference deployment. Post-implementation evaluation using Vivado 2022.2 demonstrates around 29.4% reduction in total on-chip power. Our design supports real-time detection throughput while maintaining high accuracy, making it ideal for deployment in battery-constrained environments such as drones, surveillance systems, and autonomous vehicles. These results highlight the effectiveness of RTL-level power optimization for scalable and sustainable edge AI deployment.

Keywords: BRAM; CNN accelerator; CNN architecture; FPGA RT level design; high performance; Operand isolation; low-power techniques; MAC; object detection; power consumption

1. Introduction

Object detection using Convolution Neural Networks (CNNs) has become a cornerstone of intelligent perception systems in a broad spectrum of applications, including autonomous vehicles, Unmanned Aerial Vehicles (UAVs), smart surveillance, industrial robotics, and edge devices from the Internet of Things (IoT) [1]. Among these, mobile Field Programmable Gate Arrays (FPGAs), such as the Xilinx ZCU104, PYNQ-Z2, and Ultra96, are increasingly favored due to their reconfiguration, low power consumption, and parallel computing capabilities, making them highly suitable for the real-time deployment of CNNs in constrained environments [2,3]. However, implementing high-performance object detection models like Tiny YOLOv4 on resource-limited FPGAs presents challenges, especially when balancing detection accuracy, latency, and power efficiency [4].

CNN-based object detectors are computationally intensive and involve thousands of MAC operations, large-scale feature maps, and frequent memory accesses [5]. These factors significantly increase both dynamic power consumption and latency. Although GPUs offer high computational throughput, their energy demands make them impractical for edge deployment, especially in battery-powered systems such as drones and electric vehicles. To address these challenges, researchers have explored various optimization strategies, ranging from model compression and quantization to architecture-level accelerator designs, to improve real-time inference capabilities on FPGAs [6–9].

Recent work has shifted focus to fine-grained Register Transfer Level (RTL) optimization of FPGA accelerators, which allows for more precise control over logic synthesis, signal propagation, and switching activity [10]. By applying RTL-level techniques such as adaptive clock gating, operand isolation, and enhanced gating control to core computational units such as multipliers and adders, the power consumption and resource utilization of FPGA implementations can be significantly reduced without sacrificing accuracy or throughput [6,7].

In this paper, we propose a power-aware Tiny YOLOv4 object detection system implemented on the AMD Xilinx ZCU104 FPGA. Our architecture is built using a Tensil-generated CNN accelerator as a baseline, which is then enhanced with RTL-level low-power design techniques [7,11,12]. The model is trained on the COCO dataset and compiled using the Tensil toolchain for fixed-point quantized inference. Post-synthesis analysis using Vivado 2022.2 reveals a 30% reduction in total on-chip power, with the final system demonstrating over 30× power efficiency compared to a conventional GPU-based implementation while maintaining real-time object detection capabilities [13,14].

The remainder of this paper is organized as follows. Section 2 outlines the low-power techniques applied at the RTL level and the design methodology. Section 3 presents the architecture and data flow of the proposed accelerator, including optimization and modularization strategies. Section 4 provides the results of the implementation, power profile, and comparisons with existing methods. Section 6 concludes the paper and discusses future research directions.

2. Platform-Based RTL Design Flow and Low-Power Optimization Techniques for Tiny YOLOv4 on FPGA-SoC

2.1. Background

Deploying deep learning-based object detection on mobile FPGA-SoC boards requires an efficient development flow and a hardware-aware toolchain. However, platforms such as Vivado and Quartus Prime offer standard FPGA design workflow, HLS-based direct control over RTL-level power optimization. In contrast, when combined with modular generator tools such as Tensil, platform-based RTL design flows offer enhanced customization and visibility into low-level hardware behavior, enabling power-conscious accelerator design tailored for edge AI workloads like Tiny YOLOv4 [7,11].

2.2. Platform-Based RTL Design Flow for CNN Accelerators

Xilinx Vivado offers an Integrated Development Environment (IDE) for platform-based RTL design, supporting the import and configuration of custom Verilog/VHDL modules as IP blocks. Figure 1 shows how RTL components, processing system cores, and memory interfaces are instantiated together via Vivado's IP Integrator, creating a complete hardware system with reconfigurable interconnects [15]. For user-level control and software interaction, the PYNQ framework provides Python 3.10 bindings in a Jupyter Notebook 6.x interface on embedded Linux 22.04, although it is limited in Python library support and computational efficiency. These constraints require optimized RTL design for power-constrained inference applications.

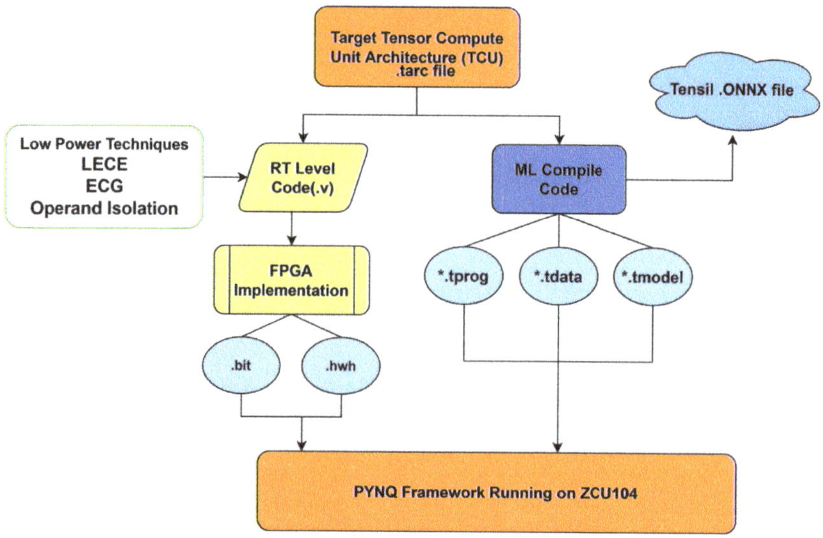

Figure 1. Tensil design flow.

2.3. *Baseline RTL Accelerator Generation Using Tensil*

To implement a CNN accelerator suitable for Tiny YOLOv4, we leverage the Tensil toolchain, as shown in Figure 1, which includes an RTL generator, compiler, and deployment runtime. Tensil enables the rapid generation of a custom accelerator from trained model representations, providing support for quantized models and memory-efficient data flow. The key advantage of Tensil lies in its flexibility and accessibility at the RTL level, enabling hardware designers to apply further optimization techniques not offered by default. However, Tensil's [14] built-in synthesis flow lacks advanced low-power capabilities, prompting us to apply additional RTL-level techniques targeting power reduction and throughput enhancement, as outlined in Section 3.

2.4. *Low-Power RTL Techniques for Tiny YOLOv4 Deployment*

Power efficiency is critical for deploying real-time object detectors, such as Tiny YOLOv4, on FPGA-SoC boards. Most of the power consumption arises from redundant toggling in MAC operations, activation layers, and memory movement [16]. To address this, we employ a suite of RTL-level low-power techniques focused on clock management and signal suppression:

- **Local Explicit Clock Enable (LECE)**
  LECE is a clock-gating technique that uses a local ENABLE signal to selectively update the output of flip-flops or pipeline registers only when valid computation is required. As illustrated in Figure 2, LECE allows finer control over bit-level register updates, significantly reducing dynamic power in pipelines where many cycles involve idle data [17].
- **Operand Isolation**
  Operand isolation prevents unnecessary signal transitions in combination logic by decoupling inactive data paths. When a computation is not needed, isolating inputs to functional units such as multipliers and adders ensures that the internal switch-

ing activity is minimized. This is implemented using control gates such as AND or MUX units placed before input operands, allowing downstream MAC units to remain inactive during idle cycles. This method proves especially effective in reducing power during memory fetches, activation layers, and sparsely populated feature map computations in Tiny YOLOv4.

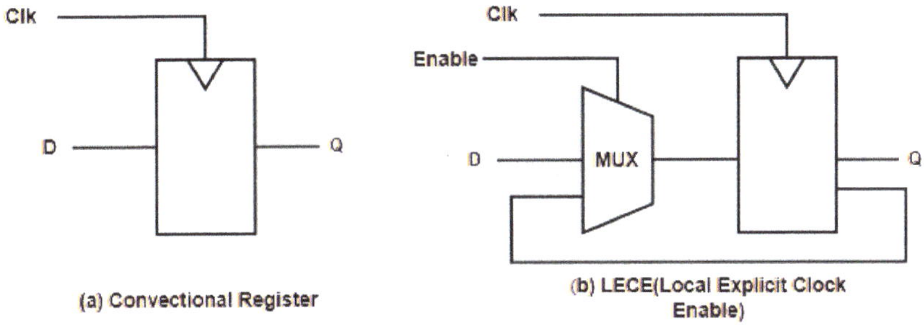

Figure 2. Conventional register with LECE technique.

- **Enhanced Clock Gating (ECG)**
  Enhanced Clock Gating (ECG) uses XOR-based gating logic to minimize unnecessary signal propagation across wide datapaths and deep pipelines. As illustrated in Figure 3, ECG applies gating at multiple stages of the processing pipeline, utilizing XOR gates for lower switching power compared to traditional AND/OR logic [18]. This makes ECG particularly suitable for MAC units and activation blocks in Tiny YOLOv4, where high bit-width operations dominate.

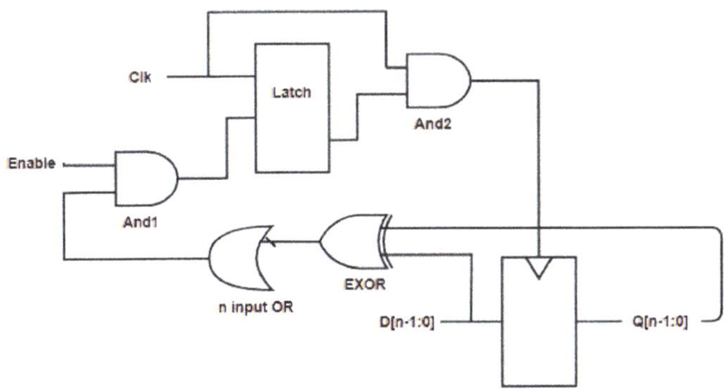

Figure 3. Enhanced clock gating.

3. Proposed Design and Optimization

3.1. Implementation of the Original Design

We utilized Xilinx Vivado 2023 for the synthesis and implementation of the RTL. Vivado handles synthesis, error checking, place, and route, and generates power and utilization summaries. The resulting bit stream configures the AMD Xilinx ZCU104 board and integrates seamlessly with the Python code to execute CNN-based object detection efficiently [14]. Our implementation included the original Tensil design [14] on the ZCU104 FPGA using the Vivado 2023 suite. This approach enabled us to measure the impact of the optimizations accurately.

3.2. Tensil Clone and Module Integration

The Tensil open-source tool was cloned using Docker and Verilog modules such as top-zcu104.v, bram1, and bram2. These modules were integrated to form a custom IP block that serves as the core of the CNN accelerator. Figure 4 illustrates the connections between various IP blocks to ensure seamless communication with the FPGA board, including Zynq IP and API Smart Connects. The 'top-zcu104' module comprises several sub-modules, where low-power techniques are applied, including MACs, POOLs, CONV, InnerDual-Port RAM, ALUs, and Counters [14]. Figure 5 presents the report of the utilization of the hardware components on the ZCU104 board after the synthesis and implementation completion [18].

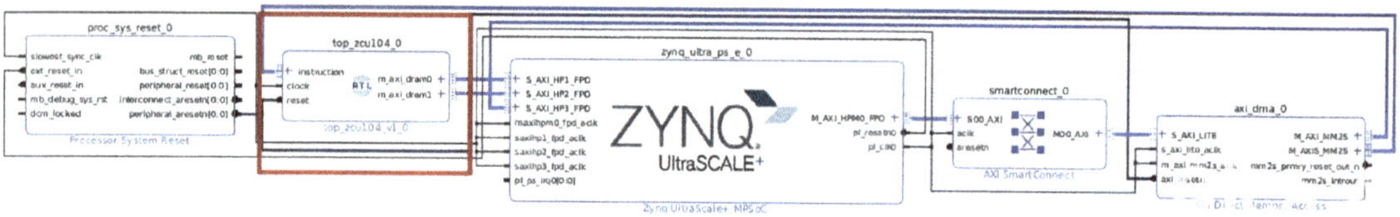

Figure 4. IP block diagram of the CNN accelerator incorporating the proposed low-power design module. The architecture emphasizes efficient data-flow, optimized memory access, and reduced dynamic power consumption, making it suitable for real-time, edge-based object detection applications.

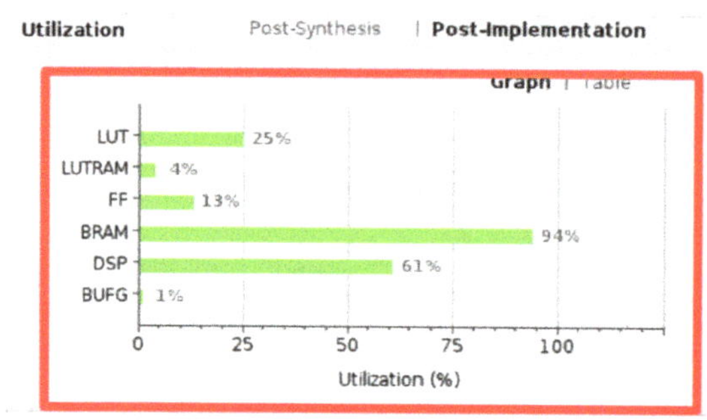

(**a**) Hardware resource utilization report

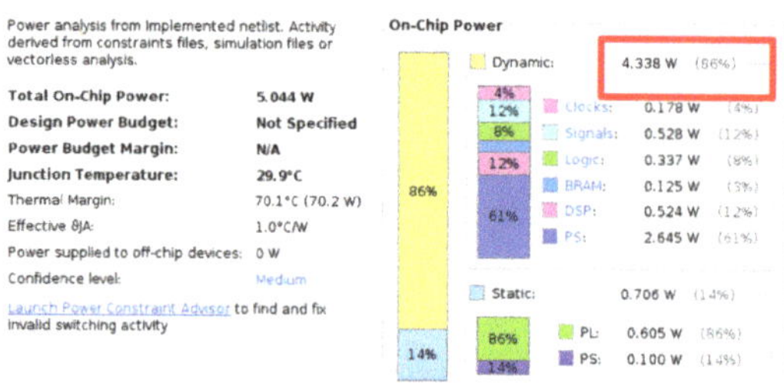

(**b**) On-chip power report

Figure 5. Hardware analysis of the original Tensil design [14]: (**a**) resource utilization and (**b**) power consumption.

3.3. Low-Power Techniques on Original Design

To enhance the energy efficiency of our baseline CNN accelerator, we integrated two RTL-level low-power design techniques: **Enhanced Clock Gating (ECG)** and **operand**

isolation. These methods were strategically implemented to reduce unnecessary switching activity, a significant contributor to dynamic power consumption in FPGA-based systems.

3.3.1. Enhanced Clock Gating (ECG)

Enhanced Clock Gating was implemented to prevent the global clock from propagating to inactive modules. Instead of relying solely on a static clock enable signal, we introduced a dynamic gating mechanism shown in Algorithm 1 by generating a gated clock `gclk` based on data activity and control logic:

```
gclk = latch_q & clock & clk_enable;
```

Here, `latch_q` captures transitions derived from `enable` and `valid_data` conditions, combined with a data toggle check (`pass-through ^ io_mulInput`). This ensures that the clock signal only reaches the compute block when there is valid data to process and when `clk_enable` is asserted. As a result, unnecessary toggling of registers and logic elements during idle cycles is avoided, reducing dynamic power.

Algorithm 1 Low-Power CNN Computation with ECG and Operand Isolation

```
Initialize latch_q ← 0
Initialize gclk ← 0
                                              ▷ On each rising edge of the main clock
if enable and valid_data then
    latch_q ← passthrough ⊕ io_mulInput
end if
                                              ▷ At every time step
gclk ← latch_q ∧ clock ∧ clk_enable           ▷ Enhanced Clock Gating
                                              ▷ On each rising edge of gated clock
if data_active then
    output ← compute_result(input_a, input_b)  ▷ Operand Isolation
end if
```

3.3.2. Operand Isolation

Operand isolation was applied to the computation stage to further minimize power consumption. By using a conditional guard (`data_active`) around the compute operation, we ensured that arithmetic functions are only executed when required:

```
if (data_active) begin
output <= compute_result(input_a, input_b);
end
```

This prevents signal transitions within the arithmetic unit (e.g., multipliers, adders) when input data are inactive, thereby reducing internal node switching and saving dynamic power.

4. Experiment and Results

4.1. ZCU104 Board Setup

We selected the ZCU104 board as our foundational hardware platform due to its high-performance FPGA-SoC architecture, which combines a quad-core ARM Cortex-A53 Processing System (PS) with extensive Programmable Logic (PL). This setup integrates effectively with the PYNQ framework and supports Jupyter Notebook for rapid software development using Python, C/C++, and libraries such as OpenCV. As shown in Figure 6, the setup consists of a ZCU104 board and a camera connected to the board using USB [19].

We employed the Tiny-YOLOv4 architecture for real-time object detection, trained on a COCO dataset, and converted it into the ONNX format. The ONNX model was compiled using the Tensil tool-chain to generate three essential artifacts: .tmodel, .tdata, and .tprog, which the CNN driver utilizes to access model weights, program instructions, and configuration data. These artifacts remain unchanged from the original, ensuring that model accuracy is preserved. After successful execution of the bit-stream on the ZCU104 board, we achieved live object detection, as illustrated in Figure 7, which shows the Jupyter environment and real-time detection results using the Tiny-YOLOv4 model on the ZCU104.

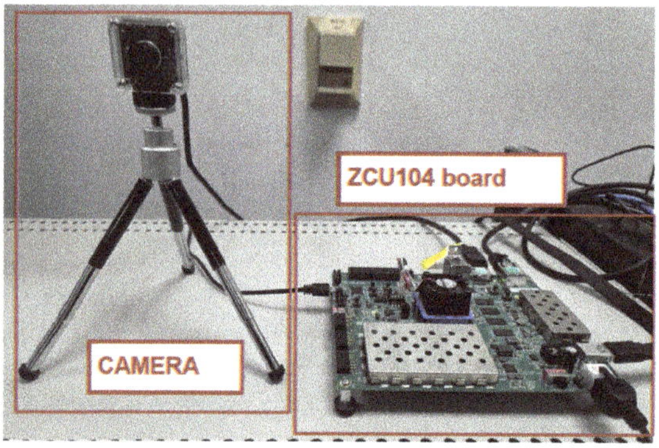

Figure 6. ZCU104 and camera setup.

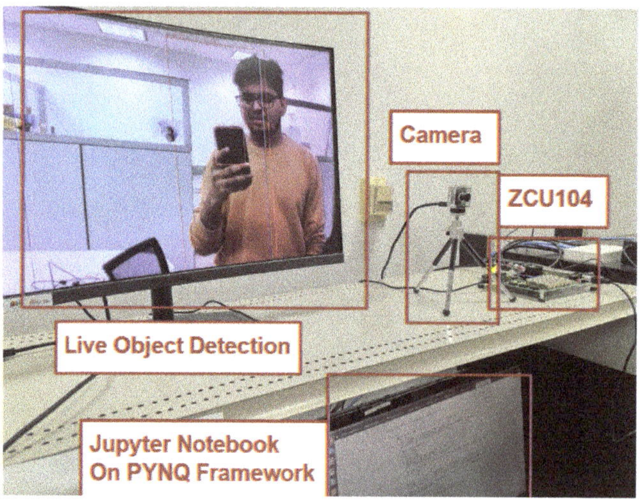

Figure 7. Live object detection on ZCU104 using Tiny-YOLOv4.

4.2. *Power Results*

Our proposed design leads to a 33.93% decrease in dynamic power consumption and a 29.4% reduction in total on-chip power, as shown in Figure 8. Additionally, this approach can handle strong fan-out signals, guaranteeing the operation of the device. Furthermore, device speed can be increased by adding intermediate flip-flops to the pipeline logic; however, using too many flip-flops increases the computational complexity. Our low-power methods surpass flip-flop-based methods in terms of performance.

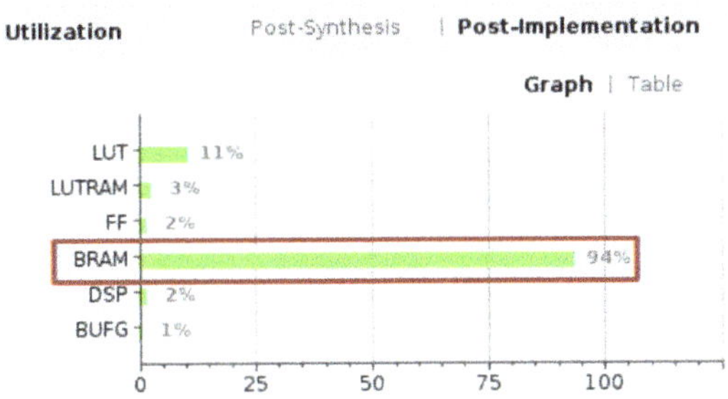

(**a**) Hardware resource utilization report

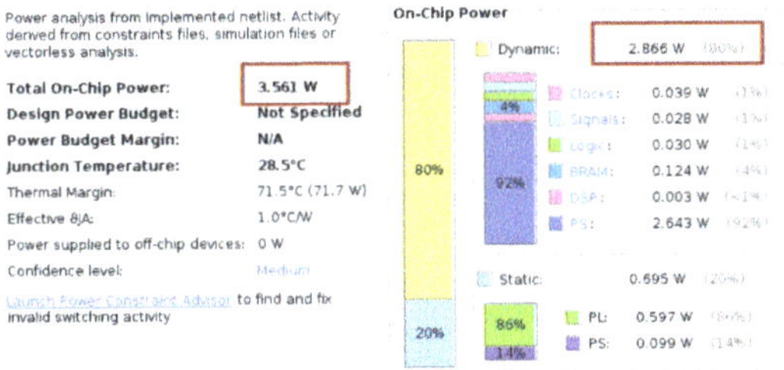

(**b**) On-chip power report

Figure 8. Hardware analysis of the proposed Tiny-YOLOv4 design on the ZCU104 FPGA: (**a**) resource utilization and (**b**) power consumption.

4.3. Combined Impact

The combined application of enhanced clock gating and operand isolation effectively reduced redundant switching activities in both the control and data-path components. This implementation resulted in a **33.94% reduction in dynamic power consumption** compared to the original design without these optimizations.

These RTL-level enhancements serve as foundational strategies in developing energy-efficient FPGA-based accelerators for real-time deep learning inference.

The power report Table 1 indicates a significant improvement in power efficiency. Specifically, the total on-chip power was reduced from 5.044 W (baseline) to 3.561 W (proposed), reflecting a 29.4% total power reduction. The dynamic power, which directly impacts energy efficiency, was reduced from 4.338 W to 2.866 W, resulting in a 33.9% dynamic power savings. Notably, the power consumed by the Processing System (PS) dropped slightly from 2.645 W to 2.643 W, confirming optimization efforts focused on the Programmable Logic (PL).

$$\text{Original Power} = 5.044\ \text{W} \tag{1}$$

$$\text{Proposed Design Power} = 3.561\ \text{W} \tag{2}$$

$$Total, Power, Reduction = \frac{5.044 - 3.561}{5.044} \times 100 = 29.4 \tag{3}$$

$$Dynamic, Power, Reduction = \frac{4.338 - 2.866}{4.338} \times 100 = 33.9 \tag{4}$$

These improvements illustrate how optimizing memory blocks, and DSP placement can directly enhance both performance and energy efficiency in FPGA-accelerated CNN inference.

Table 1. Comparison results of different low-power techniques on ZCU104.

Metric	ZCU104 Capacity [20]	Original Design [14]	Proposed Design
CLB LUTs	274,080	57,345 (20.9%)	24,744 (9.0%)
CLB Registers	548,160	59,252 (10.8%)	7718 (1.4%)
DSPs	2520	1057 (41.9%)	33 (1.3%)
Block RAM Tiles	912	293.5 (32.2%)	293.5 (32.2%)
LUT as Memory	144,000	4220 (2.93%)	3150 (2.19%)
Dynamic Power (W)	—	4.338	2.866

The performance-per-watt metric improved as well. With a target frequency of 50 MHz, the proposed design achieved 43.9 GOPs/W, representing a 1.37× increase over other FPGA board implementations. This confirms our design's superior power efficiency in real-time object detection applications [11].

Each BRAM block in the ZCU104 FPGA is 36 KB in size, which equals 4.5 KB [20]. The ZCU104 board, based on the Xilinx Zynq UltraScale+ MPSoC, contains a total of 912 BRAM blocks. From our post-implementation results, the proposed design utilizes 94% of the available BRAM. The total BRAM memory usage is calculated as follows:

$$Total\ BRAM\ memory\ used\ (\text{kB}) = 44 \times 0.94 \times 4.5\ \text{kB} = 3859.68\ \text{kB} \approx 3.77\ \text{MB} \quad (5)$$

This memory is critical for buffering feature maps, weights, and intermediate computations during real-time object detection using the Tiny-YOLOv4 model.

The total time it takes for an operation to complete is known as latency, typically expressed in clock cycles or clock periods [18]. Latency is calculated as the product of the clock period—the duration of each cycle—and the number of clock cycles required to complete a task [11]. In our experimental setup, latency measurements were conducted using a Jupyter Notebook in Python. We sequentially processed multiple images through the CNN accelerator, recording the runtime for each from the beginning of inference to the generation of the final prediction. This allowed us to capture accurate end-to-end latency for real-time object detection. The average runtime per image was then computed to determine the overall latency of the accelerator.

In Convolutional Neural Networks (CNNs), latency is inversely related to Frames Per Second (FPS). While latency measures the time required to process one image, FPS indicates how many photos can be processed per second [18]. In our experiments with Tiny-YOLOv4 running on the ZCU104 board, we observed an average processing speed of 9.87 Frames Per Second (FPS) during live object detection.

$$FPS = \frac{1}{Latency} \approx 9.87 \quad (6)$$

The rate at which operations are completed in CNNs is referred to as throughput, commonly measured in Giga-Operations Per Second (GOPS). Throughput is especially critical for real-time tasks, where computational efficiency must be maximized. In our case, the total number of Multiply-Accumulate (MAC) operations performed across the entire CNN—estimated at 6.97 billion—forms the basis for calculating GOPS. This figure was derived by summing the MAC operations across all layers of Tiny-YOLOv4. With power optimization techniques such as Enhanced Clock Gating (ECG) applied to the MAC units, our implementation achieves both high throughput and reduced dynamic power consumption.

5. Discussion

We confirmed that more register buffers and BRAM blocks are activated in our proposed Tiny-YOLOv4 implementation compared to the baseline design, as seen from the higher flip-flop and DSP utilization in Figure 8. This validates our design's improved data reuse and parallelism for CNN inference. The architecture can be further optimized at the RTL level once functional correctness and timing are validated.

From Table 2, it can be observed that while our design achieves a moderate throughput of 9.87 FPS on the ZCU104 platform, it maintains a relatively low power consumption of 2.866 W, resulting in a power efficiency of 3.44 FPS/W. Compared to other works, such as Nguyen et al. [21] (125 FPS at 26.4 W) and Valadanzoj et al. [22] (55 FPS at 13.6 W), our implementation focuses on delivering a balanced trade-off between performance and energy efficiency, which is particularly relevant for edge computing environments where thermal and power constraints are critical.

Table 2. Comparison results of FPGA implementations for YOLO models.

Author/Criteria	Year	NN Model	FPGA	Test Image Size	Accuracy (%)	Throughput (FPS)	Power (W)	Efficiency (FPS/W)
Wang et al. [23]	2023	CNN	Spartan-6	32×32	96	16	0.79	20.25
Heller et al. [24]	2022	YOLO V4 Tiny	Kria KV 260	HD	75	15	8	1.87
Corcoran et al. [25]	2023	YOLO V3 Tiny	VCU110	416×416	-	69	15.4	4.5
Nguyen et al. [21]	2024	YOLO V4 Tiny	ZCU104	HD	78	125	26.4	4.7
Valadanzoj et al. [22]	2024	YOLO V4 Tiny	ZC706	416×416	79	55	13.6	4.0
R.A.Amin et al. [26]	2024	YOLO V3 Tiny	Kria KV260	HD	99	15	3.5	4.2
This Work	2025	YOLO V4 Tiny	ZCU104	HD	-	9.87	2.866	3.44

The compact resource footprint—utilizing just 9.03% of LUTs, 1.41% of FFs, and 1.31% of DSPs—combined with a low thermal profile makes this architecture suitable for deployment in space-constrained platforms. Its design characteristics align with the requirements of AI-driven mobile applications, such as UAV-based vision systems, wearable AI devices, and battery-powered IoT cameras, where sustained real-time inference must be achieved under strict power and weight constraints.

Looking forward, further improvements could be achieved by integrating adaptive power management techniques and exploring partial reconfiguration to dynamically adjust processing capacity based on workload demands. Such enhancements would expand its applicability to a broader range of next-generation mobile AI platforms.

6. Conclusions

In this work, we presented a low-power FPGA-based Tiny-YOLOv4 accelerator on the Xilinx ZCU104, integrating RTL-level techniques such as Enhanced Clock Gating (ECG) and operand isolation. The proposed design achieved 68.4 GOPS throughput at 50 MHz with only 2.866 W PL dynamic power, offering a balanced trade-off between performance, resource usage, and energy efficiency. These characteristics make it a promising solution for real-time embedded vision tasks in power- and space-constrained environments.

Author Contributions: Conceptualization, data curation, formal analysis, investigation, methodology, validation, A.G. and Y.A.S.; writing—original draft, writing—review and editing, S.M.V.; supervision, funding acquisition, project administration, K.C. All authors have read and agreed to the published version of the manuscript.

Funding: This work was supported by the Technology Innovation Program (20018906, Development of autonomous driving collaboration control platform for commercial and task assistance vehicles) funded By the Ministry of Trade, Industry, and Energy (MOTIE, Republic of Korea).

Data Availability Statement: The original contributions presented in this study are included in the article. Further inquiries can be directed to the corresponding author.

Acknowledgments: We thank our colleagues from KETI and KEIT, who provided insight and expertise, which greatly assisted the research and improved the manuscript.

Conflicts of Interest: The authors declare no conflicts of interest.

Abbreviations

The following abbreviations are used in this manuscript:

ECG	Enhanced Clock Gating
OI	Operand Ioslation
LECG	Local Explicit Clock Gating
IP	Intellectual Property Blocks
BRAM	Block Random Access Memory
CONV	Convolution Layer
MAC	Multiply and Accumulate
RTL	Register Transfer Level
CNN	Convolutional Neural Network
FPGA	Field-Programmable Gate Array
HLS	High-Level Synthesis
Soc	System-on-Chip
ONNX	Open Neural Network Exchange

References

1. Jameil, A.K.; Al-Raweshidy, H. Efficient CNN Architecture on FPGA Using High-evel Module for Healthcare Devices. *IEEE Access* **2022**, *10*, 60486–60495. [CrossRef]
2. Zhang, Z.; Mahmud, M.A.P.; Kouzani, A.Z. FitNN: A Low-Resource FPGA-Based CNN Accelerator for Drones. *IEEE Internet Things J.* **2022**, *9*, 21357–21369. [CrossRef]
3. Li, X.; Gong, X.; Wang, D.; Zhang, J.; Baker, T.; Zhou, J.; Lu, T. ABM-SpConv-SIMD: Accelerating Convolutional Neural Network Inference for Industrial IoT Applications on Edge Devices. *IEEE Trans. Netw. Sci. Eng.* **2023**, *10*, 3071–3085. [CrossRef]
4. Nikouei, S.Y.; Chen, Y.; Song, S.; Xu, R.; Choi, B.Y.; Faughnan, T.R. Smart Surveillance as an Edge Network Service: From Harr-Cascade, SVM to a Lightweight CNN. *arXiv* **2018**, arXiv:1805.00331. [CrossRef]
5. Tamimi, S.; Ebrahimi, Z.; Khaleghi, B.; Asadi, H. An Efficient SRAM-Based Reconfigurable Architecture for Embedded Processors. *IEEE Trans. Comput. Aided Des. Integr. Circuits Syst.* **2019**, *38*, 466–479. [CrossRef]
6. Wu, X.; Ma, Y.; Wang, M.; Wang, Z. A Flexible and Efficient FPGA Accelerator for Various Large-Scale and Lightweight CNNs. *IEEE Trans. Circuits Syst. Regul. Pap.* **2022**, *69*, 1185–1198. [CrossRef]
7. Irmak, H.; Ziener, D.; Alachiotis, N. Increasing Flexibility of FPGA-based CNN Accelerators with Dynamic Partial Reconfiguration. In Proceedings of the 2021 31st International Conference on Field-Programmable Logic and Applications (FPL), Dresden, Germany, 30 August–3 September 2021; pp. 306–311. [CrossRef]
8. Wei, Z.; Arora, A.; Li, R.; John, L. HLSDataset: Open-Source Dataset for ML-Assisted FPGA Design using High Level Synthesis. In Proceedings of the 2023 IEEE 34th International Conference on Application-specific Systems, Architectures and Processors (ASAP), Porto, Portugal, 19–21 July 2023; pp. 197–204. [CrossRef]
9. Mohammadi Makrani, H.; Farahmand, F.; Sayadi, H.; Bondi, S.; Pudukotai Dinakarrao, S.M.; Homayoun, H.; Rafatirad, S. Pyramid: Machine Learning Framework to Estimate the Optimal Timing and Resource Usage of a High-Level Synthesis Design. In Proceedings of the 2019 29th International Conference on Field Programmable Logic and Applications (FPL), Barcelona, Spain, 8–12 September 2019; pp. 397–403. [CrossRef]
10. Ullah, S.; Rehman, S.; Shafique, M.; Kumar, A. High-Performance Accurate and Approximate Multipliers for FPGA-Based Hardware Accelerators. *IEEE Trans. Comput. Aided Des. Integr. Circuits Syst.* **2022**, *41*, 211–224. [CrossRef]
11. Li, S.; Luo, Y.; Sun, K.; Yadav, N.; Choi, K.K. A Novel FPGA Accelerator Design for Real-Time and Ultra-Low Power Deep Convolutional Neural Networks Compared with Titan X GPU. *IEEE Access* **2020**, *8*, 105455–105471. [CrossRef]

12. Yang, C.; Wang, Y.; Zhang, H.; Wang, X.; Geng, L. A Reconfigurable CNN Accelerator using Tile-by-Tile Computing and Dynamic Adaptive Data Truncation. In Proceedings of the 2019 IEEE International Conference on Integrated Circuits, Technologies and Applications (ICTA), Chengdu, China, 13–15 November 2019; pp. 73–74. [CrossRef]
13. Zhang, X.; Ma, Y.; Xiong, J.; Hwu, W.M.W.; Kindratenko, V.; Chen, D. Exploring HW/SW Co-Design for Video Analysis on CPU-FPGA Heterogeneous Systems. *IEEE Trans. Comput. Aided Des. Integr. Circuits Syst.* **2022**, *41*, 1606–1619. [CrossRef]
14. Tensil. Learn Tensil with ResNet and PYNQ Z1. Available online: https://k155la3.blog/2022/04/04/tensil-tutorial-for-yolo-v4-tiny-on-ultra96-v2/ (accessed on 15 December 2022).
15. Kim, Y.; Tong, Q.; Choi, K.; Lee, E.; Jang, S.J.; Choi, B.H. System Level Power Reduction for YOLO2 Sub-modules for Object Detection of Future Autonomous Vehicles. In Proceedings of the 2018 International SoC Design Conference (ISOCC), Daegu, Republic of Korea, 12–15 November 2018; pp. 151–155. [CrossRef]
16. Kim, Y.; Kim, H.; Yadav, N.; Li, S.; Choi, K.K. Low-Power RTL Code Generation for Advanced CNN Algorithms toward Object Detection in Autonomous Vehicles. *Electronics* **2020**, *9*, 478. [CrossRef]
17. Kim, H.; Choi, K. Low Power FPGA-SoC Design Techniques for CNN-based Object Detection Accelerator. In Proceedings of the 2019 IEEE 10th Annual Ubiquitous Computing, Electronics and Mobile Communication Conference (UEMCON), New York, NY, USA, 10–12 October 2019; pp. 1130–1134. [CrossRef]
18. Kim, V.H.; Choi, K.K. A Reconfigurable CNN-Based Accelerator Design for Fast and Energy-Efficient Object Detection System on Mobile FPGA. *IEEE Access* **2023**, *11*, 59438–59445. [CrossRef]
19. Zhang, Y.; Tong, Q.; Li, L.; Wang, W.; Choi, K.; Jang, J.; Jung, H.; Ahn, S.Y. Automatic Register Transfer level CAD tool design for advanced clock gating and low power schemes. In Proceedings of the 2012 International SoC Design Conference (ISOCC), Jeju Island, Republic of Korea, 4–7 November 2012; pp. 21–24. [CrossRef]
20. Advanced Micro Devices, Inc. AMD ZCU104. Available online: https://www.amd.com/en/products/adaptive-socs-and-fpgas/evaluation-boards/zcu104.html (accessed on 19 June 2024).
21. Nguyen, D.-D.; Nguyen, D.-T.; Le, M.-T.; Nguyen, Q.-C. FPGA-SoC implementation of YOLOv4 for flying-object detection. *J. Real-Time Image Process.* **2024**, *21*, 63. [CrossRef]
22. Valadanzoj, Z.; Daryanavard, H.; Harifi, A. High-speed YOLOv4-tiny hardware accelerator for self-driving automotive. *J. Supercomput.* **2024**, *80*, 6699–6724. [CrossRef]
23. Wang, Y.; Liao, Y.; Yang, J.; Wang, H.; Zhao, Y.; Zhang, C.; Xiao, B.; Xu, F.; Gao, Y.; Xu, M.; Zheng, J. An FPGA-based online reconfigurable CNN edge computing device for object detection. *Microelectron. J.* 2023, *137*, 105805. [CrossRef]
24. Heller, D.; Rizk, M.; Douguet, R.; Baghdadi, A.; Diguet, J.-P. Marine objects detection using deep learning on embedded edge devices. In Proceedings of the IEEE International Workshop on Rapid System Prototyping (RSP), Shanghai, China, 13 October 2022; pp. 1–7. Available online: https://ieeexplore.ieee.org/document/10039025 (accessed on 17 August 2025).
25. Montgomerie-Corcoran, A.; Toupas, P.; Yu, Z.; Bouganis, C.-S. SATAY: A streaming architecture toolflow for accelerating YOLO models on FPGA devices. In Proceedings of the International Conference on Field Programmable Technology (ICFPT), Yokohama, Japan, 11–14 December 2023; pp. 179–187. Available online: https://ieeexplore.ieee.org/document/10416135 (accessed on 17 August 2025).
26. Amin, R.A.; Hasan, M.; Wiese, V.; Obermaisser, R. FPGA-Based Real-Time Object Detection and Classification System Using YOLO for Edge Computing. In Proceedings of the IEEE International Conference on Consumer Electronics (ICCE), Las Vegas, NV, USA, 5–8 January 2024; pp. 1–6. Available online: https://ieeexplore.ieee.org/document/10537163/references#references (accessed on 17 August 2025).

electronics

MDPI

Article

Accelerating Deep Learning Inference: A Comparative Analysis of Modern Acceleration Frameworks

Ishrak Jahan Ratul *, Yuxiao Zhou and Kecheng Yang

Department of Computer Science, Texas State University, San Marcos, TX 78666, USA; yuxiao.zh@gmail.com (Y.Z.); yangk@txstate.edu (K.Y.)
* Correspondence: ishrakratul@txstate.edu

Abstract: Deep learning (DL) continues to play a pivotal role in a wide range of intelligent systems, including autonomous machines, smart surveillance, industrial automation, and portable healthcare technologies. These applications often demand low-latency inference and efficient resource utilization, especially when deployed on embedded or edge devices with limited computational capacity. As DL models become increasingly complex, selecting the right inference framework is essential to meeting performance and deployment goals. In this work, we conduct a comprehensive comparison of five widely adopted inference frameworks: PyTorch, ONNX Runtime, TensorRT, Apache TVM, and JAX. All experiments are performed on the NVIDIA Jetson AGX Orin platform, a high-performance computing solution tailored for edge artificial intelligence workloads. The evaluation considers several key performance metrics, including inference accuracy, inference time, throughput, memory usage, and power consumption. Each framework is tested using a wide range of convolutional and transformer models and analyzed in terms of deployment complexity, runtime efficiency, and hardware utilization. Our results show that certain frameworks offer superior inference speed and throughput, while others provide advantages in flexibility, portability, or ease of integration. We also observe meaningful differences in how each framework manages system memory and power under various load conditions. This study offers practical insights into the trade-offs associated with deploying DL inference on resource-constrained hardware.

Keywords: deep learning; PyTorch; real-time inference; TensorRT; JAX; Apache TVM

1. Introduction

In recent years, DL has experienced rapid growth and has emerged as one of the most effective techniques within the field of machine learning. This progress has fueled the integration of DL into a wide variety of applications, including computer vision, natural language processing (NLP), and autonomous control systems. Increasingly, these applications are being deployed not only on general-purpose computing platforms but also on embedded and edge systems that operate under strict power, size, and latency constraints.

Unlike traditional machine learning algorithms, which often suffer from overfitting or poor scalability in large data settings, modern deep neural networks (DNNs) can maintain high accuracy even with overparameterized architectures. For example, the parameter count in state-of-the-art image classification models has increased dramatically, from 61 million to more than 2.1 billion between 2013 and 2023, as tracked by the ImageNet leaderboard [1]. Similarly, in NLP, models like BERT [2] and its successors contain hundreds of millions of parameters, offering breakthrough performance while introducing significant computational overhead [3].

Although such large models achieve exceptional accuracy, their deployment comes at a cost. Training and especially inference can be slow, memory-intensive, and computationally expensive. This poses a major challenge in scenarios where inference must be conducted in real time while operating under limitations on size, weight, power, and cost. Embedded and edge platforms, such as those used in robotics, drones, mobile healthcare, or surveillance, must perform inference with limited processing power, memory bandwidth, and energy. These platforms often require instant responses, which makes the inefficiencies of standard DL frameworks a critical concern.

Consider autonomous vehicles as an example. They must process high-bandwidth sensor inputs such as LiDAR and video feeds in real time to ensure safe navigation. Similarly, video surveillance systems must detect incidents such as theft, fire, or physical conflict immediately, often without relying on remote cloud services. In these and similar scenarios, executing inference locally on embedded devices becomes essential due to requirements for low latency, reliability, and data privacy.

This gap between high-performing models and the constraints of real-world deployment environments has led to the development of various strategies to optimize inference. Approaches such as quantization [4], pruning [5], and neural architecture search (NAS) [6] aim to reduce the resource demand of models. Lightweight networks such as MobileNet [7] and SqueezeNet [8] are designed specifically for deployment under limited hardware resources. In addition, specialized hardware solutions including Google's TPU [9] and Intel's VPU [10] have been introduced to accelerate DL inference at low power consumption.

Despite these advances, widely used frameworks such as TensorFlow and PyTorch [11] are not inherently optimized for inference on embedded systems. To address this issue, several software-level optimization tools have emerged. For instance, NVIDIA developed TensorRT [12], a high-performance inference engine designed to transform trained models into highly efficient executables suitable for edge and automotive platforms.

In addition to TensorRT, other frameworks are increasingly used for inference acceleration. ONNX Runtime allows deployment across platforms using different execution providers [13]. Apache TVM optimizes and compiles models for specific hardware targets [14]. JAX supports high-performance computation through just-in-time compilation, although its deployment maturity on embedded platforms is still developing [15].

While many of these tools have demonstrated strong potential, there is a need for a consistent evaluation of their performance under realistic deployment conditions. The NVIDIA Jetson AGX Orin provides a modern, high-efficiency edge AI platform that integrates Ampere architecture GPUs with AI acceleration hardware [16]. This platform offers a timely opportunity to benchmark inference frameworks across critical performance dimensions.

In this study, we present a comparative evaluation of five prominent DL inference frameworks: PyTorch, ONNX Runtime, TensorRT, Apache TVM, and JAX. Our benchmarking is conducted on the Jetson AGX Orin platform, using representative models and measuring key metrics such as inference time, throughput, memory utilization, power consumption, and accuracy. The results offer insights for developers and researchers working on real-time AI applications in resource-constrained environments.

Contribution

This paper makes the following key contributions to the evaluation of DL inference performance on embedded systems:

- We conduct a comprehensive evaluation of five popular DL inference frameworks: PyTorch, ONNX Runtime, TensorRT, Apache TVM, and JAX, on the NVIDIA Jetson AGX Orin platform.
- The benchmarking covers inference time, throughput, system memory usage, power consumption, and prediction accuracy using a unified and consistent experimental setup. Both Top 1 and Top 5 classification accuracy are reported.
- All evaluations are performed using the ImageNet validation dataset comprising 50,000 images across 1000 classes, ensuring realistic and standardized performance comparison.
- The study includes both convolutional and transformer-based models, representing a diverse range of modern neural network architectures used in computer vision and general artificial intelligence.
- We present practical insights into the tradeoffs associated with each framework, offering guidance for selecting suitable inference solutions for embedded and resource-constrained deployments.
- To support reproducibility, we detail the complete benchmarking methodology, including model conversion workflows, optimization strategies, measurement protocols, and software configurations.

Organization

The subsequent sections of this paper are structured in the following manner: Section 3 offers a comprehensive introduction to PyTorch, ONNX Runtime, TensorRT, TVM, and JAX. Section 4 outlines the methodology used in our studies, which includes the models that were tested, the workflows that were followed, and the methods used to measure performance. The experimental findings and discussions may be found in Sections 5 and 6. Section 2 presented a comprehensive summary of the existing research. We conclude our article in Section 7.

2. Related Work

Numerous studies have investigated deep learning inference optimization and deployment on edge and embedded systems. Cheng et al. [17] surveyed compression and acceleration techniques such as quantization, pruning, distillation, and architecture search. Hao et al. [18] benchmarked edge AI models, demonstrating how deployment performance depends on the interplay among model structure, hardware architecture, and compiler technology.

In 2022, Shin and Kim [19] evaluated YOLO models using TensorRT on Jetson platforms, confirming real-time object detection suitability. Zhang et al. [20] assessed ONNX Runtime as a hardware-agnostic backend, emphasizing portability benefits despite limited edge-focused benchmarks. The Apache TVM compiler was introduced by Chen et al. [14], showcasing performance tuning across diverse hardware targets. Peng et al. [21] examined JAX's high-performance numerical computation on cloud and server environments, leaving its edge-inference behavior less explored. Ulker et al. [22] compared TensorFlow Lite and OpenVINO on Raspberry Pi and Jetson TX2, while Wortsman et al. [23] studied ensemble methods on high-end GPUs without embedded device focus.

More recent work continues this trend. Alqahtani et al. [24] performed extensive benchmarking of object detection models, including YOLOv8, on Jetson AGX Orin Nano and Raspberry Pi, highlighting trade-offs between accuracy, latency, and energy efficiency. Yeom and Kim [25] introduced UniForm, a vision-transformer variant optimized for edge devices like Jetson AGX Orin, achieving up to fivefold speed gains. Arya and Simmhan [26] evaluated large language model inference (2.7 B–32.8 B parameters) on Jetson Orin AGX, analyzing batch size, quantization, latency, throughput, and power, offering insight into the feasibility of edge-based LLMs.

Despite these advances, to the best of our knowledge, no prior work offers a comprehensive, multi-metric comparison across PyTorch (v2.3.0), ONNX Runtime (v1.17.1), TensorRT (v8.6.2.3), Apache TVM (v0.21.0), and JAX (v0.4.28) on the Jetson AGX Orin platform. Our research fills this gap by benchmarking both convolutional and transformer models on ImageNet across inference time, throughput, memory, power, and Top-1/Top-5 accuracy.

3. Overview of Inference Frameworks

3.1. PyTorch

PyTorch [11] is an open-source machine learning library that facilitates moving from research prototyping to production deployment rapidly. It is primarily utilized as a DL platform in Python, offering exceptional flexibility and speed for research applications.

PyTorch allows for the manipulation of Tensors (multi-dimensional arrays) across both CPUs and GPUs, significantly speeding up computations. It offers a broad spectrum of tensor operations catering to diverse scientific computing needs, including both basic arithmetic and advanced linear algebra.

Unlike other frameworks where a neural network's architecture must be predefined and reused, PyTorch employs reverse-mode auto-differentiation. This method enables users to alter network behavior on the fly without substantial computational overhead.

Enhanced by acceleration libraries like Intel MKL and NVIDIA (cuDNN, NCCL), PyTorch performs efficiently across various network sizes. It is also optimized for memory usage, enabling the training of very large DL models without the memory constraints typical of other frameworks.

3.2. ONNX Runtime

ONNX Runtime [20] is a high-performance inference engine developed by Microsoft to support the Open Neural Network Exchange (ONNX) format. It is designed to maximize inference speed and portability across a wide range of hardware platforms and environments.

ONNX Runtime allows developers to deploy trained models from multiple frameworks such as PyTorch, TensorFlow, and scikit-learn, offering backend flexibility through various execution providers. These include CPU, CUDA GPU, TensorRT, DirectML, and OpenVINO, enabling seamless adaptation to different deployment targets. The modular architecture makes it possible to switch hardware acceleration paths with minimal code changes.

To improve performance, ONNX Runtime supports optimizations such as operator fusion, constant folding, graph pruning, and quantization. It also integrates with model acceleration tools like Intel Neural Compressor and NVIDIA TensorRT to further optimize inference. ONNX Runtime is widely used in production-scale deployments for its efficient memory usage and predictable latency characteristics. It is especially well-suited for inference scenarios requiring cross-platform consistency and low deployment overhead.

3.3. TensorRT

TensorRT is a high-performance DL inference SDK, part of the NVIDIA CUDA X AI Kit. It includes an inference optimizer and runtime that achieves low latency and high throughput.

TensorRT enhances DL model performance through six optimization strategies: (1) Weight and activation precision calibration: optimizes model performance by quantizing to 8-bit integers while maintaining accuracy. (2) Layer and tensor fusion: consolidates nodes within a kernel to improve GPU memory use and bandwidth. (3) Kernel auto-tuning: optimizes based on the GPU platform to choose the best layers, algorithms, and batch sizes. (4) Dynamic tensor memory: efficiently allocates memory only when needed, reducing consumption and allocation overhead. (5) Multi-stream execution: processes multiple input streams concurrently. (6) Time fusion: optimizes RNNs by dynamically generating kernels across time steps.

TensorRT supports a broad spectrum of AI applications, from computer vision and automatic speech recognition to natural language understanding and text-to-speech. It provides ready-to-deploy inference engines for diverse applications, including autonomous driving and real-time video analytics, ensuring efficient real-time inference on edge devices and in IoT scenarios.

3.4. *Apache TVM*

Apache TVM [14] is an open-source DL compiler stack that enables the deployment of machine learning models across a diverse set of hardware backends. TVM translates high-level model representations into optimized code tailored for the target device, including CPUs, GPUs, and specialized accelerators.

TVM provides end-to-end compilation from frameworks such as PyTorch, TensorFlow, and Keras. It performs automated graph-level and tensor-level optimizations including operator fusion, memory reuse, loop unrolling, and layout transformation. These features are critical for reducing inference latency and memory consumption, especially on embedded devices.

A key feature of TVM is its AutoTVM module, which uses machine learning-based cost models to perform hardware-aware tuning. This allows TVM to search for optimal schedules that balance computation and memory usage for a specific target. The resulting compiled models are highly efficient and portable.

Due to its flexibility and performance, TVM is often used in research and production environments where fine-grained control over deployment is essential. It continues to be extended to support microcontrollers, NPUs, and custom hardware accelerators.

3.5. *JAX*

JAX [21] is a numerical computing library developed by Google Research, designed for high-performance machine learning research. It provides composable function transformations such as automatic differentiation, vectorization, and just-in-time compilation using the Accelerated Linear Algebra (XLA) compiler.

Unlike traditional DL frameworks, JAX emphasizes functional programming paradigms and offers seamless interoperability with NumPy. It supports efficient large-scale numerical computation on both CPUs and GPUs, and is particularly well-suited for gradient-based optimization and scientific simulations.

JAX compiles Python functions into optimized machine code for target devices using XLA. This compilation not only improves performance but also reduces runtime overhead. It is capable of automatically parallelizing code across multiple devices and supports distributed training through libraries such as Flax and Haiku.

Although JAX is primarily used in research, it has growing relevance for production use due to its performance and flexibility. Its suitability for inference on embedded systems is still an active area of exploration, especially in comparison to frameworks like TensorRT or TVM that offer dedicated deployment optimizations.

4. Methodology

This study conducts a systematic benchmarking of five widely adopted DL inference frameworks, PyTorch, ONNX Runtime, TensorRT, Apache TVM and JAX, on the NVIDIA Jetson AGX Orin platform. To ensure consistency across comparisons, identical models, datasets, preprocessing, and evaluation protocols were used. The experiments were carefully designed to highlight how each framework scales across a range of batch sizes and responds to hardware-aware optimizations relevant to edge computing.

4.1. Dataset and Preprocessing

All evaluations were performed using the ImageNet ILSVRC 2012 validation dataset, which includes 50,000 high-resolution natural images classified into 1000 categories. Preprocessing involved resizing images to 256 × 256 pixels, followed by center cropping to 224 × 224 pixels. Standard normalization using mean values of [0.485, 0.456, 0.406] and standard deviations of [0.229, 0.224, 0.225] was applied to align with the preprocessing pipeline of ImageNet-trained models [27]. These preprocessing steps were consistently implemented across all five frameworks to ensure input uniformity.

4.2. Model Selection and Conversion

Six pretrained models were selected to represent a diverse range of neural network architectures and computational complexities. These include ResNet-152 [28], MobileNetV2 [29], SqueezeNet [8], EfficientNet-B0 [30], VGG16 [27], Swin Transformer [31], and YOLOv5s [32]. All models were sourced from the PyTorch model zoo and initially implemented in PyTorch. For interoperability and benchmarking, models were exported to ONNX format with dynamic axes enabled, enabling execution across various inference frameworks. ONNX Runtime was evaluated using the GPU execution provider exclusively. For TensorRT, conversion was performed via ONNX using the PyTorch-to-TensorRT pipeline. Meanwhile, both JAX and TVM leveraged PyTorch models as backends for their respective optimization workflows, rather than relying on ONNX conversion. This setup ensured consistent model definitions across frameworks while allowing evaluation of native optimization strategies.

To ensure fair performance comparison, we evaluated all models across a range of batch sizes: 2, 4, 8, 16, 32, 64, and 128. However, for JAX, inference was only conducted for batch sizes 2, 4, and 8, as larger batch sizes exceeded the available memory and could not be executed. Additionally, to stabilize timing measurements, 50 warmup runs were performed prior to recording inference times for all frameworks and batch sizes. Tables 1 and 2 indicate the details of selected models and optimizations we applied for each framework, respectively.

Table 1. Details of selected models.

Model	Params (M)	Representativeness
ResNet-152 [28]	60.2	Deep, high-capacity CNN used as a benchmark for classification tasks.
MobileNetV2 [29]	3.4	Lightweight architecture optimized for mobile and edge devices.
SqueezeNet [8]	1.2	Extremely compact model suitable for highly resource-constrained environments.
EfficientNet-B0 [30]	5.3	Balances accuracy and efficiency; commonly used in edge scenarios.
VGG16 [27]	138	High-capacity model with historical significance; included for comparative completeness.
Swin Transformer [31]	29	Vision transformer model; representative of recent architectural trends.
YOLOv5s [32]	7.2	Real-time object detector widely adopted in embedded and edge AI applications.

Table 2. Optimization techniques applied for each framework.

Framework	Precision Used	Graph Optimization	Notes
PyTorch	FP16	cuDNN backend	Native inference with torch.autocast and AMP
ONNX Runtime	FP16	Graph fusion (default)	Used ExecutionProvider with graph optimizations enabled
TensorRT	FP16	Layer fusion, kernel tuning	Converted from ONNX using FP16 mode in builder config
TVM	FP16	AutoTVM tuning	Used Relax IR with tuning logs; failed for SqueezeNet
JAX	FP16	XLA JIT compilation	Enabled 16-bit precision using jax.numpy and XLA flags

4.3. PyTorch Inference

PyTorch served as the baseline framework, using models in evaluation mode with CUDA acceleration enabled. Input images were processed in batches with sizes ranging from 2 to 128 to evaluate scalability. To enhance performance, the models were converted to TorchScript using tracing, which compiles the computation graph and removes Python-level overhead. Additionally, cuDNN auto-tuner benchmarking was enabled to select the fastest convolution algorithms dynamically during runtime [11]. The inference loop was GPU-synchronized using CUDA events to ensure accurate latency measurement. Memory usage was monitored through PyTorch's built-in memory tracker, and accuracy was computed using top-k classification metrics.

4.4. ONNX Runtime Inference

Inference using ONNX Runtime was carried out using CUDAExecutionProvider backends. The ONNX format enabled the framework to apply a series of graph-level optimizations automatically. These include constant folding, operator fusion, and elimination of redundant initializers, performed via the *ORT_ENABLE_ALL* optimization level [20]. Batch sizes from 2 to 128 were evaluated for each model. NumPy was used to prepare and feed data into the ONNX Runtime sessions, and predictions were extracted from model outputs for accuracy computation. In all configurations, ONNX Runtime demonstrated competitive portability and flexibility, making it well-suited for multi-platform deployment scenarios.

4.5. TensorRT Inference

TensorRT is NVIDIA's high-performance DL inference SDK designed to optimize trained models for deployment [12]. The ONNX models were imported into TensorRT and converted into serialized engines. FP16 precision was enabled to take advantage of the Jetson AGX Orin's native hardware acceleration for half-precision operations, which reduces memory footprint and increases throughput. During engine building, we enabled advanced optimization techniques such as layer and tensor fusion, kernel auto-tuning, dynamic shape support, and memory reuse. The engines were deployed with input buffers allocated in GPU memory and executed using asynchronous inference calls managed through CUDA streams. TensorRT's ability to generate highly optimized kernels for specific batch sizes made it one of the most performant frameworks, especially under larger batch configurations.

4.6. Apache TVM Inference

Apache TVM is a DL compiler stack designed to optimize and deploy models across heterogeneous hardware platforms [14]. In our workflow, PyTorch models were directly imported into TVM via its PyTorch frontend, bypassing the need for ONNX conversion. The models were translated into TVM's Relax intermediate representation (IR) and compiled for the CUDA-enabled GPU on the NVIDIA Jetson Orin platform. TVM applied both graph-level and tensor-level optimizations, including operator fusion, memory layout transformation, and loop unrolling. AutoTVM was used to tune kernel schedules using an empirical cost model. For each tested batch size (ranging from 2 to 128), TVM recompiled the model to adapt memory allocation and computational parallelism accordingly. The compiled modules were executed using TVM's graph executor. TVM's low-level control over compilation and its backend-specific autotuning capabilities made it particularly effective for edge inference optimization on Jetson devices.

4.7. JAX Inference

JAX is a high-performance numerical computing library that compiles NumPy-compatible Python code using XLA for execution on accelerators [15,33]. In our setup, model computation graphs were restructured using functional transformations and compiled using JAX's `jit`. JAX supported mixed-precision operations using bfloat16 and enabled fusion of elementwise operations during XLA compilation. To reduce startup latency, warm-up iterations were run before recording performance measurements. The inference function was compiled just-in-time and optimized for both compute and memory efficiency. JAX's composability and XLA's backend-specific optimizations allowed it to achieve high performance with minimal framework-specific tuning.

4.8. Inference Performance Measuring

4.8.1. Model Accuracy

We evaluated the classification accuracy of models deployed across all frameworks using the ImageNet ILSVRC 2012 validation dataset, which contains 50,000 labeled images spanning 1000 classes [34]. For each model and batch size, Top-1 and Top-5 classification accuracy metrics were computed.

Top-1 accuracy quantifies the percentage of test samples for which the model's highest probability prediction matches the ground truth label. Top-5 accuracy considers a prediction correct if the ground truth label is among the model's five most probable predictions. These metrics were computed using framework-native methods such as `torch.topk` in PyTorch, `np.argsort` for ONNX Runtime, and `jax.lax.top_k` for JAX.

4.8.2. Inference Time Measurement

Inference time was measured as the average execution time of a forward pass through the model, excluding preprocessing and model loading phases. To account for runtime optimization and caching effects, we included a warm-up phase of 50 inferences prior to measurement, as supported by prior literature [22]. Timing was captured using high-resolution timestamps (e.g., `time.time()` or CUDA events) immediately before and after inference execution.

To ensure fair comparison, latency measurements were synchronized with device-specific barriers, such as CUDA stream synchronizations in PyTorch and TensorRT, and internal session synchronizations in ONNX Runtime and TVM.

4.8.3. Throughput Calculation

Throughput was defined as the number of processed inputs per second and computed as the ratio of the batch size to the average inference time per batch. This approach follows previous guidelines from work like Xu et al. [35]. We experimented with batch sizes ranging from 2 to 128, adjusting based on the available system memory capacity.

Frameworks like TensorRT and Torch-TensorRT support engine construction optimized for fixed batch sizes, which enables higher throughput. Conversely, PyTorch, ONNX Runtime, and JAX support dynamic batching and runtime kernel selection. These characteristics influence how each framework scales throughput with batch size.

To prevent memory errors during ONNX export or inference, especially at larger batch sizes, we designated the batch dimension as a dynamic axis during model conversion from PyTorch to ONNX. This strategy mitigated known memory issues linked to internal tensor duplication [36].

4.8.4. System Memory and Power Monitoring

To collect runtime telemetry on power and memory usage during inference, we employed a parallelized monitoring approach integrated with the Jetson AGX Orin's onboard sensors and external libraries.

Power draw was recorded using the `jtop` interface from the Jetson Stats toolkit. A dedicated background thread was spawned to maintain a persistent connection with the `jtop` daemon. This thread periodically queried telemetry fields such as `POM_5V_IN`, `VDD_IN`, and `VDD_SOC` from the system power dictionary, selecting the most stable reading available.

System memory usage was tracked concurrently within the same monitoring thread by accessing RAM metrics from `jtop`'s memory module. Specifically, the `used` field under the `RAM` key was queried and converted to megabytes. Given the unified memory architecture of Jetson AGX Orin, this value reflects the total DRAM consumption attributable to the inference process, encompassing both CPU and GPU allocations.

All telemetry sampling was offloaded to an isolated thread, ensuring non-blocking behavior with respect to the main inference pipeline. This allowed real-time monitoring without introducing synchronization delays or overhead to the model execution flow. All data were sampled at a frequency of 10 Hz (i.e., every 100 ms), covering the entire active inference interval for each configuration. The collected values were averaged post-execution to compute the mean during inference run.

4.9. Hardware Specifications

NVIDIA has developed a line of embedded computing devices called NVIDIA® JetsonTM, which are intended for use in machine learning and artificial intelligence applications. These are feature-rich, low-power, and compact systems that are capable of executing sophisticated DL models instantly. We do our research using the NVIDIA Jetson AGX Orin 64GB, the newest Jetson device manufactured by NVIDIA Corp., Santa Clara, CA, USA. It has a 12-core NVIDIA Carmel ARMv8.2 CPU, a 384-core NVIDIA Volta GPU, and a 32-core NVIDIA Deep Learning Accelerator (DLA) [37]. It is built on the NVIDIA Ampere architecture.

4.10. Software Specifications

All software tools used in this study were selected to be compatible with the NVIDIA Jetson AGX Orin platform, which requires strict alignment between versions of system libraries and acceleration frameworks. For instance, TensorRT 8.6.2.3 requires CUDA 12.2 and is tightly coupled with specific versions of cuDNN and ONNX parsers. Ensuring compatibility across these components is essential for stable deployment and accurate benchmarking.

The experiments were conducted using JetPack 6.0, which includes CUDA 12.2 and cuDNN 8.9.4 as part of its software stack. Python 3.10 was the base interpreter for all benchmarking scripts. Each DL inference framework used in this study was installed in versions that are stable and optimized for the Jetson Orin platform. Table 3 summarizes the key software tools and library versions used throughout this work.

Table 3. Software tools and library versions used.

JetPack	CUDA	ONNX	ONNX Runtime	PyTorch	TensorRT	Torch-TensorRT	TensorFlow	JAX	TVM
6.0	12.2	1.17.0	1.17.1	2.3.0	8.6.2.3	1.4.0	2.15.0	0.4.28	0.21.0

5. Experimental Results

5.1. Inference Output Validation

The Top-1 accuracy results are presented in Table 4, while the corresponding Top-5 accuracy scores are shown in Table 5. PyTorch, which served as the baseline framework, demonstrated consistent performance across all models. Its close integration with the original model weights ensured minimal deviation, and it provides a reference against which other backends were evaluated.

ONNX Runtime closely matched PyTorch's performance across most models, showing variations within a 1–2% range. This slight deviation is expected due to backend-specific optimizations such as operator fusion and constant folding. In certain models like MobileNet and VGG16, ONNX Runtime slightly outperformed PyTorch in Top-1 accuracy, likely benefiting from optimized execution paths.

TensorRT achieved the highest Top-1 accuracy for ResNet152 and EfficientNet, reaching 76.64% and 74.72%, respectively. These results, as highlighted in Table 4, affirm the effectiveness of its layer fusion and precision calibration strategies. However, small degradations were noted for models like SqueezeNet and Swin Transformer, indicating potential sensitivity of lightweight and transformer architectures to aggressive quantization.

Apache TVM exhibited robust accuracy in most cases and equaled or surpassed other frameworks for models like VGG16 and Swin Transformer. As seen in Table 5, TVM reported a Top-5 accuracy of 94.60% for Swin Transformer, the highest among all evaluated frameworks. The absence of results for SqueezeNet suggests potential compatibility issues during model import or relax graph lowering.

JAX displayed notably high accuracy for several models, including EfficientNet and ResNet152, as observed in both Tables 4 and 5. These elevated figures may stem from architectural differences in how JAX compiles and executes functions via XLA, as well as discrepancies in model conversion or preprocessing pipelines. These results warrant further scrutiny and may benefit from reproducibility analysis with shared checkpoints.

Table 4. Top-1 Accuracy (%).

Inference Framework	ResNet152	MobileNet	SqueezeNet	EfficientNet	VGG16	Swin Transformer	YOLOv5s
PyTorch	75.30	69.70	56.70	74.00	68.00	77.80	69.70
ONNX Runtime	72.00	70.50	55.00	73.50	69.06	76.50	67.50
TensorRT	76.64	70.60	56.06	74.72	68.06	75.68	69.80
TVM	74.26	71.20	NA	74.40	70.37	77.80	69.60
JAX	72.00	70.80	55.30	74.00	68.54	77.00	67.00

Table 5. Top-5 Accuracy (%).

Inference Framework	ResNet152	MobileNet	SqueezeNet	EfficientNet	VGG16	Swin Transformer	YOLOv5s
PyTorch	94.13	90.30	80.63	93.10	88.00	94.90	89.60
ONNX Runtime	94.50	91.00	80.57	93.00	90.87	93.50	90.50
TensorRT	93.38	89.64	78.98	91.88	88.24	92.86	89.18
TVM	93.80	90.40	NA	92.40	89.80	94.60	89.80
JAX	93.60	90.05	79.07	92.50	89.60	93.00	89.70

Observation 1. All frameworks maintained high classification accuracy, with only minor deviations from the PyTorch baseline. Overall, accuracy remained robust across frameworks, validating their use for deployment without significant accuracy loss.

5.2. Inference Time

We evaluated the average inference time per input sample across six representative DL models: ResNet152, MobileNet, SqueezeNet, EfficientNet, VGG16, and Swin Transformer. The results for each framework, PyTorch, ONNX Runtime, TensorRT, TVM, and JAX, are reported in Table 6 and visualized in Figure 1 using a logarithmic scale on the vertical axis for improved readability across orders of magnitude.

TensorRT emerged as the most efficient backend, consistently producing the lowest inference times across all models. Its performance benefits from several tightly integrated optimizations such as FP16 precision support, kernel auto-tuning, and layer fusion during static engine construction. For instance, it achieved inference times of approximately 0.66 ms for SqueezeNet and 2.28 ms for ResNet152, indicating its capability to scale well across both lightweight and heavy architectures.

PyTorch followed as the second-fastest framework, delivering moderate-to-low latency across all tested models. Its backend leverages highly optimized CUDA and cuDNN libraries but lacks static graph-level optimization. Nevertheless, inference times were within a practical range for edge deployment, with MobileNet and SqueezeNet completing forward passes in under 5 ms per sample.

In contrast, ONNX Runtime showed significantly higher latency, especially for deeper models. ResNet152 and VGG16 required over 280 ms and 158 ms, respectively, more than an order of magnitude slower than TensorRT. These results suggest that ONNX Runtime's execution providers may not be fully optimized for the Jetson Orin platform, particularly in terms of kernel fusion and hardware-specific execution planning.

TVM's performance varied by model. It achieved good latency for transformer-based and larger convolutional models such as Swin Transformer and VGG16, but performed less efficiently on MobileNet and could not successfully compile SqueezeNet. This variation reflects both the power and current limitations of AutoTVM tuning and Relax compilation on Jetson-class embedded hardware.

JAX offered moderate latency values, consistently trailing behind TensorRT and PyTorch. While its XLA-based JIT compilation allows for graph-level optimization, the general-purpose nature of the compiler and lack of hardware-specific tuning may limit its performance on edge devices. Nonetheless, it performed predictably across all models, without outliers or instability.

Table 6. Average Inference Time per Sample (ms).

Inference Framework	ResNet152	MobileNet	SqueezeNet	EfficientNet	VGG16	Swin Transformer	YOLOv5s
PyTorch	9.239	4.201	1.749	4.971	1.713	7.267	2.300
ONNX Runtime	285.534	54.402	21.270	89.842	158.146	19.813	26.287
TensorRT	2.282	1.136	0.662	1.516	2.195	3.949	0.882
TVM	7.429	9.529	NA	12.695	8.908	5.275	4.662
JAX	29.096	11.235	8.255	15.182	19.326	22.268	11.686

Observation 2. TensorRT consistently delivered the fastest inference times across all models, demonstrating its strong suitability for real-time applications on edge devices. PyTorch followed closely, offering competitive latency with minimal optimization effort. ONNX Runtime showed significantly higher latency, particularly for larger models, limiting its practicality for time-sensitive tasks. TVM and JAX exhibited variable performance, with

TVM excelling on some models but struggling with others, and JAX offering consistent yet slower inference. Overall, TensorRT clearly leads in execution efficiency on the Jetson AGX Orin platform.

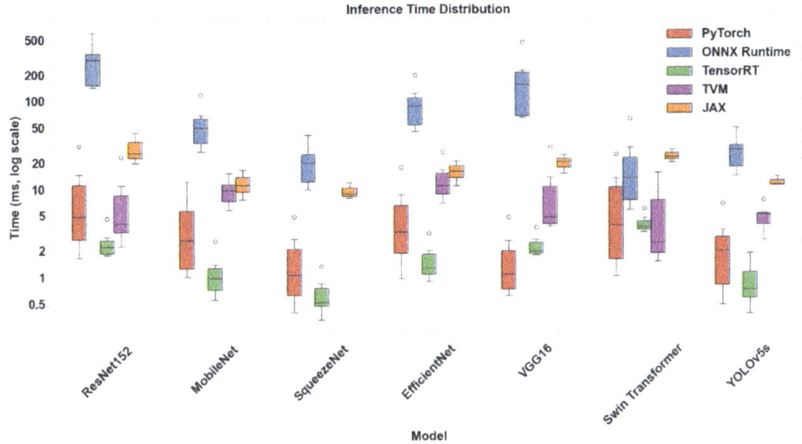

Figure 1. Inference Time Distribution (y axis in log scale).

5.3. Inference Throughput

In our evaluation, we calculated the maximum achievable throughput for each model across all frameworks by incrementally increasing the batch size until the highest sustainable rate was observed without exceeding system memory limits. The results are summarized in Table 7 and visualized in Figure 2. Additionally, Figure 3 presents a detailed view of throughput variation with batch size for MobileNet as a representative lightweight model.

TensorRT achieved the highest throughput for nearly all models, most notably reaching 3197.10 samples/s on SqueezeNet and 1382.46 samples/s on MobileNet. These results reflect TensorRT's ability to exploit static graph optimizations, layer fusion, and efficient kernel scheduling. Its performance scaled well with increasing batch sizes, owing to its use of precompiled, batch-optimized inference engines.

PyTorch also demonstrated impressive throughput, particularly on MobileNet, EfficientNet, and VGG16. Although it does not statically optimize execution graphs, PyTorch's dynamic computation engine and cuDNN-based backend allow it to benefit from increased batch size. As shown in Figure 3, PyTorch maintained high throughput even at large batch sizes, suggesting efficient GPU memory usage and parallelism.

ONNX Runtime underperformed relative to other frameworks. Its throughput peaked at only 181.46 samples/s for Swin Transformer and was significantly lower for deeper models such as ResNet152 and VGG16. This can be attributed to the lack of kernel-level fusion and less aggressive scheduling on Jetson's hardware. Despite being portable and extensible, ONNX Runtime appears limited in raw throughput performance in embedded settings.

TVM achieved moderate throughput across most models and notably surpassed PyTorch and TensorRT for Swin Transformer, reaching 874.48 samples/s. This suggests that AutoTVM tuning was particularly effective for transformer-based architectures, possibly due to efficient relay-to-CUDA scheduling. However, it failed to compile SqueezeNet, limiting its universality.

JAX reported consistent but modest throughput, with best performance on MobileNet (126.02 samples/s) and SqueezeNet (132.34 samples/s). These values suggest that JAX's general-purpose XLA compilation and runtime optimizations provide portability and correctness but fall short in low-level throughput scaling, particularly under large batch sizes.

Table 7. Maximum Acheived Throughput (samples/s).

Inference Framework	ResNet152	MobileNet	SqueezeNet	EfficientNet	VGG16	Swin Transformer	YOLOv5s
PyTorch	931.81	1058.85	1887.53	1202.90	1859.26	1250.40	2124.81
ONNX Runtime	7.45	37.63	106.02	23.50	16.34	181.46	72.84
TensorRT	651.67	1382.46	3197.10	1137.63	582.85	317.52	2691.02
TVM	456.22	171.28	NA	140.58	486.07	874.48	388.04
JAX	50.33	126.02	132.34	95.82	73.34	49.46	93.68

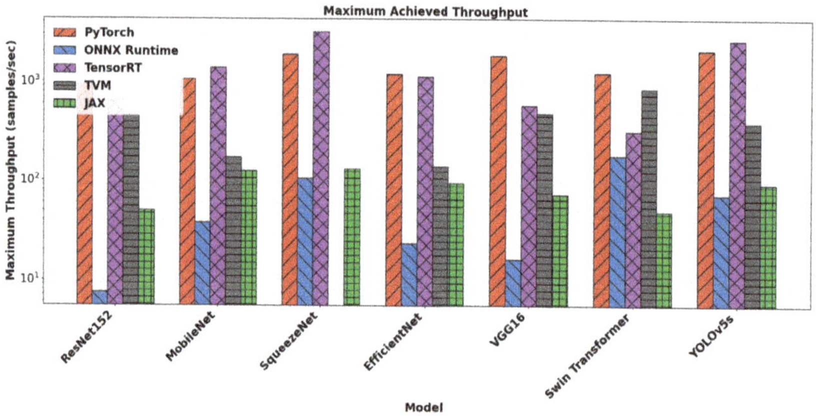

Figure 2. Maximum Achieved Throughput for All Models (y axis in log scale).

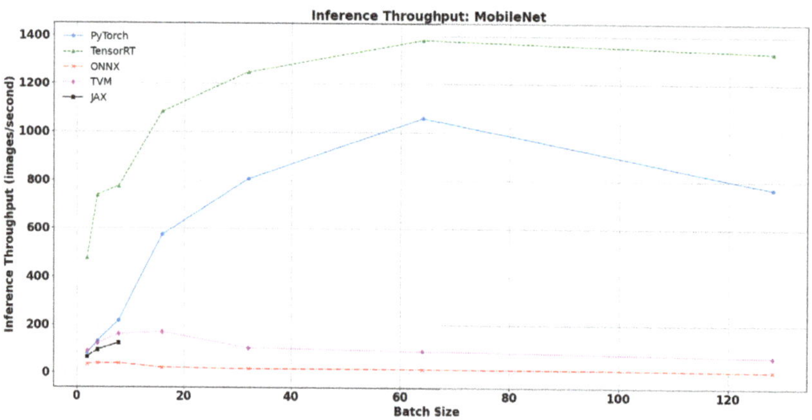

Figure 3. Inference throughput for Mobilenet with varying batch size.

Observation 3. TensorRT delivers the highest throughput across most models, driven by its batch-tuned engine and hardware-aware optimizations. PyTorch follows closely, demonstrating excellent scalability with increasing batch sizes. ONNX Runtime lags significantly in throughput, while TVM shows strength in transformer models. JAX maintains stability but does not scale as effectively. These results highlight TensorRT and PyTorch as top candidates for high-throughput deployment on embedded platforms.

5.4. System Memory Utilization

We recorded the average system memory usage (in GB) during inference across all models and frameworks, as shown in Table 8. Additionally, Figure 4 illustrates how memory usage scales with batch size for MobileNet.

TVM consistently demonstrated the most memory-efficient behavior, consuming the least memory across all test cases. For example, it maintained MobileNet inference within approximately 10.3 GB regardless of batch size, indicating effective memory planning and lightweight runtime overhead. This efficiency likely stems from TVM's static memory allocation strategies and custom graph compilation that minimizes redundant allocations.

PyTorch and TensorRT exhibited moderate and closely aligned memory footprints, with average usage between 14–16 GB across models. Their dynamic memory management, coupled with reliance on cuDNN and CUDA memory allocators, results in predictable scaling with batch size. Notably, Figure 4 shows smooth and steady increases in memory consumption for both frameworks, reflecting stable buffer reuse and kernel launch behavior.

ONNX Runtime consumed more memory than both PyTorch and TensorRT. For MobileNet, its usage hovered around 17.7 GB and showed minimal fluctuation with batch size. This higher footprint may arise from internal graph transformations or redundant buffer allocations during execution.

JAX showed significantly higher memory usage across all models, averaging nearly 29 GB. This result is consistent with its functional programming model, where immutable tensor structures and just-in-time compilation introduce memory overhead. As illustrated in Figure 4, JAX's usage remains static and elevated, indicating that it does not optimize memory use per batch dynamically.

Table 8. Average Memory Usage (GB).

Inference Framework	ResNet152	MobileNet	SqueezeNet	EfficientNet	VGG16	Swin Transformer	YOLOv5s
PyTorch	12.039	14.152	14.968	15.584	16.805	18.484	16.180
ONNX Runtime	15.420	17.693	18.164	18.745	21.134	19.853	18.537
TensorRT	12.279	14.120	14.843	15.746	17.368	17.507	14.554
TVM	7.773	10.287	NA	10.926	13.717	15.275	14.926
JAX	28.974	28.799	28.703	28.663	28.941	29.193	29.634

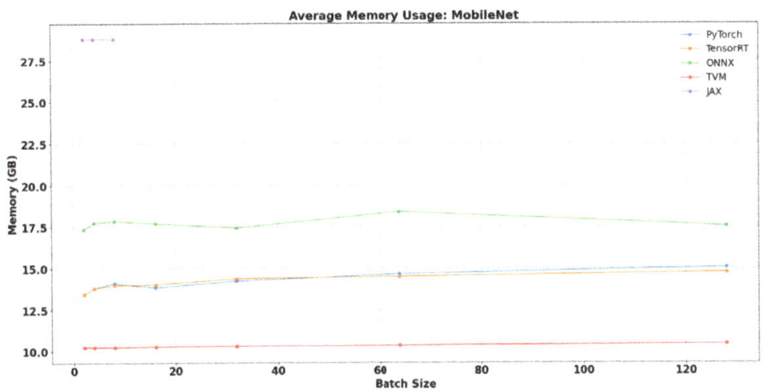

Figure 4. System Memory Usage for Mobilenet.

Observation 4. TVM offers the most efficient memory usage, making it suitable for memory-constrained environments. PyTorch and TensorRT strike a balance between performance and moderate memory overhead. ONNX Runtime uses more memory than expected, while JAX consistently consumes the most, limiting its scalability. These results underscore the importance of framework-level memory handling in real-time edge deployment.

5.5. System Power Consumption

We measured the average system power consumption during inference, using the onboard telemetry sensors of the NVIDIA Jetson AGX Orin. The results, averaged across batch sizes and inference cycles, are presented in Table 9.

TensorRT recorded the highest power draw among all frameworks, particularly when running larger models such as ResNet152 (28.30 W), VGG16 (29.85 W), and Swin Transformer (27.43 W). This elevated consumption aligns with its high throughput and low latency performance, indicating that TensorRT aggressively utilizes hardware resources, including GPU cores and memory bandwidth, to maximize inference speed. Its power profile suggests a performance-at-all-costs design philosophy, suitable for scenarios where latency is paramount and power is not a limiting factor.

PyTorch also exhibited relatively high power consumption, especially on deep CNN models like VGG16 and ResNet152, consuming 23.44 W and 21.83 W, respectively. These values reflect its use of dynamic graph execution and frequent GPU kernel launches, which, while efficient, may not fully optimize power-aware scheduling compared to compiled runtimes.

ONNX Runtime and JAX demonstrated the lowest average power consumption across most models, remaining below 15 W even for large networks. For example, ONNX Runtime drew only 14.17 W on ResNet152 and 13.96 W on EfficientNet, indicating modest GPU engagement. However, these energy savings come at the cost of higher inference latency and lower throughput, as shown in previous sections. JAX followed a similar trend, with the lowest power draw on MobileNet (11.27 W) and SqueezeNet (10.66 W), which reflects limited kernel-level parallelism despite being functionally correct and stable.

TVM's power footprint varied across models. It was competitive with PyTorch on large models, showing 23.62 W on VGG16 and 21.86 W on ResNet152, but consumed less on smaller models. This intermediate behavior suggests that TVM's auto-tuned compilation can yield efficient execution patterns but may still require hardware-specific power optimizations to match the balance achieved by TensorRT.

Table 9. Average Power Consumption (W).

Inference Framework	ResNet152	MobileNet	SqueezeNet	EfficientNet	VGG16	Swin Transformer	YOLOv5s
PyTorch	21.832	14.442	14.306	17.096	23.440	18.802	14.321
ONNX Runtime	14.166	12.459	13.312	13.962	14.213	13.783	13.176
TensorRT	28.299	13.062	11.789	17.557	29.851	27.430	12.608
TVM	21.858	13.766	NA	15.156	23.620	16.045	12.250
JAX	15.076	11.269	10.658	12.229	15.736	15.331	10.522

Observation 5. TensorRT delivers the highest inference performance with the highest power consumption, especially for large models. ONNX Runtime and JAX are the most power-efficient but also the slowest. PyTorch and TVM offer a middle ground, with moderately high power draw and good speed. These results highlight the trade-off between energy efficiency and computational performance in edge deployment scenarios.

6. Discussion

This study provides a comprehensive evaluation of modern DL inference frameworks. Our analysis spans a wide range of performance indicators, including inference accuracy, inference time, throughput, system memory utilization, and power consumption. The diversity of the selected models, encompassing both convolutional and transformer-based architectures, allows us to capture framework behavior under varying computational and memory demands.

Our results clearly illustrate that no single framework dominates across all performance dimensions. Each exhibits strengths aligned with its design philosophy, exposing important tradeoffs for deployment engineers and system architects.

TensorRT stands out in raw performance. It achieves the lowest inference latency and highest throughput across most models, demonstrating its effectiveness as a production-grade inference engine optimized for NVIDIA hardware. Its static engine construction, support for reduced precision computation (e.g., FP16), and advanced kernel fusion enable highly efficient GPU utilization [12]. However, this performance comes at the cost of power efficiency: TensorRT exhibits the highest system power draw among all frameworks. For edge devices with tight thermal envelopes or power budgets, this may necessitate tradeoffs between speed and energy efficiency.

PyTorch achieves a balance between performance and usability. Although not as fast as TensorRT, it maintains relatively low latency and strong throughput, especially when batch sizes are scaled appropriately. This performance is attributable to its mature cuDNN backend and dynamic computation graph, which allow for flexible model execution with minimal tuning. PyTorch also integrates well with deployment tools like TorchScript and Torch TensorRT, making it an accessible and adaptable solution for both development and deployment. Nevertheless, the absence of deep hardware-aware graph compilation restricts PyTorch from reaching the peak efficiency seen in statically compiled runtimes.

ONNX Runtime, while conceived as a highly portable and interoperable inference backend, significantly lags behind TensorRT and PyTorch in both latency and throughput. This performance gap becomes especially evident in deeper networks like ResNet152 and VGG16. ONNX Runtime's higher system memory usage further complicates its deployment on memory-constrained embedded devices. Despite these drawbacks, ONNX's value lies in its role as a standardized model interchange format [38], supporting cross-framework workflows and enabling interoperability across diverse hardware ecosystems. Improvements to ONNX Runtime's backend optimizations, particularly its TensorRT Execution Provider, may help bridge this performance gap in future versions.

Apache TVM presents an interesting middle ground. It demonstrates excellent system memory efficiency, likely due to its low-level code generation and memory planning strategies [14]. TVM also performs competitively in throughput, especially for transformer models like Swin Transformer, where its tuning strategies appear well matched to GPU parallelism. However, TVM's instability, evidenced by failures to compile SqueezeNet and erratic performance for certain models, exposes limitations in operator coverage and frontend robustness. This restricts its general purpose usability despite its high theoretical efficiency.

JAX, with its functional programming paradigm and XLA-backed just-in-time compilation, offers a unique inference model that emphasizes composability and reproducibility. It consistently achieved the lowest system power consumption, making it appealing for energy sensitive deployments. Yet, its high memory usage and modest throughput point to limitations in runtime execution planning and memory reuse, perhaps a result of its general purpose compiler not being fully tuned for real time inference on embedded platforms.

These characteristics suggest that JAX may be more suitable for experimental settings or academic research rather than production edge inference.

While our empirical results highlight distinct performance characteristics across inference frameworks, a theoretical analysis of their internal mechanisms offers further clarity into these outcomes. TensorRT's superior latency and throughput can be attributed to its use of aggressive optimization strategies, such as precision quantization (e.g., FP16), kernel auto-tuning, and operation fusion. These transformations reduce memory bandwidth bottlenecks and improve parallelism by lowering compute granularity and minimizing runtime overheads [12]. Unlike dynamic frameworks, TensorRT performs static compilation of ONNX graphs into highly optimized CUDA kernels, thereby bypassing Python-level execution constraints and enabling deterministic execution paths. In contrast, JAX, while demonstrating low power usage, exhibited the highest memory consumption. This can be theoretically understood through the lens of its design philosophy: JAX leverages XLA for ahead-of-time compilation, and its functional programming model emphasizes immutability. These properties, while beneficial for correctness and reproducibility, lead to extensive memory allocation, as intermediate tensors cannot be reused in-place [15,33]. This memory-intensive behavior may hinder its utility in constrained embedded environments. Apache TVM, known for fine-grained operator tuning and low-level IR transformations [14], showed commendable memory efficiency and throughput. However, its failure to compile certain models like SqueezeNet reveals architectural limitations in operator coverage, particularly within the evolving Relax IR. These limitations restrict TVM's out-of-the-box compatibility with certain ONNX-exported graphs, especially those containing custom or fused operators unsupported by the current compiler stack. Importantly, these framework behaviors are sensitive to version volatility. Both TVM and ONNX Runtime undergo rapid development cycles, which may introduce breaking changes or varying support levels for optimization passes and hardware accelerators. As such, reproducibility across future deployments may be affected unless version constraints are strictly maintained and documented. Including structured documentation of such version-dependent behaviors, along with a comparative summary of framework-specific constraints and potential mitigation strategies, would enhance the practicality of benchmarking results for deployment engineers and system designers. Table 10 summarizes the limitations of frameworks and probable mitigation strategies.

A key strength of this work lies in the reproducible and controlled benchmarking methodology. By standardizing the evaluation environment, dataset (ImageNet validation set), preprocessing pipeline, hardware platform, and metric definitions, we ensure fair and interpretable comparisons across frameworks. The use of six models from diverse architecture families strengthens generalizability, highlighting how different computational patterns (e.g., dense convolutions vs. self-attention) affect framework performance.

Furthermore, we go beyond traditional latency and accuracy measurements by incorporating throughput, system memory consumption, and power usage, which are often neglected in prior works [22,35]. These metrics are crucial for real world deployment on constrained devices, providing a holistic view of each framework's operational cost and scalability.

Despite its strengths, the study has several limitations. First, it focuses exclusively on inference; training performance, while less relevant for deployment, is important in certain edge learning scenarios (e.g., federated learning or continual learning). Second, the analysis is restricted to the Jetson AGX Orin platform. While this device is representative of modern edge accelerators, performance characteristics may differ on other embedded hardware such as Google Coral, Intel Movidius, or AMD-based systems. Extending the study across multiple hardware targets would provide broader insights into cross-platform optimization.

Additionally, the framework versions and software stacks used in this study reflect a snapshot in time. These ecosystems are evolving rapidly. For example, ONNX Runtime and TVM continue to release performance enhancements that may alter current results. Keeping benchmarks up to date is essential for ensuring relevance as frameworks improve and hardware capabilities expand. The rapid development of frameworks like ONNX Runtime and Apache TVM leads to frequent updates that can affect performance, compatibility, and operator support [14]. These changes may hinder reproducibility across versions, especially in embedded systems where software stacks are tightly integrated. To address this, documenting software versions and using containerized environments is recommended for consistent deployment.

Finally, certain runtime behaviors, such as kernel caching, compiler warm up, and background telemetry, introduce variability that may affect repeatability at a fine grained level. While our methodology includes warm up runs and averaged results, further statistical rigor (e.g., confidence intervals or variance analysis) could enhance the precision of reported metrics.

The results of this study provide actionable guidance for edge AI deployment. Developers seeking maximum speed, such as for autonomous navigation or high frame rate vision tasks, will benefit from TensorRT, provided power constraints are relaxed. For general purpose deployments, PyTorch offers a productive tradeoff between performance and portability. Memory or energy-constrained use cases may prefer TVM or JAX, depending on stability and hardware alignment. ONNX Runtime, while underperforming in this study, remains valuable for its ecosystem interoperability and may serve as a reliable fallback when framework flexibility is required.

Table 10. Framework-Specific Limitations, Causes, and Mitigation Strategies.

Framework	Limitation	Likely Cause	Mitigation Strategy
PyTorch	Moderate power and memory usage; lacks static graph-level optimization	Dynamic computation graph; no ahead-of-time compilation	Using TorchScript tracing; integrating Torch-TensorRT; optimizing memory allocators
ONNX Runtime	High latency and memory usage (e.g., 21.13 GB for VGG16)	Limited optimization for Jetson hardware; inefficient graph execution	Enabling TensorRT Execution Provider; applying manual optimization passes; avoiding very deep models
TensorRT	High power consumption (approximately 30 W for large models)	Aggressive GPU usage, kernel fusion, and FP16 throughput focus	Using INT8 quantization; limiting batch size; enforcing runtime power constraints
TVM	Compilation failure for SqueezeNet	Incomplete operator coverage or Relax IR limitations	Extending operator support; reverting to Relay IR; simplifying model architecture
JAX	Excessive memory usage (around 29 GB) across models	Functional paradigm with immutable tensors and XLA compilation overhead	Using smaller batch sizes; profiling with XLA tools; manually reusing tensors where feasible

7. Conclusions

In this study, we conducted a detailed comparative analysis of five widely used DL inference frameworks: PyTorch, ONNX Runtime, TensorRT, Apache TVM, and JAX on the NVIDIA Jetson AGX Orin platform. By evaluating diverse pretrained models on the ImageNet validation dataset, we assessed each framework across multiple dimensions, including inference accuracy, latency, throughput, system memory usage, and power consumption.

Our results show that each framework offers unique strengths depending on the deployment context. TensorRT delivered the fastest inference and highest throughput, confirming its suitability for high performance applications where speed is critical. However, this performance came with increased power consumption. PyTorch emerged as a strong general purpose framework, balancing usability with efficient runtime execution.

ONNX Runtime, while versatile in terms of model portability, showed relatively lower performance, suggesting room for further optimization. TVM demonstrated impressive memory efficiency and competitive throughput in specific scenarios, although it faced stability issues with certain models. JAX stood out for its low power consumption and functional design but lagged in memory efficiency and raw performance.

These findings emphasize the importance of selecting inference frameworks based not only on speed or accuracy but also on practical deployment factors like energy use, memory footprint, and hardware compatibility. Our work provides developers and researchers with concrete benchmarks and insights to guide framework selection for embedded AI applications.

Future work will extend this study to include additional hardware platforms, updated software stacks, and training performance metrics, offering a broader perspective on DL deployment in resource constrained environments.

Author Contributions: All authors contributed significantly to the work. All authors have read and agreed to the published version of the manuscript.

Funding: This work is supported in part by NSF grants 2104181 and 2442078.

Data Availability Statement: All experiments were conducted using publicly availble ImageNet validation dataset, which can be accessed at https://www.image-net.org.

Conflicts of Interest: The authors declare that there are no conflicts of interest regarding the publication of this paper.

References

1. Image Classification on ImageNet. Available online: https://paperswithcode.com/sota/image-classification-on-imagenet (accessed on 20 July 2025).
2. Devlin, J.; Chang, M.W.; Lee, K.; Toutanova, K. Bert: Pre-training of deep bidirectional transformers for language understanding. *arXiv* **2018**, arXiv:1810.04805.
3. Bender, E.M.; Gebru, T.; McMillan-Major, A.; Shmitchell, S. On the Dangers of Stochastic Parrots: Can Language Models Be Too Big? In Proceedings of the 2021 ACM Conference on Fairness, Accountability, and Transparency, Virtual Event, 3–10 March 2021; pp. 610–623.
4. Polino, A.; Pascanu, R.; Alistarh, D. Model compression via distillation and quantization. *arXiv* **2018**, arXiv:1802.05668.
5. Zhu, M.; Gupta, S. To prune, or not to prune: Exploring the efficacy of pruning for model compression. *arXiv* **2017**, arXiv:1710.01878.
6. Liu, C.; Zoph, B.; Neumann, M.; Shlens, J.; Hua, W.; Li, L.J.; Fei-Fei, L.; Yuille, A.; Huang, J.; Murphy, K. Progressive neural architecture search. In Proceedings of the European Conference on Computer Vision (ECCV), Munich, Germany, 8–14 September 2018; pp. 19–34.
7. Howard, A.G.; Zhu, M.; Chen, B.; Kalenichenko, D.; Wang, W.; Weyand, T.; Andreetto, M.; Adam, H. Mobilenets: Efficient convolutional neural networks for mobile vision applications. *arXiv* **2017**, arXiv:1704.04861.
8. Iandola, F.N.; Han, S.; Moskewicz, M.W.; Ashraf, K.; Dally, W.J.; Keutzer, K. SqueezeNet: AlexNet-level accuracy with 50× fewer parameters and <0.5 MB model size. *arXiv* **2016**, arXiv:1602.07360.
9. Google. Cloud Tensor Processing Units (TPUs). Available online: https://cloud.google.com/tpu/docs/tpus (accessed on 20 July 2025).
10. Intel. Intel® Vision Accelerator Design with Intel® Movidius™ Vision Processing Unit (VPU). Available online: https://www.intel.com/content/www/us/en/developer/topic-technology/edge-5g/hardware/vision-accelerator-movidius-vpu.html (accessed on 20 July 2025).
11. Pytorch. Pytorch. Available online: https://pytorch.org/ (accessed on 20 July 2025).
12. NVIDIA Corporation. NVIDIA TensorRT. Available online: https://developer.nvidia.com/tensorrt (accessed on 20 July 2025).
13. Microsoft. ONNX Runtime Documentation. 2023. Available online: https://onnxruntime.ai/docs (accessed on 20 July 2025).
14. Chen, T.; Moreau, T.; Jiang, Z.; Zheng, L.; Yan, E.; Shen, H.; Cowan, M.; Wang, L.; Hu, Y.; Ceze, L.; et al. TVM: An automated end-to-end optimizing compiler for deep learning. In Proceedings of the OSDI, Carlsbad, CA, USA, 8–10 October 2018.

15. GitHub, Inc. JAX: Composable Transformations of Python+NumPy Programs. 2023. Available online: https://github.com/google/jax (accessed on 20 July 2025).
16. NVIDIA. Jetson AGX Orin Technical Brief. 2023. Available online: https://developer.nvidia.com/embedded/jetson-agx-orin (accessed on 20 July 2025).
17. Cheng, Y.; Wang, D.; Zhou, P.; Zhang, T. A Survey of Model Compression and Acceleration for Deep Neural Networks. *arXiv* **2020**, arXiv:1710.09282.
18. Hao, T.; Huang, Y.; Wen, X.; Gao, W.; Zhang, F.; Zheng, C.; Wang, L.; Ye, H.; Hwang, K.; Ren, Z.; et al. Edge AIBench: Towards Comprehensive End-to-End Edge Computing Benchmarking. In Proceedings of the Benchmarking, Measuring, and Optimizing: First BenchCouncil International Symposium (Bench 2018), Seattle, WA, USA, 10–13 December 2018; Revised Selected Papers; Springer: Berlin/Heidelberg, Germany, 2018; pp. 23–30.
19. Shin, D.J.; Kim, J.J. Performance evaluation of YOLO models on embedded platforms using TensorRT. *Appl. Sci.* **2022**, *12*, 1154.
20. ONNX Runtime Developers. ONNX Runtime. Available online: https://onnxruntime.ai/ (accessed on 20 July 2025).
21. JAX Developers. JAX: High-Performance Array Computing. Available online: https://jax.readthedocs.io (accessed on 20 July 2025).
22. Ulker, B.; Stuijk, S.; Corporaal, H.; Wijnhoven, R. Reviewing inference performance of state-of-the-art deep learning frameworks. In Proceedings of the 23th International Workshop on Software and Compilers for Embedded Systems, St. Goar, Germany, 25–26 May 2020; pp. 48–53.
23. Wortsman, M.; Ilharco, G.; Gadre, S.Y.; Roelofs, R.; Gontijo-Lopes, R.; Morcos, A.S.; Namkoong, H.; Farhadi, A.; Carmon, Y.; Kornblith, S.; et al. Model soups: Averaging weights of multiple fine-tuned models improves accuracy without increasing inference cost. In Proceedings of the International Conference on Machine Learning (ICML), Baltimore, MD, USA, 17–23 July 2022.
24. Alqahtani, D.K.; Cheema, A.; Toosi, A.N. Benchmarking Deep Learning Models for Object Detection on Edge Computing Devices. *arXiv* **2024**, arXiv:2409.16808.
25. Yeom, S.K.; Kim, T.H. UniForm: A Reuse Attention Mechanism Optimized for Efficient Vision Transformers on Edge Devices. *arXiv* **2024**, arXiv:2412.02344.
26. Arya, M.; Simmhan, Y. Understanding the Performance and Power of LLM Inferencing on Edge Accelerators. *arXiv* **2025**, arXiv:2506.09554.
27. Stanford Vision Lab; Stanford University; Princeton University. IMAGENET. Available online: https://www.image-net.org/ (accessed on 20 July 2025).
28. He, K.; Zhang, X.; Ren, S.; Sun, J. Deep residual learning for image recognition. In Proceedings of the IEEE Conference on Computer Vision and Pattern Recognition, Las Vegas, NV, USA, 27–30 June 2016; pp. 770–778.
29. Sandler, M.; Howard, A.; Zhu, M.; Zhmoginov, A.; Chen, L.C. MobileNetV2: Inverted Residuals and Linear Bottlenecks. In Proceedings of the CVPR, Salt Lake City, UT, USA, 18–23 June 2018.
30. Tan, M.; Le, Q. EfficientNet: Rethinking Model Scaling for Convolutional Neural Networks. In Proceedings of the ICML, Long Beach, CA, USA, 9–15 June 2019.
31. Liu, Z.; Lin, Y.; Cao, Y.; Hu, H.; Wei, Y.; Zhang, Z.; Lin, S.; Guo, B. Swin Transformer: Hierarchical Vision Transformer using Shifted Windows. In Proceedings of the ICCV, Montreal, QC, Canada, 11–17 October 2021.
32. Jocher, G. YOLOv5 by Ultralytics. 2020. Available online: https://github.com/ultralytics/yolov5 (accessed on 20 July 2025).
33. Frostig, R.; Johnson, M.; Leary, C. Compiling machine learning programs via high-level tracing. *Syst. Mach. Learn.* **2018**, *4*, 1–3.
34. Deng, J.; Dong, W.; Socher, R.; Li, L.J.; Li, K.; Li, F.-F. ImageNet: A Large-Scale Hierarchical Image Database. In Proceedings of the CVPR09, Miami, FL, USA, 20–25 June 2009.
35. Xu, R.; Han, F.; Ta, Q. Deep learning at scale on nvidia v100 accelerators. In Proceedings of the 2018 IEEE/ACM Performance Modeling, Benchmarking and Simulation of High Performance Computer Systems (PMBS), Dallas, TX, USA, 12 November 2018; IEEE: Piscataway, NJ, USA, 2018; pp. 23–32.
36. Marcinkiewicz, P. ONNX Export Doubles RAM Usage. Available online: https://github.com/pytorch/pytorch/issues/61263 (accessed on 20 July 2025).
37. Karumbunathan, L. NVIDIA Jetson AGX Orin Series Technical Brief. Available online: https://www.nvidia.com/content/dam/en-zz/Solutions/gtcf21/jetson-orin/nvidia-jetson-agx-orin-technical-brief.pdf (accessed on 20 July 2025).
38. Foundation, T.L. Open Neural Network Exchange. Available online: https://onnx.ai/ (accessed on 20 July 2025).

MDPI AG
Grosspeteranlage 5
4052 Basel
Switzerland
Tel.: +41 61 683 77 34

Electronics Editorial Office
E-mail: electronics@mdpi.com
www.mdpi.com/journal/electronics

www.ingramcontent.com/pod-product-compliance
Lightning Source LLC
Chambersburg PA
CBHW061511210926
51850CB00008B/1887
9783725878550